Fortune and Elizabethan Tragedy

Fortune
and Elizabethan Tragedy
by Frederick Kiefer

THE HUNTINGTON LIBRARY
1983

Copyright 1983 by
The Huntington Library
Printed in the United States of America

Library of Congress Cataloging in Publication Data

Kiefer, Frederick, 1945-

Fortune and Elizabethan tragedy.

Includes bibliographical references and index.
1. English drama (Tragedy) — History and criticism. 2. English drama —
Early modern and Elizabethan, 1500-1600 — History and criticism.
3. English drama — 17th century — History and criticism. 4. Fortune in literature.
I. Title.

PR658-T7K5   1982   822.0512'09   82-15836
ISBN 0-87328-122-5

To
my Mother and Father

Preface

𝕴N THE NOTES to this book I have sought to record my professional debt to the many scholars who have explored the subject of Fortune. I also owe a debt of a more personal kind to friends and colleagues who have aided me, and I am pleased to express my gratitude here. G. Blakemore Evans has generously read successive drafts, as my initial ideas about Fortune assumed their present form; I owe a great deal to his incisive judgment and warm support. Richard Hosley read the manuscript in various stages, offering advice on matters stylistic and substantive; his meticulous scrutiny has improved virtually every section of this book. Roger Dahood also read and evaluated various drafts; my debt to him, both personal and professional, is inestimable. Madeleine Doran and Walter Kaiser read an early draft and provided many valuable suggestions. Finally, I am grateful to the Huntington Library for a research grant in the fall of 1979. The library staff was unfailingly helpful, and the stimulating atmosphere of the Huntington made my stay in San Marino as pleasant as it was fruitful.

Parts of Chapters 2, 3, 6, and 7 have appeared in *Studies in Philology* (University of North Carolina Press), *Comparative Literature Studies* (University of Illinois Press), *The Journal of Medieval and Renaissance Studies* (Duke University Press), and *Renaissance and Reformation* (University of Toronto). Permission to reprint this material is gratefully acknowledged. The illustrations not otherwise credited are reprinted with the permission of the Huntington Library.

In quoting primary and secondary materials, I have normalized *i:j*, *u:v*, and long *s* and have generally expanded contractions. Where a good modern-spelling edition of a Renaissance text has been available, I have used it. For the dates of sixteenth-century plays, I have been guided in most instances by *Annals of English Drama, 975-1700,* by Alfred Harbage, revised by S. Schoenbaum (London: Methuen, 1964). All citations of Shakespeare are from *The Riverside Shakespeare,* ed. G. Blakemore Evans et al. (Boston: Houghton Mifflin, 1974).

F. K.

Tucson
December 1981

Contents

LIST OF ILLUSTRATIONS

ABBREVIATIONS

Archiv	*Archiv für das Studium der Neueren Sprachen und Literaturen*	MS	*Mediaeval Studies*
		MSR	Malone Society Reprints
		N&Q	*Notes and Queries*
BuR	*Bucknell Review*	NS	*Die Neueren Sprachen*
CahiersE	*Cahiers Elisabéthains*	*PMLA*	*Publications of the Modern Language Association*
CE	*College English*		
CL	*Comparative Literature*	PQ	*Philological Quarterly*
CLAJ	*College Language Association Journal*	*RenD*	*Renaissance Drama*
		RenP	*Renaissance Papers*
CP	*Classical Philology*	RES	*Review of English Studies*
CritQ	*Critical Quarterly*	RMS	*Renaissance and Modern Studies*
E&S	*Essays and Studies*		
EETS	Early English Text Society	RORD	*Research Opportunities in Renaissance Drama*
EIC	*Essays in Criticism*		
ELH	*English Literary History*	RRDS	Regents Renaissance Drama Series
FMLS	*Forum for Modern Language Studies*		
		SEL	*Studies in English Literature*
HLQ	*Huntington Library Quarterly*	*ShakS*	*Shakespeare Studies*
		ShS	*Shakespeare Survey*
JEGP	*Journal of English and Germanic Philology*	SP	*Studies in Philology*
		SQ	*Shakespeare Quarterly*
JHI	*Journal of the History of Ideas*	SR	*Sewanee Review*
		TDR	*Tulane Drama Review*
JMRS	*Journal of Medieval and Renaissance Studies*	TEAS	Twayne's English Authors Series
JWI	*Journal of the Warburg Institute*	TSE	*Tulane Studies in English*
		TSL	*Tennessee Studies in Literature*
JWCI	*Journal of the Warburg and Courtauld Institutes*		
		TSLL	*Texas Studies in Literature and Language*
LCL	Loeb Classical Library		
MLN	*Modern Language Notes*	UTQ	*University of Toronto Quarterly*
MLQ	*Modern Language Quarterly*		
MLR	*Modern Language Review*	YR	*The Yale Review*
MP	*Modern Philology*		

Fortune is painted blind, with a muffler afore her eyes, to signify to you that Fortune is blind; and she is painted also with a wheel, to signify to you, which is the moral of it, that she is turning, and inconstant, and mutability, and variation; and her foot, look you, is fixed upon a spherical stone, which rolls, and rolls, and rolls. In good truth, the poet makes a most excellent description of it. Fortune is an excellent moral.

—Henry V

Introduction

ON THE ELIZABETHAN stage, tragic heroes commonly cry out
against Fortune. Characters in the plays of Lodge and Kyd, of
Marlowe and Jonson invoke this symbol of the arbitrary and
capricious. And some of Shakespeare's most famous creations—
Romeo, Hamlet, King Lear—exclaim over their victimization by Fortune. Spectators and readers, in considering the speeches on Fortune, have tended to minimize their significance. Most literary critics
regard references to Fortune as merely "conventional"—a label that,
once affixed, usually forecloses further discussion. Fortune's presence in
Elizabethan tragedy, they assert, represents a vestige, one perpetuated
by classical and medieval tradition. And why should Fortune have
come to seem less important? Because, it is said, in the Renaissance,
when man came increasingly to recognize the connection between his
own deeds and his success or failure in life, Fortune necessarily occupied
an ever smaller part of his world view. Man's attention turned from an
irrational Fortune to the purposeful Christian deity, who rewarded the
worthy and punished the wicked—frequently in this world, always in
the next.

Perhaps the most influential formulation of this argument appeared in
Shakespeare's Tragic Heroes (1930) by Lily B. Campbell:

> gradually the interest changed from the mere wonder and bewilder-
> ment of witnessing the tragic fall of princes to tracing the cause of the
> change of fortune. And even as the idea of the fickle goddess Fortune
> changed to that of a God just and computative in his justice, so the
> idea of the fall of princes as depending on variable fortune changed to
> the idea of sin or folly as the cause of the change from happiness to

misery; and finally the cause of the sin or folly which led to punishment was found in the passions which moved men to such deeds.[1]

Several years later Willard Farnham gave support to Campbell's view in his influential *Medieval Heritage of Elizabethan Tragedy* (1936). And he reaffirmed the argument in *Shakespeare's Tragic Frontier* (1950).[2] For half a century the conclusions of Campbell and Farnham have shaped the way Elizabethan tragedy is interpreted.

Their views, for example, lie behind Alfred Harbage's characterization of *de casibus* tragedy. Surveying the tradition from Boccaccio to the *Mirror for Magistrates*, Harbage finds the same progression:

> Since the object was moral and political admonition, the power of Fortune appears decreasingly decisive: "It is not she that pryncis gaff the fall," said Lydgate, "but viscious lyvyng." Even though Fortune is still constantly arraigned, the typical protagonist is a tyrant, or one who aspires to tyranny, or one who feeds on tyranny's nauseous fruits, often as a "remorseless, treacherous, lecherous, kindless villain." With some consternation, we observe human action becoming significant by being reprehensible, and the mystery of evil boxed up as the willful wickedness of particular men.[3]

The development that Harbage discerns in *de casibus* tragedy others have come to see in tragedy written for the stage. J. M. R. Margeson, for instance, who reports being "particularly influenced by Willard Farnham," writes that "Fortune specifies only probability, not necessity."[4] Thus Fortune seems outside the trend toward "tragic choices" and resulting "inevitability" which Margeson traces in the evolution of English tragedy. Shakespeare's plays, according to many scholars, participate in this shift from a concern with Fortune to a concern with man's decisions and their ensuing consequences. Virgil K. Whitaker, for example, finds that the dramatic action depicted by Shakespeare "differs fundamentally from that of medieval 'tragedy.' The hero's downfall results not from the caprice of fortune but, at least in part, from his own error."[5] And Larry S. Champion traces a similar progression within Shakespeare's career: "From his earliest efforts in tragedy, Shakespeare moves relatively consistently . . . toward a dramatic focus that concentrates on the flaw, the passion, the lack of wisdom within the protagonist."[6] These generalizations reflect the consensus that Shakespeare and his contemporaries turned increasingly toward what we today call "tragedies of character"; and, at the same time, that they assigned Fortune ever less significance.

Elizabethan playwrights were, to be sure, fascinated by man's psyche and by the connection between its workings and the individual's ensuing prosperity or adversity. But Fortune did not, as a consequence, die a lingering death on their stage. Indeed, to trace the development of English drama in the sixteenth century is to recognize that Fortune gradually assumed not less but more importance. Most playwrights in the first half of that century fail even to mention Fortune; not until the reign of Queen Elizabeth does Fortune loom large in the minds of tragic protagonists. And not until the sophisticated drama of Marlowe, Kyd, Jonson, and Shakespeare does Fortune gain greatest prominence. It is toward the end of the Elizabethan era, rather than at the beginning, that we find the most dramatically compelling treatment of Fortune. Similarly, it is in the latter part of Shakespeare's career that Fortune engages his imagination most fully.

Admittedly, playwrights were concerned with the operation of divine providence and with man's capacity to shape his own destiny, as Campbell, Farnham, and many others have argued. But this concern could not entirely banish the fear that man was also subject to irrational forces, that what befell him might be the consequence of chance rather than design, that despite his best efforts he could be foiled by circumstance, that not even the possession of wisdom could fend off the most horrendous adversity. This apprehension issued in a thematic concern with Fortune. Treatment of Fortune in the drama, then, represents not some literary fossil, but the profound doubts and fears of a culture whose faith in providential design was at times precarious.

The literary and iconographic impetus for the representation of Fortune in the drama was diverse, and it is, in part, the subject of this book. Individual chapters are devoted to philosophic and theological thought, the *Mirror for Magistrates*, the plays of Seneca, the native dramatic tradition, plays based on novelle, and the visual arts. These divisions are, of course, somewhat arbitrary, for traditions have a way of blending together and reinforcing one another. And tragedy was itself a more

capacious form in the Renaissance than it is today. Elizabethan tragedians were responsive to several traditions simultaneously, and it is
sometimes impossible to single out one source or another as the inspiration for a particular treatment of Fortune. Nevertheless, by examining
various genres in turn, we may better appreciate the range of
influences felt by the Elizabethan playwrights, learn what distinguishes
the portrayal of Fortune in each literary kind, and enhance our understanding of Fortune's meaning for the Elizabethans.

More important than shaping influences on the drama is the drama
itself, and, therefore, most of this book is devoted to an analysis of individual plays. I have not sought to discuss every tragedy containing some
treatment of Fortune in the period; that effort would defeat the most
indefatigable scholar. Rather, I have selected plays that are of special
significance because of their aesthetic or historic importance. Included
are discussions of the major Elizabethan dramatists: Lodge, Marlowe,
Kyd, Dekker, Jonson, and Shakespeare. If Shakespeare's plays predom-
inate, it is because he offers a more varied representation of Fortune
than any other tragedian and because he writes about Fortune more
than anyone else. It is also because Shakespeare's treatment of Fortune is
especially interesting that three of his Jacobean tragedies are included,
while other plays are excluded if written after the death of Queen
Elizabeth.

NOTES TO THE INTRODUCTION

1. *Shakespeare's Tragic Heroes: Slaves of Passion* (Cambridge: Cambridge Univ. Press, 1930), p. 37. Campbell's book has been reprinted numerous times (by Methuen in London, by Barnes and Noble in New York).

2. See *The Medieval Heritage of Elizabethan Tragedy* (Berkeley: Univ. of California Press, 1936); *Shakespeare's Tragic Frontier: The World of His Final Tragedies* (Berkeley: Univ. of California Press, 1950). *The Medieval Heritage* has been reprinted several times during the last thirty years.

3. Introduction to *Shakespeare: The Tragedies, A Collection of Critical Essays*, Twentieth Century Views (Englewood Cliffs, N.J.: Prentice-Hall, 1964), pp. 4-5.

4. *The Origins of English Tragedy* (Oxford: Clarendon Press, 1967), p. 38.

5. *The Mirror up to Nature: The Technique of Shakespeare's Tragedies* (San Marino, Calif.: Huntington Library, 1965), p. 176.

6. *Shakespeare's Tragic Perspective* (Athens: Univ. of Georgia Press, 1976), p. 266.

Chapter 1

PAGAN FORTUNE IN A CHRISTIAN WORLD

𝔄 TRAVELER IN EUROPE finds antique representations of Fortune in profusion: statues, statuettes, coins, amulets. Countless altars, moreover, bear Fortune's name. Such remnants of the pagan world are to be found in Rome, once the center of an empire that venerated Fortune, and in towns of eastern France and northern England, on the fringes of that empire two millennia ago. Pliny, the first-century naturalist, records that devotion to Fortune was as widespread and enthusiastic as the proliferation of Fortune's image would suggest:

> Everywhere in the whole world at every hour by all men's voices Fortune alone is invoked and named, alone accused, alone impeached, alone pondered, alone applauded, alone rebuked and visited with reproaches. . . .[1]

The object of this attention, Pliny notes with irony, is oblivious to man's entreaties. Fortune is "deemed volatile and indeed by most men blind as well, wayward, inconstant, uncertain, fickle in her favours and favouring the unworthy." That a capricious deity should command so great an allegiance may seem odd, but there can be no doubt of Fortune's immense appeal: "To her is debited all that is spent and credited all that is received, she alone fills both pages in the whole of mortals' account."

Although in Pliny's time there were numerous temples or shrines of Fortune in Rome[2] and although Fortune tended to absorb other deities,

I

devotion to Fortune was not universal. Pliny himself, for example, disparages the cult of Fortune, and he does so in the strongest terms. He believes that to attribute prosperity or adversity to Fortune inevitably obscures the hegemony of God. Particularly troubling is the contingency that Fortune embodies.[3] (Fortune's name was in antiquity associated with the word *fors*—signifying chance or luck—itself etymologically associated with *fero*, "I bring," by ancient authors.[4]) Pliny remarks, "we are so much at the mercy of chance that Chance herself, by whom God is proved uncertain, takes the place of God." A rational, purposeful universe, Pliny feels, is irreconcilable with an arbitrary Fortune.

While not himself a Christian, Pliny anticipates those in the Middle Ages and the Renaissance who would be similarly troubled by Fortune's popularity. Eventually, many Christians would come to accept Fortune in some fashion, as the indispensable studies by Alfred Doren, Howard R. Patch, Vincenzo Cioffari, F. P. Pickering, and others have shown.[5] Evidence of this acceptance is manifest in the important place that Fortune holds in medieval iconography; her image adorns scores of churches. Yet even in the Middle Ages there remained a residual antipathy toward this creation of pagan antiquity. Particularly with the advent of the Protestant Reformation, Fortune came to be regarded much as Pliny regarded her—as the refuge of the ignorant, as a challenge to God.

This hostility could not, however, prevent men of letters from employing a symbol that enjoyed such a long and vigorous history; nor could it prevent artists from continuing to portray Fortune in pictorial form. Whatever the moralists said, Fortune demonstrated an astonishing capacity to survive in the popular imagination. To understand this phenomenon, we need to consider some of the more influential thinkers and writers who pondered Fortune: Augustine and Boethius in the late Roman era; Dante, Petrarch, and Chaucer in the high Middle Ages; Calvin and other theologians of the Reformation. This first chapter, then, explores the efforts of Christians to come to terms with a pagan symbol of change and contingency.

I

In his youth Augustine undoubtedly used the word "Fortuna" as often as his contemporaries. But with his conversion to Christianity, Augustine felt constrained to reject the name of the pagan goddess. In his *Retractations*, Augustine speaks of his early work, *Against the Academics*, written in the fall of 386, a few months before his baptism, and he apologizes for having failed to banish Fortune from his thoughts and speech:

> I regret that, in these three books of mine, I mention fortune so often, although I did not intend that any goddess be understood by this term, but a fortuitous outcome of events in good and evil circumstances, either in our bodies or extraneous to them.[6]

Sounding much like Pliny three centuries earlier, the Church Father adds, "I regret that I spoke about fortune in this way since I realize that men have a very bad habit of saying, 'Fortune willed this' when they should say, 'God willed this.'"

In *The City of God Against the Pagans*, Augustine expresses at length his uncompromising attitude toward Fortune, and he expounds his reasons for condemning her:

> how is she really good, if she comes both to good men and bad with no consideration of justice? Moreover, why do men worship her, if she is blind, and runs into people at random, no matter who, so that she commonly passes by those who worship her and attaches herself to those who scorn her? (IV.xviii)[7]

The questions are, of course, meant to demonstrate the illogic in the propitiation of a deity so insensible to petition, so indifferent to merit. If Fortune is truly blind, Augustine argues, then to worship her is utterly pointless. The devotee is engaged in an absurd enterprise: "it is no good worshipping her if she is mere luck (*fortuna*), but if she singles out her worshippers to help them, she is not mere luck, or Fortuna" (IV.xviii).

3

Like Pliny, Augustine believes that devotion to Fortune is devotion misplaced. His jibes at Fortune are intended to lead the reader to a recognition of the sovereignty of God. Deploring men's penchant for attributing material loss or gain to Fortune, he argues that only the true God is responsible for the "good" that comes to people. By tracing all felicity back to its source in God, Augustine in effect deprives Fortune of the hegemony which she traditionally exercised over material things. He would, of course, maintain that he is not supplanting one deity (pagan) with another (Christian); he is, rather, sweeping away ignorance and placing the disposition of all things where it belonged — under the aegis of the Christian God.

Fortune supplied an explanation not only for the gain or loss of material goods but also, as Pliny recognized, for contingency — what in ordinary parlance we call chance. And this presents a problem for the Christian intent upon demonstrating the essential orderliness of the universe, since the greater the operation of chance, the less certain may appear the authority of a rational, changeless God. Sensitive to the inconsistency in affirming simultaneously fortuitous circumstance and divine design, Augustine purges his world of contingency. He claims that nothing can truly be said to happen by chance. Discussing Cicero's refutation of the Stoics, he writes: "As for those causes which he calls fortuitous (the word fortune is derived from the same root), we do not say that they are nonexistent, but that they are hidden, and we ascribe them to the will of the true God . . ." (V.ix). Augustine concedes that events may appear to be fortuitous, but he maintains that it is nonsense to claim that they are directed by Fortune. He insists that nothing is, ultimately, inexplicable. Chance is merely an illusion, Fortune a personification born of man's ignorance. What men call fortuitous is simply that part of the divine plan which they fail to comprehend in its entirety and hence construe as arbitrary. With full knowledge, man could trace all apparently random events back to "the will of the true God."

Augustine's attitude toward Fortune would seem to leave little room for compromise. Yet Fortune did not simply melt away, and Christian intellectuals of succeeding centuries would have to confront Fortune's stubborn survival. Judging from the popularity of Fortune in late Roman culture, the question facing those who followed Augustine was not whether they should accept that part of their classical heritage known as Fortune, but rather the way in which they would accommodate that heritage.

The philosopher most influential in leading the way toward a synthesis of Fortune and divine providence was Boethius, superbly qualified for this role by his education and intellectual interests. Born about 480 into a prosperous Roman family, Boethius embarked early on an ambitious scholarly career. He sought to assimilate the learning of Greece, to translate the works of Aristotle and Plato into Latin, and to write commentaries on both. This monumental project was never completed, for Boethius diverted his energies to politics and to original studies of logic, music, arithmetic, and geometry. He wrote, moreover, treatises on theological issues, which later became the subject of commentaries by such distinguished medieval theologians as Gilbert of Poitiers, Thierry of Chartres, John Scotus Erigena, and St. Thomas Aquinas. As a scholar dedicated both to the dissemination of classical philosophy and to the exploration of contemporary theological issues, Boethius has been called "the last of the Roman philosophers, and the first of the scholastic theologians."[8]

Boethius' reputation as a mediator between classical and Christian thought rests in large measure on his *Consolation of Philosophy*. Written between his arrest on political charges (in 523?) and his execution in 524, the *Consolation* is designed to assuage Boethius' grief and despair at suffering sudden, catastrophic adversity. In accomplishing this purpose, Boethius explores man's relationship to Fortune and to God. To understand how these two are related to one another, we need to look briefly at his characterization of each.

To the bewildered Boethius, it seems that God's careful regulation of the universe fails to extend to man. As he sees it, Fortune is chiefly responsible for his plight. Lady Philosophy, however, reprimands him for inveighing against Fortune. After all, she reminds him, Fortune has not really altered: "You are wrong if you think that Fortune has changed toward you. This is her nature, the way she always behaves. She is changeable, and so in her relations with you she has merely done what she always does" (II, prose 1).[9] And if Boethius is displeased by Fortune's fickleness, he is free to spurn her; to fail to do so is to remain forever vulnerable. Perhaps recalling Boethius' characterization of himself as tossed "in the stormy sea of fortune" (I, poem 5), Philosophy tells him, "If you hoist your sails in the wind, you will go where the wind blows you, not where you choose to go" (II, prose 1). Moreover, Boethius castigates Fortune unfairly, since her behavior represents the expression of her very nature: "If you try to stop the force of her turning wheel, you are the most foolish man alive. If it should stop turning, it would cease to be Fortune's wheel."

To enlighten Boethius further, Philosophy momentarily adopts the persona of Fortune, saying, "I spin my wheel and find pleasure in raising the low to a high place and lowering those who were on top. Go up, if you like, but only on condition that you will not feel abused when my sport requires your fall" (II, prose 2). If Boethius cannot blame Fortune merely for being true to her nature, neither can he expect that she will bring contentment: the gifts of Fortune are never permanent. And the more one relies on the material things that Fortune confers, the less likely is the attainment of genuine happiness. True felicity is to be found within the mind, in that region not subject to Fortune's caprice: "if you possess yourself, you have something you will never want to give up and something which Fortune cannot take from you" (II, prose 4).

Through Lady Philosophy's tutelage, Boethius gains in both understanding and confidence: "I think I may now be equal to the attacks of Fortune" (III, prose 1). The prisoner's education, however, is far from complete, for if he must repudiate Fortune he must also actively seek to know God. The theme of the dialogue thus shifts from the wiles of Fortune to the ways of the Creator.

As described by Lady Philosophy, the providence of the *Consolation* bears a close resemblance to that of Augustine. For Boethius, as for the Church Father, the universe is an expression of God's will. A benevolent deity orders all things, including mankind. He ensures that "the good are always rewarded and the wicked always punished" (IV, prose 3), even though appearances may suggest otherwise. To explain how it is that the good may seem afflicted with adversity while the wicked seem to prosper, Philosophy differentiates between the providence which God ordains and the fate (as distinguished from Fortune) which man beholds: "Providence is the unfolding of temporal events as this is present to the vision of the divine mind; but this same unfolding of events as it is worked out in time is called Fate" (IV, prose 6). It is

6

man's incomplete understanding of providence that leads him to perceive apparent injustice.

So all-encompassing is providence that no event may properly be termed purposeless or random. Admittedly, man may experience the seemingly fortuitous, but this reflects only his faulty comprehension of divine plan: "If chance is defined as an event produced by random motion and without any sequence of causes, then I say that there is no such thing as chance; apart from its use in the present context, I consider it an empty word. For what room can there be for random events since God keeps all things in order?" (V, prose 1). However, citing Aristotle's example of a man coming upon buried treasure, Philosophy makes this concession to man's ignorance: "we can define chance as an unexpected event brought about by a concurrence of causes which had other purposes in view. These causes come together because of that order which proceeds from inevitable connection of things, the order which flows from the source which is Providence and which disposes all things, each in its proper time and place" (V, prose 1).

Although this providential system of Boethius resembles Augustine's, Fortune nevertheless becomes a presence in the *Consolation* in a way that she never does in *The City of God*. To understand how Boethius can grant Fortune such prominence, let us consider more closely the relationship between Fortune and providence in his work.

Modern readers commonly infer that Boethian Fortune is subservient to God's providence. Thus F. P. Pickering writes that for Boethius, "Fortune is the instrument of Divine Providence, which at any time may place her under restraint, halt her course, bridle her."[10] And John L. Grigsby, noting that fate in the *Consolation* is subject to providence, more cautiously draws much the same inference: "God was seen limiting the power of Fortune, though she was not clearly subservient to Him."[11]

The notion that Fortune is an executrix of providence has a twofold origin. First, modern readers confuse Fortune with fate in the *Consolation* and mistakenly assume that what is said of the latter somehow applies to the former. Second, Boethius precedes the description of God's providence with a richly detailed portrait of the goddess. If Fortune does not literally appear before the prisoner in the way that Lady Philosophy does, Boethius nevertheless describes her appearance, temperament, and psychology. Philosophy even furnishes Fortune with a speech so that we may hear what Fortune would say if she were actually present. It may be natural for readers to infer that Fortune, who creates such a strong impression on the imagination, is subject to God's providence. But as Howard R. Patch observed long ago, Boethius never explicitly draws that conclusion: "An inference of such a figure in subordination to Divine Providence is easily drawn, but Boethius did not draw it."[12] Indeed, it would have made little sense for Boethius to have done so, since he deprives Fortune of a raison d'être. That is, he describes a world where Fortune has no power over the rational man. If his well-being is dependent upon his own decisions, if material things contribute nothing to his true felicity, if there exists no real contingency, and if "You can make of your fortune what you will" (IV, prose 7), what possible significance can Fortune have? Logically, none. This explains why Philosophy must impersonate her, why Fortune does not (and cannot) actually appear before the prisoner. What confuses readers of the *Consolation* is Boethius' failure to refute Fortune's existence in the rigorous way that his philosophy logically requires. Instead, he allows Fortune to fade from view as the prisoner, ignorant and anxious in Books I and II, gradually advances in his understanding of providence in Books III, IV, and V. Evidently, Fortune represents a powerful imaginative creation, too useful to obliterate with Augustinian contempt. Even if, strictly speaking, she cannot be said to exist, Fortune's representation helps to convey the grief and anguish felt by a victim of adversity.

Boethius did not singlehandedly rescue Fortune from extinction. Other influential writers created their own portraits of Dame Fortune, and popular sentiment undoubtedly helped to perpetuate her reign. The *Consolation of Philosophy*, however, had far-reaching influence, for it provided a powerful impetus to the verbal and pictorial representation of Fortune during the Middle Ages. So striking is Fortune's portrayal and so prominent the place accorded her early in the *Consolation* that anyone who read the work would necessarily be impressed by her image. Boethius' role as progenitor of later representations can scarcely be overemphasized. Howard R. Patch concludes: "He was the first among medieval writers to set forth the picture of the Goddess Fortune and her wheel with anything like a full and proper characterization. Henceforth those who wrote dialogues of the kind, short or long, or who composed apostrophes or complaints to her, are in some measure indebted to the *Consolatio*."[13] Through the inclusion of Fortune in his treatise, Boethius in effect confers a sanction on Fortune that she might not otherwise have enjoyed. He helped make it intellectually respectable, so to speak, for an exponent of providence to include the once pagan goddess among the inhabitants of his mental world.

This is not to say that the *Consolation* espouses a theological creed, for there is nothing doctrinally Christian about the work. Boethius mentions neither Christ, nor the saints, nor the Church, nor even the Bible. He seeks to assuage his anguish solely through reason. Nevertheless, much of what Boethius says is in keeping with Christian values. As Richard Green comments, "Nothing in *The Consolation* is inconsistent with patristic theology; indeed, precedent for nearly every idea which Boethius proposes can be found in the work of St. Augustine."[14] Boethius, moreover, was regarded in the Middle Ages as a Christian saint, his death as martyrdom under a heretical (Arian) emperor. So closely identified with the Church was Boethius that Dante could place him in the Circle of the Twelve Lights (*Paradiso*, Canto X) — in the company of, among others, Albertus Magnus and Thomas Aquinas.

II

Whether Boethius intended the *Consolation* chiefly for the ages or for his own solace, the treatise became a landmark of literary history. Its popularity in the Middle Ages is revealed both by the enormous number of manuscripts extant (more than 400), many of them sumptuously illustrated, and by the number of translations: "No other book, except the Bible, was so much translated in the Middle Ages."[15] Those who translated Boethius include King Alfred, Notker Labeo, Chaucer, Jean de Meun, Alberto of Florence, and Queen Elizabeth. The influence of Boethius' work on medieval literature, English and Continental, is as great as the popularity of the *Consolation* would suggest.

The fruits of Boethius' rapprochement with pagan antiquity reach perhaps their fullest literary expression in Dante, himself a reader of the

Consolation.[16] The example provided by Boethius' synthesizing cast of mind lies behind the poet's inclusion of Fortune within the Christian world of the *Commedia.* In Canto VII of the *Inferno,* when Dante reaches the circle of the avaricious and prodigal, Virgil explains that the people they encounter were in life hostages to the material gifts of Fortune. In wonderment the wayfarer turns to his guide and this dialogue ensues:

> "Master," I said, "now tell me further: this Fortune which you touch on here, what is it, which has the goods of the world so in its clutches?"
>
> And he to me, "O foolish creatures, how great is the ignorance that besets you! I would have you receive my judgment on this now. He whose wisdom transcends all, made the heavens and gave them guides, so that every part shines to every part, equally distributing the light. In like manner, for worldly splendors He ordained a general minister and guide who should in due time transfer the vain goods from race to race, and from one to another blood, beyond the prevention of human wit, so that one race rules and another languishes, pursuant to her judgment, which is hidden like the snake in the grass. Your wisdom cannot withstand her: she foresees, judges, and pursues her reign, as theirs the other gods. Her changes know no truce. Necessity compels her to be swift, so fast do men come to their turns. This is she who is much reviled even by those who ought to praise her, but do wrongfully blame her and defame her. But she is blest and does not hear it. Happy with the other primal creatures she turns her sphere and rejoices in her bliss."[17]

The nature of Virgil's reply to the wayfarer suggests the extent to which Christianity could reconcile itself to Fortune. There is nothing ambiguous about the treatment of Fortune here; instead, Dante forthrightly enlists her in his explanation of providential order. She is "a general minister and guide."[18]

The accommodation of Fortune, apparent in the *Commedia,* appears also in the physical structure of the medieval church, on whose windows, walls, and floors Fortune's image was displayed. The shape of the Gothic rose window was well suited to an adaptation of the Fortune motif. Camille Enlart has noted, "Le mot de *rose* pourrait n'être que la déformation du mot *roe*, roue. . . ."[19] And John Leyerle has shown that what we today call a rose window is just as accurately termed a wheel window.[20] Of course, the wheel could have associations entirely independent of Fortune in medieval iconography,[21] but artisans seized on the possibilities of the round window to portray Fortune's wheel and, sometimes, even Fortune herself. At the Church of St. Étienne in Beauvais a series of sculptured figures cling to the circumference of a window (north transept, c. 1120-40); and at the top, according to Helen J. Dow, appears Dame Fortune herself.[22] Similarly, windows at the Cathedral of Basel (north transept, late twelfth century) and at San Zeno in Verona (west facade, c. 1189-1200) portray men rising and falling on Fortune's wheel.[23] The Cathedrals of Trent (north transept, c. 1200-20) and Amiens (south transept, c. 1250-1300) are also adorned with such depictions.[24] And a sculptured figure in the center of the window at Trent, according to Ernst Kitzinger, "may well be Fortuna."[25] Fortune appears too at the hub of a wheel in Villard de Honnecourt's preliminary sketch (thirteenth century) for a rose or wheel window.[26]

Fortune's image is painted on the walls of many churches as well. A number of these paintings survive in England, the most famous in Rochester Cathedral (late thirteenth century). It shows Dame Fortune turning a wheel to which men cling.[27] Another painting of Fortune's wheel (also fragmentary) survives at St. Mary's Church in Kempley, Gloucestershire.[28] Still other representations of Fortune's wheel appear at Catfield Church, Norfolk; Padbury Church, Buckinghamshire; the Church of Belchamp Walter in Essex; and Old Weston in Huntingdon-shire.[29] In view of the deterioration of many churches and the damage inflicted during the Reformation, it is likely that Fortune's image once decorated many other churches as well.

Even the floors of medieval churches were adorned with pictures of Fortune and her wheel. Inlaid in the pavement of the Duomo of Siena, for example, is a wheel of Fortune dating from 1372. This design alludes to Fortune's classical origins by portraying at the corners Greek and Roman thinkers, each labeled with a truism about Fortune.[30] The same church contains another (much later) design of Dame Fortune herself. Created by Pinturicchio about 1505, the depiction on the floor shows Fortune straddling her boat and an island, onto which she has apparently just discharged some passengers.[31] The Church of St. Salvatore in Turin contains yet another representation of Fortune in its pavement.[32]

All of these representations — windows, murals, pavements — illustrate in varying ways the Christian acceptance of Fortune. Christian iconography had often been inspired by ancient gods and heroes,[33] but not since the days of imperial Rome had a classical deity been enshrined in such ecclesiastical splendor. If other pagan deities survived in attenuated form, Fortune actually flourished in the heart of Christendom.

III

The widespread representation of Fortune in medieval churches suggests that in the eyes of most people Fortune was no longer regarded as hostile to the faith. The admonitions of Augustine seem to have been largely ignored; and, ironically, some medieval manuscripts of *The City of God* contain illustrations of Fortune.[34] The acceptance of a Christianized Fortune was, however, by no means universal in the Middle Ages. The physical presence of Fortune's image in stone and paint has tended to obscure the fact that some people remained uncomfortable with Fortune, as the works of Petrarch and Chaucer reveal.

Fortune appears prominently in both Petrarch's lyric poetry and his *De Remediis Utriusque Fortunae* (written mostly between 1354 and 1357, though not completed until 1366). *De Remediis*, "of all Petrarch's works the most popular up to, and indeed well into the age of printing,"[35] is essentially a treatise on Fortune: the author discusses at considerable length the concept of the Good and the Evil Fortune and suggests strategies to be adopted in time of prosperity and adversity. At one point in his life, however, Petrarch displayed a reluctance to say anything at all about Fortune. The occasion was a banquet in honor of King John of France. Petrarch had been sent on an ambassadorial mission to Paris, his purpose to congratulate the king on his release from captivity in 1360. In his address Petrarch spoke of Fortune's role in inflicting the king's adversity, and he noted that writers and philosophers had expressed various opinions about Fortune's nature and existence. These remarks interested King John and others in attendance, and they decided to ask Petrarch his opinion of Fortune on the next day. A friend informed Petrarch about the plan to question him and that night he sought to put his thoughts in order. But even with this preparation he was not eager to speak on the topic, and the following day he took advantage of the king's preoccupation with other matters to keep silent regarding Fortune.[36]

Petrarch's reluctance to commit himself publicly suggests a difference of opinion among his auditors regarding Fortune and a desire on his part to avoid controversy. Although he apparently inclined to the view that Fortune was an "empty name" — an appropriate view for one who, upon climbing the summit of Mont Ventoux, opened his copy of Augustine's *Confessions* — Petrarch did not wish to offend those who saw Fortune as actually exerting great influence on human life. The experience at John's court, described in a letter written to Pietro de Poitiers in 1362, appears to have been troubling. As long as five years later, Petrarch was still mulling over his views of Fortune. And in another letter, to Tommaso del Garbo, Petrarch enunciates a clear-cut position. Citing Fathers of the Church — Augustine, Lactantius, Ambrose, and Jerome — he asserts that Fortune is really nothing. If he has used the word "Fortune" in his writing, he has done so only that ordinary people might better understand him.[37]

Petrarch's position, while firmly articulated, seems incongruous, in view of the attention he gives to Fortune in his literary work, especially in *De Remediis Utriusque Fortunae*. His prologue to the second book of the treatise begins with the acknowledgment that nothing he ever read impressed him more deeply than Heraclitus' vision of ceaseless change;[38] and it was apparently his reading of Heraclitus, according to Marcel Françon, that led him to transform "the trite conception of Fortune into a profound view of the world,"[39] a view that informs *De Remediis*. The discrepancy between Petrarch's declaration in his letter to del Garbo and his practice in *De Remediis*, along with the incident at King John's court, suggests that keen differences of opinion on Fortune existed.

We do not know whether Chaucer was ever as vexed as Petrarch by the subject of Fortune, but the *Monk's Tale* (c. 1393-1400), a series of accounts illustrating the operation of Fortune, meets with disapproval from the other pilgrims. Does this indicate some objection to the Monk's treatment of Fortune? Possibly. The Host, however, seems merely bored: "this Monk he clappeth lowde. / He spak how Fortune covered with a clowde / I noot nevere what" (2781-83), and turning to address the Monk, adds, "Youre tale anoyeth al this compaignye" (2789).[40] The Knight, as a man of high rank, may have more substantial reasons for objecting. Perhaps because he sees an application to himself, he protests: "I seye for me, it is a greet disese, / Whereas men han been in greet welthe and ese, / To heeren of hire sodeyn fal, allas!" (2771-73). R. E. Kaske believes that the Knight, who in his own tale demonstrates a familiarity with Boethius, finds the Monk's treatment of Fortune deficient because the Monk fails to relate Fortune to providence: "from the larger viewpoint of the *De Consolatione*, the presentation of Fortune in the *Monk's Tale* must be looked on as philosophically incomplete"; Kaske thinks that the Knight interrupts as "a protest against the philosophical limitations of the *Monk's Tale*. . . ."[41] Whether the pilgrims object chiefly to the manner of the *Monk's Tale* (its repetitive and didactic qualities) or to the matter (the fall of the mighty, often at the hands of Fortune), the narrative is indeed grim, suggesting as it does that not even virtue is proof against Fortune's afflictions.

Outwardly, the *Monk's Tale* seems a conventional injunction to beware the world's mutability. The teller is himself a cleric and his seventeen stories recount the experiences of well-known figures who enjoy prosperity for a time and then suffer disaster. The agent in most cases is Fortune, who has been interpreted as executing God's decrees. One commentator, for instance, calls Fortune "God's minister."[42] Despite the anguish inflicted by Fortune, then, the *Monk's Tale* has been seen as an affirmation of providential design.

The stories of Nero, Holofernes, Antiochus, and others. would appear to confirm such an interpretation, for these figures assuredly deserve their destruction. When Fortune turns hostile toward them, she seems to act as executrix of providence. Most stories in the *Monk's Tale*, however, do not concern heinous sinners. Especially in the so-called "modern instances"—Barnabo, Ugolino, the two Peters—we hear of virtuous men undone by the perfidy of others rather than by any fault of their own. When Fortune destroys such a man as Ugolino, she is certainly no righter of wrongs: "Allas, Fortune! it was greet cruel-tee / Swiche briddes for to putte in swich a cage!" (2413-14).

The destruction of innocence may, of course, be regarded as an object lesson in transience: the Christian should scorn the world of change and fix his attention on eternity. But if this is the Monk's intent, he has curiously little to say about divine providence. The tale contains few references to God's "governaunce"; and these seem incidental in what is essentially a story of pain, disorder, and lamentation. E. Talbot Donaldson writes of the *Monk's Tale*: "God disappears entirely; Fortune appears to exercise full control, and exercises it malignantly."[43] The tragic stories, moreover, do not seem designed to prompt a reformation of character in the listener. Instead, one is invited to contemplate the futility of action in a world that claims such mighty men and women as victims.

That a monk, presumably familiar with the writings of St. Augustine, should recount stories about Dame Fortune may be ironic; one commentator even contends that it is "rich Chaucerian humor at its best."[44] We cannot, assume, however, that Chaucer's contemporaries would necessarily have detected the irony or that they would have deemed it unsuitable for a cleric to chronicle Fortune's exploits. After all, John Lydgate—like Chaucer's Monk, a Benedictine—celebrates Fortune in his *Fall of Princes* (written in the 1430s), a work much esteemed in the fifteenth century. And Fortune's image decorated major religious structures such as Rochester Cathedral, a Benedictine establishment. What is noteworthy is not that a monk should dwell on Fortune, but that he should conceive of Fortune chiefly as a malign power rather than as a retributive agent in the service of a benevolent providence.

If the reader of Chaucer senses that Fortune is a demonic force in the *Monk's Tale* (at least in some of the tragedies), that impression seems borne out by other medieval works which explicitly describe Fortune as in league with the devil. John L. Grigsby notes that "If the personification [Fortune] appeared in a moral work, she was likely to be portrayed as an evil, rather than a godlike, force. In the *Miroir du monde—Somme le roi*, for example, she was a minion of the devil. Her wheel was under Satan's direct control. . . ."[45] Medieval iconography reflects this conception of Fortune, for related to the wheel of Fortune and probably inspired by it are representations variously called wheels of the Seven Deadly Sins or wheels of the Vices. One survives as a fresco (c. 1400) on the wall of Ingatestone Church, Essex. The spokes of the wheel divide it into seven compartments, each depicting one of the seven sins; and within the hub of the wheel is a representation of hell. Appropriately, Satan himself appears in each section to encourage villainy.[46] A variation of this design is contained in the pages of a treatise, *De Rota Verae et Falsae Religionis* by Hugh de Folieto. A late twelfth-century Austrian manuscript of the work portrays a "Rota falsae religionis" ("Wheel of false religion"), various sections of which are inscribed with the names of monastic vices while the spokes bear the names of sinful desires. Adolf Katzenellenbogen, noting the four figures that appear on the wheel in stages of rising and falling, concludes that the design is "constructed on the model of the wheel of Fortuna."[47] Contrasted with this wheel is a "Rota verae religionis" ("Wheel of true religion"), around the perimeter of which are inscribed the names of virtues.

This iconographic evidence, along with the experience of Petrarch and the *Monk's Tale* of Chaucer, suggests that the notion of a Dantesque Fortune, explicitly functioning as an agent of God's providence, was hardly universal in the Middle Ages. And, paradoxically, it may have been the persistence of a malevolent Fortune that medieval Christianity, itself rather forbidding in some ways, found useful. As G. R. Owst, discussing the gargoyles and other adornments of medieval churches, writes: "Of all such graphic caricatures of the medieval artist none made greater appeal to the pulpit than that well-known pictorial device known as the Wheel of Fortune. It illustrated with a peculiar vividness the preachers' own favourite view of life, fundamentally harsh and pagan as it had remained, the inevitable round of existence for every mortal human being, the successive stages of man's tragic journey upon the earth from cradle to grave, the varying temporal fortunes of a world that offered him no abiding security."[48]

IV

Although most Christians tolerated Fortune as a somewhat ambiguous presence within the culture of the late Middle Ages, thinkers of the Protestant Reformation generally did not. In their attitude they resemble the Church Father who so often inspires their writings — Augustine. And, like him, they adopt an antagonistic attitude toward Fortune.

What distinguishes the thinking of the Protestant Reformers is their notion of God's relationship to His creation. In *The Image of God* (1550) Roger Hutchinson acknowledges that some people, though they "grant God to be maker of all thynges," mistakenly "suppose, that as the shypwryghte when he hathe made the shypp, leaveth it to the maryners and medleth no more therwith, and as the carpenter leaveth the house that he hathe made: even so god after he had formed al thinges, lefte all his creatures to their owne governaunce, or to the governaunce of the starres, not rulinge the worlde after his providence, but lyvinge in ease and quietnes. . . ."[49] To those with faith in providence, this idea of God resting in splendid isolation from His creation is anathema. John Calvin in his *Institutes* (1561) explains: "Providence is called that, not wherwith God idlely beholdeth from heaven what is done in the world, but wherwith as guiding the sterne he sitteth and ordreth al thynges that come to passe. So doth it no lesse belong to his handes than to his eies."[50] Providence, then, entails God's continuing and undiminished direction of His creation. Calvin's is a busy God, one who not only foreknows but who actually administers: "Providence consisteth in doing: for to much fondely doo many trifle in talkyng of bare forknowledge" (Book I, fol. 58). Nor will this ever diminish. Heinrich Bullinger declares, "God hath not onelye created the world, and all thinges that are in the world, but doth also governe and preserve them at this daye, and shall governe and preserve them even till the end."[51]

In addition to being ceaselessly active, providence is all-encompassing: nothing is exempt. Andreas Gerardus Hyperius writes in *A speciall Treatise of Gods Providence* (1588?), "We call Gods Providence, a perpetuall and unchangeable disposition and administration of all thinges that be."[52] To express the breadth of God's reach, moralists sometimes use the term "universal providence," which Gulielmus Bucanus defines as "that whereby God directeth all creatures according to that secret instinct which he hath put into them at their creation, and so preserveth the order of nature, which himselfe hath appointed."[53] To those who contend that providence would be somehow tarnished by its extension to the least of God's creations, Hyperius replies: "Gods Majestie is not heere diminished, but rather becommeth more famous and notable. The mo thinges that God dooth, the more shineth foorth his power and goodnes in them. And God is no more defiled with the care of thinges earthly and vile, then the Sunne is defiled by shining even upon foulè and filthy places" (sig. B4ᵛ). To denote the specificity of providence, its application to each and every element of creation, the philosophers employ the term "special." Hyperius, for instance, writes that God administers all things, "yea even those that are esteemed least, and also directeth the actions of every thing to their appointed end. Wherupon we name it the speciall or peculiar providence of God . . ." (sig. D1). The divine hand, then, touches everything.

The Protestant notion that providence is comprehensive, extending throughout the created world and even beyond time to eternity, would probably seem familiar to most thinkers of the Middle Ages. Where Renaissance Protestants differ from many Christian thinkers in earlier centuries is in their denial that God acts through intermediaries. Adamant in the conviction that God alone supervises all activity in the cosmos, they believe that God shares His power with no one. Thus Hyperius declares: "God woorketh not by turnes or fittes, as one that is sometimes weary and requireth the enterchangeable helpe of a deputye, unto whom he might commit the office of sustaining and keeping all things upright: but he worketh continually without ceasing all in all, and onely and alone bringeth all things to their appointed end" (sig. B1ᵛ). The rejection of any go-between has, of course, profound consequences for Fortune. In the view of the moralists, the idea of a Dantesque Fortune, an executrix of providence, has no warrant in Scripture, and it smacks of paganism. Writing of the Epicureans, who assigned Fortune such a role, Calvin says: "I speake not of the Epicureans (which pestilence the worlde hath alwaye been fylled with) which dreame of an idle and slouthful God: and other as mad as they, whiche in old tyme imagined that God did so rule above the middle region of the ayre, that he left thinges benethe to Fortune . . ." (I, fol. 58ᵛ).

Protestant thinkers not only oppose Fortune as the executrix of providence, but also Fortune as the embodiment of contingency. For those who affirm providential design, nothing happens fortuitously. According to Calvin, "hys Providence so ordreth all thynges that nothyng chaunceth but by hys advised purpose" (I, fol. 57ᵛ). Therefore, no matter how adventitious some event might appear, it has in fact been ordained by God:

> If a man light among theves, or wylde beastes, if by wynde sodenly rysen he suffer shypwrack on the sea, if he be kylled wyth the fall of a house or of a tree: if an other wandryng in deserte places finde remedy for hys povertie, if having been tossed with the waves, he atteine to the haven, if miraculously he escape but a fynger bredth from death: all these chaunces as well of prosperitie as of adversitie the reason of the fleshe doeth ascrybe to fortune. But whosoever is taught by the mouth of Chryst, that all the heares of hys hed are numbred, will seke for a cause further of, and wyll fyrmelye beleve that all chaunces are governed by the secrete councell of God. (I, fol. 57)

Calvin's catalogue of mischances is intended to emphasize the gulf that separates the appearance of chance from the reality of divine design. For the faithful, seeming contingency actually confirms the surety of providence. Thus in *A frutefull treatise of predestination, and of the devine providence of God* [1561], John Veron writes: "that the scripture might the better expresse, that nothing at all is done in the worlde, without hys appoyntment and ordenaunce, it dothe adscribe and attribute unto hym those things that seme to be most casual, that seme, I say, to be of a very chaunce and fortune."[54] With supreme confidence that he perceives the order behind the disorder, Philippe de Mornay, seigneur du Plessis-Marly, says of the mutable region under the moon, "the more stirring, the more chaunge, the more disorder there is here beneath, the more doth he shew the unmoovable decree of his everlasting Providence, which (will they or nill they) directeth all the unconstancies of this world to one certeine ende."[55]

Faith in providence, however strong, is not enough for the moralists. They feel compelled to denounce Fortune as a fiction because Fortune undermines a central feature of God's providence—His retributive justice. John Veron, for instance, asks his reader to realize that "nothing can happen unto him, withoute the will and appoyntment of God, who wil suffer nothing, but that which is just, and expedient" (sig. M7ʳ). Calvin too sees that Fortune and divine justice are incompatible: "nothyng lesse agreeth with the nature of God, than to throwe awaie the governement of the world, and leave it to fortune, to wynke at the synnes of men, so as they may lyve in lycentious outrage unpunished" (I, fol. 4ᵛ).

Despite such declarations, philosophers of the Reformation were no more successful in expunging Fortune than was Augustine a millennium earlier. That they failed is hardly surprising. After all, although the moralists assured men that the world was governed by a beneficent deity who guarantees that the good will be rewarded and the evil punished (at least in the next world), earthly experience suggests that many crimes are unpunished, many wrongs unrighted in this world. Experience suggests, further, that the righteous man may suffer adversity, that virtue is no shield against calamity. How was this to be explained? Having ruled out the existence of a Dantesque Fortune, Protestant theologians had to find other ways of accounting for the seemingly accidental and for the appearance of inequity.

Most fixed on the expedient of blaming man's limited knowledge. Mornay, for example, writes, "the mischiefe is, that whereas we would not judge of a Song by one note, nor of a Comedie by one Scene, nor of an Oration by one full Sentence, we will presume to judge of the Harmony and orderly direction of the whole world, and of all that is therein, by some one action alone" (p. 172). What seems to be chance is, in reality, a misunderstanding of divine purpose. Mornay sees man's flawed comprehension behind every mention of Fortune's name. "Surely it is a word that signifieth nothing but respectively, that is to say, as having respect of some things or persons that are spoken of, and it hath no ground or beeing but of and in our owne ignorance" (p. 190). If man were to acquire the knowledge that God possesses, Fortune would vanish like the morning mist: "That which is fortune to the Childe, is no fortune to the Father: that which is fortune to the Servant, is none to the Maister: that which is fortune to the foole, is none to the wise man: that which is fortune to the wise man, is none unto God. According to the measure of our knowledge or ignorance, so doth fortune increase or abate" (p. 190).

Recognizing the tendency of some men to become victims of their incomplete knowledge, the moralists repeatedly remind their readers to beware, lest they admit of Fortune in a moment of weakness. Calvin warns: "somtyme the causes of those thynges that happen are secrete, so

20

that this thought crepeth into our myndes, that mens matters are tourned and whirled about with the blynde sway of fortune . . ." (I, fol. 61). Sir George More, sharing Calvin's concern, reconstructs the process by which an individual may falter and give credence to Fortune:

> When it pleaseth God in the secrecie of his judgment, to afflict good men, and to suffer the wicked to flourish in this world, such is our weaknes, that we stagger in mind, and seeing it often so to come to passe, we often fall into doubtfull and undutifull conceites, even of God him selfe, as if, eyther he were not, or regarded not, the dooings and deservings of men: which unjust surmise, springeth out of that old roote of unthankfulnes, wherewith mankinde was corrupted at the first; whereby fond opinions grow up in the minde, and shadow the light of reason, so that we cannot discerne true things from false, and good from evill; for so blinded by the darke mist of ignorance, we make Fortune the Author of that, whereof God is the dooer, and ascribe to Chaunce, whatsoever is performed by the providence of the Almightie.[56]

With his fragmentary understanding, man falsely construes design as accident and, even worse, confers divinity upon that figment of his imagination. The steps by which Fortune usurps the place of God in the mind also interest Hyperius, who comments on man's efforts to discover explanations for the seemingly inexplicable:

> when they could not finde what causes to alleadge in such eventes, they being overcome with admiration judged, that it must of necessitie be some divine matter, and that called they fortune or chaunce, by little and little also making it a Goddesse, by whose beck and will the greatest part of mens affaires might be guided and governed. (sig. H5)

Since Fortune has her origins in man's ignorance, she cannot, obviously, claim divinity. Accordingly, Pierre de la Primaudaye calls her a "counterfet Goddesse"; she is "nothing else but a fayned device of mans spirite, and an imagination without truth."[57]

Not content to recount the way in which Fortune takes shape in man's psyche, some moralists would actually banish her name from common parlance. Calvin forthrightly attacks what he deems pagan terminology: "wil one say, doth nothing happen by fortune or by chaunce? I answere that *Basilius magnus* hath truly said that fortune and chaunce are heathen mens wordes, wyth the signification wherof the mindes of the godly ought not to be occupied. For if every good successe be the blessing of God, & every calamitie & adversitie be his curse, now is there in mens matters no place left for fortune or chaunce" (I, fol. 60). Recalling Augustine's experience, Calvin cites the example of the Church Father: "We ought also to be moved with thys saying of Augustine. In his bokes against the Academikes he saith. It doth displease me that I have so ofte named fortune, albeit my meaning was not to have any goddesse meant therby, but only a chaunceable happening in outward things ether good or evil" (I, fol. 60).

Despite the invocation of Augustine's name, and despite their own voluminous argumentation, the Reformers' campaign against Fortune was less than an unqualified success. By the very passion of their attack, they acknowledge the persistent vitality of Fortune. Some, perhaps cognizant of Fortune's continued appeal, momentarily relax their crusade. Even those who speak out most vociferously against Fortune can be heard conceding that men may use the name of the goddess without risking opprobrium. La Primaudaye, for instance, admitting that events may at least appear to be disordered and fortuitous, writes: "I say, knowing all these things, yet bicause the order, reason, ende, and necessitie of those thinges which are so strange, uncertaine, and mutable in the world, are for the most part hidden in the counsell of God, and cannot be comprehended by the opinion and reach of man, we may call them casuall and chancing, in respect of our selves" (p. 469). Similarly, Mornay has this to say about the use of Fortune's name: "If ye meane Fortune as she is painted by the Poets, blind, standing on a bowle, and turning with every winde: it is as easie to wipe her away as to paint her. . . . But if by the word Fortune they meane as *Proclus* doth, a certeine divine power that gathereth causes farre distant one from another, al to one end: surely in that case we be more freends to fortune than they be. For we admit it, not onely in things uncertaine wandering & wavering, but also even in the things that are most certeine, yea & in al things whatsoever, as the which is but God himself disguised under another name" (p. 190). And Gulielmus Bucanus qualifies his contempt for pagan terminology when he asks, "Doth nothing come to passe by chance or fortune?" and answers, "Nothing indeed at all, if we consider the providence, power, and knowledge of all things which is in God: but in respect of ourselves who are ignorant of the true causes, and looke onely upon the inexpected events, a thing may be said to come to passe by fortune" (p. 148). Even such an ardent foe of paganism as Calvin relents sufficiently at one point to permit the use of Fortune's name. Citing the instance of a merchant entering a forest, becoming separated from his companions, and being murdered by thieves, he asks: "What shall a Christian here thinke? even this, whatsoever happened in such a death, he wil thinke it in nature chancing by fortune as it is in dede, but yet he will not doubt that the providence of God did governe to directe fortune to her ende" (I, fol. 60ᵛ). In this remarkable statement Calvin acknowledges the tendency of people to employ the name of Fortune in their everyday speech, no matter what their theological principles.

Thus constrained by the fetters of qualification, Fortune is given a very reluctant assent by La Primaudaye, Bucanus, and others. Their admission that man can, with proper safeguards, use the terms "Fortune" and "chance" represents, on one level, a concession to usage. But it also represents something more: it signals a realization that people seek a more proximate explanation for contingency than that furnished by "providence." No amount of sophisticated argumentation can make the phenomenon of chance disappear. Nor can it wholly convince men that their sensitivity to contingency represents only their own ignorance. By allowing the use of the term "Fortune," the moralists implicitly concede not only their inability to remake habits of speech, but also, in effect, the inadequacy of their philosophy to answer satisfactorily the doubts engendered by man's experience.

By their rejection of the medieval accommodation of Fortune, the Reformers, like Augustine before them, hoped to doom Fortune. Ironically, though, their efforts may have had precisely the opposite effect. For by banishing Fortune from Christendom, they unwittingly invested her with even greater independence than she enjoyed in the Middle Ages. Through their argumentation, they may actually have helped to create a climate of opinion in which pagan Fortune would flourish anew.

NOTES TO CHAPTER I

1. *Natural History*, ed. and trans. H. Rackham, LCL, 1 (Cambridge, Mass.: Harvard Univ. Press, 1944), Book II, chap. v.

2. According to tradition, the cult of Fortune was initiated by Servius Tullius, the sixth king of Rome. W. Warde Fowler, in *Roman Ideas of Deity in the Last Century before the Christian Era* (London: Macmillan, 1914), comments on Fortune's popularity: "there is no doubt that the notion of Fortuna as a cosmic force survived into the imperial period, and even gained fresh force there, especially among the common people of no special culture, who have left their thousands of records on stone in every province as well as in Italy. Those records entirely bear out the famous passage of Pliny . . ." (pp. 78-79).

3. Fortune seems originally to have been a fertility goddess, an identification that survives in some of her ancient accouterments: the cornucopia, sheaf of wheat, measure of fruit, and ear of corn. Fortune's identification with contingency apparently derives from her Greek precursor—Tyche. See F. Allègre, *Étude sur la déesse grecque Tyché* (Paris: Ernest Leroux, 1889); Howard R. Patch, "The Tradition of the Goddess Fortuna in Roman Literature and in the Transitional Period," *Smith College Studies in Modern Languages*, 3 (1922): 131-77; Roger Hinks, *Myth and Allegory in Ancient Art* (London: Warburg Institute, 1939), pp. 76-83; David M. Robinson, "The Wheel of Fortune," *CP*, 41 (1946): 207-16; John Ferguson, *The Religions of the Roman Empire* (London: Thames and Hudson, 1970), pp. 77-87.

4. On the meanings of *fors* and *fortuna* in Latin literature, see the *Oxford Latin Dictionary* (Oxford: Clarendon Press, 1971), fasc. 3: 725, 727. According to A. Ernout and A. Meillet, in *Dictionnaire étymologique de la langue latine*, 4th ed. (Paris: C. Klincksieck, 1967), "Un rapport—réel ou imaginaire—avec *ferō* était établi et a donné lieu à de nombreuses figures étymologiques" (p. 249). See also H. V. Canter, "'Fortuna' in Latin Poetry," *SP*, 19 (1922): 64-82.

5. Among the more important works dealing with Fortune in the Middle Ages are these: Alfred Doren, "Fortuna im Mittelalter und in der Renaissance," *Vorträge der Bibliothek Warburg*, ed. Fritz Saxl, 2 (1922-23), part 1, 71-151; Howard R. Patch, *The Goddess Fortuna in Mediaeval Literature* (1927; reprint ed., New York: Octagon Books, 1967); Italo Siciliano, *François Villon et les thèmes poétiques du moyen âge* (Paris: Armand Colin, 1934), esp. pp. 281-311; Vincenzo Cioffari, *Fortune and Fate from Democritus to St. Thomas Aquinas*

(New York: privately printed, 1935); F. P. Pickering, *Literature and Art in the Middle Ages* (London: Macmillan, 1970), pp. 168-222 (originally published as *Literatur und darstellende Kunst im Mittelalter* [Berlin: E. Schmidt, 1966]); Vincenzo Cioffari, "Fortune, Fate, and Chance," in *Dictionary of the History of Ideas*, ed. Philip P. Wiener, 2 (New York: Scribner's, 1973), 225-36. Also useful is G. W. Trompf, *The Idea of Historical Recurrence in Western Thought from Antiquity to the Reformation* (Berkeley and Los Angeles: Univ. of California Press, 1979).

6. *The Retractations*, trans. Mary Inez Bogan, R.S.M., The Fathers of the Church: A New Translation, 60 (Washington, D.C.: Catholic Univ. of America Press, 1968), 6-7.

7. *The City of God Against the Pagans*, ed. and trans. William M. Green, LCL, 2 (Cambridge, Mass. and London: Harvard Univ. Press, 1963).

8. H. F. Stewart and E. K. Rand, eds., *Boethius: The Theological Tractates and the Consolation of Philosophy*, LCL (New York and London: Putnam's, 1918), p. x. Major studies of Boethius include: H. F. Stewart, *Boethius: An Essay* (Edinburgh and London: William Blackwood, 1891); Howard R. Patch, *The Tradition of Boethius: A Study of His Importance in Medieval Culture* (New York: Oxford Univ. Press, 1935); Helen M. Barrett, *Boethius: Some Aspects of His Times and Work* (Cambridge: Cambridge Univ. Press, 1940); Pierre Courcelle, *La Consolation de Philosophie dans la tradition littéraire: antécédents et postérité de Boèce* (Paris: Études augustiniennes, 1967).

9. *The Consolation of Philosophy*, trans. Richard Green, Library of Liberal Arts (Indianapolis and New York: Bobbs-Merrill, 1962).

10. *Literature and Art in the Middle Ages*, p. 184.

11. Introduction to *The Middle French Liber Fortunae: A Critical Edition*, Univ. of California Publications in Modern Philology, no. 81 (Berkeley and Los Angeles: Univ. of California Press, 1967), p. 10.

12. "The Tradition of the Goddess Fortuna in Medieval Philosophy and Literature," *Smith College Studies in Modern Languages*, 3 (1922): 194.

13. *The Tradition of Boethius*, pp. 121-22.

14. Introduction to *The Consolation of Philosophy*, p. xv. The relationship of Augustine to Boethius is also discussed by F. P. Pickering, "Notes on Fate and Fortune," in *Mediaeval German Studies presented to Frederick Norman* (London: Univ. of London Institute of Germanic Studies, 1965), pp. 1-15; and Pickering, *Augustinus oder Boethius?: Geschichtsschreibung und epische Dichtung im Mittelalter—und in der Neuzeit* (Berlin: Erich Schmidt, 1967).

15. Gilbert Highet, *The Classical Tradition: Greek and Roman Influences on Western Literature* (Oxford: Clarendon Press, 1949), p. 571, *n*63.

16. For the influence of Boethius on Dante, see Rocco Murari, *Dante e Boezio* (Bologna: Nicola Zanichelli, 1905); Angelo Gualtieri, "Lady Philosophy in Boethius and Dante," *CL*, 23 (1971): 141-50.

17. *The Divine Comedy*, trans. Charles S. Singleton, 2nd printing with corrections, Bollingen Series, 80 (Princeton: Princeton Univ. Press, 1977), Canto VII, ll. 67-96.

18. In his commentary on the word *ministra*, Singleton writes: "In applying the term to Fortune here in *Inf.* VII, the poet is already beginning to represent Lady Fortune as an angelic creature or Intelligence assigned to a sphere" (2: 115). For Dante's treatment of Fortune, see also Vincenzo Cioffari, *The Conception of Fortune and Fate in the Works of Dante* (Cambridge, Mass.: Dante Society, 1940).

19. *Manuel d'archéologie française depuis les temps mérovingiens jusqu'à la renaissance* (Paris: Alphonse Picard, 1902), 1: 310, *n2*.

20. See "The Rose-Wheel Design and Dante's *Paradiso*," *UTQ*, 46 (1977): 280-308.

21. For example, a thirteenth-century manuscript from Verona depicts Christ sitting above a wheel; He holds in his mouth the sword of justice. On the right side of the wheel, three figures fall toward hell; on the left, virtuous men rise toward their heavenly reward. Reproduced by Richard Salomon, *Opicinus de Canistris* (London: Warburg Institute, 1936), pl. XLII, fig. 72. For another instance of the wheel employed in connection with Christ, see A. N. Didron, *Christian Iconography; or, The History of Christian Art in the Middle Ages*, trans. E. J. Millington (London: Henry G. Bohn, 1851), 1: 117, fig. 39. Other wheels that figure in medieval iconography include those of Ezekiel and St. Catherine.

22. "The Rose-Window," *JWCI*, 20 (1957): 269. The window is reproduced as pl. 14, fig. c.

23. The window at Basel is reproduced by Doren, "Fortuna im Mittelalter und in der Renaissance," pl. III, fig. 8; the window at Verona, by Leyerle, illus. 1.

24. The window at Trent is reproduced by Leyerle, illus. 2; the window at Amiens, by Maurice Eschapasse, *Notre-Dame d'Amiens* (Paris: Hachette, 1960), pl. 68.

25. "World Map and Fortune's Wheel: A Medieval Mosaic Floor in Turin,"

Pagan Fortune in a Christian World

Proceedings of the American Philosophical Society, 117 (October 1973): 364, n132.

26. Reproduced in *The Sketchbook of Villard de Honnecourt*, ed. Theodore Bowie (Bloomington and London: Indiana Univ. Press, 1959), pl. 64.

27. Reproduced by Tancred Borenius and E. W. Tristram, *English Medieval Painting* (Paris: Pegasus Press, 1927), pls. 38 and 39.

28. See C. E. Keyser, "The Mural Paintings at Kempley Church, Gloucestershire," *Archaeological Journal*, 34 (1877): 271.

29. Reference to the wheel of Fortune at Catfield Church is made by Dawson Turner, "Mural Painting in Catfield Church," *Norfolk Archaeology*, 1 (1947): 137. Reference to the wheel of Fortune at Padbury Church is made by C. E. Keyser, *A List of Buildings in Great Britain and Ireland*, 3rd ed. (London: Eyre and Spottiswoode, 1883), p. 194. For description of Fortune at Belchamp Walter, see E. W. Tristram, *English Wall Painting of the Fourteenth Century*, ed. Eileen Tristram (London: Routledge and Kegan Paul, 1955), p. 140. The painting at Old Weston is described by the Royal Commission on Historical Monuments (England), *An Inventory of the Historical Monuments in Huntingdonshire* (London: His Majesty's Stationery Office, 1926), pp. 288-90.

30. Reproduced by Robert H. Hobart Cust, *The Pavement Masters of Siena (1369-1562)* (London: George Bell, 1901), p. 30, pl. VI.

31. Ibid., p. 27, pl. V.

32. See Kitzinger, figs. 3, 4, 11.

33. See, for example, Erwin Panofsky and Fritz Saxl, "Classical Mythology in Medieval Art," *Metropolitan Museum Studies*, 4 (1933): part 2, 228-80; Jean Seznec, *The Survival of the Pagan Gods: The Mythological Tradition and Its Place in Renaissance Humanism and Art*, trans. Barbara F. Sessions, Bollingen Series, 38 (New York: Pantheon Books, 1953); and André Grabar, *Christian Iconography: A Study of Its Origins*, Bollingen Series, 35 (Princeton: Princeton Univ. Press, 1968).

34. See Alexandre de Laborde, *Les Manuscrits à peintures de la Cité de Dieu de Saint Augustin* (Paris: Édouard Rahir, 1909), 3: pls. XIX, XXII, XXX, LXIV, and LXV.

35. Nicholas Mann, "Petrarch's Role as Moralist in Fifteenth-Century France," in *Humanism in France at the End of the Middle Ages and in the Early Renaissance*, ed. A. H. T. Levi (Manchester, England and New York: Barnes and Noble, 1970), p. 7.

27

36. This incident is recounted by Alfred Barbeu du Rocher, "Ambassade de Pétrarque auprès du Roi Jean le Bon," in *Mémoires présentés par divers savants à l'Académie des Inscriptions et Belles-Lettres de l'institut impérial de France*, 2nd Series (Paris: The Imperial Press, 1854), 3: 172-228. See also Carlo Godi, "L'Orazione del Petrarca per Giovanni il Buono," *Italia medioevale e umanistica*, 8 (1965): 45-83.

37. For the text of the letter to Pietro de Poitiers (in Italian translation), see *Lettere di Francesco Petrarca delle cose familiari*, ed. Giuseppe Fracassetti, 4 (Florence: Le Monnier, 1866), Book 22, letter 13, 475-77. For the text of the letter to Tommaso del Garbo, see *Lettere senili di Francesco Petrarca*, ed. Giuseppe Fracassetti, 1 (Florence: Le Monnier, 1892), Book 8, letter 3, 463-74.

38. In the English translation by Thomas Twyne, *Phisicke against Fortune, as well prosperous, as adverse, conteyned in two Bookes* (London, 1579), that second book begins: "Of all the thinges wherein I ever toke delight, either in reading or hearing, there is nothing almost more firmelie setled, or more deepelie imprinted, or that more often commeth into my remembrance, than the saying of *Heraclitus, That all things are made by disagrement*" (fol. 153).

39. "Petrarch, Disciple of Heraclitus," *Speculum*, 11 (1936): 271. For a useful introduction to Petrarch's work, see F. N. M. Diekstra, Introduction to *A Dialogue between Reason and Adversity: A Late Middle English Version of Petrarch's De Remediis* (Assen: Van Gorcum, 1968).

40. *The Canterbury Tales*, in *The Works of Geoffrey Chaucer*, ed. F. N. Robinson, 2nd ed. (Boston: Houghton Mifflin, 1957).

41. "The Knight's Interruption of the *Monk's Tale*," *ELH*, 24 (1957): 261.

42. James Smith, "Chaucer, Boethius and Recent Trends in Criticism," *EIC*, 22 (1972): 31, *n*15.

43. *Chaucer's Poetry: An Anthology for the Modern Reader*, 2nd ed. (New York: Ronald Press, 1975), p. 1102.

44. Rodney K. Delasanta, "'Namoore of this': Chaucer's Priest and Monk," *TSL*, 13 (1968): 123.

45. Introduction to *The Middle French Liber Fortunae: A Critical Edition*, p. 9.

46. Reproduced by John Piggot, "Notes on the Polychromatic Decoration of Churches, with Special Reference to a Wall Painting Discovered in Ingatestone Church," *Transactions of the Essex Archaeological Society*, 4 (1866-69): 137-43.

47. *Allegories of the Virtues and Vices in Mediaeval Art from Early Christian*

Times to the Thirteenth Century, trans. Alan J. P. Crick (1939; reprint ed., New York: Norton, 1964), p. 71. For the illustration, see pl. XLIV, fig. 70. For a later variation of this motif, see "The Round Table of Vices" by Matthias Gerung (1546). Reproduced in *Hollstein's German Engravings, Etchings and Woodcuts*, ed. Fedja Anzelewski, compiled by Robert Zijlma, 10 (Amsterdam: Van Gendt, 1975), 40, fig. 45.

48. *Literature and Pulpit in Medieval England* (Cambridge: Cambridge Univ. Press, 1933), pp. 238-39.

49. *The Image of God, or laie mans booke, in whyche the ryghte knoweledge of God is disclosed, and diverse doutes besydes the principall matter* (London, 1550), sig. H1^V.

50. *The Institution of Christian Religion, wrytten in Latine by maister John Calvin, and translated into Englysh according to the authors last edition*, trans. [Thomas Norton] (London, 1561), Book I, fol. 58.

51. *Fiftie Godlie and Learned Sermons, divided into five Decades, conteyning the chiefe and principall pointes of Christian Religion*, trans. H. I. (London, 1577), p. 638. The author's name is given as Henrie Bullinger on the title page of this translation.

52. *A speciall Treatise of Gods Providence, and of comforts against all kinde of crosses & calamities to be fetched from the same*, trans. I. L. = J. L[udham] (London, 1588?), sig. A6^V.

53. *Institutions of Christian Religion, framed out of Gods word, and the writings of the best Divines, methodically handled by Questions and Answers*, trans. Robert Hill (London, 1606), p. 140. The author's name is given as William Bucanus on the title page of this translation.

54. *A frutefull treatise of predestination, and of the devine providence of God* (London, [1561]), sigs. L6^V-L7.

55. *A Woorke concerning the trewnesse of the Christian Religion, written in French: Against Atheists, Epicures, Paynims, Jewes, Mahumetists, and other Infidels*, trans. Sir Philip Sidney and Arthur Golding (London, 1587), p. 162.

56. *A Demonstration of God in his workes. Against all such as either in word or life deny there is a God* (London, 1598), p. 122.

57. *The French Academie, wherin is discoursed the institution of maners, and whatsoever els concerneth the good and happie life of all estates and callings*, trans. T. B. [Thomas Bowes?] (London, 1586), p. 468. The author's name is given as Peter de la Primaudaye on the title page of this translation.

Chapter 2

FORTUNE AND PROVIDENCE IN THE
MIRROR FOR MAGISTRATES

IN SIXTEENTH-CENTURY literary tradition, Fortune occupied an anomalous position dictated by the conflicting claims of classical and Christian cultures. The Elizabethans were heirs to an ancient and medieval tradition which extolled Fortune's power. But they were also admonished by contemporary moralists that the very name of the goddess constituted an affront to God's providence. Poets and dramatists, at once Christians and humanists, were forced to wrestle with the conflict. Their perplexity is nowhere more apparent than in the *Mirror for Magistrates* (1559), a work whose full title speaks of unstable prosperity, "even of those whom Fortune seemeth most highly to favour."[1] The editor's Preface to the Reader reveals that the authors had not chosen exclusively between literary convention and theological orthodoxy. William Baldwin, explaining how he came to supervise the compilation of the *Mirror*, writes that he had been asked

> to have the storye contynewed from where as Bochas [Boccaccio] lefte, unto this presente time, chiefly of suche as Fortune had dalyed with here in this ylande: whiche might be as a myrrour for al men as well noble as others, to shewe the slyppery deceytes of the wavering lady, and the due rewarde of all kinde of vices.[2]

This passage suggests that Fortune represents something more than the "superstition" decried by Christian apologists. At the same time,

30

the reader is left uncertain whether Fortune represents the awesome embodiment of contingency and change envisioned by antiquity. In fact, the stories of the *Mirror* raise a number of questions about the goddess. Did Fortune retain the meaning she possessed in antiquity? Was Fortune responsible for what Baldwin calls "the due rewarde of all kinde of vices"? And to what extent could Fortune be pressed into the service of the Christian God?

For most of the past half-century, the idea has prevailed that Fortune in the *Mirror* had become less capricious than previously.[3] According to Willard Farnham, "Fortune is more and more plainly made to surrender the mystery of her ways and to work according to laws which men may analyze and understand."[4] This diminution in Fortune's irrationality is generally attributed to the didacticism of the Elizabethan poets who, in the view of Lily B. Campbell, endeavored to substitute "an analysis of divine justice for the older philosophizing on the uncertainty of fortune."[5] Under the impact of this retributive emphasis, Fortune, it is thought, was inevitably incorporated into providential design and assigned a judicial function. Irving Ribner undoubtedly speaks for most readers when he concludes that "Fortune in the *Mirror* usually served as an agent by which God visited retribution upon evil rulers for their sins. . . ."[6]

Farnham, Campbell, and Ribner rightly underscore the role of providence in the *Mirror for Magistrates*. And the belief that, within such a framework, Fortune performed a retributive function gains support from the fact that Renaissance iconographers sometimes conflated Fortune and Nemesis, the classical goddess of justice. However, the very recognition of the centrality of providential justice to the *Mirror* has colored the modern interpretation of Fortune. The iconographic evidence, after all, proves inconsistent if not contradictory. And a careful reading of the poems themselves suggests that Fortune was no thoroughgoing executrix of God's will. On the contrary, Fortune generally retained the identity conferred by the ancients and, to a considerable extent, resisted absorption by Christian providence.

I

Baldwin and his associates were perhaps more interested in establishing accurate historical accounts than their predecessors in the *de casibus* tradition. But their interest did not lie exclusively or even principally in the assemblage of names, dates, and places. Of much greater consequence was recording the lessons that history taught. They assumed that human events were divinely ordained and that through the study of those events man might progress in his understanding of God's purposes. In other words, political history had significance in so far as it transcended what one character, the earl of Worcester, calls "the face / Of time and dedes" (22-23).[7] The causality that most interested the authors of the *Mirror* was of a moral kind.

In keeping with the political and moral objectives of the *Mirror*, the contributing poets are often led to a preoccupation with retributive justice, itself a manifestation of providence. Indeed, the retributive theme pervades Baldwin's work, leaving scarcely a story untouched. The tragic complaint of King James I of Scotland illustrates this insistent emphasis on the consequences of wrongdoing. The headnote sets the tone for the narrative: "How king James the first for breaking his othes and bondes, was by gods suffrauns miserably murdred of his owne subjectes" (p. 155). Like so many of his fellow penitents in the *Mirror*, James begins his lament with the customary address to his interlocutor, proceeds to sketch his personal history, and concludes by offering his story as a warning to others:

> See Baldwin Baldwin, the unhappy endes,
> Of suche as passe not for theyr lawfull oth:
> Of those that causeles leave theyr fayth or frendes,
> And murdre kynsfolke through their foes untroth. (148-51)

Despite the brutal manner of his death and the fact that his wife too was "sore wounded," James does not hesitate to attribute his demise to providential design. Avoid "lyke sinnes," he admonishes us, "For God hates hyghly suche as are forsworne" (154). A sense of God's constant watchfulness permeates the entire narrative. Not a shred of doubt ever enters James's mind that, given his crimes, his end could or should have been other than it was. There is no sense of capricious change at work. James inhabits a world rigorously ordered by the divine will. The repentant monarch has an Augustinian faith in the goodness and justice of providence and confidence that he discerns its logic.

So pronounced is the emphasis on retributive justice in accounts such as James's that other concerns are necessarily subordinated and assimilated. Under the burden of the providential framework, even Dame Fortune seems at times to become a partner of providence. When, for instance, the poets make a series of references to the goddess, each one of which is connected with some misdeed of the tragic figure, they imply that Fortune's behavior is congruent with God's purposes. This handling of Fortune can be observed in its simplest form in James's narrative. There he refers to Fortune in the first stanza and then, later, after confessing his part in the murder of innocents, reflects:

> And while sly Fortune at my doinges smiled,
> The wrath of God which I had wel deserved,
> Fell on my necke, for thus loe was I served. (131-33)

The goddess plays a similar role in the tragedy of Robert Tresilian, whose fall came about "for misconstruyng the lawes, and expounding them to serve the Princes affections" (p. 73). Tresilian opens his account with a reference to Fortune and then goes on to record his worldly attainments. About midway through the narrative, he chronicles his road to vice and foreshadows his future doom when he says:

> Thus clymyng and contendyng alway to the top
> From hye unto hygher, and than to be most hye,
> The hunny dewe of Fortune so fast on us dyd drop
> That of kinge Richards counsayle we came to be full nye.
> (78-81)

The comments of James and Tresilian imply a relationship of character to Fortune that is not ethically neutral. That is, their references chronicle not only a character's rise to power but also his fall from virtue. The allusions to Fortune thus serve as a kind of index of that figure's changing moral status. As he plunges more deeply into crime, his position with respect to Fortune rises. Fortune, or Fortune's wheel, becomes a means by which the poet can graphically display the declining moral probity of his character.

That the authors of the *Mirror for Magistrates* sometimes conceive of Fortune's activity as an expression of God's will is clear enough. Henry VI, for instance, declares that he will admit Fortune to his cosmology only with the proviso that she serve as an agent of God (49-52). That Baldwin and his compatriots did not originate this notion is equally plain. As we have seen, Dante had, centuries earlier in the *Commedia*, envisioned Fortune as an executrix of providence. And in his *Fall of Princes*, John Lydgate had written that "God above hath the sovereynte, / And off Fortune the power may restreyne, / To save and spille lik as folk disserve."[8] Many iconographic representations during the Renaissance demonstrate the survival of this notion. In a woodcut that appears in a German translation of Petrarch's *De Remediis Utriusque Fortunae* (1532), Hans Burgkmair the Elder portrays Fortune sitting on a throne which is suspended from heaven by ropes.[9] Thus the artist indicates the subjection of Fortune to God's will. Similarly, in a woodcut by George Pencz (1534) depicting Dame Fortune turning her wheel on which men rise and fall, God's hand, which extends out of a cloud, holds a bridle and reins which are attached to Fortune (Chew, fig. 52). Pencz means to demonstrate that, while Fortune may have the power to direct human destiny, ultimately she acts under the aegis of God.

The relationship between Fortune and God implicit in such designs suggests that Fortune exercises a function not unlike that of Nemesis, the classical goddess of retribution for wrongdoing.[10] Renaissance thinkers actually comment upon this correspondence, mythographers finding a precedent for it in the literature of antiquity. Richard Linche, for example, while noting that Fortune and Nemesis could be quite disparate, also points out that "Among the Ancients and among the old writers, Fortuna and Nemesis were oftentimes taken to bee all one. . . ."[11] During the Renaissance Fortune and Nemesis continued to be linked at times, and there seems to have been some uncertainty about how to differentiate the two.[12] This confusion, apparent in the iconography of the period, is epitomized in Albrecht Dürer's engraving of Nemesis (c. 1501-2). The design shows a winged woman holding in one hand a bridle symbolic of both restraint and chastisement and, in the other, a goblet or vase symbolic of temperance and reward (fig. 1). But

Fig. 1. Albrecht Dürer, engraving of Nemesis, c. 1501-1502.

35

Nemesis stands upon a globe not unlike that which appears in representations of Fortune. That Dürer intended to represent Nemesis is clear from the references he makes to this engraving in his diary.[13] That he incorporated a symbol that belongs to Fortune seems equally obvious, for Dürer's engraving has been called "Das grosse Glück" since at least the seventeenth century and probably earlier.[14]

A variety of other pictorial designs shows that Dürer was not alone in associating Nemesis with Fortune. Nemesis borrows an accouterment of Fortune in Andrea Alciati's *Viri Clarissimi . . . Emblematum Liber* (Augsburg, 1531). There the goddess again holds a bridle but she stands upon a wheel resembling that of Fortune (fig. 2).[15] Nemesis

NEC VERBO NEC FACTO
quenquam lædendum.

*A ſſequitur, Nemeſisq; uirum ueſtigia ſeruat
Continet & cubitum, duráq; frena manu
Ne male quid facias, néue impròba uerba loquaris
Et iubet in cunctis rebus adeſſe modum.*

Fig. 2. Andrea Alciati, Viri Clarissimi . . . Emblematum Liber

acquires not only Fortune's wheel but also her rudder in Vincenzo Cartari's *Imagini de i Dei de gli antichi* (Venice, 1556; first illustrated edition, Venice, 1571). Cartari's Nemesis carries a bridle in one hand and a cubit-rule in the other; she stands upon a wheel that, in turn, leans against a rudder (Panofsky, fig. 12). Sixteenth-century poets and playwrights also reflect this iconographic conflation. Thus, for example, Nemesis acquires the rudder in the play *Respublica* (1553), where Nemesis appears as a character:

> Her cognizance therefore is a wheel and wings to fly,
> In token her rule extendeth far and nigh.
> A rudder eke she beareth in her other hand,
> As directory of all things in every land.[16]

In such representations, pictorial and verbal, Nemesis clearly usurps the properties of Dame Fortune. The relationship between the two was, however, reciprocal, for Fortune could occasionally borrow the trappings of Nemesis. Hans Holbein's woodcut of the *Table of Cebes* (c. 1521), often used as a frontispiece, depicts a figure labeled "Fortuna" holding the bridle of Nemesis (Panofsky, fig. 16). And on the title page of the 1642 edition of Francis Bacon's *Historia Regni Henrici Septimi*, Cornelis Van Dalen represents Fortune with both wheel and bridle (Chew, fig. 68). This exchange of implements between Nemesis and Fortune came about, of course, not only because mythographers had found some classical precedent for the iconography but also because the artistic and literary creators of these figures in the Renaissance saw them as sharing certain traits. Just as Fortune could perform a retributive function (akin to that of Nemesis), so too Nemesis could represent mere vicissitude (usually embodied in Fortune) as well as retribution. Francis Bacon explains in *The Wisedome of the Ancients* (1619),

> Her name *Nemesis* doth plainly signifie Revenge or Retribution, her office and administration being (like a Tribune of the people) to hinder the constant & perpetuall felicity of happy men, and to interpose her word, *veto*, I forbid the continuance of it, that is, not onely to chastice insolency, but to intermix prosperity (though harmles and in

37

a meane) with the vicissitudes of adversity, as if it were a custome, that noe mortall man should be admitted to the Table of the Gods but for sport.[17]

Both Fortune and Nemesis, moreover, possess the power to inflict adversity, no matter how high an individual's station. And Nemesis could act with the malice commonly associated with Fortune: in Thomas Kyd's *Spanish Tragedy* (c. 1587), Horatio speaks of "wrathful Nemesis, that wicked power."[18] There was, then, a conceptual basis for the iconographic parallels.

The designs of Burgkmair and Pencz, of Dürer and Van Dalen, together with such narratives as those of James and Tresilian in the *Mirror*, might well lead us to suppose that Christian artists and poets had successfully harnessed the pagan goddess, that Fortune had become one with Nemesis, that the ambiguity seemingly inherent in Baldwin's Preface to the *Mirror for Magistrates* had been neatly resolved by subordinating Fortune to providence and by assigning the goddess a retributive function. There is even a passage in the *Mirror* which appears to confirm such assumptions. In the prose link following the story of William de la Pole, duke of Suffolk, Baldwin says that the poets were pleased to see the man punished, "For though Fortune in many poyntes be injurius to Princes, yet in this and such lyke she is moost righteous: And only deserveth the name of a Goddes, whan she provideth meanes to punish & distroye Tyrantes" (p. 170). These words, in all likelihood written by the editor of the *Mirror*, have an authoritative air. It is questionable, however, whether they accurately and fully characterize Fortune's role in the *Mirror*. In fact, there is some question whether they apply even to Suffolk's story, for nowhere in the narrative is there any explicit description of Fortune corresponding to that which appears in the prose link. Nor, for that matter, is there such a statement in any of the poems of the 1559 *Mirror*. Moreover, the epithet with which Baldwin chooses to describe Fortune — "righteous" — is never applied to the goddess anywhere in the poems. On the contrary, Fortune is consistently described in the opposite terms. Tresilian calls her "frowarde" (35), Northumberland "double" (14), Warwick "false" (8), and Henry VI "fel" (118). The various narratives thus fail to confirm in practice what

Baldwin asserts in theory: although Fortune could be employed to de-lineate a character's dedication to vice and his imminent demise, and, although Fortune might also effect a person's fall, nevertheless, the poets were not entirely comfortable with Fortune in the guise of Nemesis. To discover why they were uneasy, let us consider what Suffolk has to say about Fortune.

In the course of his lament, the duke makes a number of comments about the goddess, the first of which reads: "My only life in all poyntes may suffise / To shewe howe base all baytes of Fortune be, / Which thaw like yse, through heate of envies eyes" (8-10). Like many of the other ghostly narrators, Suffolk speaks of Fortune's capacity for deceiving and entrapping man. In similar fashion, we have already seen James suggest-ing that Fortune led him on to a life of crime. And Tresilian opens his ac-count by announcing sadly: "In the rufull Register of mischief and mishap, / Baldwin we beseche thee with our names to begin, / Whom unfrendly Fortune did trayne unto a trap" (1-3). Mortimer too suggests Fortune's treachery: "whyles that Fortune lulde me in her lap, / And gave me gyftes mo than I dyd requyre, / The subtyll quean behynde me set a trap, / whereby to dashe and laye all in the myre" (99-102). In the eyes of Suffolk and the others, Fortune not only conceals her true nature for a time, she also takes advantage of man's ignorance to encourage his transgressions. In short, Fortune represents an enticement to evil. This conception of the goddess constitutes a modification of the way in which Fortune was normally viewed in an-tiquity. If Fortune was primarily a test of virtue for Seneca, she represents a temptation to vice for the Christian. The transformation of adversary into full-fledged temptress was one price that Fortune had to pay for adaptation to a Christian world. It was an appealing solu-tion for poets because, by portraying Fortune in this fashion, they were able to preserve a pagan symbol which still had the capacity to evoke an emotional response in a contemporary audience. Moreover, they could depict harsh adversity without seeming to undermine a benevolent providence; like other embodiments of temptation, Fortune helped to explain the existence of evil in a divinely ordered world. Undoubtedly, such an adaptation of the pagan goddess pleased those who sought to slip the yoke of the Christian God upon Fortune. However, it also tended, ultimately, to undercut the identification of Fortune with Nemesis. For as a cunning, treacherous, and cruel tempter, Fortune could not possibly be an embodiment of rationality, fairness, and justice. Indeed, to be true to her nature, Fortune had to represent exactly the opposite qualities. Logically, Fortune could no more be an emblem of righteousness than could Satan.

Given the conceptual contradiction involved in merging tempter and justicer, it is not surprising that poets and artists in the Renaissance more often than not sought to discriminate between Fortune and Nemesis. Emblem books provide the most graphic evidence of this phenomenon. We have, above, noted several designs which seem to conflate Fortune and Nemesis, including that of Alciati in 1531. Only five years after the publication of his *Viri Clarissimi*, however, another edition appeared with a picture of Nemesis very different from the first. Although the motto and poem remain the same in both editions, and although the woodcut still shows Nemesis holding a bridle, the wheel that she had stood upon in the 1531 edition has disappeared (fig. 3). There is now nothing in the emblem to link Nemesis with Fortune. Similarly, in Gilles Corrozet's *Hecatomgraphie* (1543), Nemesis appears with a bridle and the palm of victory, but without a single accouterment of Fortune.[19] Again, Achille Bocchi's *Symbolicarum Quaestionum . . . Libri Quinque* (1555) depicts Nemesis as winged and holding a bridle and cubit-rule, but without any specific attributes of Fortune.[20] (The wings of Nemesis are thought to derive not from those that appear in some representations of Fortune, but rather from those of the classical Victory.[21]) Geoffrey Whitney's depiction of Nemesis in *A Choice of Emblemes* (1586) also shows the goddess without any implements associated with Fortune,[22] and the Nemesis of Otho Vaenius (Octavio van Veen) carries a bridle and whip but no property of Fortune.[23] Especially interesting is the design by Hans Holbein for the wall of the guildhall of the London Steelyard Merchants (1532-33). Called "The Triumph of Riches," the picture portrays, in one corner, Nemesis hovering in the clouds with her bridle; in the center, Fortune holds her billowing cloak and sits upon her globe.[24] Although Holbein could merge features of Fortune and Nemesis, as he seems to do in his engraving for the *Table of Cebes*, cited above, he could also represent the two in a single painting as utterly different.

Nec uerbo nec facto quenquam
lædendum.

Affequitur, Nemesisꝗ; uirum uestigia feruat,
Continet & cubitum duráꝗ; frena manu.
Ne malè quid facias, néue improba uerba loquaris:
Et iubet in cunctis rebus adeffe modum.
B

Fig. 3. Andrea Alciati, Emblematum Libellus

II

Fortune's assimilation by providence was frustrated not only by her transformation into a temptress, which effectively precluded a successful fusion with Nemesis, but also, even more importantly, by Fortune's pagan inheritance, especially her ancient identification with contingency. To understand why this association made it awkward to assign Fortune a providential function, let us return to Suffolk's narrative. There we learn that the duke, guilty of heinous crimes, is exiled by the king. On his way to the Continent, Suffolk's ship accidentally encounters another vessel manned by his enemies. The poet takes pains to link Suffolk's apprehension and subsequent death with his manner of living. With these words he opens the stanza which recounts the duke's capture: "marke howe vengeaunce wayteth upon vice" (162). But the poet must also concede that the meeting of ships on the high seas was adventitious: "The Earle of Devonshires barke, of litle price, / Encountred me upon the seas by chaunce" (164-65). This creates a problem for a poet intent on demonstrating the providential nature of his character's end, for as ancient, medieval, and Renaissance thinkers recognized, the operation of chance can seriously undercut a sense of heavenly design.

The author of Suffolk's story might have followed the strategy employed in another narrative that deals with chance, that of Lord Clifford. The villainous Clifford, struck by an arrow while adjusting his armor in battle, addresses himself directly to the issue when he asks, "Was this a chaunce?" and replies, "no suer, gods just award, / Wherin due justice playnly doth appere" (57-58). Clifford's shrill question and answer arise out of his eagerness to disallow the phenomenon of chance which he clearly sees as a threat to God's justice. So anxious is the poet to trumpet the operation of providence that he excludes even an incidental reference to Fortune lest the presence of this traditional embodiment of contingency blunt the impact of his aggressively retributive poem. The author of Suffolk's narrative also seeks to maximize the sense of design and minimize the aura of contingency. But he takes a more oblique approach: he simply refuses to confront directly the problem that the existence of chance poses to his just world. And he quietly banishes Fortune from the poem. By the time he relates the capture of Suffolk, the poet has already alluded to Fortune four times. As soon as he recounts the fortuitous encounter of ships, however, Fortune disappears from the narrative. Were the poet secure in associating Fortune with justice and providential design, he would not have deemed it necessary to exclude Fortune from the last third of the poem. That part of the narrative is, in a sense, the heart of the poem because it is there that Suffolk's arrest is described and the moral drawn. On the basis of his handling of Fortune, particularly his care to remove the goddess from the poem when a fortuitous event is recounted, it would appear that the author of Suffolk's tale saw Fortune as an emblem of contingency and contingency as a threat to providence. The poem itself, then, fails to corroborate the editorial comments that follow it. Instead of representing a considered evaluation of Fortune, Baldwin's remark about "righteous" Fortune seems to have been something of an afterthought. His tone is defensive, as though he felt obliged to explain the presence of Fortune in a narrative that chronicles God's justice. Fortune's role in Suffolk's story and in the *Mirror for Magistrates* generally is a good deal more anomalous than Baldwin concedes.

In evaluating the relationship between Fortune and providence, it is useful to consider not only where Fortune is excluded from the poems, but also where she gains the greatest prominence. No story in the 1559 *Mirror* accords Fortune more attention than that of Thomas Montague, earl of Salisbury. Like Clifford and Suffolk, Salisbury meets his end through apparent mischance. The headnote calls attention to the element of contingency when it announces that the earl "in the middes of his glory, was chaunceably slayne with a piece of ordinaunce" (p. 143). A man of war, Salisbury is unaccountably killed during a peaceful interlude. Surveying the siege of Orleans, he suffers a mortal wound when struck in the face by a pellet shot from the city. The circumstances of the earl's death seem neither more nor less fortuitous than those surrounding the deaths of Suffolk and Clifford. Yet Fortune assumes an extraordinary importance in Salisbury's narrative. Nor is Fortune excluded from the conclusion as she is in Suffolk's story. On the contrary Salisbury continues to inveigh against the goddess even as he draws the moral. The reader may well wonder why, if Fortune is an embodiment of contingency and if contingency is felt to threaten providence, the poet here tolerates the presence of the pagan goddess.

The prominence that Fortune achieves in the poem seems directly related to the predominant tone. In contrast to Clifford's doctrinaire pronouncements, Salisbury strikes a tentative, querulous note. This, in turn, springs from the poet's obvious uncertainty over how to account for his subject's death. The author would undoubtedly like to see God's hand in this occurrence. The protagonist utters such wise saws as, "To every vice due guerdon doth belong" (77). But such remarks seem grossly inappropriate to Salisbury's death, for the poet has to concede that the earl has led an exemplary life. Guilty of no wrongdoing and at a moment of seemingly complete safety, he is struck down in his prime for no apparent reason. Salisbury does not address himself specifically to the questions raised by his untimely death. But during the course of the narrative, we find passages which suggest that the poet is wrestling with the puzzle of the protagonist's death. Early in the poem, for example, Salisbury ponders his father's wrongful death:

> And God doth suffer that it should be so,
> But why, my wit is feble to decise,
> Except it be to heape up wrath and wo
> Upon their heades that injuries devise.
> The cause why mischiefes many times arise,
> And light on them that wold mens wronges redresse,
> Is for the rancour that they beare, I gesse. (64-70)

His words could, of course, apply just as easily to his own fate as to his father's, for he is equally perplexed by his own death. This uncertainty and confusion are especially manifest at the close of the poem. Unlike most of the other narrators, who conclude in leisurely fashion as they delineate the meaning inherent in their falls, Salisbury continues for only a single stanza after relating his death. Embarrassed by his inability to offer a convincing explanation for his end, he breaks off abruptly:

See Baldwin see the uncertaynty of glory,
How sodayne mischief dasheth all to dust.
And warne all princes by my broken story,
The happiest Fortune chiefly to mistrust.
Was never man that alway had his lust.
Than such be fooles, in fancy more then mad,
Which hope to have that never any had. (274-80)

Denied the opportunity to attribute Salisbury's end to villainy, the poet
in his bafflement falls back upon Fortune as an explanation for an inexplicable occurrence. Here, as elsewhere throughout the narrative, the
poet introduces Fortune to fill the vacuum left by a providence conspicuous by its absence.

Salisbury's story, together with those of Suffolk, Clifford, and others,
permits some generalizations about the use of Fortune in the *Mirror for
Magistrates*. When a poet is most confident that he understands the justice of God's ways, he aggressively denies the phenomenon of chance.
And he implicitly rejects Fortune by severely restricting the role she
plays or by totally excluding her from the narrative. However,
when the poet is genuinely mystified by the fate of his protagonist, when
injustice seems to prevail, and when the character's death lends itself to
no easy explanation, then he refrains from explicitly raising the issue of
contingency. He foregoes a too strident assertion of providential design.
And he allows Fortune to become the presiding deity of the poem.
Fortune, who stubbornly refused to relinquish her association with
chance, may not have represented any ultimate explanation for contingency. However, this personification at least allowed the inexplicable
and the irrational to be localized and objectified.

Only in a few cases do the authors of the *Mirror* speak openly of the
tension between Fortune and providence. One such instance occurs in
the 1563 edition, where Lord Hastings relates his richly deserved fall and
asks rhetorically about God:

And hath he erst restraynd his provydence?
Or is he nygard of his free dispence?
Or is he uncertayne foresett dryfts to dryve?

That not Dame Chaunce but he all goods may gyve?
A heathen god they hold, whoe fortune keepe,
To deal them happs, whyle god they ween a sleepe.
Mock godds they are, and many Gods induce,
Whoe fortune fayne to father theyr abuse. (521-28)

Occasionally, as here, the poets concede the fundamental incompatibility of providence and Fortune. More frequently, though, we sense that the authors of the *Mirror* are intuitively but silently aware of the dissonance. It is no coincidence that they nearly always refrain from proclaiming God's justice and Fortune's power in the same breath. Providential design may be conspicuous in one story and the vagaries of Fortune in another. But there is a definite correlation between the relative prominence accorded providence and that given Fortune. Invariably, those poems that seek to emphasize divine justice also restrain the scope of Fortune. Thus, in the narratives of James, Tresilian, and Clifford—all strongly retributive in orientation—Fortune plays a decidedly secondary role or none at all. The authors of the *Mirror for Magistrates* carefully orchestrate the two themes in order to avoid any overt clash. Providence and Fortune may appear on the same stage, but they do so in an artistically controlled manner.

III

If the authors of the *Mirror* were, on account of doctrinal conviction, inclined to assert divine providence, they were drawn to Fortune for pragmatic reasons. As writers who, according to the prose links, discussed the strengths and weaknesses of one another's work, they must have known that a poem more readily engages the reader or listener and fosters identification with the tragic figure when it employs rather than ignores or dismisses Fortune. Such poetry, in short, becomes more emotionally compelling as it makes of Fortune an impressive antagonist. This principle is vividly illustrated by Thomas Sackville's complaint of Henry, duke of Buckingham, which first appeared in the *Mirror* of 1563. The celebrated poem, unusual in its length, treats of providence for a time before turning to Fortune; it thus enables us to examine the very different poetic effects achieved by each of these formulations.

Although the opening stanzas speak of Fortune's guile, the first third of Sackville's poem is concerned chiefly with Buckingham's career in crime. In some detail the tragic figure recounts his path to perdition. He tells how he went to the aid of Richard, duke of Gloucester, and how he helped this aspirant destroy his rivals. Making scarcely any attempt to extenuate his guilt for heinous acts, Buckingham portrays himself as a craven accomplice: "What he thought best, to me so seemde the same, / My selfe not bent so much for to aspyer, / As to fulfyl that greedy dukes desyre" (61-63). Describing himself as "drowned in the depth / Of diepe desyre to drinke the gylteles blud" (169-70), he seems almost inhuman in his viciousness.

The reader or auditor is, during this recital, somewhat detached. Although Buckingham may be the speaker, it is in effect divine judgment that we hear: "So just is God in al his dreadfull doomes" (105). But after nearly two hundred lines illustrating the extent of his wrongdoing, Buckingham adopts a more human viewpoint. If we have been made to sense the wrath of God looking down on the miscreant, now we begin to learn of his suffering. He speaks movingly of his mental torment: "we diepe wounded with the bluddy thought, / And gnawing wurme that grieved our conscience so, / Never tooke ease" (239-41). And he recounts his growing sense of horror at Richard's ruthlessness: "alas I weepe in thought, / To thinke on that which this fel wretche hath wrought" (363-64).

As the perspective of the speaker shifts, Dame Fortune begins to assume greater prominence.[25] Indeed, once he begins to reveal his misgivings, scarcely an incident occurs that is not somehow related to Fortune. She is on Buckingham's mind, for instance, even as he experiences the first stirrings of conscience: "Loe sée the fine, when once it felt the whele / Of slipper Fortune, stay it mought no stowne, / The wheele whurles up, but strayt it whurleth downe" (250-52). And, after his break with Richard, Fortune plays a key role in Buckingham's undoing. Significantly, he brackets the account of his followers' defection with pointed reminders of Fortune's treachery. Before relating the sudden desertion, Buckingham comments:

while I nowe had Fortune at my becke
Mistrusting I no earthly thing at all,
Unwares alas, least looking for a checke,
She mated me in turning of a ball. (407-10)

And of the soldiers' cowardly action, he concludes, "such is Fortune
when she lyst to frowne, / Who seemes most sure, him soonest whurles
she down" (419-20).

By the time we reach this desperate stage in Buckingham's career,
providence is little in evidence; in fact, it has diminished nearly to the
vanishing point. Meanwhile, the representation of Fortune has been
enlarged until Buckingham is no longer the scourge of God but the prey
of the goddess. This transition has a direct bearing on our response to
the character, for as the assertion of providential design gives way to the
recognition of Fortune's perversity, so too our indignation at Buckingham's transgression yields to compassion at his plight. He comes to
seem less a culprit and more a casualty of the overwhelming
odds against him. Because he is a sufferer, especially of Fortune's
caprice, we are drawn more closely to him and share his tribulation to a
far greater extent than we might if he were merely an exemplum of
God's wrath.

As the complaint draws to a close, Sackville's protagonist lavishes
ever more attention on Fortune's role in his demise. And as he does so,
the poem becomes still more affecting. With keen psychological
insight, the poet converts Buckingham's pain at Fortune's hostility into
anger at Fortune, and in this way he taps the reservoir of feeling that can
only be released by the rhetoric of denunciation. Buckingham's passion
intensifies as he relates his betrayal at the hands of one of his oldest and,
ostensibly, most loyal retainers. So apoplectic does Buckingham
become that he actually breaks off his account; the poet then steps in
with a description of the anguished figure. Regaining his composure,
Buckingham excoriates Fortune: "false Fortune whan I suspected
least, / Dyd turne the wheele, and wyth a dolefull fall / Hath me bereft of
honour life and all" (747-49). His riches and position – the gifts of Fortune – were of no avail, for "Whan Fortune frounde the feller made my
fall" (756). The ruined duke stands a monument to Fortune's

48

deceit: "on whom but me dyd she most smyle? / And whom but me lo, dyd she most begyle?" (769-70). Despite his once great power, he could not hope to contend with the antipathy of the goddess:

> Now hast thou heard the whole of my unhap,
> My chaunce, my chaunge, the cause of all my care:
> In wealth and wo, how Fortune dyd me wrap,
> With world at will to win me to her snare. (771-74)

With each salvo against Fortune, Buckingham embellishes a self-portrait that flatters more than it indicts him. There is little affirmation of providential justice in these stanzas and necessarily so: to dwell on God's righteousness at this point would undercut the heroism of a man whose antagonist is Fortune herself. For the purpose of enhancing Buckingham's stature and thus of enlisting our sympathies, the caprice and malignity of Fortune serve the poet's needs more effectively than the justice and benevolence of God.

Had Sackville banished Fortune from his poem, he might still have created an interesting narrative, but one with less capacity to move us. This, at least, seems a likely inference since those poems most concerned to minimize Fortune's role tend to be among the least affecting in the *Mirror for Magistrates*. Consider, for example, Jack Cade's lament, included in the 1559 edition.

At the outset Cade bluntly raises the question of Fortune's existence. In an effort to redefine Fortune, he asks if what men call Fortune is not the culmination of their own desires, judgments, and actions: "Shal I cal it Fortune or my froward folly / That lifted me, and layed me downe below?" (1-2). And, after speaking briefly of God's providence and man's free will, he formulates this conclusion about Fortune:

> Now if this happe wherby we yelde our mynde
> To lust and wyll, be fortune, as we name her,
> Than is she justly called false and blynde,
> And no reproche can be to much to blame her:
> Yet is the shame our owne when so we shame her,
> For sure this hap if it be rightly knowen,
> Cummeth of our selves, and so the blame our owne. (29-35)

By emphasizing man's liberty to choose his own destiny and by arguing for the providential ordering of the world, Cade implicitly shrinks Fortune's realm. Indeed, he not only seeks to take away her status as a kind of quasi-divinity, but he also virtually disallows Fortune as an embodiment of change and chance when he declares: "Fortune is the folly and plage of those / Which to the worlde their wretched willes dispose" (41-42).

In his uncompromising attitude toward Fortune, Jack Cade gives eloquent voice to the sentiments of many sixteenth-century thinkers. And in the prose link at the conclusion of the poem, the assembled writers allude to the speaker's intellectual attainments. One listener compliments Cade's erudition, saying, "By saint mary . . . yf Jacke wer as well learned, as you have made his oracion, What so ever he was by byrth, I warraunt hym a gentylman by his learnyng. Howe notably and Philosopher like hath he discrybed Fortune and the causes of worldly cumbraunce?" (p. 178). With some justice this observer points to the merit of the poem: its shrewd analysis of man's responsibility for his condition and his penchant for rationalizing his folly.

What the speaker leaves unsaid, however, is also important. Although he praises the poem as philosophy, he says nothing about its being particularly well liked by the auditors.[26] And with good reason. For just as surely as we acknowledge the philosophic orthodoxy of the poem, we must also admit that Cade's narrative lacks dramatic impact. In fact, the deficiency of the poem arises largely from that very orthodoxy. So concerned is the poet to demonstrate the man's villainy that Cade emerges merely as an exemplum of divine justice. He comes before us a penitent, offering a subdued admission of guilt and a redefinition of Fortune. While perhaps satisfying from a philosophic standpoint, this is plainly deficient as human drama. In order for the reader or auditor to become involved, he must share, however briefly, the protagonist's frustrated aspirations and sense of bitter disappointment. Such identification is made difficult by Cade's attribution of everything that befalls him to his own culpability and to God's judgment.

Surely Cade's lament would have greater emotional force if he were to come before us a martyr to hostile circumstance, struggling to endure in the face of adversity. Or if he were defiant, challenging the yoke of a hostile deity. And perhaps the author of the narrative himself realized this, for midway through the poem Fortune, whose existence had earlier been denied, is unexpectedly revived. Describing his progress in crime, Cade says, "Se here how Fortune setting us a flote / Brought to our nettes a porcion of our pray" (71-72). And in the last stanza, Cade bids his listeners not be slaves of Fortune:

> There is no trust in rebelles, raskall knaves,
> In Fortune lesse, whiche wurketh as the waves:
> From whose assautes who lyst to stande at large,
> Must folowe skyll, and flye all worldly charge. (165-68)

These references to Fortune, following the earlier repudiation, do not signify that the poet has suddenly overcome his philosophic misgivings about Fortune. Rather, they suggest an effort to enhance Cade's stature by creating a more impressive antagonist than "raskall knaves." The poet, then, temporarily banishes his scruples about Fortune in the interests of good storytelling.

Intellectual subtlety of the kind displayed in Cade's complaint and dramatic effectiveness of the kind displayed in Buckingham's are sometimes joined in a single poem. There is no finer instance than Jane Shore's lament, written by Thomas Churchyard and included in the *Mirror for Magistrates* of 1563.

The opening lines herald the role that Fortune plays in Jane Shore's story: "Among the rest by Fortune overthrowen, / I am not least, that most may wayle her fate" (1-2). What might be passing references to Fortune in another poem become elaborate set pieces here. Thus the second stanza offers a brief discourse on Fortune's capacity to deceive:

> This wandryng worlde bewitched me with wyles,
> And wonne my wittes wyth wanton sugred joyes,
> In Fortunes frekes who trustes her when she smyles,
> Shal fynde her false, and full of fyckle toyes,
> Her tryumphes al but fyl our eares wyth noyse,
> Her flatteryng gyftes are pleasures myxt wyth payne.
> Yea al her wordes are thunders threatnyng rayne. (8-14)

Such passages, like those in Buckingham's account, suggest the precariousness of the human condition. They guide our response toward compassion rather than censure, for although we know that Jane Shore has transgressed moral law, we cannot fail to appreciate her distress. We tend to understand rather than condemn.

This is not to say that the poem absolves Jane Shore of culpability. On the contrary, the poem exposes her flaws of character. It does so, however, in oblique fashion — by suggesting her similarity to the Fortune she decries. For example, Jane relates her wielding of great power in words that Fortune herself might speak: "I strake the stroke that threwe the mightye downe" (175). And she recalls the sugared lips of Fortune when she says, "With my sweete wordes I could the kyng perswade" (177). Moreover, like Fortune, notorious for her smiles and frowns, Jane revels in the flattery of her subjects: "Yf I did frowne, who then did looke awrye? / Yf I dyd smyle, who would not laugh outryght?" (183-84). Finally, Jane recalls one of Fortune's most common accouterments, the rolling sphere: "when the ball was at my foote to guyde, / I played to those that fortune did abide" (209-10). (Buckingham says of Fortune, "She mated me in turning of a ball" [410].)

What Churchyard has done is to apply Jack Cade's insight about Fortune ("Shal I cal it Fortune or my froward folly / That lifted me, and layed me downe below?"), but in such a way that Jane Shore's lament has all the dramatic appeal of Buckingham's. By depicting her as the victim of hostile Fortune, the poet enlists our sympathies. At the same time, the poet suggests that Jane Shore came, like Fortune, to relish the exercise of power, that she bent others to her will through guile, and that, in her actions, she could be indifferent to reason and virtue. Her admission that "for the time a Goddesse place I had" (217) seems a clear indication of the connection between her character and Fortune's.

Churchyard has drawn his portrait of Jane Shore with extraordinary skill. Although he fills the poem with references to Fortune, he avoids condoning Jane's actions. And although he suggests her culpability, he avoids reducing the tragic figure to the status of mere exemplum. The poet recognizes how complex a matter is responsibility: he knows that culprit and victim may be one and the same.

IV

The stories of Jane Shore, Jack Cade, Buckingham, and the others in the *Mirror* had, collectively, a profound impact on Elizabethan tragedy. Their significance is explained by Lily B. Campbell: "probably the most far-reaching influence of the *Mirror for Magistrates* came through the fact that it acted as the bridge by which medieval tragedy crossed over into the literature of the Renaissance."[27] As a literary bridge, the *Mirror* reached back to the precursor of medieval tragedy in the Roman world, where Fortune was an integral part of tragedy. Fortune herself asks in the *Consolation of Philosophy*, "What else does the cry of tragedy bewail but the overthrow of happy realms by the unexpected blow of Fortune?"[28] This same query could be made of most *de casibus* tragedies in the Middle Ages. The genre takes its name from Boccaccio's *De Casibus Virorum Illustrium*, written in Latin prose between 1355 and 1360.[29] Like Roman tragedy, this too celebrates Fortune's power. "The *De Casibus*," writes Derek Pearsall, "is a history of Fortune, of the crushing blows dealt to the most illustrious characters in history and mythology, based mostly on Biblical and classical sources, with the object of teaching princes wisdom and virtue by showing them the misfortunes brought on by pride, ambition, and sin, or simply the salutary lesson of misfortune."[30] Largely through the influence of Boccaccio, Fortune remained part of the very definition of tragedy. Thus in *The Canterbury Tales* the Monk says:

> I wol biwaille, in manere of tragedie,
> The harm of hem that stoode in heigh degree,
> And fillen so that ther nas no remedie
> To brynge hem out of hir adversitee.
> For certein, whan that Fortune list to flee,
> Ther may no man the cours of hire withholde.[31]

John Lydgate, adapting Laurent de Premierfait's paraphrase of Boccaccio, went on to compile more instances of tragedy than even Chaucer's garrulous Monk envisioned. And, like his predecessors, Lydgate makes

Fortune central to his tragedies. In *The Fall of Princes,* written in the 1430s, Lydgate writes of Laurent:

> Ful weel he felte the labour was notable,
> The fall of nobles, with everi circumstau*n*ce,
> From ther lordshippes, dreedful and unstable,
> How that thei fill to putte in remembrau*n*ce,
> Therin to shewe Fortunys variau*n*ce,
> That othre myhte as in a merour see
> In worldly worshepe may be no surete.[32]

At one point in *The Fall of Princes* (Book VI), Fortune actually takes over the narration of tragical stories. Dame Fortune does not play the same role in the *Mirror for Magistrates,* but Baldwin's work, conceived as an extension of Lydgate's, also chronicles Fortune's exploits.[33] Indeed, no other Elizabethan book provides so comprehensive and varied a treatment of Fortune.

As a bridge the *Mirror for Magistrates* proved extraordinarily sturdy. Upon successful publication in 1559,[34] it quickly became a literary phenomenon, going through new editions in 1563, 1571, 1574, 1575, 1578, and 1587. Supplementing Baldwin's efforts, John Higgins and Thomas Blenerhasset added stories of ancient Rome and pre-Christian Britain to accounts of the more recent past. By the time that Richard Niccols compiled his edition in 1610, the *Mirror* had grown from its original nineteen poems to over ninety. In addition, the *Mirror* inspired a small library of similar works, many bearing the words "mirror" or "complaint" in the title.[35] Among the writers to emulate Baldwin were Daniel, Drayton, and Lodge. That they were also playwrights suggests the close relationship between the world of *de casibus* tragedy and the stage. Francis Meres speaks implicitly of that connection when he includes "the Authour of the *Mirrour for Magistrates,*" along with Marlowe, Kyd, Shakespeare and others, as among "our best for Tragedie."[36]

For dramatists who themselves wrote *de casibus* poems or who were merely readers of the *Mirror for Magistrates* and its progeny, Fortune was virtually inseparable from tragedy. Often in their plays when a character experiences mutability or contingency or adversity, his mind turns naturally to Fortune. The importance of the *Mirror* in fostering this representation can scarcely be overemphasized. Perhaps no other work played a greater role in shaping the Elizabethan concept of tragedy. If, as Lily B. Campbell suggests, the *Mirror* was a literary bridge, it was one across which Fortune walked onto the Elizabethan stage.

NOTES TO CHAPTER 2

1. The full title reads: *A Myrroure for Magistrates. Wherein may be seen by example of other, with howe grevous plages vices are punished: and howe frayle and unstable worldly prosperitie is founde, even of those whom Fortune seemeth most highly to favour.* For the origin of the *Mirror* and its publishing history, see the Introduction to Lily B. Campbell's edition, *The Mirror for Magistrates* (1938; reprint ed., New York: Barnes and Noble, 1960).

2. *The Mirror for Magistrates*, p. 68.

3. William Peery, however, has challenged this assumption, in "Tragic Retribution in the 1559 *Mirror for Magistrates*," *SP*, 46 (1949): 113-30. More recently, Henry Ansgar Kelly implicitly questioned the notion that Fortune in the *Mirror* was more tame than she had once been (*Divine Providence in the England of Shakespeare's Histories* [Cambridge, Mass.: Harvard Univ. Press, 1970], pp. 163-82). Both of these writers seem to reject the idea that Fortune is merely an extension of providential design. Neither, however, fully explores the relationship between Fortune and providence.

4. *The Medieval Heritage of Elizabethan Tragedy* (1936; reprint ed. with corrections, Oxford: Basil Blackwell, 1970), p. 285.

5. *The Mirror for Magistrates*, p. 56.

6. *The English History Play in the Age of Shakespeare*, rev. ed. (London: Methuen, 1965), p. 99. Similarly, Hiram Haydn, in *The Counter-Renaissance* (New York: Scribner's, 1950), writes, "the *leit-motifs* of such books as Boccaccio's *De Casibus* and the English *Mirror for Magistrates* merged harmoniously the concept of Fortune and that of a retributive justice which it was easy to equate (or at least associate) with Providence..." (p. 435). J. M. R. Margeson, in

The Origins of English Tragedy (Oxford: Clarendon Press, 1967), writes: "In *Mirror* tragedy the dominant power is sometimes fortune, but fortune too operates under the rule of providence" (p. 83).

7. *The Mirror for Magistrates*, ed. Campbell. All citations from this edition are identified by line number except for headnotes and prose links, which are identified by page number.

8. *Lydgate's Fall of Princes*, ed. Henry Bergen (Washington, D. C.: The Carnegie Institution, 1923), part 1, Book I, ll. 4977-79.

9. Reproduced by Samuel C. Chew, *The Pilgrimage of Life* (1962; reprint ed., Port Washington, N.Y. and London: Kennikat Press, 1973), fig. 53.

10. Studies of Nemesis include: Éd. Tournier, *Némésis et la jalousie des dieux* (Paris: A. Durand, 1863); Ch. Daremberg, Edmond Saglio, E. Pottier, *Dictionnaire des antiquités grecques et romaines d'après les textes et les monuments* (Paris: Hachette, 1877-1919), 4: part 1, 52-55; Pauly-Wissowa-Kroll, *Real-Encyclopädie der classischen Altertumswissenschaft* (Stuttgart: J. B. Metzler, 1893-1919), 16: part 2, cols. 2338-80; W. H. Roscher, *Ausführliches Lexikon der griechischen und römischen Mythologie* (Leipzig: B. G. Teubner, 1884-1937), 3: cols. 117 ff.; Bernhard Schweitzer, "Dea Nemesis Regina," *Jahrbuch des Deutschen Archäologischen Instituts*, 46 (1931): 175-246.

11. *The Fountaine of Ancient Fiction. Wherein is lively depictured the Images and Statues of the gods of the Ancients, with their proper and perticular expositions* (London, 1599), sig. Aa4^V. This work is a partial translation of Vincenzo Cartari's *Imagini de i Dei de gli antichi* (1580 edition).

12. For studies of Nemesis in the Renaissance, which in part deal with the relationship to Fortune, see Hans Kauffmann, "Dürers 'Nemesis,'" in *Tymbos für Wilhelm Ahlmann* (Berlin: Walter De Gruyter, 1951), pp. 135-59; Erwin Panofsky, "'Virgo et Victrix': A Note on Dürer's *Nemesis*," in *Prints: Thirteen Illustrated Essays on the Art of the Print*, ed. Carl Zigrosser (New York: Holt, Rinehart and Winston, 1962), pp. 13-38; David M. Greene, "The Identity of the Emblematic Nemesis," *Studies in the Renaissance*, 10 (1963): 25-43. Panofsky, in his essay, explores the important role that Politian played in fostering the conflation of Nemesis and Fortune.

13. See Wilhelm Waetzoldt, *Dürer and His Times*, trans. R. H. Boothroyd (New York: Phaidon, 1955), p. 63.

14. Of the engraving of Nemesis Waetzoldt writes, "[Joachim von] Sandrardt called it the 'Great Fortune,' in order to distinguish it from the 'Little Fortune'

of the engraving of 1497" (p. 63). Joachim von Sandrardt lived from 1606 to 1688.

15. Because Fortune and Nemesis share certain implements, it is impossible to say that the wheel, for example, belongs only to Fortune or the bridle only to Nemesis. However, since most representations in the Renaissance give Fortune the wheel and Nemesis the bridle, we can say that these are the more proper associations. In his *Attributs et symboles dans l'art profane, 1450-1600* (Geneva: E. Droz, 1958), Guy de Tervarent lists the wheel as a common attribute of Fortune but not of Nemesis (cols. 325-26). He also lists the bit and bridle as most frequently assigned to Temperance and Nemesis, and less often to Fortune (cols. 277-78). Similarly, Tervarent cites the globe or ball (of the kind that appears in Dürer's engraving) as a common symbol of Fortune, and less often a symbol of Nemesis (cols. 51-52).

16. *Respublica*, in *English Morality Plays and Moral Interludes*, ed. Edgar T. Schell and J. D. Schuchter (New York: Holt, Rinehart and Winston, 1969), ll. 1915-18.

17. *The Wisedome of the Ancients*, trans. Sir Arthur Gorges (London, 1619), pp. 99-100.

18. *The Spanish Tragedy*, ed. Philip Edwards, The Revels Plays (London: Methuen, 1959), I.iv.16.

19. *Hecatomgraphie* (Paris, 1543), sig. F4^V. 1540 ed., reprint ed., Ilkley, England: Scolar Press, 1974.

20. *Symbolicarum Quaestionum . . . Libri Quinque* (Bologna, 1555), p. cxxxviii. 1574 ed., reprint ed., Stephen Orgel, New York and London: Garland, 1979.

21. See Panofsky, p. 38, *n*70.

22. *A Choice of Emblemes, and Other Devises, For the most parte gathered out of sundrie writers, Englished and Moralized* (Leyden, 1586), part 1, p. 19. Reprint ed. Henry Green, London: L. Reeve, 1866.

23. *Quinti Horatii Flacci Emblemata* (Antwerp, 1612), p. [27]. Reprint ed. Stephen Orgel, New York and London: Garland, 1979.

24. Reproduced by Paul Ganz, *The Paintings of Hans Holbein* (London: Phaidon, 1950), fig. 57.

25. Some readers feel that Sackville fails to differentiate between Fortune and providence. Normand Berlin, for instance, in *Thomas Sackville*, TEAS (New York: Twayne, 1974), writes that "Sackville fuses the ideas of Fortune, indivi-

dual responsibility, and God's justice..." (p. 121). Paul Bacquet, in *Un Contemporain d'Elisabeth I: Thomas Sackville, l'homme et l'oeuvre* (Geneva: Droz, 1966), argues that "si Buckingham est victime de la Fortune, celle-ci ne fait que traduire les volontés de la Justice Divine" (p. 124).

26. Among the stories praised in the prose links are those of Lord Mowbray, Owen Glendower, and William de la Pole, duke of Suffolk. In addition, the stories of Richard II and Lord Salisbury move the auditors, not unagreeably, to melancholy.

27. *Tudor Conceptions of History and Tragedy in "A Mirror for Magistrates"* (Berkeley: Univ. of California Press, 1936), p. 16.

28. Boethius, *The Consolation of Philosophy*, trans. Richard Green, Library of Liberal Arts (Indianapolis and New York: Bobbs-Merrill, 1962), II, prose 2.

29. Boccaccio's work is available in the Paris edition of 1520, edited by Louis Brewer Hall (Gainesville, Fl.: Scholars' Facsimiles and Reprints, 1962).

30. *John Lydgate* (Charlottesville: Univ. Press of Virginia, 1970), p. 231.

31. *The Monk's Tale*, in *The Works of Geoffrey Chaucer*, ed. F. N. Robinson, 2nd ed. (Boston: Houghton Mifflin, 1957), p. 189. For a discussion of the Monk's words, see D. W. Robertson, Jr., "Chaucerian Tragedy," *ELH*, 19 (1952): 1-37. Alfred Harbage, in his Introduction to *Shakespeare: The Tragedies, A Collection of Critical Essays*, Twentieth Century Views (Englewood Cliffs, N.J.: Prentice-Hall, 1964), writes of the Monk's formulation: "Chaucer's definition of Tragedy, several times repeated, is that of Donatus . . ." (pp. 3-4). For a discussion of Donatus, see Madeleine Doran, *Endeavors of Art: A Study of Form in Elizabethan Drama* (Madison: Univ. of Wisconsin Press, 1954), pp. 106-9.

32. *Lydgate's Fall of Princes*, part 1, Book I, ll. 50-56. Studies of Lydgate include: Walter F. Schirmer, *John Lydgate: A Study in the Culture of the XVth Century*, trans. Ann E. Keep (Berkeley and Los Angeles: Univ. of California Press, 1961), pp. 206-27; Alain Renoir, *The Poetry of John Lydgate* (London: Routledge and Kegan Paul, 1967).

33. See A. S. G. Edwards, "The Influence of Lydgate's *Fall of Princes* c. 1440-1559: A Survey," *MS*, 39 (1977): 424-39.

34. The first edition of the *Mirror*, most likely printed in 1555, was suppressed by Queen Mary's chancellor.

35. For the influence of the *Mirror*, see Louis R. Zocca, *Elizabethan Narrative Poetry* (New Brunswick, N.J.: Rutgers Univ. Press, 1950); Lily B. Campbell,

Divine Poetry and Drama in Sixteenth-Century England (Berkeley and Los Angeles: Univ. of California Press, 1959), pp. 108-21.

36. *Palladis Tamia, Wits Treasury, Being the Second Part of Wits Commonwealth* (London, 1598), fol. 283. Reprint ed., pref. Arthur Freeman, New York and London: Garland, 1973.

Chapter 3

FORTUNE AND SENECA:
THE ELIZABETHAN TRANSLATIONS

T ABOUT THE SAME time that William Baldwin was readying the *Mirror for Magistrates* for the press, Jasper Heywood was completing his translation of Seneca's *Troades*. This work, published in 1559, was the first of the Senecan translations. In subsequent years the other plays of the Roman tragedian were Englished, and in 1581 they were gathered together by Thomas Newton and published under the title, *Seneca His Tenne Tragedies Translated into English*. That interest in the translations should have coincided with the popularity of the *Mirror* and its progeny may be merely accidental. But it is fitting that the two projects should have been carried out during the same period, for the *Mirror* and the *Tenne Tragedies*, different in so many ways, express a similar tragic vision. By closely examining the translations of Seneca, we shall see that the translators intensify and broaden the same themes that dominate the *Mirror for Magistrates*— the mutability of Fortune and the severity of retributive justice. These changes were inspired not only by the translators' understanding of Seneca's purposes, but also by their own conception of tragedy, as it developed from the *de casibus* tradition. The plays in translation, then, have a distinctly medieval flavor.[1]

Because the thematic modifications wrought by the translators are more readily apparent in the works most freely translated, this chapter treats those plays within the *Tenne Tragedies* that make the boldest departures from their originals: Alexander Neville's *Oedipus* and Jasper Heywood's *Troades* and *Thyestes*.[2]

I

In his Preface to *Oedipus* Alexander Neville concedes that the translation is "in word and verse somewhat transformed, though in Sense litle altered: and yet oftentimes rudely encreased with mine owne simple invention . . ." (I, 190).[3] Neville's tone of self-deprecation, like that of his fellow translators, might well lead the unsuspecting reader to assume that only modest changes have been made. Actually, Neville's "invention" is at times considerable. However, it is lavished not on the delineation of character and incident, but chiefly on the choral passages. And to appreciate Neville's contribution, we must begin by considering briefly the function of the chorus.

The Senecan chorus frequently reflects upon the nature of man's world and his conduct within it. Much of the choral material is philosophic in nature; Seneca the philosopher has left his traces throughout the plays.[4] In particular, the chorus is implicitly concerned with the paradox that lies at the heart of Seneca's Stoicism: on the one hand, the world is assumed to be rationally ordered, a benevolent deity immanent, and evil merely apparent; on the other hand, observation of man's experience suggests that the world's design is baffling, that powerful and even hostile forces impinge upon man, that adversity is an inescapable part of the human condition.[5]

This paradox is reflected in two of the seemingly contradictory formulations that make up the Senecan cosmos. To the extent that the cosmos is conceived as ultimately coherent and purposeful, its workings are ascribed to fate. Impersonal, inflexible, and remote, fate connotes fixity, permanence, pattern. Man's conduct, the Senecan chorus urges, must be aligned with that pattern: man must submit. To the extent, however, that the cosmos is conceived as perilous and unstable, a menace to man's security, its workings are ascribed to Fortune.[6] Envisioned as a mercurial woman, Fortune signifies fluctuation, change, caprice. According to the chorus, Fortune must be vigorously contested. These disparate formulations — and strategies — bespeak a fundamental tension between Seneca's mind and heart.[7] By incorporating fate and Fortune in the choral passages (and elsewhere in the plays), Seneca seeks to account both for his intellectual conviction of a rational, purposeful universe and, at the same time, for his visceral sense of unreason and adversity. Such issues are important to *Oedipus* where, for example, the chorus appears midway through the last act to issue its final admonition:

> Fatis agimur; cedite fatis.
> non sollicitae possunt curae
> mutare rati stamina fusi.
> quidquid patimur mortale genus,
> quidquid facimus venit ex alto,
> servatque suae decreta colus
> Lachesis nulla revoluta manu.
> omnia secto tramite vadunt
> primusque dies dedit extremum.
> non illa deo vertisse licet
> quae nexa suis currunt causis.
> it cuique ratus prece non ulla
> mobilis ordo. multis ipsum
> metuisse nocet, multi ad fatum
> venere suum dum fata timent.

(By fate are we driven; yield ye to fate. No anxious cares can change the threads of its inevitable spindle. Whate'er we mortals bear, whate'er we do, comes from on high; and Lachesis maintains the decrees of her distaff which by no hand may be reversed. All things move on in an appointed path, and our first day fixed our last. Those things God may not change which speed on their way, close woven with their causes. To each his established life goes on, unmovable by any prayer. To many their very fear is bane; for many have come upon their doom while shunning doom [ll. 980-94].)[8]

Here the chorus dwells on the idea that all things in the universe are connected one to another, that they constitute an ineluctable pattern, and that the shape of that pattern is an expression of fate. Neville alters both the substance and tone of Seneca's lines:

Mans lyfe with tumbling fatal course of fortunes wheele is rowld,

To it give place, for it doth run all swiftly uncontrowld.
And Cares and teares are spent in vayn, for it cannot be stayed,
Syth hie decree of heavenly powers perforce must be obayed.
What mankind bydes or does on earth it cometh from above,
Then wayling grones powrd out in griefe do nought at all behove.
Our life must have her pointed course, (alas) what shall I say:
As fates decree, so things do run, no man can make them stay.
For at our byrth to Gods is known our latter dying day.
No Prayer, no Arte, not God himselfe may fatall fates resist.
But fastned all in fixed course, unchaunged they persist.
Such ende them still ensues as they appointed were to have,
Than fly all feare of Fortunes chaung, seeke not to lyve a slave
Enthrald in bondage vyle to feare. For feare doth often bring
Destnies that dreaded ben and mischiefs feard upon us fling.

(I, 226)

If Seneca's choral speaker stresses the absolute inviolability of fate and draws comfort from the doctrine, Neville, by contrast, appears uneasy at the prospect of external compulsion. His reference to man's "Cares and teares" implies a grudging acceptance of constraint imposed from without and a knowledge of the cost which it exacts in human terms. The fear of contingency expressed by Neville's chorus outweighs any confidence in man's ability to scorn change. What concerns Neville most is not the Senecan notion that all things move along on their appointed paths, but rather that they are "uncontrowld."

In Neville's hands the Senecan injunction to submit to fate becomes an elegiac complaint about the "tumbling" course of Fortune's wheel and of man's life. Characteristically, Seneca speaks of Lachesis, one of the Fates; Neville twice names Fortune.[9] And where Seneca invokes the specter of the "inevitable spindle," held by Lachesis, Neville introduces Fortune's wheel, the most famous of the goddess' implements. These symbols typify the divergent attitudes of Roman tragedian and English translator: Seneca emphasizes the force of fate along with the human accommodation it demands; Neville accentuates the suffering that hostile circumstance inflicts, stressing caprice over plan, confusion over purpose, Fortune the harsh antagonist over fate the impersonal arbiter.

Similarly disparate emphases mark the Latin and English versions of the fourth-act chorus, where man's relationship to his world is explored. In the original, Seneca acknowledges the phenomenon of adversity, but he suggests that hardship can be borne through a spirit of acceptance and its worst ravages avoided by an adherence to the *via media*. The chorus counsels:

> Fata si liceat mihi
> fingere arbitrio meo,
> temperem zephyro levi
> vela, ne pressae gravi
> spiritu antennae tremant.
> lenis et modice fluens
> aura nec vergens latus
> ducat intrepidam ratem;
> tuta me media vehat
> vita decurrens via.

(Were it mine to shape fate at my will, I would trim my sails to gentle winds, lest my yards tremble, bent 'neath a heavy blast. May soft breezes, gently blowing, unvarying, carry my untroubled barque along; may life bear me on safely, running in middle course [ll. 882-91].)

And to exemplify its moral, the chorus goes on to cite the history of Icarus, who ignored the middle way and perished.

Neville, evincing no interest in Seneca's cautionary story, substitutes a chorus of his own devising. Instead of a hymn to the *via media*, he presents a discourse on the susceptibility of every man to swift and sudden change:

> Fortune the guide of humaine lyfe doth al things chaunge at will.
> And stirring stil, with restles thoughts our wretched minds doth
> fill.
> In vayn men strive their stars to kepe when hideous tempests
> rise:
> And blustring windes of daungers deepe sets death before their
> eyes.

Who saith he doth her fauning feele? and chaungeth not his
    minde,
When fickle fight [i.e., flight] of Fortunes wheele doth turne by
  course of kinde. (I, 222)

From Seneca's chorus Neville adopts only the metaphor of navigation,
and he alters even that. Where Seneca speaks of the "soft breezes" that
propel the ship of life, Neville talks of "hideous tempests" and the
"blustring windes of daungers deepe." Where Seneca invokes the ideal
of the middle way, Neville composes a general lament on the precariousness of man's existence. Where Seneca outlines a method by which man
can escape the threat posed by external circumstance, Neville calls
attention to the seriousness of that menace. And where Seneca
champions a strategy of moderation as a means of averting suffering,
Neville bewails the insufficiency of any strategy.

A mixed fear and wonder at the sheer turbulence of the world has replaced Seneca's spirit of submission. Concerned with man's peril,
Neville concentrates his attention not on fate that disposes, but rather on
Fortune who threatens man's security. So complete is Neville's modification of his materials that he can name Fortune "the guide of humaine
lyfe."

The fragility of man's prosperity also occupies Neville in the third-act
chorus. There he dispenses with lines 709 to 763 of the original, which
recount the prodigies that occurred in Thebes during the plague,
substituting a didactic reflection on the dangers of princely state. His
chorus begins:

See, see, the myserable State of Prynces carefull lyfe.
What raging storms? what bloudy broyles? what toyle?
    what endlesse stryfe
Doe they endure? (O God) what plagues? what griefe do they
    sustayne?
A Princely lyfe: No. No. (No doubt) an ever duringe payne.
A state ene fit for men on whom Fortune woulde wreke her will.
                         (I, 215)

Seneca is not unconcerned with the vulnerability of greatness; in fact, he alludes to the hazard of high estate at the very beginning of the play where Oedipus notes that the loftiest peaks sustain the most severe blasts. But what Seneca treats in passing, Neville elevates to prominence. He intensifies the theme of impermanence by dwelling, in the third-act chorus, on the king's anguish and by describing with singular fervor Oedipus' lost happiness:

> Let Oedipus example bee of this unto you all,
> A Mirrour meete, A Patern playne, of Princes carefull
> > thrall.
> Who late in perfect Joy as seem'de, and everlasting blis,
> Triumphantly his life out led, a Myser now hee is,
> And most of wretched Misers all. . . . (I, 216)

The shattering fall from eminence, the swiftness of that collapse, and the brittleness of worldly "blis" — all these assume an urgency in the translation that they do not possess in the original.

Neville's fellow translator, Jasper Heywood, expresses a similar preoccupation with those forces that impinge upon man's security. In his translation of *Troades*, for example, Heywood adds these lines of his own devising to the first-act chorus:

> Who weneth here to win eternall welth,
> Let him behold this present perfite proofe.
> And learne the secrete stoppe of chaunces stelth,
> Most nere alas, when most it seemes aloofe.
> In slipper joy let no man put his trust:
> Let none dispayre that heavy haps hath past:
> The swete with sowre she mingleth as she lust
> Whose doubtful web pretendeth nought to last. (II, 15)

Heywood's personification, "chaunce," evidently represents essentially what Neville means by Fortune, for the epithets "sweet" and "sour" were traditionally applied to Fortune, personified (like Heywood's "chaunce") as a woman. The identification of "chaunce" with Fortune is further indicated by Heywood's borrowing of part of a chorus from Seneca's *Hippolytus*, which reads:

Res humanas ordine nullo
Fortuna regit sparsitque manu
munera caeca, peiora fovens;
vincit sanctos dira libido,
fraus sublimi regnat in aula.

(Fate [the Loeb mistranslation of *Fortuna*] without order rules the
affairs of men, scatters her gifts with unseeing hand, fostering the
worse; dire lust prevails against pure men, and crime sits regnant in
the lofty palace [ll. 978-82].)

Heywood uses Seneca's words as the basis for this third-act chorus in
Troades:[10]

Chaunce beareth rule in every place and turneth mans estate at
    will.
She geves the wronge the upper hand, the better part she doth
    oppresse,
She makes the highest low to stand, her Kingdome all is
    orderlesse.
O parfite profe of her frailty, the princely towres of Troy beat
    downe,
The flowre of Asia here ye see with turne of hand quight
    overthrowne. (II, 41)

By such alterations and adaptations of the Latin text, Heywood, like
Neville, develops his thematic concern with the forces of flux and contingency.[11]

Of course, in his treatment of Fortune neither translator introduces a
theme foreign to Seneca's drama; Fortune is no less important to
Seneca's tragedies than to his philosophic treatises.[12] What the translators effect through their changes is the representation of a world even
more precarious and unstable than that of the original. In their
handling of the theme of change, then, the translators out-Seneca
Seneca.

That this alteration by the translators had anything to do with making
the plays more stageworthy, as has been claimed, seems highly dubious.

It is true that the translators usually shorten the choral passages and such shortening might, as H. B. Charlton suggests, make for more effective theater.[13] However, the translators' adaptation of the choral passages consists of no mere condensation or deletion. Rather, it represents a significant modification of thematic emphasis.

II

The other major change made by the translators — an emphasis on retributive justice — has, similarly, little or nothing to do with preparing the plays for the stage. To be sure, this thematic concern results in the addition of a vengeful ghost to Heywood's version of *Troades*, and such a ghost would, of course, be theatrically effective. But the emphasis on justice in the translations is far broader and takes a more subtle form than any single apparition would suggest.

In *Oedipus* Neville accentuates the theme of justice practically everywhere he finds it. Consider, for instance, the speech of Manto, who explains the sight of a frightening omen to her blind father: "neque ista, quae te pepulit, armenti gravis / vox est nec usquam territi resonant greges; / immugit aris ignis et trepidant foci." ("Nor is that sound which strikes thy ears the deep lowing of the herd, nor are frightened cattle bellowing anywhere; it is the lowing of the altar-fires, the affrighted murmurings of the hearth" [ll. 381-83].) Neville brings his version to a higher pitch:

> The fearefull noyse and sound you heere is not of beasts, but fier
> That roaring on the Alters makes, presaging wrekefull yre
> Of angry Gods who doe foretell some purpose that they have,
> For to revenge some foule misdeede that vengeance just doth
> crave. (I, 206)

The alterations that Neville makes produce a marked shift in tone. He converts the image of angry gods into a more certain and purposeful "wrekefull yre" and "vengeance just." Moreover, in keeping with the emphasis on divine wrath, Neville broadens the individual's awareness of his transgression. Seneca's Nuntius announces Oedipus' discovery of his identity in these terms: "Praedicta postquam fata et infandum genus / deprendit ac se scelere convictum Oedipus / damnavit ipse, regiam infestus petens / invisa propero tecta penetravit gradu." ("When Oedipus grasped his foretold fate, and his breed unspeakable, he condemned himself as convicted of the crime and, seeking the palace with deadly purpose, he entered within that hateful roof with hurried step" [ll. 915-18].) Neville begins the lines:

> When Oedipus accursed wretch, his fatall fals had spied,
> To hell he damnd his wretched soule and on the Gods he cryed
> For vengeaunce due. (I, 223)

Once again, the translator embroiders his text, and this time he adds a sense of remorse to self-condemnation. In Neville's hands, Oedipus' admission of guilt becomes a plea for his own destruction.

Perhaps even more indicative of the translator's particular concern with the theme of retribution are some lines added by Neville to the middle of the choral passage in Act I:

> O God withhold thy fury great, thy Plagues from us remove.
> Ceasse of afflicted Soules to scourge, who thee both serve and
> > love.
> Powre downe on them diseases fowle, that them deserved have.
> A Guerdon just for sinne (Oh God) this this of thee wee crave,
> And onely this. (I, 196-97)

There can be no mistaking the sentiment underlying the composition of these lines — the quest for justice, the self-reproach of the guilty, the psychological weight of sin. Nor is this the only intrusion of such elements in the translation. In similar fashion Neville adds an interpolation to the messenger's speech in the last act. Didactically, the messenger points to Oedipus and cries: "Beware betimes, by him beware, I speake unto you all: / Learne Justice, truth, and feare of God by his unhappy fall" (I, 226). These additions suggest that while Neville preserves the sense of cosmic doom that characterizes Seneca's tragedy, he also modifies it by making that doom appear more personal, more clearly related to specific human transgressions; man's responsibility and the guilt which it entails gain greater prominence.

The concern with justice evident in *Oedipus* is shared by Jasper Heywood in *Thyestes*. In fact, Heywood outdoes Neville in his handling of this theme by adding a long speech for the protagonist, whose sons have been cruelly murdered. Thyestes' words, appearing at the very end of the play, constitute an eloquent plea for justice. He says, in part,

Yet turne agayne yee Skyes a while, ere quight yee goe fro mee,
Take vengeance fyrst on him, whose faulte enforceth you to flee.
If needes yee must your flight prepare, and may no longer bide,
But rolle yee must with you forthwith, the Gods and Sunne a
    syde,
Yet slowly flee: that I at length, may you yet overtake,
While wandring wayes I after you, and speedy jorney make.
By seas, by lands, by woods, by rockes, in darke I wonder [i.e.,
    wander] shall:
And on your wrath, for right rewarde to due deserts, will call.
Yee scape not fro me, so yee Gods, still after you I goe,
And vengeaunce aske on wicked wight, your thunder bolte to
    throe. (I, 95)

In *Troades*, too, Heywood enlarges upon the quest for vengeance. In this play Seneca was content to allow a messenger to report his vision of the angry Achilles. But Heywood seeks a more vivid embodiment of revenge. He actually brings the ghost of Achilles on stage and furnishes him with a lengthy harangue. The warrior insists that "Hel will now just vengeance have," "Vengeance and bloud doth Orcus pit require," "Ditis deepe on you shall vengeance take," "ye must the sprightes and hell appease," "So shal the wrath of Hel appeased bee" (II, 17-18). What lends the warnings special significance is the idea that those who commit crimes must answer not only to their human antagonists but also to superhuman powers as well. The wrath of hell—not simply the wrath of Achilles—is the chief threat to the warrior's foes. Achilles' revenge is, then, not merely personal; it has a higher sanction.

Heywood fails to specify the motivation for these alterations, although he does mention in the Preface to *Troades* that he has added "the speache of Achilles Spright," and he says of his additions: "forasmuch as this worke seemed unto mee in some places unperfite, whether

70

left so of the Author, or parte of it loste, as tyme devoureth all thinges, I wot not, I have (where I thought good) with addition of myne owne Penne supplied the wante of some thynges . . ." (II, 4).

Neville's Preface to *Oedipus* is more illuminating. Although he does not discuss the individual changes he has made, he does declare that Oedipus has left behind "unto all posterities, a dreadfull Example of Gods horrible vengeaunce for sinne" (I, 190). And Neville goes on to say this of his overall purpose: "Myne onely entent was to exhorte men to embrace Vertue and shun Vyce, according to that of the right famous and excellent Poet Virgil. 'Discite justiciam moniti, et non temnere divos'" (I, 191) — "Be warned; learn ye to be just and not to slight the gods!" (*Aeneid*, VI, 620). The accentuation of justice in the translated play is certainly in keeping with this declaration; Neville's contribution, then, would seem at least partly an expression of his own didacticism.

III

When considered individually, the thematic modifications wrought by the Elizabethan translators of Seneca present no particular problem for a modern reader seeking to understand their inspiration. That both themes, however, should have been the subject of the translators' invention may seem anomalous, for the two are not only disparate but even inconsistent. After all, the strict cause-and-effect relationships dictated by the operation of retributive justice are undercut by the exploits of an arbitrary Fortune. The one implies the existence of a reasonable, vigilant, and fundamentally benign deity; the other suggests irrationality and caprice on a cosmic scale.

Senecan tragedy itself, however, suggests an explanation for the twofold form which the translators' invention takes. That tragedy reflects the inconsistency of the Stoic vision which informs so much of the drama. On the one hand, the chorus speaks at times of an overarching cosmic design, one which, in effect, guarantees the purposefulness of life. A modern editor of Seneca remarks, "the choruses, with their Stoic calm, often have the effect of removing us for a moment from scenes of blood and horror and giving us a new perspective. We glimpse an ordered universe, the ongoing cosmos whose laws have been violated but whose serenity is undisturbed."[14] Perhaps man cannot always discern this order clearly, but he can at least find comfort in the conviction that things do not just happen, they are directed; adversity tests the mettle of the good and requites the iniquity of the wicked.[15] On the other hand, even though man may find consolation in the notion that he participates in some larger design, he still confronts evidence of apparent disorder around him; characters in the plays sometimes exhibit a bewildered incomprehension of their world. Senecan tragedy, then, asserts the existence of a rational order and yet portrays irrationality. And the English translators, accentuating both, intensify disparate elements already present in Seneca's work. Their "inconsistency," then, may be rooted in the original text.

This is not to say, however, that the translators' emphasis upon Fortune and justice is inadvertent, for the poets perceive both themes as central to Seneca's tragic vision. In the dedicatory epistle to his translation of *Oedipus*, Neville describes his purpose as similar to Seneca's,

> Which was by the tragicall and Pompous showe upon Stage, to admonish all men of their fickle Estates, to declare the unconstant head of wavering Fortune, her sodayne interchaunged and soone altered Face: and lyvely to expresse the just revenge, and fearefull punishments of horrible Crimes, wherewith the wretched worlde in these our myserable dayes pyteously swarmeth. (I, 187-88)

This declaration represents something more than a pious bromide on Neville's part, for precisely the same interpretation of Senecan tragedy is expressed elsewhere in Elizabethan literature. George Puttenham, for instance, seems to echo Neville when, in *The Arte of English Poesie* (1589), he explains why tyrants were portrayed in ancient tragedy:

> their infamous life and tyrannies were layd open to all the world, their wickednes reproched, their follies and extreme insolencies derided, and their miserable ends painted out in playes and pageants, to shew the mutabilitie of fortune, and the just punishment of God in revenge of a vicious and evill life.[16]

Other Elizabethans describe Senecan tragedy in essentially similar terms. Sir Philip Sidney, in his *Apology for Poetry* (printed 1595), declares that it is "high and excellent Tragedy"

> that openeth the greatest wounds, and showeth forth the ulcers that are covered with tissue; that maketh kings fear to be tyrants, and tyrants manifest their tyrannical humours; that, with stirring the affects of admiration and commiseration, teacheth the uncertainty of this world, and upon how weak foundations gilden roofs are builded; that maketh us know,
>
> > *Qui sceptra saevus duro imperio regit,*
> > *Timet timentes, metus in auctorem redit.*
> > [Who harshly wields the sceptre with tyrannic
> > sway, fears those who fear; terror recoils upon
> > its author's head.][17]

Sidney's remark about kings fearing to be tyrants clearly implies the workings of a retributive justice that will requite their wrongdoing. And the reference to the "uncertainty of this world" corresponds to what Neville and Puttenham call the mutability of Fortune. That Sidney has Senecan tragedy in mind is evident from the source of the Latin quotation: lines 705-6 of Seneca's *Oedipus.*

Taken together, the remarks of Neville, Puttenham, and Sidney show that Elizabethans perceived Senecan tragedy to have a twofold thematic import. And this perception undoubtedly helped to inspire the changes made by the translators. Indeed, Neville, having declared that his purpose coincides with Seneca's desire to depict "just revenge" and Fortune's fickleness, goes on to say: "This caused me not to be precise in following the Author, word for word: but sometymes by addition, sometimes by subtraction, to use the aptest Phrases in geving the Sense that I could invent" (I, 188). And Jasper Heywood in his Preface to *Troades*, while conceding his additions and subtractions, declares that he too has been guided by a desire to remain true to the spirit of the original: "In the rest I have for my slender learninge endevored to keepe touch with the Latten, not worde for woorde or verse for verse, as to expounde it, but neglectynge the placinge of the wordes, observed their sence" (II, 4).[18]

73

The translators' invention, however, was inspired not only by what they believed they saw in Seneca, but also by their own concept of tragedy, shaped by the Middle Ages. As heir to a long cultural tradition, the Christian tragedian almost certainly assumed the existence of providence, much as Seneca had. He believed in a righteous God, one who punishes wrongdoing in this world as well as the next. At the same time, he undoubtedly perceived apparent injustice and contingency. He saw that mutability is the property of every living thing, that flux and accident take an awesome toll. And he customarily embodied those forces in a symbol sanctioned by medieval tradition: Fortune.

The attitudes and experience of a Christian culture issued in the tragical stories of Boccaccio, Chaucer, and Lydgate, who trace the fall of eminent men to the same causes that Neville describes in his Preface to *Oedipus*: namely, the caprice of Fortune or the just punishment of God. This *de casibus* vision sustained its power and appeal at the time that Neville, Heywood, and the others were busy with their translations. For as we have seen, the *Mirror for Magistrates*, conceived as an extension of Lydgate's work, enjoyed great popularity from the time of its first successfully published edition in 1559. And the very title proclaims the centrality of the twin themes: *A Myrroure For Magistrates. Wherein may be seen by example of other, with howe grevous plages vices are punished: and howe frayle and unstable worldly prosperitie is founde, even of those, whom Fortune seemeth most highly to favour.*

The basic assumptions of the *de casibus* writer, whether in Boccaccio's day or William Baldwin's, are in some respects strikingly similar to Seneca's. Both share the conviction that the cosmos is ultimately rational, that behind the facade of appearances lies divine purpose. Both also share a fear of mutability, a hostility toward contingency, a sense that the irrational constitutes a powerful and dangerous foe. Their worlds, then, are linked by a common affirmation of rationality and a reluctant concession to the irrational. In short, the inconsistency of Seneca's tragic vision is not so very different from that of his Christian counterparts.

This underlying similarity had important ramifications both for *de casibus* tragedy and for Seneca in English. It led to the reinforcement of those themes in *de casibus* tragedy that were discovered to have a classical precedent.[19] Thus, for example, a tragedian in the *Mirror for Magistrates* invokes Seneca:

O Morall Senec true find I thy saying,
That neyther kinsfolke, ryches, strength, or favour
Are free from Fortune, but are ay decaying.[20]

Similarly, another *de casibus* poet, Thomas Storer, speaks of drawing inspiration from Seneca:

Now write *Melpomene* my tragicke mone,
Call Neroes learned maister, he will ayd,
Thy failing quill with what himselfe once sayd:
  Never did Fortune greater instance give,
  In what fraile state prowd Magistrates do live.[21]

Conversely, the translators of Seneca were led to accentuate those themes in the plays that had become part of their own tragic vision. Reuben A. Brower speaks of the translators' "way of reading the plays as if they were 'tragedies' of the *Mirror* type."[22] This tendency may have been inevitable, given the translators' admiration for *de casibus* literature. Thomas Newton, editor of the collected translations, contributed a commendatory poem to the *Mirror for Magistrates* of 1587.[23] And Jasper Heywood, in his Preface to *Thyestes*, salutes the accomplishment of William Baldwin. Heywood reports seeing in a dream the spirit of Seneca, who asks him to undertake the translation; modestly the Englishman replies that more celebrated men of letters are to be found at the Inns of Court:

There heare thou shale a great reporte,
  of Baldwyns worthie name,
Whose Myrrour dothe of Magistrates,
  proclayme eternall fame.[24]

Willard Farnham, noting that Thomas Sackville contributed to both the *Mirror for Magistrates* and (as co-author) to the Senecan play *Gorboduc* (1562), speaks of the confluence of Senecan and metrical tragedy: "This coloring of classic tragedy with *De Casibus* tragedy and this uniting of admiration for the one with admiration for the other was natural. For the cultivated Elizabethan the classic art of tragedy was usually well represented, even represented preëminently well, by the plays attributed to Seneca. In these plays he could find something of the same spiritual satisfaction that he had found in the *Fall of Princes* or the *Mirror for Magistrates* because he was uncovering there an important source of Christian tragical moralizing."²⁵ Farnham's view finds support in the words of the translators of Seneca, who attest to the Roman dramatist's Christian credentials. Neville, in his Dedication of *Oedipus,* speaks of the play as having been written by "the most grave, vertuous & Christian Ethenicke (For so doubteth not *Erasmus* to terme him) *Lucius Anneus Seneca.*"²⁶ Similarly, John Studley, in his Dedication of *Medea,* speaks of the "pearlesse Poet and most Christian Ethnicke *Seneca.*"²⁷

There are, to be sure, differences in emphasis between the Senecan and *de casibus* world views. The author of metrical tragedy seems to have a surer sense of divine vigilance over all creation. Where Seneca chronicles divine wrath against nations and families, the *de casibus* writer prefers to depict God's avenging justice against individuals; he more readily connects specific punishments with particular transgressions. His system of retributive justice is thus more rigid than that of his ancient forebear. At the same time, he sees the world as even more tumultuous than does Seneca. Fortune seems to loom even larger in the *de casibus* world than in Seneca's.

These differences in outlook are to a large extent responsible for divergences between the Latin text of Seneca and the English text of the translations. For the Englishmen invariably manifest in their work the strength of their own native tradition, one that placed the most wanton caprice and the most severe retribution at the very center of the tragic experience. True to their own cultural propensities, the translators present a dramatic world that might best be described as a "heightened" version of Seneca's.

Significant as these differences may be, we should not lose sight of the underlying concept of tragedy shared by Seneca and his translators. And that idea, while permitting the translators to depart from the original in many particulars, ultimately leads the Englishmen to remain fairly close to Seneca in spirit. The consanguinity is perhaps even sufficient to justify John Studley's remark that the "Tragedies which are set furthe by *Jasper Heiwood* and *Alexander Nevyle,* are so excellently well done (that in reading of them it semeth to me no translation, but even SENECA hym selfe to speke in englysh). . . ."²⁸

NOTES TO CHAPTER 3

1. Modern editors of the translated plays devote most of their commentary to matters of style. See H. De Vocht, ed., *Jasper Heywood and his Translations of Seneca's Troas, Thyestes and Hercules Furens* (Louvain: A. Uystpruyst, 1913); Evelyn M. Spearing, ed., *Studley's Translations of Seneca's Agamemnon and Medea* (Louvain: A. Uystpruyst, 1913). These works are, respectively, volumes 41 and 38 of W. Bang's *Materialen zur Kunde des älteren Englischen Dramas*. John W. Cunliffe, in *The Influence of Seneca on Elizabethan Tragedy* (London and New York: Macmillan, 1893), comments only briefly on the translations (pp. 4-5). Even the two major studies, by Ernst Jockers (*Die englischen Seneca-Uebersetzer des 16. Jahrhunderts* [Strassburg: Druckerei der Strassburger Neuesten Nachrichten, 1909]) and by Evelyn M. Spearing (*The Elizabethan Translations of Seneca's Tragedies* [Cambridge: W. Heffer, 1912]) limit their discussion of the translators' alterations chiefly to diction, meter, grammar, and style. In his Introduction to *The Poetical Works of Sir William Alexander, Earl of Stirling,* ed. H. B. Charlton and L. E. Kastner, 2 vols. (Manchester: Manchester Univ. Press, 1921, 1929), Charlton observes that in addition to "straining to outdo Seneca in rhetorical bombast" the translators shorten choruses and accentuate melodrama for "dramatic effect" (pp. cliii-clviii), but he scarcely touches upon the overall thematic import of the changes. Charlton's Introduction was reissued under the title *The Senecan Tradition in Renaissance Tragedy* (Manchester: Manchester Univ. Press, 1946). B. R. Rees, in "English Seneca: A Preamble," *Greece and Rome*, 2nd Series, 16 (1969): 119-33, characterizes the translators' contribution as "sensationalism and bombast." However, Bruce R. Smith, in "Toward the Rediscovery of Tragedy: Productions of Seneca's Plays on the English Renaissance Stage," *RenD*, NS 9 (1978): 3-37, devotes several pages of perceptive commentary to the thematic changes. See also J. W. Binns, "William Gager's Additions to Seneca's *Hippolytus,*" *Studies in the Renaissance,* 17 (1970): 153-91.

2. Neville's translation of *Oedipus*, made in 1560 and first published in 1563, was considerably revised for the 1581 edition of the *Tenne Tragedies*. Evelyn M. Spearing discusses the differences between the two versions, in "Alexander Nevile's Translation of Seneca's 'Oedipus,'" *MLR*, 15 (1920): 359-63. I have read both versions of the translation and quote from the 1581 edition. Heywood's *Troades* went through two editions in 1559; a third edition bears no date. *Thyestes* first appeared in 1560.

3. *Seneca His Tenne Tragedies Translated into English*, ed. Thomas Newton, Intro. T. S. Eliot, 2 vols. in 1 (1927; reprint ed., Bloomington and London: Indiana Univ. Press, 1966). References are by volume and page number.

4. The correspondence between Seneca's philosophic thought and his tragedies is discussed by R. B. Steele, "Some Roman Elements in the Tragedies of Seneca," *American Journal of Philology*, 43 (1922): 1-31; T. S. Eliot, "Shakespeare and the Stoicism of Seneca," in *Selected Essays* (1932; reprint ed., New York: Harcourt, Brace and World, 1960), pp. 107-20; Berthe Marti, "Seneca's Tragedies. A New Interpretation," *Transactions of the American Philological Association*, 76 (1945): 216-45; Norman T. Pratt, Jr., "The Stoic Base of Senecan Drama," *Transactions of the American Philological Association*, 79 (1948): 1-11; Norman T. Pratt, Jr., "Tragedy and Moralism: Euripides and Seneca," in *Comparative Literature: Method and Perspective*, ed. Newton P. Stallknecht and Horst Frenz (Carbondale: Southern Illinois Univ. Press, 1961), pp. 189-203.

5. General studies of Stoicism include: Willard Farnham, *The Medieval Heritage of Elizabethan Tragedy* (1936; reprint ed., Oxford: Basil Blackwell, 1970), esp. pp. 14-20; Basil Willey, *The English Moralists* (1964; reprint ed., Garden City, N.Y.: Doubleday, 1967), pp. 54-60; Ludwig Edelstein, *The Meaning of Stoicism* (Cambridge, Mass.: Harvard Univ. Press, 1966); John M. Rist, *Stoic Philosophy* (Cambridge: Cambridge Univ. Press, 1969); F. H. Sandbach, *The Stoics* (New York: Norton, 1975); John M. Rist, ed., *The Stoics* (Berkeley and Los Angeles: Univ. of California Press, 1978).

6. As a consequence of her dual heritage, Fortune has sometimes been confused with fate. Originally an agricultural deity, the goddess who later came to be known as Fortune assumed many characteristics of the Greek Tyche. From this assimilation she acquired her role as the deity presiding over the unforeseen and contingent. For Fortune's relationship to her Greek progenitor, see Roger Hinks, *Myth and Allegory in Ancient Art* (London: Warburg Institute, 1939), pp. 76-83; John Ferguson, *The Religions of the Roman Empire* (London: Thames and Hudson, 1970), pp. 77-87. Fortune also acquired an association with determinism, largely from the Etruscan deity Nortia into whose temple a nail was driven each year to symbolize "the acceptance of the inevitability of divine fate" (Otto-Wilhelm von Vacano, *The Etruscans in the Ancient World*, trans. Sheila Ann Ogilvie [New York: St. Martin's Press, 1960], p. 12). Horace has this relationship in mind when, addressing Fortune, he writes: "Before thee ever stalks Necessity, grim goddess, with spikes and wedges in her brazen hand" (*Horace: The Odes and Epodes*, trans. C. E. Bennett, LCL [1927; reprint ed., Cambridge, Mass.: Harvard Univ. Press, 1960], p.

93). It is interesting that the person generally credited with introducing the cult of Fortune to Rome, Servius Tullius, was of Etruscan origin.

7. There is no basis for Clarence Mendell's contention, in *Our Seneca* (1941; reprint ed., Hamden, Conn.: Archon Books, 1968), that "Seneca the philosopher believed in predestination; the poet Seneca saw constantly in the world the caprice of Fortune" (p. 153). One need only read Seneca's *De Providentia* to see that both Fortune and fate are part of his philosophic system. For a refutation of Mendell's distinction, see Norman T. Pratt, Jr., "The Stoic Base of Senecan Drama," pp. 5-6.

8. *Seneca's Tragedies*, ed. and trans. Frank Justus Miller, LCL, 2 vols. (1917; reprint ed., Cambridge, Mass.: Harvard Univ. Press, 1968). The Loeb edition, used here for convenience, differs in some respects from the Elizabethan editions of Seneca available to the translators. I have consulted several Renaissance editions and I have checked the Loeb against the edition edited by Rudolf Peiper and Gustav Richter (*Tragoediae* [Leipzig: B. G. Teubner, 1921]) and found no variants that would significantly affect my conclusions about the nature of the changes made by the Elizabethan translators.

9. Fortune and fate are usually differentiated in the Renaissance, as they were in the ancient world. The emblematist Claude Paradin uses a wheel to distinguish the two. In his *Dévises heroiques* (Lyons, 1551), he depicts a wheel that resembles conventional representations of Fortune's wheel. However, the rim of the wheel is spiked to prevent it from moving, and a heavy block hangs from the wheel, thereby locking it in place. The motto reads, "Fata obstant" (sig. g4^V). A variation of this design appears in George Wither's *A Collection of Emblemes, Ancient and Moderne* (London, 1635), Book Four, p. 248. Wither's *Collection* has been reproduced in facsimile, Intro. Rosemary Freeman (Columbia: Univ. of South Carolina Press [for the Newberry Library], 1975). Samuel C. Chew discusses the iconographic relationship between Fortune and fate, in *The Pilgrimage of Life* (1962; reprint ed., Port Washington, N. Y. and London: Kennikat Press, 1973), pp. 55-60.

10. In his Preface to *Troades*, Heywood writes of Seneca's third-act chorus: "For as much as nothing is therein but a heaped number of farre and straunge Countries, . . . I have in the place therof made another. . . . Which alteration may be borne withall, seynge that Chorus is no part of the substaunce of the matter" (II, 4). Here the translator perhaps indulges in hyperbole, but it is true that Seneca's chorus seems at least outwardly unrelated to the dialogue of the characters at that point in the play.

11. Throughout the plays, the English translators consistently endow Fortune with greater prominence than she enjoys in the original. One evidence of this tendency is their penchant for supplementing the features of her personification. For example, where Seneca writes in *Oedipus*, "haud est virile terga Fortunae dare," ("'Tis not a manly thing to turn the back to Fortune" [l. 86]), Neville renders the line, "It is no poinct of courage stout to yeelde to fortunes frown" (I, 195). The translators also introduce Fortune's wheel where it is not mentioned in the original. In *Medea* Seneca writes: "Fortuna opes auferre, non animum potest," ("Fortune can take away my wealth, but not my spirit" [l. 176]). Studley renders this: "Full well may fortunes welting wheele to begging bring my state, / As for my worthy corage, that shee never shall abate" (II, 63). And in the same play Medea complains: "rapida fortuna ac levis / praecepsque regno eripuit, exilio dedit," ("Swift and fickle is fortune and, swooping down, has torn me from royalty and given me o'er to exile" [ll. 219-20]). Studley translates: "Rashe, ficle, pevish, undiscreete, and wavering Fortunes wheele, / Hath cast me out, the crusshing cares of banishment to feele" (II, 65). Fortune's countenance and wheel are together added in the translation of this line from *Octavia*: "Crede obsequenti parcius; levis est dea." ("Indulgent fortune trust more cautiously; she is a fickle goddess" [l. 452]). Thomas Nuce's version reads: "Geve slender trust to Fortunes flattring face: / She topsie turvy turnes her wheele apace" (II, 166).

12. Fortune in Seneca's tragedy is discussed by P. R. Coleman-Norton, in "The Conception of Fortune in Roman Drama," in *Classical Studies Presented to Edward Capps* (Princeton: Princeton Univ. Press, 1936), pp. 61-71.

13. As evidence that the translators were preparing the plays for the stage, Charlton cites Neville's assertion that his purpose was "onely to satisfy the instant requests of a few my familiar frends, who thought to have put it to the very same use, that Seneca himselfe in His Invention pretended: Which was by the tragicall and Pompous showe upon Stage . . ." (I, 187). It is entirely possible, however, that Neville is here speaking figuratively, not literally. In any event, there is no convincing evidence that Neville's work or any of the other translated plays was ever performed.

14. Eric C. Baade, Introduction to *Seneca's Tragedies: Oedipus, Troas, Agamemnon*, The Classics of Greece and Rome Series, ed. Dudley Fitts (London: Macmillan, 1969), p. xix.

15. On the Stoic view of divine punishment, see E. Zeller, *The Stoics, Epicureans and Sceptics*, trans. Oswald J. Reichel, rev. ed. (London: Longmans, Green, 1880), pp. 192-93.

16. *The Arte of English Poesie*, ed. Gladys Doidge Willcock and Alice Walker (1936; reprint ed., Cambridge: Cambridge Univ. Press, 1970), p. 33.

17. *An Apology for Poetry*, ed. Geoffrey Shepherd (London: Thomas Nelson, 1965), pp. 117-18.

18. A few years later Heywood became less free in translation. In his Preface to *Hercules Furens*, first printed in 1561, he writes: "Neither coulde I satisfie my self, til I had through oute thys whole tragedye of Seneca a grave and wise writer so travailed that I had in englysh geven verse for verse, (as far as the englysh tongue permitts) and word for word wyth the latyn. . . ." See *The first Tragedie of Lucius Anneus Seneca, intituled Hercules furens* (London, 1561), sig. A3. To aid his readers and perhaps to demonstrate his proficiency, Heywood published his translation with the Latin on facing pages.

19. The influence of Stoicism in general and of Seneca in particular has been examined by Léontine Zanta, *La Renaissance du Stoicisme au XVIe siècle* (Paris: Honoré Champion, 1914); R. M. Wenley, *Stoicism and Its Influence* (1924; reprint ed., New York: Cooper Square Publishers, 1963); André Bridoux, *Le Stoicisme et son influence* (Paris: J. Vrin, 1966).

20. *The Mirror for Magistrates*, ed. Lily B. Campbell (1938; reprint ed., New York: Barnes and Noble, 1960), p. 132.

21. *The Life and Death of Thomas Wolsey Cardinall* (London, 1599), sig. I1.

22. *Hero and Saint: Shakespeare and the Graeco-Roman Heroic Tradition* (New York and Oxford: Oxford Univ. Press, 1971), p. 169. W. F. Trench, in *A Mirror for Magistrates: Its Origin and Influence* (privately printed, 1898), writes: "Except in that they were not written to be acted, there was little difference between the poems of the *Mirror* and plays on the Senecan model . . ." (p. 18, n 1). Also, J.M.R. Margeson, in *The Origins of English Tragedy* (Oxford: Clarendon Press, 1967), observes that John Studley speaks of tragedy, in his Preface to *Agamemnon*, as displaying the instability of Fortune, while Thomas Nuce, in a prefatory poem to the same translation, sees the action as a demonstration of retribution. Margeson comments: "the very mixture of fortune and retribution is in the tradition of the metrical tragedies" (p. 78).

23. See *Parts Added to The Mirror for Magistrates by John Higgins and Thomas Blenerhasset*, ed. Lily B. Campbell (Cambridge: Cambridge Univ. Press, 1946), pp. 225-26.

24. *The Seconde Tragedie of Seneca entituled Thyestes* (London, 1560), sig. *7^V.

25. *The Medieval Heritage of Elizabethan Tragedy* (1936; reprint ed., with corrections, Oxford: Basil Blackwell, 1970), p. 343.

26. *The Lamentable Tragedie of Oedipus the Sonne of Laius Kyng of Thebes out of Seneca* (London, 1563), sig. a3.

27. *The seventh Tragedie of Seneca, Entituled Medea* (London, 1566), sig. A2^V.

28. *The Eyght Tragedie of Seneca, Entituled Agamemnon* (London, 1566), sigs. A3^V-A4.

Chapter 4

FORTUNE AND THE
NATIVE DRAMATIC TRADITION

IN ENGLISH DRAMA of the Middle Ages and early Renaissance, Fortune enjoys none of the prominence accorded her in *de casibus* literature of the period. Indeed, Fortune did not become a truly important part of the drama until more than midway through the sixteenth century. There are, of course, earlier plays which treat Fortune's impact on man's life, but these are exceptions to the prevailing dramatic practice. Not until about the time of Elizabeth's accession did Fortune begin to emerge as a major motif; not until then did Fortune come to the stage as a character.

Although not exactly a fixture of the drama in the early and middle sixteenth century, Fortune merits consideration during that period nonetheless. After all, Fortune first appears as a character in the moral interludes. There she contributes not only to the spectacle, but also to the doctrinal meaning of the drama. And even in plays where Fortune fails to appear on stage, she sometimes has a significant role in the lives of the characters. In the interludes, moreover, Fortune's moral significance is clarified, largely through her relationship to the Vice. It seems appropriate, then, to provide an overview of Fortune in the native dramatic tradition. To that end this chapter examines the treatment of Fortune in the first half of the sixteenth century; Fortune's portrayal when, in the 1550s and 1560s, she was brought to the stage as a character; Fortune's off-stage presence in several interludes which deal with contingency; and the influence of the native tradition on Fortune's appearance as a character in later Elizabethan plays.

I

At a time when Chaucer and Lydgate were writing of her perversity, dramatists virtually ignored Fortune. The nature of the fourteenth- and fifteenth-century scriptural plays suggests a likely explanation. Although they may depict a world of cruelty and suffering, they also temper the desolation of adversity. Consider, for instance, the drama of *Abraham and Isaac*, wherein the pain of loss is balanced by religious certainty. The audience, which of course knows the outcome, sees and hears God instructing His angel; the trial of Abraham and Isaac thus appears as part of a divine scheme. Moreover, both father and son possess a faith which enables them to approach the sacrifice without despair, if not entirely without trepidation. And their confidence is handsomely repaid when, at the end of the drama, God congratulates Abraham on his loyalty. J. M. R. Margeson comments: "The play of *Abraham and Isaac* contains in miniature the divine comedy of the whole cycle, in which the tragic moment is swallowed up in a final triumph."[1] Implicit in such a drama is the assurance that the suffering of the virtuous is only temporary, that patience will be rewarded, that redemption awaits those who come to recognize and submit to the divine will. Within such a set of assumptions, providence is deemed of itself a sufficient explanation for adversity. History, the mystery plays assert, constitutes a divinely ordained progression.[2]

The morality plays of the fifteenth century would seem to offer greater opportunities for the treatment of Fortune, for they have as protagonists the kind of heedless figures who, if transposed to the world of metrical tragedy, would invite the ravages of Fortune. *The Pride of Life*, for instance, demonstrates an "alliance with *De Casibus* story," according to Willard Farnham, who draws this parallel with Chaucerian tragedy: "There is much the same erection of mortal achievement into 'nonesuch' position as we have found in Chaucer's *Monkes Tale*. . . ."[3] Yet the fragmentary play (c. 1400-25) never mentions Fortune. Nor does the extant summary of *The Cradle of Security*. *The Castle of Perseverance* (c. 1400-25) alludes to a wheel, but whether it belongs to Fortune is uncertain. *Mankind* (c. 1465-70) contains the word "fortune," and Henry Medwall's *Nature* (before 1500) the term "fortunes," but in both plays the word is not a personification, simply a reference to man's condition. *Everyman* (c. 1500) does not mention Fortune. Only *Wisdom* (c. 1460-70) devotes so much as a few lines to Fortune.[4] The comparative absence of Fortune from the moralities, as from the mystery plays, reflects their essentially comic world. In the words of Madeleine Doran, "The morality play . . . was not in itself tragic; its concern was not to show the inevitability of failure in the contest, but the ever-renewed possibility of success — certainty, indeed, if one followed the formula. It was, therefore, nearer comedy in the medieval sense than tragedy . . . ."[5]

Not until the early years of the sixteenth century, in John Skelton's political satire *Magnificence* (c. 1515-23), does Fortune receive significant attention in the drama. The subject matter of the play — the right use of wealth — undoubtedly fostered the representation of Fortune. Skelton's story draws inspiration from the *Nichomachean Ethics* of Aristotle: the playwright seeks to explore the attainment of the golden mean — the avoidance of the threat posed by excess and deficit.[6] Specifically, he focuses on the possession of wealthful felicity; the character Felicity announces near the beginning of the play, "Wealth is of wisdom the very true probate" (4).[7] Since the management of material prosperity lies at the thematic center of the drama and since Fortune was popularly believed to govern the distribution of wealth, it is not surprising that Fortune should assume prominence in the play, if only as an off-stage presence.

The comparatively secular spirit of this play may also have led Skelton to grant Fortune greater prominence than had earlier playwrights. Admittedly, he employs many of the conventions of his predecessors: his characters consist of personified abstractions; virtues contend with vices; at the center of the conflict stands a representative figure who commits error, suffers for his mistakes, and finally repents. But there is much less theologizing here than in earlier drama. In the framework of the play error is less a matter of sin than it is of incompetence. When Magnificence sets Liberty free from the control of Measure, hands Felicity over to Liberty and Fancy, and finally dismisses Measure altogether from the court, he violates not so much the law of God as the principle of moderation. Robert Lee Ramsay observes, "In the earlier plays the issue had been between good and evil; in *Magnificence* it is simply between prudence and folly."[8] *Magnificence,* writes F. P. Wilson, is a cautionary tale with a markedly secular flavor: "the play is not so much a mirror for man as a mirror for princes, a lesson in the art of good government, but also a lesson in the art of preserving worldly prosperity."[9]

Magnificence thus shares with *de casibus* tragedy a concern with princes and prosperity. And Skelton, like authors of that kind of tragedy, employs Fortune to dramatize the protagonist's exaltation and to suggest the imminence of his fall. At the height of his prosperity, for example, Magnificence asserts his power by repudiating Fortune:

> Fortune to her laws cannot abandon me,
> But I shall of Fortune rule the rein;
> I fear nothing Fortune's perplexity.
> All honour to me must needs stoop and lean;
> I sing of two parts without a mean;
> I have wind and weather over all to sail,
> No stormy rage against me can prevail. (1460-66)

Magnificence defiantly scorns the *via media* that might ensure some safety from the ravages of Fortune. Disaster leads to a wiser perception. After his fall, the character named Poverty advises him:

> Sir, remember the turn of Fortune's wheel,
> That wantonly can wink, and winch with her heel.
> Now she will laugh, forthwith she will frown;
> Suddenly set up and suddenly plucked down;
> She danceth variance with mutability,
> Now all in wealth, forthwith in poverty;
> In her promise there is no sickerness;
> All her delight is set in doubleness. (2023-30)

His confidence shattered, his friends gone, his prosperity vanished, Magnificence has no difficulty perceiving the merit of Poverty's counsel:

> O good lord, how long shall I endure
> This misery, this careful wretchedness?

86

Of worldly wealth, alas, who can be sure?
In Fortune's friendship there is no steadfastness.
She hath deceived me with her doubleness.
For to be wise all men may learn of me,
In wealth to beware of hard adversity. (2154-60)

In such speeches the play approaches the world of *de casibus* tragedy.
The ruined prince is eloquent testimony of man's vulnerability to
change. What he experiences is not the loss of life, of course, but rather—
to one who relishes the creature comforts something nearly as serious—
the loss of those things regarded as the "gifts" of Fortune.[10]

It would be inaccurate, however, to claim that Skelton's didacticism is
directed principally to a warning about Fortune. For although the education of Magnificence takes the form, in part, of learning about Fortune's treachery, the playwright goes further. He suggests, in the
conversation between Magnificence and Poverty, the need to see
beyond Fortune. When a self-pitying Magnificence cries, "Alas, of Fortune I may well complain," Poverty directs his attention heavenward:

Yea sir, yesterday will not be called again.
But yet, sir, now in this case,
Take it meekly, and thank God of his grace;
For now go I will beg for you some meat.
It is folly against God for to plete. (2032-36)

Fortune is not forgotten; the character of Circumspection will have yet
more to say of Fortune's mutability later. But the dramatist, at an important moment of recognition for the protagonist, effects a shift of emphasis from Fortune to God. The character of Poverty clearly diverts
Magnificence's attention—and hence that of the audience—from one to
the other.

This suggests that Skelton, for all his secularism, remains rooted in the
assumptions of his dramatic predecessors. Like them, he seeks to demonstrate that what befalls a man results from his own actions and that
the relationship between cause and effect is ineluctable. The force that
blights Magnificence's happiness is Adversity, identified chiefly not
with the Fortune whom Magnificence laments but with the punishment

of a vigilant and just God. Admittedly, when Adversity arrives to smite Magnificence, he announces, "Take heed of this caitiff that lieth here on ground; / Behold how Fortune of him hath frowned" (1947-48). However, in his long speech Adversity stresses that the fall results not merely from the mutability of the world, but from divine displeasure.[11] Adversity begins the speech by declaring: "I am Adversity, that for thy misdeed / From God am sent to quite thee thy meed" (1877-78). And he strongly affirms his role as divine servant:

> The stroke of God, Adversity, I hight;
> I pluck down king, prince, lord, and knight;
> I rush at them roughly and make them lie full low;
> And in their most trust I make them overthrow. (1883-86)

The insistence on Adversity's divine mission arises out of Skelton's desire to point a retributive moral. While employing Fortune as a symbol of mutability and as an antagonist of the prince, Skelton refrains from naming Fortune as the primary agent of Magnificence's undoing. The audience must be made to feel that the downfall represents God's retribution, not merely the result of transience.

Skelton's treatment of Fortune is unusual in its extent: most interludes in the first half of the sixteenth century grant Fortune scarcely more prominence than she enjoys in the moralities of the preceding century. More typical of the dramatic handling of Fortune is that of *Hickescorner* (c. 1513-16), written at about the same time as *Magnificence*. In this anonymous play Contemplation, one of the virtues, admonishes the rascally Freewill:

> Freewill, forsake all this world wilfully here,
> And change by time; thou oughtest to stand in fear;
> For fortune will turn her wheel so swift,
> That clean fro thy wealth she will thee lift.[12]

For the next four decades, this kind of isolated allusion, rather than Skelton's more detailed treatment, would typify the drama. As often as not, Fortune is mentioned only in passing. In John Redford's *Wit and Science* (1531-47), for example, the character Worship says, "Truth binding me ever to be true, / How so that fortune favoreth my chance."[13] Such references have a perfunctory air about them, for they lead to no wider inquiry into the ways of Fortune and her relationship to man.

The reluctance to employ Fortune more often may have arisen, in part, from uncertainty over the doctrinal value of pondering Fortune's mutability. Her nature can, of course, constitute a fit subject of meditation when one reflects upon the vagaries of life in a spirit of *contemptus mundi*; contemplation of caprice may lead one to seek more fervently the surety of the next world where justice prevails and virtue is rewarded. But not everyone will find the same inspiration in the evidence of turmoil and uncertainty. For some, the meditation may shake confidence in the essential order of a providentially administered world; and, if sustained, it may even call into doubt the very existence of a providence presumed responsible for all things. Perhaps this explains why the authors of the moral interludes are usually reluctant to dwell for long on Fortune.

Forty years after Skelton wrote *Magnificence*, playwrights continued to trace assiduously the workings of providential design; Fortune remained a distinctly secondary theme. Consider *The Comedy of Patient and Meek Grissell* (1558-61) by John Phillip. Like *Magnificence* the play is secular in tone; at issue is not sin and repentance but the general question of how best to confront adversity. The protagonist is a young woman who, while wretchedly poor, epitomizes the virtues of obedience, reverence, and filial affection. So devoted is she to her father, the aged Janickle, that she has to be urged by him to accept the marriage proposal of Gautier, the Marquis. For some time following their marriage, the couple live happily. But the villainous Politic Persuasion manages to sow doubts in Gautier's mind about his wife's virtue. Deciding to test her character, Gautier professes to be troubled by his wife's humble background. He tells her that their children must be put to death. And he claims that he has decided to marry someone befitting his social station; Grissell, therefore, must return to the home from which she came.

In this story of virtue tested, Fortune, it seems initially, operates in conjunction with providence. At least, this may be inferred from Janickle's urging his daughter to accept the offer of marriage:

Comfort thy selfe my childe, for mee God will provide,
Hee is my Rocke, my stafe, my stay, my trust and perfect
guid,
And sith that hee by providence, respected hath thy state,
And to the top of Fortunes wheele, in mercie elevate,
Lament no more, distill no teares, though thou departe
mee froe,
For God that rules both heaven and earth, hath wild it
shold be so. (761-66)[14]

Later, however, Fortune is identified less with God than with the villainy of Politic Persuasion. The Vice, recognizing that the reported deaths of her son and daughter have failed to shake Grissell's virtue, ponders his next move:

I am minded ageinst hir a new assault to prove,
Which shall exempt hir from the top of fortunat
prosperitie,
And plounge hir deepe in the floods of adversytie.
(1483-85)

Moreover, the comments of Rumor, not unlike those of Poverty and Circumspection in *Magnificence*, underscore the treachery of Fortune:

From the top of honor, the Marquis will her exile,
For Fortune is fickle, although shee do smyle,
Her chaunges unstable, full of mutabylitie,
Her wheele is full glyding, and of no certaintie,
Her freshe vissage, full soone chaungeth cheare,
As nowe by Lady Grissill, doth playnly appeare,
For shee is nowe throwne, from the top of prosperytie,
And with old Jannickle, must suffer paynfull povertie.
(1678-85)

In the speeches of Politic Persuasion and of Rumor, we hear of a power that delights in destruction, victimizes the innocent, and inspires fear and dismay in her prey. Such characteristics seem ill-suited to an executrix of a benign providence.

Although Phillip moralizes at some length on Fortune, he also draws the audience's attention toward God. The turning point occurs in a conversation between Grissell and her father, and it sounds very much like a similar conversation between Magnificence and Poverty. Janickle laments the return home of his daughter, cast out by her husband:

> Oh froward Fortune, all together disceaveable,
> Full of Gerishe flatterye, all together varyable:
> The chaunges of thy hawtie wheele, to Luna I may
>   compare,
> Who so trusteth thee hath often cause of care:
> From prosperytie to adversitie the simple thou doste
>   throe,
> Phie on thee Fortune, which art cause of my woe.
>
> (1756-61)

This tirade follows in the vein of earlier allusions to Fortune, but the heroine fails to reply in kind. Instead, she directs her father's thinking from Fortune's malice to God's benignity:

> Oh father bee joyfull & prayse God for my fall,
> For hee that gave prosperitie, can send adversitie:
> And at his prescript pleasure hee can swaidge the thrall,
> Of such as bee aflicted with needfull povertie,
> Imbrace Pacience, let go rashe timeritie:
> Blame not Fortune for my overthroe,
> It was the will of God, that it should be so:
> And what creature living, can withstand his providence,
> This Crosse is to trye us, as hee doth his elect,
> Therfore good father, arme your selfe with Pacience.
>
> (1762-71)

Although willing throughout most of the play (and immediately before this point) to ascribe change in condition to Fortune, the dramatist here fails to attribute Grissell's devastating setback to Fortune. Indeed, he explicitly rejects the notion that Fortune has dictated her fall; as Grissell herself says, "Blame not Fortune for my overthroe." Within the framework of the play, it is a sign of insight that Grissell should repudiate Fortune as an explanation for what has transpired. And, equally, it is a sign of her father's growth in understanding that he too should cease to credit Fortune for Grissell's lot. Thus, later, when Grissell rejoins her husband, the aged father—taking to heart his daughter's instruction—speaks only of God's mercy: "God be blessed, which from so great adversitie, / Hath ellevated us to great prosperitie" (2078-79).

Phillip's tracing of adversity back to its source in the divine will bears a notable resemblance to Skelton's practice in *Magnificence.* Though separated by a half century, the two playwrights evince a nearly identical attitude toward Fortune. Both employ Fortune for a time while chronicling the career of the protagonist; both decline to address directly the relationship of Fortune to God; both reject Fortune as an ultimate explanation for the adversity suffered by the protagonist; both, after dramatizing adversity, seek to turn the audience's attention from Fortune to God; both affirm, at the denouement, the justice of God's ways.

In the work of dramatists like Skelton and Phillip, the desire to affirm providential design leads to some restriction in the use of Fortune. In the hands of other dramatists, this didactic purpose leads to the virtual suppression of Fortune. A case in point is Thomas Preston's *Cambises* (c. 1558-69), the story of a tyrant who behaves cruelly toward even his closest advisers and kin. The protagonist richly deserves his comeuppance, which occurs at the very end of the play. There he meets his death through apparent mischance, when he is fatally wounded in a riding accident. Cambises himself calls attention to the contingency when he says, "Out! alas! What shal I doo? My life is finished! / Wounded I am by sodain chaunce; my blood is minished" (1159-60).[15] And before he expires, he adds, "A marvels chaunce unfortunate, that in this wise should be!" (1168).

The reader might well expect some reference to Fortune since chance plays so important a role in Cambises' death, since Fortune embodies contingency, and since, earlier in the play, a character has already alluded to Fortune.[16] Yet the reader finds no such explicit reference. The explanation may be implicit in the last words spoken by the King: "A just reward for my misdeeds my death doth plaine declare" (1172). Evidently,

Preston seeks to stress the purposefulness of Cambises' demise, even though it appears to have been brought about by chance. He refrains from personifying Fortune while he is busy affirming, somewhat clumsily, the justice of divine providence.[17]

Fortune might have become more conspicuous in *Cambises* and in other plays if she could easily have been assigned a retributive function. The interludes, after all, are replete with figures who must pay for their transgressions. However, as Preston's play suggests, there was a difficulty in employing Fortune as a righter of wrongs. Fortune's capacity for overthrowing the wicked, we must remember, does not depend on any antipathy to vice. Fortune spurns anyone who enjoys too much, aspires too high, or simply attains security for too long. And she is as likely to afflict the virtuous as the villainous. Thus in *Cambises* the one figure who complains against Fortune is not a culprit, but the innocent child of a man executed by the tyrannical king.

From the treatment of Fortune in plays until Preston's time, it would have been difficult to predict that Fortune would shortly assume a far more prominent role in the drama. But Fortune was, in fact, finally beginning to take her place among the personified abstractions of the moral interludes. What dramatists were discovering was a way to employ Fortune as a character without compromising their didactic purpose.[18]

II

To employ Fortune effectively in a drama of moral abstractions, playwrights needed to present a characterization that was relatively straightforward and consistent. That is, they could not very well portray Fortune as powerful and menacing on stage and then, later, suggest that Fortune was merely an illusion, a product of man's faulty perception—at least not without risking a jarring inconsistency. Nor, if Fortune was to function as a character, could they leave ill-defined the relationship between Fortune and providence. After all, the Psychomachia encouraged the division of characters into competing sides. Was Fortune to be aligned with the virtues or with the vices? The playwrights needed, in short, a conceptual framework within which Fortune could function as a genuinely dramatic figure. And they found it in the ancient topos that opposed Fortuna and Virtus.[19] They applied the topos, however, in a way that ancient dramatists never envisioned. The Christian playwrights of the mid-sixteenth century conceive Fortune not only as a foe of Virtus (in the sense of moral virtue), but also as an ally of vice. Invariably hostile to reason and reward, Fortune becomes an enemy of the providence whose ways the dramatists explicate.

Fortune's antagonism toward virtue is apparent in W. Wager's *The Longer Thou Livest, the More Fool Thou Art* (c. 1559-68), an interlude concerned with material prosperity and spiritual poverty. The play traces the history of Moros from youth to manhood to old age. From the beginning Moros seems past redemption, for he is handicapped by a seriously deficient upbringing. His parents, utterly remiss about his education, have failed to instill in him any saving moral values. As a consequence, the youth is not only obstreperous and uncivil but irreverent and blasphemous. He neither knows nor seeks to understand what constitutes a Christian life. In an effort to repair Moros' deficient education, three figures of virtue—Discipline, Piety, and Exercitation— undertake to instruct him in religious doctrine. Despite their dedication, however, they fail: Moros proves a thoroughly recalcitrant pupil. More interested in personal pleasure than spiritual enlightenment, he lightheartedly sings, mimics his teachers, and disregards the need for reformation. He is admonished: "Grace will not enter into a foolish heart" (217).[20] But Moros refuses to take heed. And, to make matters worse, he falls in with three brigands—Idleness, Incontinence, and Wrath—who present themselves under false names and divert him from the course advocated by the virtues; under the tutelage of the vices, Moros indulges in drinking, gambling, and carnality.

In the story of Moros' ruin, Fortune assumes a major role. Entering the stage at a point when Moros is on the brink of adulthood, Fortune demands that her sovereignty be acknowledged:

> No God's mercy? no reverence? no honor?
> No cap off? no knee bowed? no homage?
> Who am I? is there no more good manner?
> I trow, you know not me nor my lineage.
> I tell you, I rule and govern all;

I advance and I pluck down again;
Of him that of birth is poor and small,
As a noble man I can make to reign;
I am she that may do all things. (1038-46)

Irritated because she has failed to receive the respect owed her by the audience, Fortune contrives a vivid demonstration of her might:

A popish fool will I place in a wiseman's seat.
By that you shall learn, I trow,
To do your duty to a lady so high;
He shall teach you Fortune to know
And to honor her till you die. (1065-69)

She will, then, affirm her power by rewarding the unworthy. And she decides that she can best assert the irrationality that is her essence by elevating Moros. No matter how vile, foolish, proud, or impious he may be, Fortune is determined to bestow her gifts upon him. In an action that literalizes the adage, "Fortune favors fools," Dame Fortune sets out to bring Moros to a bad eminence.

To help carry out her purposes, Fortune enlists a formidable host of servants, who wholeheartedly approve the elevation of Moros. Incontinence tells Fortune, "O Empress, O Goddess omnipotent, / I render you praises manifold" (1092-93). Wrath too rejoices in Fortune's activity: "Ha, ha, ha! I must laugh to see Fortune's dalliance. / Lord, how she hath this fool enhanced" (1201-2). The vices that make their appearance during the middle part of Moros' life also announce their commitment to Fortune. Ignorance says that she has conspired with the goddess: "Lady Fortune did tell me her mind" (1251). Impiety, assigned to play a role in Moros' career, tells him: "Fortune appointed me to be governor, / Of your own person you to direct" (1329-30). And Cruelty also carries out the will of Fortune: "me she appointed them to correct / Which should do ought against your mind, / Yea, and your profits and rents to collect / And to seek narrowly where we may them find" (1333-36). Collectively, the vices endorse Dame Fortune's purposes through their deeds. Fortune, for her part, seems to orchestrate their activities.

The relationship of the vices to Fortune renders the latter's moral significance clear. Fortune contributes to Moros' neglect of virtue; elevating him, she distracts him from proper spiritual concerns. She is no partner of providence; indeed, Fortune's activity has the effect of momentarily frustrating the divine will. God, of course, is not a character in the play, and so we cannot say unequivocally how Fortune and the Deity might have interacted on stage. But God is an unseen presence in the drama; He is the source of the grace that could redeem Moros, the source of the instruction that the virtues seek to impart. In His reason God represents the very antithesis of Fortune. The division of characters in the play underscores that antipathy: the virtues look to God for their sustenance; the vices collaborate with Fortune. What the audience witnesses, then, is a conflict between the righteousness and authority of God, on the one hand, and the perversity and power of Fortune, on the other.

In this contest Fortune achieves a kind of victory, if only in the sense that the elevation of a wastrel demonstrates her might. The chagrin of the virtues is testimony to Fortune's power as well as to Moros' fatuity. Yet despite her impact during Moros' manhood, Fortune makes no appearance in the third and final section of his history. At that point People enters to declare that nothing is more intolerable than "A fool wealthy, a wicked man fortunable" (1689). The audience may expect Fortune to destroy Moros as swiftly as she raised him, but the playwright credits God with Moros' destruction, not Fortune. Like his predecessors, Wager wishes to affirm the workings of retributive justice.

When we see Moros in old age, it is clear that the passage of time has brought neither self-knowledge nor a beneficial change in his attitude. To the last he remains the cavorting prankster. Even the appearance of God's Judgment fails to work any salutary transformation. This minister of God tells Moros:

> The longer thou livest, the more fool thou art.
> This to thee hath been often recited;
> For so much as thou hast play'd such a fool's part,
> As a fool thou shalt be justly requited. (1759-62)

Having delivered the indictment, God's Judgment smites the fool: "With this sword of vengeance I strike thee" (1791). Moros, *in extremis*, even now fails to grasp the seriousness of his predicament. Although shaken, he comprehends neither the nature nor the cause of his malady. Ignoring advice that he call upon God for mercy, Moros instead believes that his plight can be remedied by drink: "I lack nothing but a cup of good wine" (1804). Shortly afterward, he is carried off on the back of Confusion to his eternal punishment.

The lesson that Wager inculcates is not so very different from that of his predecessors. Why, then, should he employ Fortune as a character when they did not? The answer probably lies in the characterization of the protagonist. Moros is not a figure who wavers between good and evil. He represents, rather, a type of error. His very name suggests this: "Moros" is derived from the Latin word for folly. He seems, in Calvinist terms, predestined. Wager obviously needs to account for the unmerited prosperity of this flawed character. To ascribe that prosperity directly to God might seem to compromise the justice of the Deity, especially since the very possession of wealth contributes to Moros' perdition. No such obstacle stands in the way of attributing prosperity to Dame Fortune who, on account of her perverse nature, customarily showers her favors on the undeserving. Calvin may have disdained the use of Fortune's name, but Protestant playwrights found Dame Fortune useful since she helps to account for the seemingly inexplicable prosperity of the undeserving. Fortune's employment in the drama, then, preserves the putative fairness of an inscrutable God.

III

Few playwrights emulate Wager in his extensive use of Fortune. Nevertheless, Fortune plays a role, if only off-stage, in a number of interludes, including *Impatient Poverty*, *Apius and Virginia*, and *The Tide Tarrieth No Man*. In each play we find a prominent Vice, and in each instance the Vice aligns himself with the contingency that Fortune embodies. By this alignment the Vice seeks to destroy the protagonist.

The association of Fortune with the Vice must have seemed natural to dramatists, for the figures have much in common.[21] Fortune and the Vice are deceitful; they are both two-faced.[22] Both Fortune and the Vice, moreover, typically raise their victims to temporary prosperity, and they revel in the unexpected adversity that ensues. (In *Common Conditions* [S.R. 1576] the Vice says that he is "Nere kinde [i.e., near kin] to dame fortune to raise and to let fall.")[23] Fortune and the Vice are also notoriously inconsistent. In *The Tide Tarrieth No Man* the Vice, named Courage, declares:

> Thus may you see Courage contagious
> And eke contrarious—both in me do rest,
> For I, of kind, am always various
> And change as to my mind seemeth best.[24]

Fortune, of course, never loses an opportunity to indulge her whimsicality. As she says in *The Longer Thou Livest*, "I change all in the turning of a hand; / Whatsoever I will, do it I may" (1056-57). It was, then, an essentially similar nature that fostered the symbiotic relationship between the Vice and Fortune.

The dependence of the Vice upon Fortune is implicit in *Impatient Poverty* (c. 1547-58), a story of wealth won and lost and won again. The virtuous Peace leads Poverty to the attainment of riches and to his new name, Prosperity. The protagonist is pleased with his new status, but Peace cautions him against the danger of vice and, in particular, the threat to his security posed by games of chance: "Beware of misrule in any wise; / Play not at cailes, cards, nor dice."[25] When the heedless Prosperity falls in with Envy and Misrule, Peace once again admonishes him: "Eschew evermore these rioters' company, / And be ruled by reason, as I thee bade" (p. 335). Prosperity, however, disregards the counsel and is inveigled into gambling with Colhazard. What this character represents seems clear enough, for the *OED* defines "cole" as "A deceiver, cheat, sharper (at dice)." True to his name, Colhazard promptly relieves Prosperity of his money, much to the amusement of Envy and Misrule. The protagonist, once again named Poverty, exclaims woefully, "As a man all mortified, and mased in my wit, / I, a captive in captivity, lo, fortune is my foe!" (p. 341). Poverty's exclamation could not be more apt, for although Fortune does not materialize in the shape of a character, contingency is very much in evidence; it is through chance that Prosperity loses his wealth.

R. B.'s *New Tragical Comedy of Apius and Virginia* (1559-67) bears a close resemblance to *Impatient Poverty* in the character of its Vice. He is called Haphazard, a name that underscores his identification with contingency. Bernard Spivack observes: "His name defines a code of behavior accommodated to the belief that all things are governed by chance, and that, accordingly, reward and punishment have no essential relation to virtue and vice but proceed indiscriminately from the caprice of blind fortune."[26] Unlike his counterpart in *Impatient Poverty,* Haphazard seeks to deprive his victim of spiritual integrity rather than material prosperity. The Vice's method, however, is not dissimilar, for Haphazard would entice Apius, the lustful judge, to embark on a risky enterprise. Specifically, Haphazard suggests that Apius can take custody of Virginia if he finds a man who will claim that she is not the daughter of Virginius. She will thus be separated from her father, and Apius may attain his desires. The words of the Vice demonstrate the element of chance which the action entails:

> Well then, this is my counsell, thus standeth the case,
> Perhaps such a fetche, as may please your grace:
> There is no more wayes, but hap or hap not,
> Either hap, or els haplesse, to knit up the knot:
> And if you will hazard, to venter what falles,
> Perhaps, that *Haphazard,* will end al your thralles. (472-77)[27]

Convinced by this appeal, Apius meditates upon his course in a speech which shows that he has adopted not only the language but also the values of the Vice:

> Well hap as can hap, or no,
> In hazard it is but let that goe,
> I wyll what so happen persue on still,
> Why none there is living, can let me my wyll:
> I will have *Virginia,* I will hir defloure,
> Els rigorous sword, hir hart shall devoure. (999-1004)

Ironically, by the time that Apius speaks these words, Virginia is already dead, slain by her father to prevent her rape. Apius, having overreached himself, is soon apprehended, the victim of his own lustful desires and the encouragement of Haphazard. At no point does Fortune set foot on the stage, but the contingency (in the form of chance-taking) that helps to destroy Apius is almost palpable. While not a character, then, Fortune in effect plays a crucial role. As Bernard Spivack points out, Fortune is "responsible for the whole moral significance of the Vice."[28]

The capacity of a Vice to persuade a man to risk his future for personal gain is also central to the dramatic pattern of George Wapull's *The Tide Tarrieth No Man* (published in 1576). And, again, Fortune seems closely allied to the character of the Vice. Here the Vice, named Courage, seeks to waylay a young courtier, Willing-to-Win-Worship. The courtier, pondering a departure from the court, is importuned by the Vice:

> Sir, are you so foolish the court for to leave
> When the time is that worship you should win?
> For in times of triumphing we always perceive
> The Courtier's worship doth first begin.
> Therefore do you from such foolishness stray,
> And Fortune may chance give you as you wish. (542-47)

Like many of his brethren in the interludes, the Vice extends the prospect of Fortune's favor, and the argument is appealing. The courtier, however, also recognizes the danger inherent in Courage's advice. Willing-to-Win-Worship counters with this argument: "But the wheels of Fortune, as Socrates doth say, / Are like the snares wherewith men take fish" (548-49). Armed with this knowledge, the protagonist seems poised to expose the specious reasoning of the Vice. But Courage recovers the initiative, pursuing the same strategy that worked for Haphazard. He suggests that the prospective reward outweighs any risk and that it would surely be folly to throw away such an opportunity:

> Well, whatever it cost it must needs be had.
> Therefore withstand not thy fortunate chance,
> For I will count thee fool, worse than mad,

100

If thou wilt not spend money thyself to advance.
Now is the time of hap, good or ill—
Venture it therefore, while it is hot,
For the tide will not tarry for any man's will.
Never shalt thou speed if now thou speed not. (578-85)

The courtier, needing money to purchase the attire expected at court, is convinced by the Vice to pledge his land as security. This decision soon proves to be his undoing, and he expresses his dismay:

They promised me my friends for to stand,
And to help me to that which I did crave,
Until that I had obligated my land,
And then was I subject to every knave;
The merchant for loan, the broker for his pain,
And the scribe for writing, each man had a gain.

(997-1002)

In adversity the courtier experiences the truth of something that he knew intellectually all along—that Fortune is a snare, her friendliness a delusion.

In Wapull's play and in those of his contemporaries, the *modus operandi* of the Vice includes a reliance upon the contingency embodied in Fortune. By employing that contingency to further his ends—whether he merely induces the protagonist to indulge in a game of chance or to take a risk in a more profound sense and commit a crime—the Vice allies himself with Fortune. This alliance was, of course, facilitated by Fortune's traditional opposition to Virtus (in the sense of moral virtue). The progression of Fortune from enemy of virtue to friend of vice in general, and to ally of the Vice in particular, must have had a certain inevitability about it.

This affinity also had important implications for the theatrical use of Fortune, since the Vice could perform much the same function as Fortune. In *Common Conditions*, as we have seen, the Vice says that he is "Nere kinde to Dame Fortune to raise and to let fall." It may have been this very similarity which precluded Fortune's prominence on the stage, for the Vice in his vitality was undoubtedly more interesting theatrically than Dame Fortune. Since a playwright could readily locate the immediate source of a character's adversity in the activity of the Vice, he had less need to cite the hostility of Fortune. Perhaps significantly, Fortune appears as a character only in interludes which lack a chief Vice.

IV

As the drama became more realistic in the last two decades of the sixteenth century, the use of abstractions as characters diminished sharply. Yet Fortune was more often brought to the stage as a character in the second half of Elizabeth's reign than in the first. Fortune appears in two plays of the 1580s and 1590s dealing with romantic love— *The Rare Triumphs of Love and Fortune* (c. 1582) and *Soliman and Perseda* (c. 1589-92) — both of which will be discussed in a later chapter. Moreover, Fortune appears in two other plays that were staged at the turn of the century: the anonymous *Contention between Liberality and Prodigality* and Thomas Dekker's *Old Fortunatus*.[29]

Both of these resemble such earlier works as *The Longer Thou Livest* and *Impatient Poverty* in that they are concerned with material prosperity and spiritual decline. *Liberality* and *Fortunatus* are more secular in tone than the others; both were evidently written, at least in their present form, as much for the amusement of a courtly audience as for moral edification. Yet they reflect the impact of the moral interludes, for each deals with the relationship of Fortune to virtue and vice. Considered together, the two plays demonstrate the continuity of the dramatic tradition, even if, in Dekker's work, there is considerable experimentation.

By far the more conventional of the two plays is *Liberality and Prodigality*, originally performed "probably in 1567-1568 during the Christmas revels."[30] It is thought to have been revised for a performance at court in 1601. Because only the revision, printed in 1602, survives, we cannot say exactly how it differs from the original. However, since the conception of Fortune in the extant play closely resembles that presented by Wager in *The Longer Thou Livest*, it seems probable that the representation of Fortune in the extant play is not very different from that in the earlier version.

In *Liberality and Prodigality*, as in Wager's drama, Fortune stands opposed to goodness and rectitude. The antinomy takes shape in the first speech of the play when Vanity, who calls Fortune "my most sove-raigne dame," speaks of the hostility between Fortune and Virtue and promises the audience: "'twixt their states, what difference will be, / Your selves shall judge, and witnesse when you see" (40-41). [31] Shortly afterward, Virtue herself appears and characterizes her antagonist:

> Whilome hath bin taught that fortunes hold is tickle,
> She beares a double face, disguised, false, and fickle,
> Full fraughted with all sleights, she playeth on the pack,
> On whom she smileth most, she turneth most to wracke.
> The time hath bin, when virtue had the soveraignety
> Of greatest price, and plaste in chiefest dignity:
> But topsie-turvy now, the world is turn'd about:
> Proud Fortune is preferd, poore Vertue cleane thrust out.
>
> (116-23)

Virtue's vituperative portrait of her adversary heralds the conflict to come. And when Fortune enters, mounted on a chariot drawn by kings, she confirms the intensity of the struggle:

> Well is it knowne, what contrary effects,
> Twixt Fortune and dame Vertue hath beene wrought:
> How still I her contemne, she me rejects;
> I her despise, she setteth me at nought:
> So as great warres are growne for soveraignty,
> And strife as great, twixt us for victorie. (269-74)

Anxious to demonstrate her hegemony (like Fortune in *The Longer Thou Livest*), Fortune announces that the antipathy between herself and Virtue is about to issue in a test:

> Now is the time of triall to be had,
> The place appoynted, eke in present here:
> So as the trueth to all sorts, good and bad,

More cleere then light, shall presently appeare.
It shall be seene, what Fortunes power can doe,
When Vertue shall be forst to yeeld thereto. (275-80)

So begins the contest that will pit Fortune against Virtue, unreason against rationality, excess against moderation.

Although the play opposes Virtue and Fortune, the chief rivalry actually witnessed by the audience is that of Prodigality and Tenacity. (The title of the play is therefore a little misleading.) These two characters are not to be taken as the supernumeraries of Fortune and Virtue. Rather, they both represent errant behavior, inconsistent with rationality. The play, then, deals not with a single figure representing mankind, but with characters representing contrasting forms of immoderation.

Prodigality and Tenacity, anxious to acquire wealth, petition Fortune for the possession of her child Money. Their pleas fall on deaf ears, for the goddess is unaffected by rational argument. Indeed, she renders a decision which, by its indifference to reason, provides a vivid demonstration of her nature:

> Dame Fortune dealeth not by merit, but by chance:
> He hath it but by hap, whom Fortune doth advance;
> And of his hap as he hath small assurance:
> So in his hap likewise is small continuance.
> Therefore at a venture, my deare sonne Money,
> I doe commit you unto Prodigalitie. (462-67)

The eagerness of men to seek the gifts of Fortune suggests that the goddess may prevail in the contest with Virtue, but Liberality, the "steward" of Virtue, predicts that the victory is only temporary:

> Men see without most just desert, of vertue nought is got,
> To Fortune therefore flie they still, that giveth all by lot;
> And finding Fortunes gifts, so pleasant, sweet and savery,
> They build thereon, as if they should endure perpetually.
> But this is sure, and that most sure, that Fortune is
> unsure,
> Herselfe most fraile, her giftes as fraile, subject to every
> shewre:

And in the end, who buildeth most upon her suerty,
Shall find himselfe cast headlong downe, to depth of
    miserie. (626-33)

Those who put their faith in the gifts of Fortune are destined to be disappointed, for happiness of a lasting kind cannot be gained from Fortune
alone; it is achieved only through virtuous action. And this entails a
moderation which neither Prodigality nor Tenacity possesses.

At the hands of Prodigality, Money fares badly. Although initially
prized, Money finds himself "cruelly handled." Escaping the control of
Prodigality, Money makes his way to Liberality and reports:

now how my case is altered suddenly;
You would not beleeve, unlesse you saw it apparantly.
Ifaith since ye saw me, I have bin turmoyled
From post to piller: see how I am spoyled. (731-34)

Having no desire to repeat this experience, Money resolves to return to
Fortune: "To my mother in haste againe I will get me, / And keepe at
home safely: from thence let them set me" (745-46). However, when
Money is reunited with his mother, Fortune expresses the wish that he
accompany Tenacity. Money is reluctant, but Tenacity promises him
better treatment than he has hitherto received: "Let Prodigalitie goe to
the gallowes tree: / Why man, he and I are cleane contrary?"
(827-28). So off goes Money with his new master and new hopes. It is
not long, however, before Money once again seeks release. This time his
complaint is the opposite of what it was formerly: "Ah, that wretch
Tenacitie hath brought mee to all this woe. / 'Twas he indeed that sought
to destroy me, / In that he would never use to employ me" (1018-
20). When, finally, Money is entrusted to Liberality, he looks back and
finds that each of his previous masters erred by excess. Of Tenacity,
Money says:

He would never let me abroad to goe,
But lockt me up in coffers, or in bags bound me fast,
That like a Bore in a stie, he fed me at last.

Thus Tenacitie did spoile me, for want of exercise:
But Prodigalitie, cleane contrarywise,
Did tosse me, and fleece me, so bare and so thinne,
That he left nothing on me, but very bone and skinne.
(1182-88)

After such bitter experience, Money is only too happy to be placed in the care of Liberality, who will avoid both excess and deficiency: "Sir, I like you well, and therefore willingly, / I am contented with you to remaine, / So as you protect me from the other twaine" (1193-95).

Liberality and Prodigality expresses its conventionality by the nature of its didacticism. The play advocates essentially what John Skelton advocated nearly a century earlier in *Magnificence*: namely, that Fortune's gifts should be handled prudently. Although the author of *Liberality and Prodigality* suggests the value of spare simplicity when he portrays Virtue's "homely bower," he affirms, in the play as a whole, the judicious management of wealth rather than ascetic withdrawal from life. The play, which purports to chronicle a struggle between Virtue and Fortune, suggests that the gifts of Fortune are not to be contemned: money is to be used wisely. The lesson to be drawn, then, is much like that of *Magnificence*—the importance of Aristotelian measure. Liberality, called the "steward" of Virtue, is a mean between extremes.

The author of *Liberality and Prodigality* is conventional in another sense as well, for he is reluctant to allow Fortune the prominence that would seem her due. Although Fortune enters splendidly in her chariot, judges the pleas of Prodigality and Tenacity, awards Money first to Prodigality, then Tenacity, and appears on stage ensconced in her palace, the playwright sharply restricts Fortune's role in the latter part of the play. This seems particularly curious since Fortune may rightly claim some part in the demise of Prodigality. After all, when the latter loses Money and angrily storms Fortune's palace, the goddess vows revenge:

For here as now I will no longer stay,
But prosecute this foe of mine so fast,

By mischiefes all I may, that at the last,
He shall arrive unto a wretched end,
And with repentance learne how to offend
A goddesse of my state and dignitie. (946-51)

However, it is not Fortune but Equity, the Sheriff, and the Judge who are most responsible for the undoing of Prodigality. Thus when a robbery and murder are committed, Virtue directs Equity to investigate the crime. The Sheriff quickly apprehends Prodigality and brings him to court where he pleads guilty. The penitent Prodigality looks back over his career and concedes his folly: "I finde the brittle stay of trustlesse Fortunes state. / My heart now thirsteth after Vertue, all too late" (1302-3). But the Fortune whom he names, the Fortune who has played so important a role in Prodigality's story, has disappeared from the drama. Evidently, it would have undercut the playwright's instruction to have allowed Fortune a direct part in Prodigality's undoing. After all, the audience is meant to recognize the connection between cause and effect, error and retribution; and Fortune, by her own testimony, "dealeth not by merit, but by chance."

Thomas Dekker's *Pleasant Comedy of Old Fortunatus* was written four decades after *The Longer Thou Livest* and nearly as long after the original version of *Liberality and Prodigality*. The portrayal of Fortune differs markedly, in some respects, from that which typifies other plays of the sixteenth century. Nevertheless, Dekker's treatment of Fortune shows signs of being shaped by the legacy of the moral interludes: although the story derives from Germanic folklore, Dekker is concerned with the relationship of Fortune to good and evil.[32]

The first scene seems to promise that Dekker's play will resemble other plays in which Fortune appears. Like her namesake in *Liberality and Prodigality*, Fortune enters in splendor; and she treads upon the kings who lie at her feet. Like Fortune in *The Longer Thou Livest*, moreover, she determines to assert her power by elevating the unworthy. She tells the princes whom she has overthrown, "Stand by; now rise, behold, here lies a wretch, / To vex your soules, this begger ile advaunce" (I.i.140-41).[33] The object of Fortune's beneficence is the aged Fortunatus, to whom the goddess offers a choice:

Six gifts I spend upon mortalitie,
Wisedome, strength, health, beautie, long life, and riches:
Out of my bountie, one of these is thine,
Choose then which likes thee best. (210-13)

The impoverished Fortunatus selects the last of these, saying, "My choice is store of gold; the rich are wise" (286). Fortune fulfills her pledge by giving him a magic purse:

Thou shalt spend ever, and be never poore:
For proofe receive this purse: with it this vertue,
Still when thou thrusts thy hand into the same,
Thou shalt draw foorth ten pieces of bright gold. (298-301)

Having made his decision and received his prize, Fortunatus is almost immediately spurned by Fortune, who calls him a "vaine covetous foole" (308). Like Moros, Fortunatus will enjoy temporary prosperity but eventually be destroyed by his infatuation with the things of this world. This much of *Old Fortunatus* is reminiscent of Wager's drama.

Dekker also recalls Fortune's traditional antagonism toward virtue. In the very first scene, for example, Fortune makes remarks designed to slight Virtue who, along with Vice, will appear as a character: Fortune boasts that she sets "an Ideots cap on vertues head" (I.i.120). Fortune also suggests a fundamental antipathy to Virtue when, later, she says to Virtue: "Poore foole, tis not this badge of puritie, / Nor *Sibi sapit*, (painted on thy breast,) / Allures mortalitie to seeke thy love" (I.iii.58-60). Fortune advises:

Then *Vertue*, buy a golden face like *Vice*,
And hang thy bosome full of silver Moones,
To tell the credulous world, As those increase,
As the bright Moone swelles in her pearled Spheare,
So wealth and pleasures them to heaven shall reare.
(69-73)

In this same scene when Vice suggests that she, by means of her "Saint-like forme," will lure some fool to taste of the tree she has planted, Fortune relishes the prospect (94). The very garment worn by Vice ("painted before with silver halfe moones, increasing by litle and litle, till they come to the full") suggests a kinship with Fortune, whose mutability was traditionally associated with the waxing and waning moon.

Fortune, however, assumes an unaccustomed role in her treatment of Ampedo and Andelocia, the sons of Fortunatus, who inherit their father's magic purse and magic hat. Like pairs of characters in the interludes, the brothers are a study in contrast. Ampedo is prudent and temperate; Andelocia foolishly dedicates himself to the pursuit of pleasure. At one point Ampedo is called "brother vertue" and Andelocia "brother Vice" (I.ii.91-92). The appellations suggest that the brothers are the supernumeraries of Virtue and Vice. Toward these latter figures — and hence toward Ampedo and Andelocia — Fortune professes indifference. When Virtue and Vice plant their trees, Fortune declares:

> Florish or wither, *Fortune* cares not which,
> In eithers fall or height our Eminence
> Shines equall to the Sunne: the Queene of chance
> Both vertuous soules and vicious doth advance. (I.iii.36-39)

So disinterested is Fortune that she will decide the outcome of the strife between Virtue and Vice: "*Fortune* shall judge who winnes the soveraigntie" (103).

To a reader of the moral interludes, Dekker's portrayal of a neutral Fortune seems curious, for in those earlier plays the contingency of Fortune is usually presented as hostile to reason, justice, goodness.[34] That Fortune, out of caprice, may at some point aid a virtuous individual does not alter this basic pattern. Even though, theoretically, Fortune may be indifferent to virtue, this very indifference is construed by the authors of the interludes as tantamount to hostility.

Equally puzzling is the unexplained shift in attitude that overtakes Fortune further on in *Old Fortunatus*. Late in the play, despite her declared neutrality, Fortune reproves Andelocia for eating from the tree of Vice. And she urges him to pursue Virtue:

> Runne after her, sheele give thee these and these
> Crownes and Bay-garlands: (honours victories:)
> Serve her, and shee will fetch thee pay from heaven,
> Or give thee some bright office in the starres.
>
> (IV.i.194-97)

In the last scene Fortune reiterates this advice. She actually defers to Virtue when she tells the king, who now possesses the magic purse, "*Vertue* pardond you, and so doth *Fortune*" (V.ii.224). Encouraging him to follow Virtue's course, Fortune promises: "*England* shall ne're be poore, if *England* strive, / Rather by vertue, then by wealth to thrive" (259-60).

What the audience witnesses, then, is the transition of Fortune from impartial observer of the struggle between Virtue and Vice (in the first act) to friend of Virtue (in the last) — a transition for which the play offers no explanation. No wonder modern readers have been perplexed.[35] How are we to account for Dekker's unconventional treatment of Fortune?

The answer may lie in the complicated circumstances surrounding the composition of the play. Henslowe's *Diary* records that a drama called *The First Part of Fortunatus* was performed by the Admiral's Men early in 1596; it is not known whether Dekker had a hand in this work. Evidently the play underwent revision in 1599 when Dekker received payment for *The Whole History of Fortunatus*. In all likelihood, Dekker combined *The First Part*, already written, with additional material (a *Second Part* perhaps already written?) and thereby created a new play. This was not, however, the final version, for near the end of 1599 Dekker revised the play yet again for presentation before Queen Elizabeth. Finally, in 1600 *Old Fortunatus* was printed.

This theatrical history has led Dekker's modern editor, Fredson Bowers, to conjecture that the scenes involving Fortune together with Virtue and Vice may have been added only in the final version. Noting the size of the last payment to Dekker, Bowers reasons: "Since the substantial sum of £2 would scarcely be warranted merely for the closing compliment to Elizabeth and the epilogue, and ought to have included more than the court prologue, it is not impossible that this payment covered further work on the text, perhaps in the expansion of the masque element dealing with Fortune, Virtue, and Vice."[36] The composition of such additional material must have presented Dekker with an artistic problem: how to handle the relationship of Fortune to Virtue and Vice. His principal source, the *Volksbuch*, offered little help, for it does not present Fortune in the company of the other two figures. Dekker had, in the native dramatic tradition, the precedent of Fortune's close relationship to the Vice and, as noted above, he appears to follow this in several scenes of the play. But for the most part Dekker seems to have relied upon his own ingenuity.

Early in the play Dekker underscores Fortune's contingency. In the first scene the kings whom she has overthrown address her as the "Accursed Queene of chaunce" (I.i.91). And Fortune emphasizes the caprice which constitutes her nature by moralizing on one of her accouterments, the globe:

> Behold you not this Globe, this golden bowle,
> This toy cal'd worlde at our Imperiall feete?
> This world is *Fortunes* ball wherewith she sports. (99-101)

It is this identification of Fortune with sportiveness that seems to guide her relationship to Virtue and Vice early in the play. Had Dekker somehow managed to preserve this characterization of Fortune, the inconsistencies noted above might have been avoided. But he transforms Fortune into an ally of Virtue and, as a result, the logic of the play breaks down.

What led Dekker to compromise his portrait of a neutral Fortune is not known with certainty. To account for the dramatist's practice, I propose what is admittedly a speculation: that Dekker's need to pay homage to the Queen caused an inconsistency in his treatment of Fortune. Let us begin with what we know: in the final version of the play, performed before the court, Elizabeth is to be complimented. Conceivably, Fortune could pay the compliment. Indeed, there was even a precedent for this in *The Rare Triumphs of Love and Fortune*, where Love and Fortune put aside their strife and Fortune says, "God save her Majestie, that keepes us all in peace."[37] But the issue is much more complicated in Dekker's play, where the supremacy of Virtue or Vice is at stake, where Virtue presumably must emerge victorious, and where

Fortune, because of her central role in the story, is to play some part. To allow Fortune to declare Virtue the winner might seem to undercut the courtly compliment, for it would suggest Virtue's inferiority to the goddess of caprice. Dekker must have been aware of this problem since, in an arch designed to honor James I in 1604, he takes pains to ensure that Fortune appears inferior to Virtue. According to Dekker's description, depicted on the arch "was *Arete* (Vertue) inthronde, her garments white, her head crowned, and under her *Fortuna*: her foote treading on the Globe, that movde beneath her: Intimating, that his Majesties fortune, was above the world, but his vertues above his fortune."[38] To avoid overtly undercutting the supremacy of Virtue in *Old Fortunatus*, Dekker might have emulated the author of *Liberality and Prodigality* and in effect banished Fortune from the latter part of the play; in that interlude Virtue delivers the epilogue praising the Queen. But Dekker chooses another solution: he has Fortune relinquish her position as judge (which she has held since I.iii) and descend into a three-way contest with Virtue and Vice.[39] Thus in the final scene Fortune says to the others, "see here's a court / Of mortall Judges, lets by them be tride, / Which of us three shall most be deifide" (V.ii.302-4). Elizabeth, of course, will do the deciding. By having Fortune incline to Virtue long before the contest comes to issue, Dekker evidently felt that he would make more plausible and inevitable the victory of Virtue, a moral quality embodied in the Queen.

Whatever his intent, the plausibility of Virtue's triumph is strained. It certainly cannot be based on the career of Andelocia who, practically to the end, maintains his quest for riches. Admittedly, he says, shortly before his death, "Riches and knowledge are two gifts divine. / They that abuse them both as I have done, / To shame, to beggerie, to hell must runne" (V.ii.173-75). But he can scarcely be said to have reformed: although Andelocia momentarily inclines to Virtue when he loses the magic purse and hat, he remains essentially egocentric and avaricious. His whole life constitutes a neglect of Virtue, and his fate is appropriately damnation. The victory of Virtue, similarly, can scarcely rest upon the career of Ampedo. Throughout the play he has seemed on his way to eventual triumph; when he is spurned by Andelocia, we feel that Ampedo (who has consistently disdained wealth) will surely reap a heavenly reward. Yet in a bizarre turn of events, Virtue lambastes

Ampedo on the grounds that his virtue has been insufficiently aggressive:

> The Idiots cap I once wore on my head,
> Did figure him, those that (like him) doe muffle
> *Vertue* in clouds, and care not how shee shine,
> Ile make their glorie like to his decline:
> He made no use of me, but like a miser,
> Lockt up his wealth in rustie barres of sloth:
> His face was beautifull, but wore a maske,
> And in the worlds eyes seemd a Blackamore.
> So perish they that so keepe vertue poore. (V.ii.271-79)

This criticism makes it sound as though Ampedo has played Tenacity to Andelocia's Prodigality. But Virtue's criticism of Ampedo is not anticipated by anything that the audience has witnessed or heard earlier. Indeed, in a previous version of the play, as Sidney R. Homan, Jr. suggests, Ampedo may have "emerged as the hero, thus showing Virtue's triumph"; Virtue's speech "looks like a hurried attempt by Dekker to clear the stage of any rivals for Elizabeth."[40] Aesthetically, the play suffers for this dramatic legerdemain. James H. Conover remarks, "Dekker has produced a witty compliment to Queen Elizabeth and to England, but has marred his play in the process."[41]

V

Basic to *Old Fortunatus* is this unresolved contradiction: money is dangerous, yet it may be used to good purpose. On the one hand, Dekker suggests that Fortunatus makes a terrible mistake in choosing wealth over wisdom. Fortune tells the character: "thou wilt repent, / That for the love of drosse thou hast despised / Wisedomes divine embrace" (I.i.308-10). And Ampedo's rejection of the magic purse seems throughout most of the play a mark of his spiritual integrity. On the other hand, Dekker suggests at several points that it is not so much wealth but its ill use that is blameworthy. Thus just before Fortunatus dies, Fortune tells him: "Thou hast eaten Metals, and abusde my giftes, /

Hast plaid the Ruffian, wasted that in ryots, / Which as a blessing I bestowed on thee" (II.ii.235-37). And still later the equally prodigal Andelocia comes to this recognition: "I have abuzde two blessings, welth and knowledge, / Wealth in my purse, and knowledge in my Hat" (IV.i.101-2). Finally, at the end of the play, Fortune restores to the purse the power to create money and gives it to the king with this admonition: "take heede how thou my gifts doest use" (V.ii.258). Throughout the play Dekker oscillates between an outright condemnation of wealth and an injunction to handle it wisely.

Dekker's contradictory counsel is implicit in many of the plays that we have considered, if perhaps in less stark form. Magnificence comes very close to utterly destroying himself, but he is eventually restored to power. Grissell renders herself vulnerable to disaster when she accepts the proposal of the wealthy Marquis, but she finally returns to a position of privilege. Poverty, for a time at least, is ruined, but he resolves to mend his ways and returns to prosperity. Prodigality and Tenacity destroy themselves, but a relieved Money is entrusted to Liberality. In each instance the audience is invited to rejoice in the happy ending. Yet the audience is also left to ponder how narrowly tragedy is averted. These plays indicate that ambivalence over money was by no means confined to Dekker, that it was manifest throughout the sixteenth century. Evidently, despite a lingering feeling that the mere possession of wealth could be injurious to one's soul, many people were coming to accept a different view. For them the accumulation of money was entirely compatible with spiritual integrity.

A century and more before the composition of *Old Fortunatus*, we find in the drama a general disdain for the amassing of material possessions; they are deemed useless to spiritual progress. Everyman, for instance, discovers that Goods is unwilling to accompany him at the last, and in any case that figure exerts a pernicious influence: "my Goods sharply did me tell / That he bringeth many into hell."[42] Only a few years later, in *Magnificence*, material things are regarded as at least potentially good. And by the middle of the sixteenth century, they are even seen as a mark of divine favor. Thus in Thomas Lupton's *All for Money* (1559-77) the prologue opens with the question, "What good gift of God but may be misused?" and goes on to announce: "Money ill-used is the devil's snare and hook / Whereby many are brought to endless damnation, / But the godly do bestow it to their salvation."[43] And in *The Trial of Treasure* (published in 1567) the virtuous Trust bids his auditors:

> Flee from love of treasure, catch hold of me, Trust;
> And then double felicity at the last you shall possess,
> And in all earthly doings God shall give you success.[44]

This is the inevitable corollary of a world view well on its way to overcoming a moral objection to money.

Traditional attitudes did not of course disappear. The survival of older values alongside the new is evident in *Impatient Poverty* (c. 1547-58), which has been called "a patched revision of an even earlier play."[45] Peace approvingly cites the conditions which may facilitate the acquisition of riches:

> I speak for this cause: daily ye may see
> How that, by envy and malice, many be destroyed;
> Which, if they had lived in peace with patient humility,
> Riches and prosperity with them had been employed.
> For thereas is peace, no man is annoyed;
> For by peace men grow to great richesse;
> And by peace men live in great quietness. (p. 313)

Within the play, however, this attitude is not sustained. In fact, after the protagonist has strayed from the virtuous path and lost his money, the playwright lapses into an assertion of *contemptus mundi*:

> Sovereigns! here may ye see proved, before you all,
> Of this wanton world the great fragility;
> Ever mutable of the turning, as a ball.
> Now, flood of riches; now, ebb of poverty:
> What should men set by this world's vanity?
> Think on this lesson, and do it not forget:
> The gayest of us all is but worms' meat. (p. 347)

Appearing near the end of a play so unashamedly devoted to the getting of money, this speech seems incongruous. In the warning about the "world's vanity," there is no suggestion that wealth derives from God's beneficence, that it may be a mark of His favor. Indeed, the allusion to the ball suggests the globe upon which Fortune stands. (In *Old Fortunatus* the globe is borne onto the stage by one of Fortune's servants.) The sentiment expressed at the end of *Impatient Poverty* belongs to an earlier time when both Fortune and her gifts were spurned as injurious to man's moral welfare.

We must, of course, beware of imagining a consistent historical progression. As early as the 1560s, when Wager wrote *The Longer Thou Livest*, a character in Ulpian Fulwell's *Like Will to Like* (1562-68) says, "virtue and fortune be not at strife. / Where virtue is, fortune must needs grow."[46] And as late as the turn of the century, in *Old Fortunatus*, several scenes recall Fortune's traditional kinship with vice. Nevertheless, attitudes toward wealth were changing, generally from severity to indulgence, and as they did they created difficulties for dramatists who sought to employ Fortune. For where moral objection to material bounty diminished, so too did the tendency to regard Fortune as the source of moral peril. Thus at the very time that the Psychomachia was fostering a portrayal of Fortune as evil, an increasingly receptive attitude toward Fortune's gifts was tending to blur Fortune's alignment with vice. As the Elizabethan era drew to a close, Fortune was becoming a more neutral figure than in the heady days when she exalted young Moros. Dekker, by continuing to address so directly Fortune's relationship to good and evil, brought to focus a problem which other playwrights preferred to evade and which he himself had not the wit to resolve.

NOTES TO CHAPTER 4

1. *The Origins of English Tragedy* (Oxford: Clarendon Press, 1967), p. 14.

2. Similarly, the saints' plays or conversion plays generally eschew Fortune. However, World, a character in *Mary Magdalene* (from the Digby MS),

mentions the wheel of Fortune. See *Medieval Drama,* ed. David Bevington (Boston: Houghton Mifflin, 1975), p. 699.

3. *The Medieval Heritage of Elizabethan Tragedy* (1936; reprint ed. with corrections, Oxford: Basil Blackwell, 1970), p. 186.

4. See *The Castle of Perseverance,* in *The Macro Plays,* ed. Mark Eccles, EETS, no. 262 (New York: Oxford Univ. Press, 1969), l. 1073; *Mankind,* in *The Macro Plays,* l. 203; *Nature,* in *Recently Recovered "Lost" Tudor Plays with Some Others,* ed. John S. Farmer (1907; reprint ed., New York: Barnes and Noble, 1966), p. 69; *Wisdom,* in *The Macro Plays,* ll. 574-80.

5. *Endeavors of Art: A Study of Form in Elizabethan Drama* (Madison and London: Univ. of Wisconsin Press, 1954), p. 104.

6. The Aristotelianism of *Magnificence* has been treated by Robert Lee Ramsay in his Introduction to the play, EETS, Extra Series 98 (New York: Oxford Univ. Press, 1908). William O. Harris has challenged Ramsay's interpretation, in *Skelton's Magnyfycence and the Cardinal Virtue Tradition* (Chapel Hill: Univ. of North Carolina Press, 1965). Harris argues that the design of the play is based upon "the doctrine of the cardinal virtue of Fortitude (sometimes called Magnificence or Magnanimity) which required of a man— especially a ruler—that he resist by temperate action the temptations of both prosperity and adversity" (p. 10). It seems to me that one can accept the influence of the "cardinal virtue tradition" without disallowing the influence of Aristotle. Renaissance drama, after all, draws inspiration from both native and classical traditions. As for the treatment of Fortune in the play, even Harris concedes that "the emphasis on Fortune and a contempt for worldly felicity has, of course, far wider currency than any exclusive association with the concept of Fortitude" (p. 155).

7. *Magnificence,* ed. Paula Neuss, The Revels Plays (Manchester and Baltimore: Johns Hopkins Univ. Press, 1980).

8. Ramsay, ed., *Magnyfycence: A Moral Play,* p. xxviii.

9. *The English Drama, 1485-1585,* ed. G. K. Hunter, Oxford History of English Literature (Oxford: Clarendon Press, 1969), p. 13.

10. Howard R. Patch, in *The Goddess Fortuna in Mediaeval Literature* (1927; reprint ed., New York: Octagon Books, 1974), writes of Fortune's gifts: "These possessions are of various kinds; but first and foremost there is a general notion that Fortune deals in the mundane, the temporal, in goods of mortal concern. These we may subdivide appropriately as (1) dignities—honor, fame, glory, and the like; (2) riches, which are of course the mundane gifts *par excellence*" (pp. 63-64).

11. As scholars have long noted, the relationship between Fortune and providence is not clearly defined in the play. Margeson writes that "the fickleness of fortune is a more important theme than retribution, though the two are linked when Adversity announces that he comes from God" (p. 47). David Bevington, in *Tudor Drama and Politics: A Critical Approach to Topical Meaning* (Cambridge, Mass.: Harvard Univ. Press, 1968), comments: "Though Magnificence's decline on Fortune's wheel appears to contradict the idea of causality in his misfortunes, the ending is notwithstanding integral to the play's *speculum* intent" (p. 63). Robert Potter, in *The English Morality Play: Origins, History and Influence of a Dramatic Tradition* (London and Boston: Routledge and Kegan Paul, 1975), speaks of "a general and retributive mutability which fulfills God's providence" (p. 74). Paula Neuss, in her edition of *Magnificence*, writes: "Skelton's inclusion of the characters Felicity and Adversity (aspects of Fortune, rather than qualities of mankind), in his allegory gives the play at times a tone similar to tragedies like Lydgate's. But prosperity is lost by the prince's own actions, through his submission to will rather than reason, and Adversity is seen not as an undeserved visitation of Fortune, but as a punishment for sin, coming from God . . ." (p. 21).

12. *Hickescorner*, in *Six Anonymous Plays: First Series* (c. 1510-1537), ed. John S. Farmer (1905; reprint ed., New York: Barnes and Noble, 1966), p. 151.

13. *Wit and Science*, in *English Morality Plays and Moral Interludes*, ed. Edgar T. Schell and J. D. Shuchter (New York: Holt, Rinehart and Winston, 1969), ll. 648-49.

14. *The Play of Patient Grissell*, ed. Ronald B. McKerrow and W. W. Greg, MSR (Oxford: Chiswick Press, 1909).

15. *Cambises*, in *Chief Pre-Shakespearean Dramas*, ed. Joseph Quincy Adams (Cambridge, Mass.: Houghton Mifflin, 1924).

16. Otian, the son of Sisamnes, after pleading unsuccessfully for his father's life, asks: "O false and fickle frowning dame, that turneth as the winde, / Is this the joy in fathers age thou me assignest to finde?" (449-50).

17. Most readers of the play agree that the ending is something of a muddle. J.M.R. Margeson, in *The Origins of English Tragedy*, writes, "The end of the play is an accident, even if it is interpreted as the intervention of Providence" (p. 52). David Bevington, in *From Mankind to Marlowe: Growth of Structure in the Popular Drama of Tudor England* (Cambridge, Mass.: Harvard Univ. Press, 1962), observes that "an ambiguity exists, because the death of Cambises is sudden and accidental. It comes only in the last few lines of the action, and its moral function is underplayed" (p. 214).

18. John Isaac Owen, in *An Edition of The Rare Triumphs of Love and Fortune*, Renaissance Drama: A Collection of Critical Editions (New York and London: Garland, 1979), suggests a connection between the treatment of Fortune in medieval poetry and the employment of Fortune on the stage: "It would appear that one of the stages in this transition is to be found in the disguisings, or mummings, and in the pageants of the fifteenth century and the early years of the sixteenth century" (p. 123). For the text of such mummings and pageants, see *The Minor Poems of John Lydgate*, ed. Henry Noble Mac-Cracken, EETS, Original Series, 192 (London: Oxford Univ. Press, 1934), part 2, 630-48, 682-91, and 698-701.

19. The history of the Fortuna-Virtus topos is treated by Ida Wyss, *Virtù und Fortuna bei Boiardo und Ariost* (Leipzig and Berlin: B. G. Teubner, 1931); Klaus Heitmann, *Fortuna und Virtus: Eine Studie zu Petrarcas Lebensweisheit* (Cologne: Böhlau, 1958); Oskar Roth, *Studien zum "Estrif de Fortune et Vertu" des Martin Le Franc* (Bern: Herbert Lang, 1970); Gottfried Kirchner, *Fortuna in Dichtung und Emblematik des Barock: Tradition und Bedeutungswandel eines Motivs* (Stuttgart: Metzler, 1970).

20. *The Longer Thou Livest and Enough is as Good as a Feast*, ed. R. Mark Benbow, RRDS (Lincoln: Univ. of Nebraska Press, 1967).

21. The typical features of the Vice are enumerated by Bernard Spivack, in *Shakespeare and the Allegory of Evil: The History of a Metaphor in Relation to His Major Villains* (New York and London: Columbia Univ. Press, 1958), esp. chap. 6.

22. In *Magnificence*, for example, a vice named Cloaked Collusion says, "Two faces in a hood covertly I bear" (710). Fortune's faces are discussed by Samuel C. Chew, *The Pilgrimage of Life* (1962; reprint ed., Port Washington, N.Y. and London: Kennikat Press, 1973), pp. 45-51; and Jesús Gutiérrez, La *"Fortuna Bifrons" en el teatro del Siglo de Oro* (Santander: Sociedad Menéndez Pelayo, 1975), esp. pp. 3-88.

23. *Common Conditions*, ed. Tucker Brooke, Elizabethan Club Reprints, no. 1 (New Haven and London: Yale Univ. Press, 1915), l. 166.

24. *The Tide Tarrieth No Man*, in *English Morality Plays and Moral Interludes*, ed. Schell and Shuchter, ll. 640-43.

25. *Impatient Poverty*, in *Recently Recovered "Lost" Tudor Plays*, ed. Farmer, p. 320.

26. *Shakespeare and the Allegory of Evil*, p. 271.

27. *Apius and Virginia,* ed. Ronald B. McKerrow and W. W. Greg, MSR (Oxford: Oxford Univ. Press, 1911).

28. *Shakespeare and the Allegory of Evil,* p. 270.

29. Fortune also appears on the Jacobean stage. She is a character in two Latin plays performed at Oxford in 1607-1608 as part of the revels at St. John's College: *Ara Fortunae* and *Ira Fortunae.* For the texts of the plays, see *The Christmas Prince,* ed. Frederick S. Boas and W. W. Greg, MSR (Oxford: Oxford Univ. Press, 1922), pp. 14-27 and 198-226. Fortune has a long speech at the beginning of R. A.'s *The Valiant Welshman* [1610-15], ed. Valentin Kreb, in *Münchener Beiträge zur romanischen und englischen Philologie,* 23 (Leipzig: A. Deichert, 1902). Fortune appears in a dumb show in Thomas Middleton's *Hengist, King of Kent; or The Mayor of Queenborough* [1615-20], ed. R. C. Bald (New York and London: Scribner's, 1938), pp. 12-13.

30. Bevington, *From Mankind to Marlowe,* p. 29.

31. *The Contention between Liberality and Prodigality,* ed. W. W. Greg, MSR (Oxford: Oxford Univ. Press, 1913). The play is discussed by T. W. Craik, *The Tudor Interlude: Stage, Costume, and Acting* (Leicester: Leicester Univ. Press, 1958), pp. 203-19.

32. The relationship of the play to its source is discussed by Charles H. Herford, in *Studies in the Literary Relations of England and Germany in the Sixteenth Century* (Cambridge: Cambridge Univ. Press, 1886), pp. 203-19.

33. *Old Fortunatus,* in *The Dramatic Works of Thomas Dekker,* ed. Fredson Bowers (Cambridge: Cambridge Univ. Press, 1953), vol. 1.

34. George R. Price has argued, in *Thomas Dekker,* TEAS (New York: Twayne, 1969), that "For a Renaissance audience familiar with the abundant literature and iconography of the goddess, nothing in Dekker's representation of her is inconsistent . . . with the traditional indifference of Fortune to moral quality in human beings" (p. 47). However, this assertion is not supported by a reading of the moral interludes.

35. Una Ellis-Fermor, in *The Jacobean Drama: An Interpretation,* 4th ed. (1957; reprint ed., New York: Vintage Books, 1964), finds "inconsistencies" in the relationship of Fortune to Virtue and Vice (p. 121, *n2*). Mary Leland Hunt, in *Thomas Dekker, A Study* (1911; reprint ed., New York: Russell and Russell, 1964), calls that relationship "befogging" (p. 34).

36. *The Dramatic Works of Thomas Dekker,* 1: 107.

37. *An Edition of The Rare Triumphs of Love and Fortune,* ed. John Isaac Owen, l. 1851.

38. *The Magnificent Entertainment Given to King James*, in *The Dramatic Works of Thomas Dekker*, 2: 295.

39. David M. Bergeron, in *English Civic Pageantry, 1558-1642* (Columbia: Univ. of South Carolina Press, 1971), makes a relevant observation about progress entertainments and royal entries for Elizabeth: "Mythological gods and goddesses surrender their claims on deity in her presence, the one who seemingly embodies all virtue" (p. 63).

40. "*Doctor Faustus*, Dekker's *Old Fortunatus*, and the Morality Plays," *MLQ*, 26 (1965): 501.

41. *Thomas Dekker: An Analysis of Dramatic Structure* (The Hague and Paris: Mouton, 1969), p. 81.

42. *Everyman*, in *Everyman and Medieval Miracle Plays*, ed. A. C. Cawley (1956; reprint ed., with revisions, London: J. M. Dent, 1974), ll. 474-75.

43. *All for Money*, in *English Morality Plays and Moral Interludes*, ed. Schell and Shuchter, ll. 75-77.

44. *The Trial of Treasure*, in *Dodsley's Old English Plays*, ed. W. Carew Hazlitt, 4th ed. (London: Reeves and Turner, 1874), 3: 286.

45. Bevington, *From Mankind to Marlowe*, p. 142.

46. *Like Will to Like*, in *Four Tudor Interludes*, ed. J. A. B. Somerset (London: Athlone Press, 1974), ll. 769-70.

Chapter 5

FORTUNE IN THE
DRAMA OF LODGE, MARLOWE, AND KYD

ONSIDERED IN RETROSPECT, Fortune's prominence in Elizabethan tragedy may seem to have been inevitable. Almost everywhere the dramatists turned for material, they encountered representations of Fortune. It is only natural that they should have carried over into their plays so ubiquitous a symbol. This was not, however, mere mechanical replication, Fortune in the source being dutifully rendered in the drama; significantly, the plays frequently assign a far greater role to Fortune than the sources warrant. Although it is sometimes possible to see an unmistakable connection between Fortune in a given play and in its source, Fortune's general prominence in the drama can be traced to no single source—indeed, to no one tradition. Thus a writer largely indebted to the native dramatic tradition and its treatment of Fortune may find inspiration in Seneca and in *de casibus* tragedy as well. Typically, the representation of Fortune in any given play is something of a pastiche; it constitutes creative borrowing from diverse antecedents.

Such inventiveness is apparent in the plays that are the subject of this chapter: *The Wounds of Civil War* by Thomas Lodge; *Tamburlaine* and *Edward II* by Christopher Marlowe; and *The Spanish Tragedy* by Thomas Kyd. Written in the period 1586-91, before Shakespeare had progressed very far in his own dramatic career, these plays exhibit a marked eclecticism. To the representation of Fortune in such immediate sources as Plutarch and Holinshed, the playwrights add images and ideas garnered from Seneca and the *Mirror for Magistrates*, even lines from Ovid and Alanus de Insulis. Collectively, the plays demonstrate how nimble the dramatists were in adapting traditional attitudes toward Fortune and giving them dramatic form.

Never hostage to a source, each playwright forges a personal vision; each tragedy represents Fortune in a distinctive fashion. In one play Fortune poses a formidable threat to even the most skilled and resourceful of men. In another, Fortune is part of the cosmic furniture, to be pushed aside as the protagonist flexes his power. In yet another, Fortune is an ambivalent force, aiding an aspirant's climb to great estate before claiming him as victim. Finally, Fortune is an unmistakably sinister force with whom the villains are in league.

If Fortune is so variously conceived, various strategies, it follows, are required to combat her. These range from passive acceptance to intellectual resolution to fierce aggressiveness. The relationship between man and Fortune is never exactly the same in any two plays. Each suggests a different answer to the question: How is man to grapple with Fortune's challenge?

I

The Wounds of Civil War, lively set forth in the true tragedies of Marius and Scilla (c. 1586) has considerable significance as the earliest surviving Roman tragedy. Seven or eight years before Shakespeare's first experiment with a Roman setting, Lodge's play expresses the Elizabethan playwrights' fascination with classical antiquity, especially with Roman history and culture. That culture was, of course, an important inspiration for the representation of Fortune on the Elizabethan stage. In particular, it was Rome which had popularized what became one of the most common of Renaissance topoi — Fortuna and Virtus — and it is this which underlies *The Wounds of Civil War.*

Lodge's work, however, illustrates the difficulty of locating specific origins for the treatment of Fortune. For the Fortuna-Virtus topos is not especially prominent in either of the sources that Lodge consulted: Appian's *Roman History*, translated into English in 1578, and Plutarch's *Lives*, translated in 1579. Where, then, did Lodge find the topos? Perhaps in other works by classical writers: essays by Plutarch on Fortuna and Virtus; or the moral essays of Seneca, translated by Lodge himself and published in 1614; or the tragedies of Seneca. Lodge could also have found his inspiration closer to home in the *Mirror for Magistrates*; the poems in this work often pit the individual against Fortune. The playwright was almost certainly familiar with all of these works, and we shall probably never know which was the most influential in shaping his tragic vision. By the 1580s, the Fortuna-Virtus topos was so much a part of European culture that it is impossible to single out a particular inspiration for Lodge's treatment of Fortune. This need not, however, prevent us from appreciating his achievement. The important point is that Lodge impresses upon historical materials a topos developed in Roman literature, and he makes it the very basis of his characterization. He constructs a response to Fortune on the foundations of Stoic thought: in the face of adversity, his characters embrace an even-tempered self-sufficiency.

Lodge found in Appian and Plutarch much that was potentially stageworthy: the story of a conflict that shook Rome for a decade (from 88 to 78 B.C.), a plethora of vivid and sometimes violent incidents, and, in Marius and Scilla (Sulla in Latin), two personalities of extraordinary forcefulness. Lodge had, then, the makings of a stirring drama. He chose, however, not to stress the color and excitement; Lodge "astonishes us by his failure to make use of picturesque incidents which he must have known."[1] In place of them, he presents Roman life as a field of competing ideologies. His handling of the first scene is illustrative. There he portrays the conflict between the two antagonists, each of whom seeks to lead the military expedition against Mithridates. The antipathy is fierce, but it is conveyed largely through the stately speeches of their adherents. When Scilla is replaced as commander by Marius, the men confront one another. Their speeches, however, have the patina of high-mindedness; there is much talk of "honor," "courage," and "the mind." And even though the stage directions at the beginning of scene ii signal violence (as Scilla drives Marius from Rome), the action seems perfunctory, and Lodge hurries past it to his real interest: the impact of the upheaval on the psyches of Marius and Scilla.

Neither Appian nor Plutarch speaks of Marius as possessing a philosophic cast of mind. By contrast, Lodge's Marius is preoccupied with searching out the underlying reasons for his defeat at the hands of Scilla.

When Marius reaches the temporary safety of Minturnum and ponders the meaning of what has happened, he blames neither his own weakness chiefly nor Scilla's strength. Instead, expostulating over the timidity of the Minturnians, who fear for their city as long as he remains there, Marius singles out Fortune as blameworthy:

> Thou wretched stepdame of my fickle state
> Are these the guerdons of the greatest minds,
> To make them hope and yet betray their hap,
> To make them climb to overthrow them straight?
> Accurst thy wreak, thy wrath, thy bale, thy wheel,
> That mak'st me sigh the sorrows that I feel. (II.ii.46-51)[2]

Scilla may be Marius' chief opponent among men, but his greatest foe is an adverse Fortune; and he must somehow come to terms with this adversary. The struggle, though, is largely internal, Marius' desire for power contending with his need to adapt to present circumstance.

Marius' plight is dire: the Minturnians, fearful of offending Scilla, place Marius in custody and plan to execute him. Alone and in peril, Marius resembles Boethius in the *Consolation of Philosophy*. The Roman general, however, makes his way to enlightenment without the help of Dame Philosophy. His interlocutor is a simple jailer who inquires about Marius' state of mind. Were he Marius, the jailer suggests, he could not endure the deprivation of what Fortune once conferred:

> The high estate your lordship once did wield,
> The many friends that fawn'd when fortune smil'd,
> Your great promotions, and your mighty wealth,
> These, were I Marius, would amate me so
> As loss of them would vex me more than death. (III.ii.11-15)

Prompted by the jailer's melancholy assessment, Marius is led to reply that his keeper is short-sighted, for he fails to appreciate that "lordship" has its burdens which must be borne like any others: "These stales of fortune are the common plagues / That still mislead the thoughts of simple men" (22-23). Everything in the world is unstable, Marius reasons. Why should political power be different? —"lordship, friends, wealth, spring and perish fast, / Where death alone yields happy life at last" (30-31). Adversity, it seems on reflection, is simply a part of life; and a noble death is not to be feared since it ensures that fame will live.

Although she poses the supreme challenge in this play, Fortune may, Lodge suggests, be successfully countered by self-discipline of the sort that Marius displays. The jailer, contemplating the attitude and words of his captive, points the way for the audience's response:

> The most undaunted words that ever were.
> The mighty thoughts of his imperious mind
> Do wound my heart with terror and remorse. (III.ii.59-61)

Marius may be frustrated by the fearful Minturnians and by his own recent defeat. But he is able to put aside rancor and self-criticism. He attains serenity of mind. In his Stoic determination to accept his lot, he transcends Fortune.

It may seem that Marius' resolution is too easily attained. But Lodge tests it, revealing self-doubts on the part of the general. After leaving Minturnum for the mountains of Numidia, Marius finds himself completely alone and, once again, ponders his deprivation. This time he concedes that he misses the authority he once held: "none but fortune all these mischiefs knows" (III.iv.4). By exercising "virtues of the mind" (20), he hopes to quell his uneasiness. Pomp and power, however, have not lost their allure. And after he has spent "six hundreth suns" in the wilderness, his resolve to preserve self-mastery by isolation wanes. An opportunity to alter his condition presents itself when he is discovered by his son. Young Marius brings word that Cinna has become Consul, that Marius is welcome to return to Rome; Scilla remains in the East. And so Marius returns, setting up the final test of his Stoic discipline.

The man who earlier cherished equanimity of spirit now embarks on a bloody revenge against his enemies, the desire for vengeance becoming an obsession. Marius' suppression of his foes, his consolidation of power, his election to the consulship — these events portrayed by Lodge conform in general outline to the histories of Appian and Plutarch. In the play, however, Marius undergoes a profound change before dying, one that ensures his final victory over Fortune. The catalyst for the transformation is an action that has no precedent in the classical accounts of Marius' life: a conversation with Cornelia and Fulvia, the wife and daughter of Scilla.

Even though Marius could condemn them with a word, the two women strike an aggressive pose. Their tone is distinctly hostile, Cornelia calling him "Vile monster, robb'd of virtue" (IV.i.296). Yet he finds himself admiring their courage. When Fulvia says fatalistically, "We wait our ends with Roman constancy" (335), Marius must be reminded of his own fortitude in Minturnum and Numidia. Fulvia, like Marius himself earlier, must struggle to attain self-mastery. When Cornelia tells her daughter to prepare for death, Fulvia momentarily gives way to emotion and suggests that their end might have been avoided: "Yet had my father known the course of change, / Or seen our loss by lucky augury, / This tyrant nor his followers had lived / To joy the ruin of fierce Scilla's house" (369-72). Himself once the victim of regret, Marius observes that anyone who enjoys great estate must expect to pay a price: "they that dwell on Fortune's call, / No sooner rise but subject are to fall" (373-74).

In this conversation Marius, perhaps unconsciously, plays the role of the jailer in Minturnum. At once interlocutor and prompter, he seems to evoke the best in both women. And, in consequence, he finds himself— like his jailer earlier—overcome with admiration. Impressed by the fearlessness of the women, Marius finds his own dormant virtue reawakened. He decides to free them both and send them back to Scilla. Their nobility has led Marius to remember his own better nature:

> Virtue, sweet ladies, is of more regard
> In Marius' mind where honor is enthron'd,
> Than Rome or rule of Roman Empery. (IV.i.390-92)

Although his enmity toward Scilla is not diminished, Marius has succeeded in putting aside his personal bitterness. His virtue reaffirmed, he demonstrates once again superiority to Fortune. Now in prosperity, as formerly in adversity, he summons the strength to prevail.

Scilla presents a very different relationship to Fortune. He believes himself to be as favored by Fortune as Marius feels victimized. When he drives his antagonist from Rome, Scilla declares:

> You Roman soldiers, fellow mates in arms,
> The blindfold mistress of incertain chance
> Hath turn'd these traitorous climbers from the top
> And seated Scilla in the chieftest place,
> The place beseeming Scilla and his mind. (II.i.1-5)

In this portrayal the playwright is essentially faithful to his sources. Lodge read in Appian's *History* that Scilla was considered exceptionally lucky. To honor him the Romans erected a golden statue bearing the title, "Cornelius Sylla the happy Captayne":

> For so did Flatterers use to call him in his fortunate fightes againste his foes, whiche name beginning of flattery, remayned firme and stable. I have seene in some writings, that he was called by decree *Sylla* the gratious, whiche thing is not incredible to me, bycause he was after named the Fortunate, which be names very nigh to lucky and gratious.[3]

Plutarch attributes even greater significance to Fortune. Scilla, he writes,

> did not only paciently abide their wordes that sayed, he was a happy man, and singularly beloved of fortune: but also increasinge this opinion, and glorying as at a speciall grace of the goddes, did attribute the honor of his doings unto fortune, either for a vaine glory, or for that he had in fansy, that the goddes did prosper him in all his doinges.[4]

In this and other passages, Plutarch draws the portrait of a man singularly favored by Fortune — and eager to foster his reputation as Fortune's favorite.

What Lodge adds is a counter-theme, articulated by Anthony and Granius. In the first scene, these two acknowledge the might of Fortune, her penchant for working her caprice through the ambition of men. In Granius' words, "our gods, our temples, and our walls, / Ambition makes fell Fortune's spiteful thralls" (I.i.316-17). In Scilla they recognize such ambition, a driving force which brooks no dissent. Concerned to deter him from civil carnage when he comes to power, they warn that mutability is everywhere, that prudence, therefore, should dictate his actions, even when he is most confident of Fortune's favor. Granius' argument takes the form of historical evidence: "Even here in Rome the fencer Spectacus / Hath been as fortunate as thou thyself, / But when that Crassus' sword assayed his crest, / The fear of death did make him droop for woe" (II.i.91-94). Anthony, for his part, cites the evidence of natural phenomena. Everything in nature, he observes, is subject to change:

> Old Anthony did never see, my lord,
> A swelling shower that did continue long,
> A climbing tower that did not taste the wind,
> A wrathful man not wasted with repent. (II.i.150-53)

While expressed with Anthony's customary eloquence, the advice has little effect; Scilla utterly rejects it. Granius, a supporter of Marius, fares worse; Scilla orders him executed.

For a time Scilla seems to defy with impunity the admonitions; he succeeds brilliantly in the Mithridatic wars. This stage direction indicates his supremacy: "Enter *Scilla* in triumph in his chair triumphant of gold, drawn by four Moors . . ."(III.iii). Whether this precedes or follows Marlowe's similar presentation of Tamburlaine on the Elizabethan stage, the effect is unmistakable: it is to exalt Scilla's stature. Lodge may even intend the audience to see Scilla as so favored by Fortune that he actually commands her chariot. Members of Lodge's audience could have seen at least two previous Elizabethan plays in which Fortune appears in a chariot. Two decades earlier, Gascoigne and Kinwelmershe in *Jocasta* (1566) brought Fortune on stage in her chariot. Fortune also rides a chariot in *Liberality and Prodigality*, originally written about 1567 though not published until 1602. Either precedent could have inspired Lodge's stagecraft.[5]

Although he is Fortune's favorite, Scilla has, paradoxically, greater difficulty coming to terms with Fortune than does Marius. Rejecting the advice of Granius and Anthony, he somehow manages to forget that fickleness is Fortune's most conspicuous trait. Subconsciously, though, he finds change threatening. Hence he castigates in others the mutability which he so fears. When he returns to Rome, for example, he locates the cause of the people's suffering in their caprice: "The reasons of this ruthful wrack / Are your seditious innovations, / Your fickle minds inclin'd to foolish change" (V.i.8-10). To Scilla, any variation in others represents a personal threat. His quest for permanence leads him even to find fault with the very Romans who proclaim him Dictator:

> You name me your Dictator, but prefix
> No time, no course, but give me leave to rule,
> And yet exempt me not from your revenge. (V.v.36-38)

His desire is clear: "Either let Scilla be Dictator ever, / Or flatter Scilla with these titles never" (43-44). What others experience as transitory, Scilla would fix forever. And until he achieves this security, he will not rest.

The historical Scilla, having returned to Rome and assumed absolute authority, did in fact rest: he voluntarily relinquished power and left the capital. Such a repudiation of great estate baffles the historians no less than it does us today. To Appian the decision seems extraordinary: "It seemeth beyond reason, that he, who by violence, passing so many perils, hadde made himselfe a Prince, should so freely leave it, & beyond al mens opinions, have no feare of the alteration" (p. 62). Appian goes on to speculate that perhaps sheer fatigue was responsible; Scilla "was weery of war, weery of dominion, & weery of the Citie, & therfore sought a vacation as it were, and quietnesse in the Countrey" (p. 63). Plutarch passes over the decision almost without comment. This silence, probably reflecting the same uncertainty felt by Appian, allows Lodge the opportunity to provide his own explanation of the change which overtook Scilla. And this Lodge does—in such a way that Scilla reenacts, in a sense, the history of Marius.

What triggers Scilla's abdication in the play is an event which receives cursory mention in the histories: the suicide of Marius' son.[6] Lodge represents it as having a chastening effect on Scilla, who reflects:

> I needs must pity thee,
> Whose noble mind could never mated be.
> Believe me, countrymen, a sudden thought,
> A sudden change in Scilla now hath wrought. (V.v.78-81)

Until now Scilla has cherished his position as Fortune's favorite, refusing to admit the possibility that he, like others, might succumb to mutability. Inwardly fearful of change, he was reluctant to acknowledge it as a natural and inevitable part of all things. Now in Young Marius he sees a man who experienced catastrophic change, yet managed to retain his nobility:

> Old Marius and his son were men of name,
> Nor Fortune's laughs nor lowers their minds could tame;
> And when I count their fortunes that are pass'd,
> I see that death confirm'd their fames at last. (82-85)

This recognition has a liberating effect on Scilla, who for the first time is willing to pause in his struggle to dominate others: "Then he that strives to manage mighty things / Amidst his triumphs gains a troubled mind" (86-87). Content of mind takes precedence over wielding power. And that content derives from acknowledging limitation, something he was formerly unable to concede.

Scilla has come to see that Anthony was correct, that everyone—regardless of rank—is subject to mutability, that the only effective strategy is acceptance. And so to himself he says:

> O, Scilla, see the ocean ebbs and floats,
> The springtime wanes when winter draweth nigh;
> Ay, these are true and most assured notes.
> Inconstant chance such tickle turns hath lent,
> As who so fears no fall must seek content. (V.v.99-103)

Hence his decision to abdicate. And with an intimation of approaching death, he remarks,

the man that made the world to stoop,
And fettered Fortune in the chains of power,
Must droop and draw the Chariot of Fate
Along the darksome banks of Acheron. (315-18)

The phraseology suggests Marlowe's Tamburlaine, but the attitude underlying Scilla's speech is very different. Unlike Tamburlaine, Scilla willingly renounces worldly attainments. He rejects continued aspiration in favor of tranquillity. And while, as the classical historians report, he may go to his death still congratulating himself on being Fortune's favorite, he no longer clings to power in a vain effort to find security. He has found something more durable, more valuable.

Despite the intensity of their struggle, Marius and Scilla seem almost to move in separate spheres of action. This has led to the charge that Lodge's play lacks unity. Admittedly, with the exception of the opening scene, Marius and Scilla do not appear on stage together. And since Marius dies before Scilla returns to Rome, the play lacks a spectacular face-to-face meeting. There is nothing here to match the climactic confrontation of Edward and Mortimer in *Edward II* or of Richard and Bolingbroke in *Richard II*. Yet the play does possess a kind of unity, one that derives from the dramatist's central purpose. What interests Lodge is not the clash of personality in the Senate or the clash of arms on the battlefield — not the civil wars at all — but rather the change that takes place within the minds of the two generals. The one must confront Fortune's outright hostility; the other, the prospect of Fortune's mutability. The unity that the play possesses lies in the essential similarity of the strategy which each man adopts in the face of this challenge. The nature of that strategy explains why Lodge declines to exploit the histrionic possibilities of the story: he seeks to focus attention on the transformation, psychological and philosophic, that the two characters experience. Of distinctly secondary importance is the military and political action that lies behind the psychic change.

Although Lodge was certainly not the last of Elizabethan playwrights to base his characters on the Stoic model, he can scarcely be said to typify the practice of most tragedians. In a theater that dramatized aspiration and worldly achievement, the values of detachment and denial must have seemed ill-suited to the construction of compelling characters. The cool, restrained attitude of a Marius is surely at odds with the flamboyance enjoyed by the Elizabethan audience. Perhaps the stage was itself inimical to the presentation of Stoicism: the successful Stoic seems to inhabit a private world, remote from other people — and perhaps from the audience as well. Witness Clermont D'Ambois in Chapman's play. To be sure, dramatists continued to celebrate the Stoic ideal: Shakespeare's Horatio is an attractive instance. But the demands of the theater and the taste of the audiences led away from Lodge's austere vision to something more engaging.

II

Although critics have pointed out similarities of style, phrase, and even staging between *The Wounds of Civil War* and *Tamburlaine the Great* (c. 1587), Lodge's work and Marlowe's differ sharply in spirit.[7] One concerns the acceptance of the human condition; the other, the denial of any thralldom. Tamburlaine sweeps aside every impediment; like some irresistible, elemental force he rolls from victory to victory. *Part 1* ends not with his demise but with his unquestioned supremacy. And his death at the conclusion of *Part 2* may be merely the consequence of old age. Marlowe's protagonist, moreover, achieves his greatest success on the battlefield rather than within his own mind. Unlike Marius, he bests Fortune by sheer force rather than restraint. And unlike Scilla, he chooses never to forsake worldly dominion. Until the very end Tamburlaine's quest for hegemony continues unabated, fired by his enormous ambition.

So buoyant is Marlowe's play — at least *Part 1* — that it seems inaccurate to call it a tragedy; some scholars prefer the term "epic biography" or "conqueror play." Nevertheless, the reader is invited to see *Tamburlaine* within a tragic framework. The title page of the 1590 edition calls *Tamburlaine, Parts 1* and *2* "Tragical Discourses," and the printer in his address to the reader uses the same expression. The prologue too speaks of tragedy: "View but his picture in this tragic glass, / And then applaud his fortunes as you please."[8] Near the end of *Part 1* the protagonist himself adopts the image of the "glass"; he says of his victims, "such are objects fit for Tamburlaine, / Wherein, as in a mirror, may be seen / His honor . . ." (V.i.475-77). The use of the words "glass" and "mirror" in a drama about gaining and losing power can scarcely have been accidental at a time when the *Mirror for Magistrates* was giving rise to a vast progeny. Marlowe surely means his audience to recall the assumptions and attitudes of *de casibus* tragedy.[9]

Near the beginning of the play, Mycetes evokes the experience of the *de casibus* world when he bids Theridimas, "Return with speed, time passeth swift away, / Our life is frail, and we may die today" (I.i.67-68). Likewise, Meander resembles those speakers in the *Mirror* who once enjoyed supreme confidence. He tells the soldiers of Mycetes, "Strike up the drum and march courageously. / Fortune herself doth sit upon our crests" (II.ii.72-73). Mycetes, of course, is the first monarch to be overthrown. He will be followed by Cosroe, Agydas, Bajazeth, the Soldan of Egypt, and the King of Arabia. By their fates (and by their sententious reflections) these figures, collectively, recall the seemingly endless procession of the fallen in *de casibus* tragedy. Harry Levin remarks, "To watch this parade is to see the *Mirror for Magistrates* come to life, to hear the sad stories of their deaths acted out. . . ."[10]

Tamburlaine himself experiences unprecedented success, something that baffles his enemies. Meander, for example, is led to conjecture that Tamburlaine "was never sprung of human race" (II.vi.11). Such puzzlement is understandable, for as Una Ellis-Fermor observes, Tamburlaine "is built in proud defiance of all that the accumulated wisdom of the ages has declared to be the lot of man."[11] While his victims may belong to the *de casibus* world, Tamburlaine himself does not; he repudiates it. Clearly, Marlowe portrays the protagonist against a *de casibus* background in order to demonstrate Tamburlaine's uniqueness: only this man defies the hitherto universal laws of change and decay. To the extent that the "tragic glass" of the play reflects Tamburlaine, then, it represents a negation of the tragic spirit. In him the audience witnesses triumph instead of defeat, aspiration instead of limitation.

In keeping with the exaltation of the protagonist, Fortune's power is circumscribed.[12] At no point does she possess the authority that she wields in most other Elizabethan plays or poems. Tamburlaine is decribed as "His fortune's master" (II.i.36). Fortune neither deceives him, nor blights his progress, nor even intimidates him. She is not to be feared because her hegemony is limited. As Tamburlaine explains to Theridimas,

> I hold the Fates bound fast in iron chains,
> And with my hand turn Fortune's wheel about,
> And sooner shall the sun fall from his sphere
> Than Tamburlaine be slain or overcome. (I.ii.174-77)[13]

If this bold assertion about controlling Fortune's wheel appeared in an earlier drama, we would naturally interpret it as the speaker's delusion, a sure prelude to downfall. In *Tamburlaine* it represents no foolish boast, merely a realistic claim apparently borne out by events. The Fortune of Marlowe's play actually seems subject to Tamburlaine.[14]

To demonstrate Tamburlaine's unparalleled stature, Marlowe employs a vivid theatrical stratagem: Tamburlaine in *Part 2* enters the stage in a chariot drawn by kings (V.iii.41).[15] Possibly this entry was inspired by Roman custom — the return of a victorious general — or by various iconographic traditions; Petrarch's *Triumphs*, for instance, was widely known. It seems more likely, however, that Marlowe was inspired by precedent on the Elizabethan stage, precedent involving Fortune. If Lodge's play preceded *Tamburlaine*, then *The Wounds of Civil War* could have inspired Marlowe's stagecraft. If Lodge's play followed *Tamburlaine*, then Marlowe could have found his inspiration in *Jocasta* or *Liberality and Prodigality*. In any case, Marlowe's use of the chariot may signal that Fortune has been displaced by Tamburlaine, by what the Italian humanists call *virtù*. T. W. Craik suggests, "the whole significance of Tamburlaine's chariot, as I see it, is that he is usurping Fortune's attributes."[16]

Tamburlaine's vanquished enemies find comfort only in the expectation that their antagonist too will succumb to Fortune. The mighty Bajazeth, for instance, firmly believes that Tamburlaine will be the next to fall:

> Great Tamburlaine, great in my overthrow,
> Ambitious pride shall make thee fall as low,
> For treading on the back of Bajazeth
> That should be horsed on four mighty kings. (IV.ii.75-78)

If Bajazeth, why not Tamburlaine? Even Zenocrate is convinced that Tamburlaine cannot sustain his string of successes, that disaster must inevitably overtake him as it has his victims. She sees in the fate of Bajazeth and Zabina a prelude to the fall of her beloved: "Those that are proud of fickle empery / And place their chiefest good in earthly pomp, / Behold the Turk and his great emperess!" (V.i.352-54). Believing that Tamburlaine will surely suffer for his heedlessness and impiety, she addresses "mighty Jove and holy Mahomet," beseeching them to forgive his temerity: "O, pardon his contempt / Of earthly fortune and respect of pity" (364-65). But her fear proves unjustified. And at this point her maid, Anippe, offers reassurance:

> Madam, content yourself, and be resolv'd
> Your love hath Fortune so at his command
> That she shall stay and turn her wheel no more
> As long as life maintains his mighty arm
> That fights for honor to adorn your head. (V.i.372-76)

Anippe's confidence, rather than her mistress' apprehension, epitomizes the judgment of the play. Zenocrate's reflection on mutability, it would seem, has been introduced only to underscore the novelty of Tamburlaine's achievement. He alone escapes the constraints of the sublunary world. He alone holds Fortune "at his command."

Even in *Part 2*, where Tamburlaine dies, his dominance over Fortune is never directly challenged. When afflicted by an unexplained, fatal illness, Tamburlaine holds the heavenly gods, not Fortune, responsible: "What daring god torments my body thus / And seeks to conquer mighty Tamburlaine?" (V.iii.42-43). And he bids his followers, "Come, let us march against the powers of heaven / And set black streamers in the firmament / To signify the slaughter of the gods" (48-50). His illness, coming so soon after he ridicules Mahomet, suggests divine retribution. But Marlowe leaves the matter of causation enigmatic, for the characters seem not to agree on the responsibility for Tamburlaine's demise. Theridimas charges the infernal powers and Death: "Hell and Darkness pitch their pitchy tents, / And Death, with armies of Cimmerian spirits, / Gives battle 'gainst the heart of Tamburlaine" (V.iii.7-9). Techelles, while speaking vaguely of "powers that sway eternal seats," identifies Tamburlaine's final opponent as Death: "Then let some god oppose his holy power / Against the wrath and tyranny of Death" (V.iii.220-21). Since neither Tamburlaine nor his lieutenants single out Fortune for blame, it seems that Marlowe does not wish us to construe the ailing conqueror as yet another victim of Fortune's spite.

III

Edward II (c. 1591), so different in structure and tone from *Tamburlaine*, contains a figure very much like the Scythian warrior. Mortimer seems immune from the usual pitfalls of the *de casibus* world. Like Tamburlaine, he combines strength and shrewdness. Like Tamburlaine, moreover, he boasts the capacity to meet every challenge. When he takes up arms against the king, it seems that he will depose Edward as easily as Tamburlaine usurped Cosroe's throne. Through his confident bearing, he promises another successful defiance of Fortune.

Even when captured by the royal forces, Mortimer remains undaunted:

> What, Mortimer, can raggèd stony walls
> Immure thy virtue that aspires to heaven?
> No, Edward, England's scourge, it may not be;
> Mortimer's hope surmounts his fortune far. (III.iii.72-75)[17]

It does not surprise us that he should escape from prison and rally his comrades to break the king's power. Nor is it out of character for Mortimer to utter a Tamburlaine-like boast, claiming that he "now makes Fortune's wheel turn as he please" (V.ii.53). In context this seems not arrogance but prediction. The English baron, with his assertion about controlling Fortune's wheel, appears a true counterpart of the victorious Scythian.

That Marlowe was fascinated by the qualities inherent in Mortimer cannot be doubted: the character is almost entirely the playwright's invention. His chief source, Holinshed's *Chronicle* (1587 ed.) has relatively little to say of Mortimer. And although Marlowe follows the chronicler closely, even sometimes using "the actual words of the chronicle,"[18] he is not content to let Mortimer remain a shadowy figure. He invests Mortimer with great importance, elevating him to a position of prominence equal to the king's. The title of the play, *The Troublesome Reign and Lamentable Death of Edward the Second King of England with the Tragical Fall of Proud Mortimer*, underscores Mortimer's stature.

Although Marlowe is drawn to the creation of a Tamburlaine-like figure, his intention in *Edward II* is not to extoll the character but to dramatize his vulnerability to those forces which Tamburlaine successfully flaunts. Among them is Fortune, whom Mortimer claims to be subject to his will. Near the end of the play he says:

> Now is all sure; the queen and Mortimer
> Shall rule the realm, the king, and none rule us.
> Mine enemies will I plague, my friends advance,
> And what I list command who dare control?
> *Major sum quam cui possit fortuna nocere.* (V.iv.65-69)

The Latin comes from Ovid's *Metamorphoses*: "I am too great for Fortune to harm" (VI.195). The words, spoken in Ovid by Niobe just before the death of her children, here in Marlowe's tragedy signal to the alert reader or playgoer that Mortimer will not enjoy Tamburlaine's success, that the course of his career will, rather, coincide with that of Fortune's wheel.

Since Marlowe is interested in demonstrating Mortimer's vulnerability to circumstance, it is appropriate that he should have consulted the *Mirror for Magistrates* when writing the play; in its 1559 edition the *Mirror* relates the story of Sir Roger Mortimer.[19] And in its account the *Mirror*, unlike Holinshed, makes considerable reference to Fortune. Mortimer is described as one "Whom Fortune brought to boote and efte to bale" (9), one "In whom dame Fortune fully shewed her kynde, / For whom she heaves, she hurleth downe as fast" (45-46).[20] The poem also tells the story of a kinsman, similarly named Roger Mortimer, and again Fortune plays a role in the narrative. The speaker records Fortune's initial friendliness: "Fortune lulde me in her lap, / And gave me gyftes mo than I dyd requyre" (99-100). Eventually, his delusion becomes apparent, and he concludes, "Se here the staye of fortunate estate, / The vayne assurance of this britell lyfe" (141-42).

Marlowe's Mortimer is markedly different from Mortimer in the *Mirror*, for the character in the play exudes greater forcefulness and bravado. Yet the poem, with its iteration of Fortune's power and its depiction of Mortimer's susceptibility, undoubtedly helped to shape Marlowe's conception.[21] Much the same limitations of time and circumstance described in the *Mirror* also prevail in the play. The Mortimer of both poem and play disdains obstacles, reaches for power, attains temporary success — and then is destroyed.

Marlowe's treatment of the character is especially interesting because his invention takes a seemingly contradictory form. On the one hand, Marlowe departs from Holinshed to create in Mortimer a figure of extraordinary daring and power; Mortimer's temperamental kinship with Tamburlaine is readily apparent. On the other hand, Marlowe also departs from Holinshed by greatly increasing the role of Fortune; onto the chronicler's story Marlowe grafts a *de casibus* meditation about implacable Fortune. Having created a Tamburlaine-like character, Marlowe subjects him to the limitations of the *de casibus* world.

Subtly altering virtually everything he draws upon, Marlowe in this play recasts the *de casibus* mode itself. Most notably, he allows no room whatsoever for the role of divine providence. To be sure, there are those in *Edward II* who speak of God. Mortimer himself at one point says:

> Lords, sith that we are by sufferance of heaven
> Arrived and armèd in this prince's right,
> Here for our country's cause swear we to him
> All homage, fealty, and forwardness. (IV.iv.17-20)

This seems, however, a statement calculated for public consumption; by the time Mortimer utters these words, his personal ambition has become abundantly clear. Similarly, Isabella's references to the Deity (IV.v.28-31) appear insincere. Her words can scarcely be accepted at face value; her actions belie them. F. P. Wilson writes: "In public she is full of concern for the state of the country and the King's misfortunes, of thanks to 'the God of kings' and 'heaven's great architect'; in private, there is no villainy of Mortimer's which she does not aid and abet."[22] Even Edward manifests no real concern for the heavens. He neither ascribes his adversity nor credits his success to divinity. Significant-

ly, the issue of the divine right of kings, so important to Shakespeare's
Richard II, never finds expression in Marlowe's tragedy.

Man's destiny, the play suggests, is the product of two forces: his own
will and Fortune's might. In the words of Wilbur Sanders, "Marlowe
appears to have assimilated the naturalistic trend of Renaissance histo-
riography so thoroughly as to exclude altogether the providential tradition."[23] By purging the play of providence, Marlowe in effect heightens
the significance of Fortune. Indeed, Fortune is the only hostile force
whose hand Mortimer perceives in his fall. His last speech begins:

> Base Fortune, now I see that in thy wheel
> There is a point, to which when men aspire,
> They tumble headlong down. That point I touched,
> And, seeing there was no place to mount up higher,
> Why should I grieve at my declining fall? (V.vi.59-63)

Some critics insist that the speech indicates a new appreciation of justice
on the part of Mortimer — and Marlowe: "he has learned that men are
mortal and cannot successfully defy either God or God's agent [i.e.,
Fortune]."[24] Nowhere in the play, however, does any character suggest
that Fortune is an executrix of providence. Nowhere in the play is
Fortune said to perform a retributive function. And, as we have
just seen, nowhere in the play is there even a convincing assertion of
providential design. What Mortimer has "learned," then, is simply acquiescence: he has achieved everything possible in the particular circumstances dictated by Fortune. Now he must accept the inevitable.

Marlowe, to be sure, is not without concern for the workings of retributive justice. He means us to see that Mortimer overreaches himself
and that Edward's foolishness and weakness contribute to his own
downfall. Following Holinshed, Marlowe explores what Eugene M.
Waith calls the "practical and political."[25] Nevertheless, even in his treatment of the king, Marlowe is as interested in delineating the sheer spectacle of defeat and in wringing from it every possible theatrical effect as
he is in chronicling the human failures which have contributed to that
miserable end. The *de casibus* mood is pervasive. Edward may have no
great speeches on Fortune, but the cadence of metrical tragedy is heard
in his lines:

Stately and proud, in riches and in train,
Whilom I was powerful and full of pomp;
But what is he whom rule and empery
Have not in life or death made miserable? (IV.vi.12-15)

The words, which seem to echo Zenocrate's, have their origin, ultimately, in *de casibus* literature; Edward's speech is scarcely distinguishable from complaints in the *Mirror*. We find the same contrast between prosperity and adversity, the same rueful recognition that power is evanescent, that misery is the inevitable lot of the living.

In his portrait of the king, moreover, Marlowe emulates the practice of William Baldwin and the other authors of the *Mirror*, embellishing the *de casibus* theme with Senecan coloring. Thus when Leicester seizes the king, he comments,

Alas, see where he sits, and hopes unseen
T'escape their hands that seek to reave his life.
Too true it is, *Quem dies vidit veniens superbum*,
Hunc dies vidit fugiens jacentem. (IV.vi.51-54)

The Latin is from Seneca's *Thyestes* (lines 613-14), translated by Ben Jonson in *Sejanus* as "For whom the morning saw so great and high, / Thus low and little, 'fore the 'even doth lie" (V.902-3). In *Edward II*, as in the *Mirror*, the Senecan and the *de casibus* merge. In the words of Harry Levin, "Classical or medieval, the peripety is the same, the overturn from grandeur to misery."[26]

Why Marlowe should have turned from such an exuberant play as *Tamburlaine* to one so grim as *Edward II*, only a few years later, is a matter for conjecture. Perhaps he sought a new challenge: having treated conspicuous success, he may have wanted to examine those forces that frustrate human achievement, to dramatize the psychological toll they take. Or perhaps he had come to doubt man's capacity to bend the world to his will. Whatever his motive, the adoption of Fortune as the paramount external force in the lives of the characters enables Marlowe to achieve powerful theatrical effects. As the authors of the *Mirror for Magistrates* had demonstrated, Fortune's antipathy toward the mighty readily engages the emotions of the reader or listener. And on stage,

Marlowe recognized, defeat can be as affecting as victory. Ironically, then, the dramatist renowned for his iconoclasm and skepticism perpetuates in what may be his finest play the legacy of medieval tragedy.

IV

The Spanish Tragedy (c. 1587) differs from *The Wounds of Civil War*, *Tamburlaine*, and *Edward II* in that it is not essentially a story of ambition. "Where *Tamburlaine* and other plays following more or less closely the usual *De Casibus* tradition tend to give the effect of biography," Willard Farnham writes, *The Spanish Tragedy* "and its kind tend to give the effect of the crowded romantic novel."[27] Thomas Kyd's play is in fact one of elaborate intrigue which, as T. S. Eliot remarked, resembles a "detective drama."[28] This departure from the theatrical fare of the 1580s immediately created a new vogue. For almost the next half century, this most influential of Elizabethan tragedies would, directly or indirectly, inspire other plays of intrigue, especially stories of revenge.

Since the focus of interest is the convoluted story rather than the gain or loss of power and position, it may seem that Fortune would play a comparatively small role in *The Spanish Tragedy*. And in fact Fortune figures most obviously not in the main plot but in the subplot, where the allusions to Fortune may appear as gratuitous as the action itself. Moody E. Prior argues: "the reflections on Fortune in the irrelevant Portuguese episodes presumably acknowledge the expectation of sententious or eloquent expression of certain conventional themes, though the idea of fickle Fortune has no essential bearing on anything involved in the main action."[29] In this contention Prior underestimates the importance of both Fortune and the subplot. The speeches on Fortune in those Portuguese scenes create a mood which prepares the audience for the ensuing dramatic action. And that action, involving the intriguer Villuppo and his machinations against an innocent man, parallels that of the main plot.

In the first Portuguese scene, the Viceroy, contemplating his military loss to Spain, speaks three lines in Latin, then goes on to apply them to his present situation:

Qui jacet in terra non habet unde cadat.
In me consumpsit vires fortuna nocendo,
　Nil superest ut jam possit obesse magis.
Yes, Fortune may bereave me of my crown:
Here take it now: let Fortune do her worst,
She will not rob me of this sable weed:
O no, she envies none but pleasant things:
Such is the folly of despiteful chance!
Fortune is blind and sees not my deserts,
So is she deaf and hears not my laments:
And could she hear, yet is she wilful mad,
And therefore will not pity my distress. (I.iii.15-26)[30]

The characterization of Fortune as indifferent to man is familiar. And the sources, classical and medieval, which Kyd draws upon are well known: the first Latin line is from the *Liber Parabolarum* of Alanus de Insulis; the second is from Seneca's *Agamemnon* (line 698); the third may be of Kyd's own composition.[31] The verbal picture of Fortune is similarly commonplace:

Suppose that she could pity me, what then?
What help can be expected at her hands,
Whose foot is standing on a rolling stone
And mind more mutable than fickle winds? (27-30)

When we listen to these lines, we may well feel that we have heard such speeches before. Kyd, drawing from diverse sources, creates a speech in the *de casibus* mold. Indeed, it might almost have been lifted out of the *Mirror for Magistrates*. The resemblance may help to explain why the speech on Fortune initially seems so irrelevant: it constitutes a meditative and essentially non-dramatic element in the midst of a swiftly-moving drama. With its curiously static quality, the speech seems at odds with the larger story of intrigue and retribution.

Much the same may be said of the second Portuguese scene and its treatment of Fortune. In this instance the speech on Fortune is adapted from Seneca's *Agamemnon* (lines 57-73):

Infortunate condition of kings,
Seated amidst so many helpless doubts!
First we are plac'd upon extremest height,
And oft supplanted with exceeding heat,
But ever subject to the wheel of chance:
And at our highest never joy we so,
As we both doubt and dread our overthrow.
So striveth not the waves with sundry winds
As fortune toileth in the affairs of kings,
That would be fear'd, yet fear to be belov'd,
Sith fear or love to kings is flattery. (III.i.1-11)

Although the lines have their source in a drama, they do not really advance the dramatic action here. The discussion of the burdens of kingship, the vulnerability to chance, the peril of high place — all this looks back to the Viceroy's speech in Act I. And, like that earlier speech, this one seems to stand apart from the surrounding material. No wonder some readers find the disquisitions on Fortune extraneous.

Actually, though, the speeches on Fortune are entirely appropriate, given the Viceroy's situation: he has suffered defeat at the hands of his enemies and he has (as he supposes) lost his son. In addition, the speeches have relevance for the chief business of the subplot: the intrigue of Villuppo against the virtuous Alexandro. Although neither of these characters talks about Fortune, the speeches of the Viceroy help to establish the atmosphere of a world in which Villuppo's intrigue can so easily succeed — where caprice and deceit flourish, where a thorough-going villain can victimize the innocent, where injustice seems to prevail. If there is a presiding deity in the subplot, the Viceroy would seem to have identified it in his speeches on Fortune.

The subplot, moreover, with its intrigue and its treatment of Fortune, is directly related to the main plot, to which it bears a marked similarity. In both, a villain perpetrates an attack: in the subplot the attack is verbal; in the main plot, physical. Both plots dramatize the sudden discovery of the villainy: one, by the timely arrival of an ambassador; the other, by the timely arrival of a letter. Both culminate in assurances that the malefactors will be punished and the virtuous rewarded: in one, by the head of state; in the other, by supernatural power. In addition, there is a further similarity involving the character of the intriguer: in both plots he takes a gamble (actually a series of gambles in the main plot). In this he resembles the Vice of the moral interludes, for he aligns himself with the contingency embodied in Fortune.

Villuppo's resemblance to the Vice is apparent in the first Portuguese scene. There he concocts a story intended to discredit and doom Alexandro. The miscreant claims that during the battle he witnessed Alexandro shoot the Viceroy's son in the back. Like the Vice of old, Villuppo is a superbly convincing dissembler. And, like the Vice, he confides his villainy to the audience:

> Thus have I with an envious forged tale
> Deceiv'd the king, betray'd mine enemy,
> And hope for guerdon of my villainy. (I.iii.93-95)

In the second Portuguese scene, Villuppo is poised to reap the reward of his perfidy. The Viceroy, convinced of the charges, would execute Alexandro without delay: "Why linger ye? Bring forth that daring fiend / And let him die for his accursed deed" (III.i.38-39). The words "fiend" and "accursed" accurately apply not to Alexandro, of course, but to his accuser. Villuppo's mask of probity, like the Vice's, is difficult to penetrate; only the entry of the Ambassador, with news that the Viceroy's son lives, saves the intended victim. Confronted with his treachery, Villuppo confesses his reckless chance-taking: "for reward, and hope to be preferr'd, / Thus have I shamelessly hazarded his life" (95-96).

Lorenzo is Villuppo writ large. His similarity to the Vice, particularly his facility for constructing a false show of innocence, has long been recognized. Douglas Cole writes that "Like the Vice of the morality play, Lorenzo reveals himself as villain to the audience. . . ."[32] Bernard Spivack observes that Lorenzo has another characteristic of the type: his "motivation seems slight."[33] Other similarities to the Vice may be noted. For example, this speech of Lorenzo's, with its metaphor of bird-catching, seems to echo the speeches of particular Vices:

> I lay the plot, he prosecutes the point,
> I set the trap, he breaks the worthless twigs
> And sees not that wherewith the bird was lim'd.
> (III.iv.40-42)

In *Nice Wanton* (printed in 1560), Worldly Shame exults: "I have caught two birds; I will set for the dame."[34] And in *The Conflict of Conscience* (printed in 1581), Hypocrisy says, "We have now caught him as bird is in lime."[35]

Even Lorenzo's physical appearance may have evoked that of the Vice to a contemporary audience. Consider the title page of the 1615 edition, which depicts the scene of Horatio's murder.[36] On the left side of the woodcut, the dead Horatio hangs in the arbor. In the middle stands Hieronimo with sword and torch, crying, "Alas, it is my son Horatio." And on the right is Bel-imperia, saying, "Murder, help Hieronimo." Grabbing her arm is a man who says, "Stop her mouth" — words uttered by Lorenzo (II.iv.63). What makes this figure especially noteworthy is his black face: either he is wearing some sort of dark makeup or he is wearing a mask. If the woodcut accurately represents the appearance of the actors on stage, then the actor playing Lorenzo must have had a black face in the murder scene. Such an appearance would probably recall to an audience the Vice of the interludes, who sometimes blackened his face.[37]

Lorenzo's mode of action also evokes that of the Vice. He numbers among his dramatic ancestors Colhazard in *Impatient Poverty*, Haphazard in *Apius and Virginia*, and Courage in *The Tide Tarrieth No Man*, for he uses contingency as a weapon against others. In murdering Horatio, Lorenzo takes a great risk; and the possibility that his identity will be revealed haunts him. To ensure that his villainy remains secret, he concocts a plan to do away with those who might implicate him. He begins by enlisting Pedringano to shoot Serberine. Lorenzo will then allow Pedringano to be apprehended and, later, executed. No witnesses to the murder of Horatio will remain, except of course for Balthazar, Bel-imperia, and Lorenzo himself.

Throughout the perpetration of this scheme, a powerful sense of contingency pervades Lorenzo's speech: "Thus must we work that will avoid distrust, / Thus must we practise to prevent mishap" (III.ii.105-6). Having arranged for Serberine to be at a park where he will find Pedringano, Lorenzo realizes that his machinations have reached a precarious stage. And he reflects upon his effort to transfer his vulnerability to subordinates:

> They that for coin their souls endangered,
> To save my life, for coin shall venture theirs:
> And better it's that base companions die,
> Than by their life to hazard our good haps. (III.ii.113-16)

Chance seem uppermost in his mind: he fears "mishaps," will "venture" the lives of others, and hastens to "hazards our good haps." His words recall those of Haphazard to Apius:

> There is no more wayes, but hap or hap not,
> Either hap, or els haplesse, to knit up the knot:
> And if you will hazard, to venter what falles,
> Perhaps, that *Haphazard*, will end al your thralles.[38]

Like Haphazard and other Vices, Lorenzo has an unusual sensitivity to chance and a willingness to profit from its operation.

He never loses, however, a sense of apprehension. When Balthazar (after the shooting of Serberine) asks why he cannot sleep, Lorenzo replies: "Fear of preventing our mishaps too late" (III.iv.2); a moment later he adds that "inexpected harms do hurt us most" (5). And when he gives the Page the box ostensibly containing the promised pardon for Pedringano, Lorenzo is at his most uneasy: "Now stands our fortune on a tickle point, / And now or never ends Lorenzo's doubts" (78-79). Hazard is a way of life for Lorenzo, chance his unseen partner in crime. Fortune is not only a part of his vocabulary, but an almost palpable force with which he allies himself.[39]

If Lorenzo's words recall those of the Vice in the interludes, so too does his action on stage. When in III.xii he stands head to head with Hieronimo, the Knight Marshal, their struggle recalls those of the moral interludes, where the guardians of justice confront and vanquish those who entice others to submit themselves to contingency.[40] In *Apius and Virginia*, for example, Justice and Reward seize the villainous Haphazard and sentence him to be hanged. In *The Tide Tarrieth No Man*, Authority and Correction physically restrain Courage and carry him off to punishment. In Kyd's drama it is the Knight Marshal, chief judicial officer of the kingdom, who foils the Vice-like Lorenzo.

Their struggle reaches a culmination of sorts in III.xii, where Hieronimo seeks to bring his grievance before the king, and Lorenzo seeks to frustrate him at every turn. Hieronimo, a man whose office and temperament identify him with justice, cries out, "Justice, O justice to Hieronimo!" (27). Lorenzo physically and verbally interposes himself: "Back! seest thou not the king is busy?" (28). Moments later Hieronimo renews his plea: "Justice, O justice, justice, gentle king!" (63). Once again, Lorenzo blocks the attempt: "Hieronimo, you are not well-advis'd" (67). The man who cries justice is defeated directly by Lorenzo and indirectly by his own incipient madness.

In a conflict far more agonizing than those of the interludes, Hieronimo goes on ultimately to requite the malefactor, but not before the most extraordinary effort. During the play the Knight Marshal is forced to adopt a variety of strategies, depending upon his knowledge and state of mind. First, he is wary, uncertain of Lorenzo's guilt. When that is finally ascertained, Hieronimo essays a direct appeal to the king. Unsuccessful and reeling from the psychic strain of grief and frustration, he moves to guile, eventually dispatching Lorenzo at the banquet. While he struggles, the Knight Marshal gives no speeches akin to the Viceroy's on Fortune, but he is no less obsessed with injustice and disorder.[41] The difference is that while the Viceroy deplores blind and deaf Fortune, Hieronimo appeals to the heavens, which ought to guarantee justice but which, too, seem indifferent. Each of Hieronimo's appeals, expressed in a series of anguished soliloquies, raises by implication the same issues addressed by the Viceroy. Hieronimo may be less ready to surrender his faith in divine justice; perhaps he never does entirely. But when the distance between his ideal of justice and the reality of his situation becomes too great, he behaves as though the gods had abandoned him. He takes justice into his own hands and becomes a killer.

If we view Hieronimo and Lorenzo in admittedly schematic terms— the one, a minister of justice; the other, a manipulator of contingency— then we may interpret the struggle between these two figures not only as the reenactment of a dramatic pattern bequeathed by the moral interludes, but also, in thematic terms, as a contest between Revenge, the symbol of retributive justice in the play, and Fortune, the embodiment of contingency.[42] Unlike Revenge, Fortune never actually appears on stage, but her agents, Lorenzo and Villuppo, do. And her image is vividly evoked in the speeches of the Viceroy. Eventually, Fortune is vanquished. By Hieronimo's final victory, chance may not be entirely banished from the world of the play, but those who seek to take advantage of contingency for personal gain are requited. And there is a parallel with the subplot, for when the villainy of Villuppo is revealed, there are no further speeches on Fortune. Instead, the Viceroy turns to an assertion of retribution for wrongdoing and the reward of the virtuous. In thematic terms, Fortune gives way to justice and revenge.[43]

V

Were such ancient writers as Plutarch and Seneca somehow to witness the performance of Elizabethan plays, they would no doubt be struck by a basic similarity to their own literary work. For in the drama of Lodge, Marlowe, and Kyd the world remains turbulent, unjust, threatening. Even so great a soldier as Scilla can be displaced from his command, and Marius from his. All the powers of kingship cannot prevent Edward II from being tortured and brutally murdered; the manifold skills of Mortimer, likewise, confer no immunity from arrest and execution. And the chief judicial officer of Spain finds it virtually impossible to secure justice when his own son is killed. Even the seemingly invincible Tamburlaine in *Part 2* suffers the disappointment of his wife's death and his son's inadequacy. To his way of thinking, death itself is a reproach.

To a large extent the dramatic world of these Elizabethan plays is shaped by Fortune, whose exploits the ancients chronicle at length. The Fortuna-Virtus topos that underlies Lodge's play would be immediately recognizable to Plutarch, himself the author of essays on Fortuna and Virtus.[44] The Greek historian, moreover, would be compatible with Lodge's confidence in man's ability to contest Fortune's might, for in his moral essays Plutarch generally favors the claims of Virtus over Fortuna. Seneca would naturally be flattered by Marlowe's citation of his own work in *Edward II*, and Seneca would feel an instinctive kinship with a dramatist who could portray the degradation of Edward and the overthrow by Fortune of one so powerful as Mortimer. There is also much for Seneca to admire in *The Spanish Tragedy*. He would doubtless be intrigued to see that Kyd had adapted an entire speech on Fortune from *Agamemnon*, along with other lines from the Latin tragedies. He would see in the Knight Marshal's madness a state similar to that of his own characters overcome by adversity. And the Viceroy's speeches on Fortune, with their melancholy verging on despair, would similarly find a sympathetic response in the Roman tragedian.

To be sure, a momentous difference separates the ancient world from that of Elizabethan England: the dominance of Christianity, with its promise of redemption and its confidence in divine plan. But not one of the four plays treated in this chapter presents a fully Christian milieu. Lodge's play is, of course, set in the first century B.C.; neither Tamburlaine nor his opponents (at least in *Part 1*) belong to Christianity; neither Mortimer nor Edward seems to be a believing Christian; and Kyd's drama, although set in a vaguely Renaissance Spain, features a pagan underworld, complete with ancient gods and Elysian fields. Christian audiences would doubtless bring to the theater certain religious assumptions that would help shape their response to the plays. But could they fail to notice that in *Tamburlaine* the gods are either powerless or intimidated by the protagonist? that in *Edward II* the concept of providence seems merely a tool of political propaganda? that the character with the firmest conviction of divine solicitude in *The Spanish Tragedy* (Isabella) is the first to go mad and ends a suicide?

In the absence of a Christian world view, the Fortune of Lodge, Marlowe, and Kyd can scarcely be construed as simply an extension of Christian providence. Nor can one easily imagine Fortune as an executrix of retributive justice ordained by God. Like their forebears, the Elizabethans sometimes conflate Fortune and Nemesis, but that identification is not obvious in the plays considered here. The characters either steel themselves to Fortune's assault or try to cudgel her into submission or curse her. It is difficult to imagine their adopting these attitudes if Fortune were truly an emblem of justice. In these plays Fortune retains the capricious nature so familiar to the ancients. Despite the inventiveness of Lodge, Marlowe, and Kyd, their plays demonstrate the survival, after a millennium and a half, of an essentially pagan Fortune.

NOTES TO CHAPTER 5

1. M. W. MacCallum, *Shakespeare's Roman Plays and Their Background* (1910; reprint ed., London: Methuen, 1967), p. 63. Similarly, Charles W. Whitworth, in "The Plays of Thomas Lodge," *CahiersE*, 4 (1973): 3-14, writes: "Lodge's inexperience caused him to pass over some opportunities of clear dramatic potential . . ." (8).

2. *The Wounds of Civil War*, ed. Joseph W. Houppert, RRDS (Lincoln: Univ. of Nebraska Press, 1969).

3. *An Auncient Historie and exquisite Chronicle of the Romanes warres, both Civile and Foren*, trans. W. B. [William Barker?] (London, 1578), p. 58. For a useful introduction to this work, see Ernest Schanzer, *Shakespeare's Appian* (Liverpool: Liverpool Univ. Press, 1956). For the original Greek, see *Appian's Roman History*, ed. and trans. Horace White, LCL, 4 vols. (New York and London: Macmillan, 1912-13).

4. *The Lives of the Noble Grecians and Romanes, Compared together by that grave learned Philosopher and Historiographer, Plutarke of Chaeronea*, trans. Thomas North (London, 1579), p. 503. For the original Greek, see *Plutarch's Lives*, ed. and trans. Bernadotte Perrin, LCL, 11 vols. (New York and London: Putnam's, 1914-26). Volume 4 contains the *Life of Sulla*, volume 9 the *Life of Caius Marius*.

5. In *Jocasta* Fortune appears in the dumb show preceding the last act: "First the Stillpipes sounded a very mournful melody, in which time came upon the Stage a woman clothed in a white garment, on hir head a piller, double faced, the formost face fair & smiling, the other behinde blacke & louring, muffled with a white laune about hir eyes, hir lap ful of Jewelles, sitting in a charyot, hir legges naked, hir fete set upon a great round bal, & beyng drawen in by .iiij. noble personages, she led in a string on hir right hand .ij. kings crowned, and in hir lefte hand .ij. poore slaves very meanly attyred." For the remainder of the description see the text of *Jocasta*, in *Early English Classical Tragedies*, ed. John W. Cunliffe (Oxford: Clarendon Press, 1912), p. 139. For the stage direction concerning Fortune in *The Contention between Liberality and Prodigality*, see the edition by W. W. Greg, MSR (Oxford: Oxford Univ. Press, 1913), I.vi.

6. Appian speaks in passing of the youth's death: "[Young] Marius hidde him-

selfe in a Cave, and shortly after killed hymselfe" (p. 56). Plutarch offers little more detail: "In the end he was shut in, and besieged by *Sylla* in the city of Perusia, where he did what he could possible to save his life, but all was in vaine: & lastly, seeing no way to escape, the city being taken, he slew him selfe with his owne handes" (p. 479). By contrast, Lodge dwells on the suicide and chooses to portray it as a victory over Fortune. Addressing the goddess, Young Marius says:

> Thy colored wings steeped in purple blood,
> Thy blinding wreath distain'd in purple blood,
> Thy royal robes wash'd in my purple blood,
> Shall witness to the world thy thirst of blood.
> And when the tyrant Scilla shall expect
> To see the son of Marius stoop for fear,
> Then, then, O then my mind shall well appear,
> That scorn my life and hold mine honor dear. (V.ii.21-28)

7. Most scholars assume that *Tamburlaine* preceded the composition of Lodge's play, which was not printed until 1594. See Willard Farnham, *The Medieval Heritage of Elizabethan Tragedy* (1936; reprint ed. with corrections, Oxford: Basil Blackwell, 1970), pp. 376-79; William A. Armstrong, "'Tamburlaine' and 'The Wounds of Civil War,'" *N&Q*, 203 (1958): 381-83; Wolfgang Clemen, *English Tragedy before Shakespeare: The Development of Dramatic Speech*, trans. T. S. Dorsch (London: Methuen, 1961), pp. 134-40; Joel B. Altman, *The Tudor Play of Mind: Rhetorical Inquiry and the Development of Elizabethan Drama* (Berkeley and Los Angeles: Univ. of California Press, 1978), pp. 283-88. However, N. Burton Paradise, in *Thomas Lodge: The History of an Elizabethan* (1931; reprint ed., Hamden, Conn.: Archon Books, 1970), argues that "Lodge, in this play at least, owed nothing to Marlowe" (p. 130). Paradise's arguments that Lodge's tragedy precedes *Tamburlaine* have been accepted by Wesley D. Rae, *Thomas Lodge* (New York: Twayne, 1967), pp. 39-42; and Charles W. Whitworth, "'The Wounds of Civil War' and 'Tamburlaine': Lodge's Alleged Imitation," *N&Q*, NS 22 (1975): 245-47. I too find Paradise's reasoning convincing. I feel that if Lodge had written the play to capitalize on the success of Marlowe's, he would have emulated such works as *Alphonsus, King of Aragon* and *Selimus, The Battle of Alcazar* and *Locrine*, plays that celebrate martial prowess. Lodge, by contrast, has written a drama that celebrates victory within man's psyche.

8. *Tamburlaine the Great, Parts I and II*, ed. John D. Jump, RRDS (Lincoln: Univ. of Nebraska Press, 1967).

9. Marlowe's sources, containing *de casibus* elements, undoubtedly encouraged his treatment. In *The English Myrror* (London, 1586), for example, George Whetstone writes: "... a notable example of the incertaintye of worldly fortunes: *Bajazet*, that in the morning was the mightiest Emperor on the earth, at night, and the residue of his life, was driven to feede among the dogs, and which might most grieve him, he was thus abased, by one that in the beginning was but a poore sheepheard" (p. 81). Marlowe's handling of his sources is discussed by W. L. Godshalk, *The Marlovian World Picture* (The Hague: Mouton, 1974), pp. 102-17 and 137-50.

10. *The Overreacher: A Study of Christopher Marlowe* (Cambridge, Mass.: Harvard Univ. Press, 1952), p. 34. See also Robert Kimbrough, "*1 Tamburlaine*: A Speaking Picture in a Tragic Glass," *RenD*, 7 (1964): 20-34.

11. *Christopher Marlowe* (1927; reprint ed., Hamden, Conn.: Archon Books, 1967), p. 24.

12. Relevant discussions of Fortune include those by Roy W. Battenhouse, *Marlowe's Tamburlaine: A Study in Renaissance Moral Philosophy* (Nashville: Vanderbilt Univ. Press, 1941), pp. 86-98; and Irving Ribner, "The Idea of History in Marlowe's *Tamburlaine*," *ELH*, 20 (1953): 251-66.

13. M. C. Bradbrook, in *Themes and Conventions of Elizabethan Tragedy* (Cambridge: Cambridge Univ. Press, 1935), collects a number of passages in other Elizabethan plays which resemble Tamburlaine's lines (pp. 95-96).

14. Tamburlaine's supremacy over Fortune makes it unlikely, in my judgment, that he is to be construed as one of the *fortunati*, as Don Cameron Allen has suggested in "Renaissance Remedies for Fortune: Marlowe and the *Fortunati*," *SP*, 38 (1941): 188-97. Unlike the *fortunati*, Tamburlaine is the sort of man envisioned by Machiavelli in *The Prince*: he would cudgel Fortune into submission.

15. Marlowe's use of such "dramatic emblems" as the chariot is the subject of Jocelyn Powell's "Marlowe's Spectacle," *TDR*, 8 (1964): 195-210. See also Alice S. Venezky, *Pageantry on the Shakespearean Stage* (New York: Twayne, 1951), pp. 196-97; Samuel C. Chew, "The Allegorical Chariot in English Literature of the Renaissance," in *De Artibus Opuscula XL: Essays in Honor of Erwin Panofsky*, ed. Millard Meiss (New York: New York Univ. Press, 1961), 1: 37-54; Robert Cockcroft, "Emblematic Irony: Some Possible Significances of Tamburlaine's Chariot," *RMS*, 12 (1968): 33-55.

16. *The Tudor Interlude: Stage, Costume, and Acting* (Leicester: Leicester Univ. Press, 1958), p. 96.

17. *Edward II*, in *The Complete Plays of Christopher Marlowe*, ed., Irving Ribner (New York: Odyssey Press, 1963).

18. H. B. Charlton and R. D. Waller, ed., *Edward II* (1933; reprint ed., New York: Gordian Press, 1966), p. 52.

19. Alwin Thaler, in "Churchyard and Marlowe," *MLN*, 38 (1923): 89-92, first suggested that Marlowe in *Edward II* was indebted to the poem in the *Mirror* about the two Mortimers.

20. *The Mirror for Magistrates*, ed., Lily B. Campbell (1938; reprint ed., New York: Barnes and Noble, 1960).

21. Marlowe's treatment of Fortune in *Edward II* may also have been influenced by Lucan's *Pharsalia*, the first book of which Marlowe translated. See D. J. Palmer, "Marlowe's Naturalism," in *Christopher Marlowe*, ed. Brian Morris, Mermaid Critical Commentaries (New York: Hill and Wang, 1969), pp. 161-62.

22. *Marlowe and the Early Shakespeare* (Oxford: Clarendon Press, 1953), p. 98.

23. *The Dramatist and the Received Idea: Studies in the Plays of Marlowe and Shakespeare* (Cambridge: Cambridge Univ. Press, 1968), p. 121. Sanders' discussion of Marlowe is indebted to that of Irving Ribner, in *The English History Play in the Age of Shakespeare*, rev. ed. (New York: Barnes and Noble, 1965), pp. 123-33.

24. Harry Morris, "Marlowe's Poetry," *TDR*, 8 (1964): 148.

25. "*Edward II*: The Shadow of Action," *TDR*, 8 (1964): 61.

26. *The Overreacher*, p. 102.

27. *The Medieval Heritage of Elizabethan Tragedy*, p. 392.

28. Introduction to *Seneca His Tenne Tragedies Translated into English*, ed. Thomas Newton (1927; reprint ed., Bloomington and London: Indiana Univ. Press, [1966]), p. xxv.

29. *The Language of Tragedy* (1947; reprint ed., Bloomington and London: Indiana Univ. Press, 1966), p. 49.

30. *The Spanish Tragedy*, ed. Philip Edwards, The Revels Plays (London: Methuen, 1959). Edwards translates the Latin of the Viceroy: "If one lies on the ground, one can fall no further; in me, Fortune has exhausted her power of hurting; there is nothing left that can harm me more" (p. 17).

31. The sources have been identified by Wilfred P. Mustard, "Notes on Thomas Kyd's Works," *PQ*, 5 (1926): 85.

32. *Suffering and Evil in the Plays of Christopher Marlowe* (1962; reprint ed., New York: Gordian Press, 1972), p. 137.

33. *Shakespeare and the Allegory of Evil: The History of a Metaphor in Relation to His Major Villains* (New York and London: Columbia Univ. Press, 1958), p. 360. Spivack, however, goes on to say that Lorenzo "is not radically complicated by the traits of the convention we are tracing"; he thus declines to discuss the character in any detail.

34. *Nice Wanton*, in *English Moral Interludes*, ed. Glynne Wickham (London and Totowa, N.J.: Rowman and Littlefield, 1976), l. 434.

35. *The Conflict of Conscience*, in *English Morality Plays and Moral Interludes*, ed. Edgar T. Schell and J. D. Shuchter (New York: Holt, Rinehart and Winston, 1969), l. 1420. Fortune, who shares with the Vice the ability to deceive, is sometimes described in much the same terms. Petrarch begins one of his lyric poems: "The more desirously I spread my wings toward you, O sweet flock of friends, the more does Fortune with birdlime entangle my flight and make me go astray" (*Petrarch's Lyric Poems: The Rime sparse and Other Lyrics*, ed. and trans. Robert M. Durling [London and Cambridge, Mass.: Harvard Univ. Press, 1976], poem 139, p. 282.) And John Lydgate, in his *Troy Book*, ed. Henry Bergen, EETS, Extra Series, 97 (London: Kegan Paul, Trench, Trübner, 1906), part 1, ll. 1869-72, writes of Fortune:

> Sche is so sleighty with hir gynny snare,
> That sche can make a man from his welfare,
> With hir panter, that is with fraude englued,
> Whan he lest weneth for to be remewed.

In the sixteenth century this metaphor found expression in the visual arts. An emblem by Jean Cousin, in *The Book of Fortune, Two Hundred Unpublished Drawings*, ed. Ludovic Lalanne, trans. H. Mainwaring Dunstan (London and Paris: Librairie de l'art, 1883), portrays Fortune practically covered with twigs; they seem to spring from her arms, legs, and head. The caption reads, "Fortuna viscata" (Sticky Fortune), pl. CXXXIX. The manuscript of Cousin's emblem book, *Liber Fortunae*, indicates that the work was to have been published in 1568. It is unclear why the manuscript, now in the Library of the Institute of France (Paris), never found its way into print during Cousin's lifetime.

36. The title page is reproduced as the frontispiece of Edwards' edition (Revels Plays).

37. See Francis Hugh Mares, "The Origin of the Figure Called 'the Vice' in Tudor Drama," *HLQ*, 22 (1958): 11-29. It is interesting that Fortune too was sometimes depicted with a black face or a face half white and half black. See Marie Tanner, "Chance and Coincidence in Titian's *Diana and Actaeon*," *Art Bulletin*, 56 (1974): 540-41; and figs. 10 and 11.

38. *Apius and Virginia*, ed. Ronald B. McKerrow and W. W. Greg, MSR (Oxford: Oxford Univ. Press, 1911), ll. 474-77.

39. Lorenzo's agent, Pedringano, speaks of Fortune just before shooting Serberine: "Now, Pedringano, bid thy pistol hold, / And hold on, Fortune! once more favour me, / Give but success to mine attempting spirit, / And let me shift for taking of mine aim!" (III.iii.1-4).

40. For a discussion of Justice as a personified abstraction, see J. Wilson McCutchan, "Justice and Equity in the English Morality Play," *JHI*, 19 (1958): 405-10.

41. Willard Farnham, in *Medieval Heritage*, notes the existence of a seventeenth-century ballad which "throws Kyd's drama into the simplest terms of *De Casibus* story. Here Hieronimo is a complaining ghost. He tells briefly of his rise to honor under Fortune's smiles . . . and then tells at some length of his fall under Fortune's frown . . ." (pp. 394-95).

42. In his *Liber Fortunae* (pl. XCV), Jean Cousin portrays the conflict between Fortune (carrying her wheel and a sword) and Justice (carrying her scales and a sword).

43. Studies of the theme of justice in the play include the following: Ernest de Chickera, "Divine Justice and Private Revenge in 'The Spanish Tragedy,'" *MLR*, 57 (1962): 228-32; Ejner J. Jensen, "Kyd's *Spanish Tragedy*: The Play Explains Itself," *JEGP*, 64 (1965): 7-16; G. K. Hunter, "Ironies of Justice in *The Spanish Tragedy*," *RenD*, 8 (1965): 89-104.

44. For the original Greek (with English translation), see "Chance," in Plutarch's *Moralia*, ed. and trans. F. C. Babbitt, LCL, 2 (New York and London: Putnam's, 1928): 74-89; "On the Fortune of the Romans," in Plutarch's *Moralia*, ed. and trans. F. C. Babbitt, LCL, 4 (Cambridge, Mass.: Harvard Univ. Press, 1936): 320-77. See also "Of Fortune" and "Of the Romans Fortune," in *The Philosophie, commonlie called, The Morals*, trans. Philemon Holland (London, 1603): pp. 229-33 and 627-39. For a discussion of Fortune in the moral essays, see C. P. Jones, *Plutarch and Rome* (Oxford: Clarendon Press,

1971), pp. 67-71. For a discussion of Fortune in the *Lives*, see Alan Wardman, *Plutarch's Lives* (Berkeley and Los Angeles: Univ. of California Press, 1974), pp. 179-89.

Chapter 6

FORTUNE AND THE TRAGEDY OF LOVE

S THOUGH MINDFUL of Giraldi Cinthio's advice to seek stories in modern fiction rather than in myth or history, Elizabethan playwrights turned increasingly to the novelle of Italy and France.[1] In the tales of Boccaccio, Bandello, Boaistuau, and others, they discovered stories of romantic love, rich with possibilities for the stage. They found Fortune, too, in those narratives, and so when the playwrights transformed novelle into drama they had at hand a strong impetus for the representation of Fortune.

To writers of love tragedies, Fortune in the novelle presented a somewhat different inspiration from the Fortune of Seneca or of *de casibus* literature. For in the novelle Fortune is closely linked with another personification—Love—and sometimes with Death as well. As a result, the dramatists usually treat Fortune not in isolation but in relation to Love and Death. In some plays the relationship becomes an important part of the dramatic action, and it will require our attention in the pages that follow.

Important as the Continental stories are in fostering the representation of Fortune, a dramatist's decision to base his play upon a novella does not in itself guarantee Fortune a place in his love tragedy. As we shall see in our consideration of three tragedies, a playwright's attitude toward his subject chiefly determines whether Fortune will flourish on the stage. Disapproval of young love tends to limit Fortune's appearance while a more sympathetic attitude generally enhances the portrayal of Fortune. Thus in the severe *Gismond of Salerne* Fortune receives scant attention, though prominent in the source. In the more indulgent

Soliman and Perseda, Fortune actually appears as a character. And in *Romeo and Juliet*, which portrays the lovers in sympathetic fashion while also suggesting their responsibility for their demise, Fortune plays an intermediate role. Neither the lifeless abstraction of *Gismond* nor the colorful character of *Soliman*, Fortune becomes in Shakespeare's drama an unseen but vivid presence.

I

In 1566 or 1568 Robert Wilmot and four colleagues at the Inner Temple pooled their talents and brought to the stage a story from Boccaccio's *Decameron* (4.1).[2] Their play, *Gismond of Salerne*, possesses considerable historical significance, for it is both the earliest surviving English play based upon a novella and the earliest extant tragedy of romantic love in English. In choosing to adapt an Italian narrative, the playwrights displayed the penchant for seeking love stories in Continental novelle that governed so many of their successors. And in profoundly altering their source, Wilmot and his collaborators anticipated the dramaturgy of writers in the later Elizabethan period who also adapted Italian and French stories. What sets *Gismond of Salerne* apart from such later plays as *Soliman and Perseda* and *Romeo and Juliet* is the complete transmutation of the tale which inspired it. The general indifference of Wilmot and his colleagues to the spirit of the source has been noticed, but the underlying attitudes responsible for their curious dramatic adaptation have not been fully explored.[3] Here we shall examine the divergent values that shaped the novella and the play, and the disparate treatments of Love and Fortune that resulted.

What the authors of *Gismond of Salerne* found in Boccaccio's novella was a tale of fervent, youthful love temporarily winning out against parental opposition but ultimately succumbing to adversity. With considerable sensitivity the Italian writer characterizes Ghismonda, the widowed daughter of Tancredi, and Guiscardo, the man of inferior social station with whom she falls in love. Scarcely less important to Boccaccio than the lovers themselves, however, is the nature of their love. For love, powerful and benevolent, emerges as the chief preoccupation of the story. Guiscardo affirms the might of love when he appears before Tancredi to answer for his illicit assignation with Ghismonda. After listening quietly to the Prince's indictment, he "gave no other answere, but that Love was of greater force, then either the Prince, or hymself" (fol. 103).[4] The awesome intensity of love thus mitigates any personal culpability; the lovers are driven irresistibly along. Yet, mighty as that force may be, it is not a destructive passion. For Boccaccio, love does not wrench the lover's personality, leaving him or her emotionally contorted and wasted. Rather, it represents entirely natural and humanizing behavior. Boccaccio's wholly sympathetic treatment of the mutual affection of Ghismonda and Guiscardo extolls the positive value of love and sex.

Love constitutes an extraordinary force in the world of Boccaccio's novella, but alone love is insufficient to bring Ghismonda and Guiscardo together. Their actual rendezvous depends upon a felicitous conjunction of time and place. And, just as Boccaccio personifies love, rendering it as both an internal disposition and an external entity, so too he personifies the force of circumstance. If Love furnishes the motivating impulse for the couple, Fortune arranges the conditions under which they consummate their desire. Fortune and Love thus assume, in effect, the status of participants — indeed, machinators — in the story. Together, they preside over the destiny of the lovers.

The relationship between Love and Fortune proves to be a volatile one, although the lovers learn this only gradually. Initially, they view the two powers as cooperative. Confronted by her father with evidence of her transgression, Ghismonda explains that "pitifull Love, and gentle Fortune have founde out, and shewed a waie secrete enough, whereby without knowledge of any man, I am come to the effect of my desires" (fol. 104). And when she explains her choice of a lover, Ghismonda again cites external agency. In answer to her father's objection to Guiscardo's social rank, she observes, "you doe not consider, that the fault is not mine, but rather to be ascribed to Fortune who ought to bee blamed, bicause many tymes she exalteth the unworthie, and treadeth under foote, those that be moste worthie" (fol. 104ᵛ). What neither Ghismonda nor Guiscardo realizes at first is how frail must be a human relationship dependent upon the continued amity of two such powers. Only later do the lovers come to see that Love and Fortune are not always solicitous of human well-being. They learn that Fortune in particular may employ her power to destroy love as well as to foster it. Indeed, even as she brings the lovers together, Fortune lays the groundwork for their downfall. The author explains how, once united, the lovers become the prey of the capricious deity: "Fortune envious of that pleasure, so long and greate, with dolorous successe, tourned the joye of those twoo lovers, into heavie and sorrowfull ende" (fol. 102). Fortune attains her purpose by having Tancredi fall asleep in his daughter's chamber and awaken to catch the lovers *in flagrante delicto*. Later Ghismonda alludes to Fortune's hostility when she addresses the heart of the slain Guiscardo: "Thou hast finished thy course, and by that ende, whiche Fortune vouchsaufed to give thee thou art dispatched, and arrived to the ende, whereunto all men have recourse" (fol. 106). Much to her dismay, Ghismonda has discovered that Fortune is as puissant as Love though not nearly so indulgent.

The duel between Love and Fortune is not so obtrusive that it ever obscures the relationship of Ghismonda and Guiscardo. And we would be justified in describing the story simply as one in which two lovers, caught between the demands of their own emotions on the one hand and the circumstance of parental opposition on the other, become martyrs to the cause of innocent affection crossed by adversity. Boccaccio's treatment of Love and Fortune, however, is hardly superfluous; it must have evoked in the minds of his readers memories of other such combats. For centuries writers had said that human affection blossomed under the joint hegemony of Love and Fortune.[5] The two are linked as early as the composition of *Octavia*, a Roman tragedy formerly ascribed to Seneca.[6] Toward the end of the Middle Ages, this conjunction became a literary commonplace, finding perhaps its best known expression in the *Roman de la Rose*. In fact, John V. Fleming notes that "it is probably to the *Roman*, if a particular source is to be adduced, that the widespread popularity of the Love-Fortune *topos* in late medieval and Renaissance literature is to be traced."[7] Boccaccio, by locating the love affair of Ghismonda and Guiscardo under the aegis of Love and Fortune, relates his own brief narrative to the canon of medieval love literature. In so doing he must have satisfied the expectations of his readers. Moreover, Boccaccio's representation of the topos is directly related to the impact of the story, for the interplay of Love and Fortune heightens the poignancy of the lovers' plight even as it seals their doom.

Love and Fortune thus help to create the aura of pathos and sentimentality which undoubtedly contributed to the great popularity of Boccaccio's tale.

Wilmot and his colleagues could not have chosen a more affecting story on which to base a tragedy of romantic love. They were, however, little interested in its charm or pathos. Their purposes are perhaps most clearly revealed in their treatment of Love, whom they bring to the stage as a full-fledged character named Cupid.[8] In so doing they profoundly alter the spirit of Boccaccio's novella, for their Cupid is a savage creature, bristling with hostility and fury. We gain some inkling of the metamorphosis wrought by Wilmot and his collaborators when, in the first scene of the play, Cupid announces that his purpose is not to unite the lovers but rather to refurbish his own tarnished reputation. To this end he will enter the palace "and there enflame the faire Gismonda soe, / in creping thorough all her veines within, / that she thereby shall raise much ruthe and woe" (I.i.62-64).[9] His intent at once characterizes the god of love as cruel and malicious:

> Loe, this before your eyes so will I showe,
> that ye shall justly say with one accord,
> we must relent and yeld: for now we knowe,
> Love rules the world, Love onely is the Lorde. (65-68)

In the English adaptation the benevolent deity of the Italian story is converted into a fiercely destructive force.

Those under the spell of such a power will necessarily bear little resemblance to the lovers depicted by Boccaccio. Thus in *Gismond of Saleme* the young woman no longer yields to natural, innocent impulse. Now she is seized by a dangerous and uncontrollable passion, one which violates the spirit of temperance. Throughout the play the dramatists enlist the chorus to urge the virtues of restraint and moderation, and, by implication, to condemn Gismond. The opprobrium which attaches to her actions is suggested when, at the conclusion of Act II, the chorus laments the diminution of virtue that has occurred since the end of the golden age. With pointed reference to Gismond, the chorus cites exempla of feminine virtue: "Ulysses wife (such was her stedfastnesse) / abode his slow returne whole twenty yeres, / and spent her youthfull dayes in pensivenesse, / bathing her widowes bed wth often teres" (25-28). Deploring the disappearance of such figures as Penelope, the chorus reflects,

> I think those good ladies, that livëd here
> a mirrour and a glasse to womankinde,
> and in their lives their vertues held so dere,
> had them to grave, and left them not behinde:
> ells in so many yeres we might have seen
> as good and vertuous dames as they have ben. (45-50)

Not only are the unchaste reproached but so too evidently are any who fall prey to Cupid. At the conclusion of Act III, the choral speaker warns against the "slye snake" that "lurkes under those flowers gay," concluding aphoristically, "seldome times is Cupide wont to send / unto a joyfull love a joyfull end" (49-50). Perhaps even more astonishing in this love story is the idea that "Cupide is but a childe, and can not daunte / the minde that beares him on his vertues bold" (39-40).

Choral admonitions are reinforced by the comments of Gismond's aunt and father. Lucrece presents her niece's case for remarriage to Tancred. But when the Prince explains his objections, Lucrece returns to Gismond with this counsel:

> And therfore myne advise shalbe, to stere
> no farther in this case: but sins his will
> is grounded on his fatherly love to yow,
> and that it lieth in yow to save or spill
> his old forwasted age, yow ought t'eschue
> to seke the thing that shold so much agreve
> his tender hart: and in the state yow stand
> content yor self: and let this thought releve
> all your unquiet thoughtes, that in yor hand
> yor agëd fathers life doeth rest and stay,
> sins without yow it may not long endure,
> but runne to ruthefull ruine and decay. (II.iii.24-35)

Even the insensitive Tancred, so highhanded in dealing with his daughter, movingly pleads his case. Reflecting upon his discovery of Gismond and Guishard in bed together, he cries,

> O daughter (whome alas most happy had I ben
> if living on the earth the sonne had never seen)
> is thys my hoped joy, my comfort, and my stay,
> to glad my grefefull yeres that wast and wear away?
> For happy life, that thow receivëd hâst by me,
> ten thousand cruel deathes shall I receive by thee?
>
> (IV.ii.17-22)

Such speeches have the effect of fundamentally altering the orientation of Boccaccio's narrative. No longer is love a force to be embraced but rather a menace to familial loyalty and even a potential threat to one's moral probity.[10]

The remarks of the chorus and principals make clear that the god of love is an outward manifestation of the passion that overwhelms Gismond and her lover. If the sinister character of Cupid seems monstrous to us, so too should the spectacle of those figures wracked by violent emotion. In this treatment of the god of love, the English playwrights display their lack of sympathy with Boccaccio's purposes. The *Decameron*, one writer has observed, is characterized by a "complete absence of the sense of sin."[11] Such a sense of wrongdoing, by contrast, pervades *Gismond of Salerne*. What was a forthright celebration of love in the Italian novella has in the English play become a severe warning against vice.

If Love undergoes a transformation at the hands of the English playwrights, so too does Fortune. Unlike Love, however, Fortune is not brought to the stage as a dramatic character. In fact, the dramatists eschew for the most part any effort to make Fortune a viable presence in the play. This is not to say that they exclude Fortune entirely, for in a lengthy refrain the first-act chorus expounds upon the instability of all things earthly:

> Here fortune rules, whoe, when she list to play,
> whirleth her whele and bringes the hye full lowe,

to morrow takes what she hath geven to day,
to shew she can advaunce and overthrowe. (37-40)

And when in the last act Renuchio delivers his eyewitness account of
Guishard's death, he punctuates his speech with frequent allusions to
Fortune. While more elaborate perhaps than Boccaccio's references,
these actually convey less thematic import. For the invocations or de-
precations of Fortune are confined chiefly to a single choral interlude
following the first act and to the single speech of a minor character in the
last. The protagonists themselves fail to convey any real sense of
being threatened by Fortune's power.

The disparity between Boccaccio's handling of Fortune and that of
the dramatists is epitomized in the first-act chorus. There we learn that
Fortune cannot tyrannize the virtuous individual:

> he may scorne fortune, that hath no power
> on him that is content with his estate.
> He seketh not her swete, ne feares her sower,
> but lives alône within his bounded rate,
> and marking how these worldly thinges do wade,
> rejoiseth to him self, and laughes to see
> the follie of mortal men, how they have made
> Fortune a god, and placed her in the skye. (53-60)

A greater contrast with Boccaccio can scarcely be imagined. Whereas for
the Italian narrator Fortune is a wily manipulator of events, she possesses no real power for Wilmot and his colleagues. As far as they are
concerned, she lacks any true divinity; Fortune exists merely as a figment of the foolish man's imagination.

Clearly, Fortune cannot play the vital role in *Gismond of Salerne* that
she did in Boccaccio's novella. Stripped of her authority, she no longer
can account satisfactorily for the adversity that overtakes the lovers. The
dramatists therefore must work a major alteration in their materials. If
the fickle goddess foils the lovers in the novella, the just vengeance of the
gods brings about their demise in the play. Nearly everyone, including
the god of love, is affected by the spirit of revenge. For instance, when
Cupid appears at the beginning of Act III, he tells the audience that he

plans to ascend to heaven where he will report to Jove how "by sharp revenge on earthly wightes" he has restored his formidable reputation and will "hensefourth ceasse unserved to sitt in vaine / a God whome men unpunished may disdaine" (III.i.31-32). *Gismond of Salerne,* however, concerns itself not primarily with the pique of any single deity. Purely personal revenge gives way to a corporate quest for divine vengeance against human malefactors. This is demonstrated by Megaera, a Fury apparently adapted from Seneca's *Thyestes,* who appears in Act IV to sanction the destruction of the royal family: "Vengeance and blood out of the depest helles / I bring the cursed house where Gismond dwelles" (IV.i.1-2). She comes not as a fiend who capriciously torments mankind, but rather as an executrix of justice. Her presence represents the general condemnation of the lovers by a synod of deities; the gods are offended because "Love that blinded boy" has induced Gismond to "throw away / chastnesse of life, to her immortal shame" (22-23). The Fury goes on to explain that the gods of the underworld have directed her to rise

> above the earth, with dole and drere to daunt
> the present joyes wherwith Gismonda now
> fedes her disteinëd hart, and so to make
> Cupide Lord of his will. (34-37)

Megaera's mission is thus one of chastisement: "Furies must aide, when men will ceasse to know / their Goddes: and Hell shall send revenging paine / to those, whome Shame from sinne can not restraine" (42-44).

Even Gismond, so gentle by temperament in the novella, is touched by the spirit of retribution. If her life and love represent a nearly complete antithesis to that described by Boccaccio, so too does her death. Boccaccio's heroine takes her own life so that she may join her slain lover. By contrast, the young woman in Wilmot's play commits suicide largely to spite her father. She even frames her own epitaph to memorialize her motive:

> Loe here within one tombe whear harbour twaine,
> Gismonda Quene, and Counte Palurine:

She loved him, he for her love was slayen,
for whoes revenge eke lyes she here in shrine. (V.iii.45-48)

This is surely an appropriate conclusion not only for Gismond's life but also for a drama that is at least as concerned with retribution as it is with eroticism and love. Justice in the shape of revenge informs the play from beginning to end; practically every character is either a revenger or a victim of revenge.

Without question, the dramatists have decisively altered the topos bequeathed them by Boccaccio; Love and Fortune no longer are the adversaries they were in the novella. Instead, the playwrights substitute a contrariety of their own: they recast the opposition delineated by the author of the *Decameron* and counterpose concupiscence with the retribution which it invites. The protagonists, instead of being victimized by the strife between Love and Fortune, are now pinioned between the impulse of passion and the claims of retributive justice.

The inspiration for the modifications wrought by Wilmot and his colleagues probably cannot be identified with any certitude. We can, however, at least speculate about their motives in so profoundly modifying Boccaccio's story. And, given their use of the revenge motif, the chorus, such stock characters as the messenger and confidant, such stylistic features as stichomythic dialogue, long speeches, and sententious precepts, and, of course, their borrowing from *Thyestes*, our conjecture may well begin with Seneca, who seems to have had a considerable impact on *Gismond of Salerne*, directly and perhaps indirectly as well through Renaissance Italian tragedy.[12] That the play should have a distinctly Senecan flavor is not at all surprising since it was written for the same kind of sophisticated audience at the Inns of Court that enjoyed the performance of such Senecan plays as *Gorboduc* and *Jocasta*. Indeed, William Webbe, in his prefatory epistle to Wilmot's revision of the play, printed in 1592, writes that the original performance was "of the whole honorable audience notably applauded: yea, and of al men generally desired, as a work, either in statelines of shew, depth of conceit, or true ornaments of poeticall arte, inferior to none of the best in that kinde: no, were the Roman *Seneca* the censurer."[13] In addition to certain character types and stylistic features, the English playwrights may also have adopted Seneca's characteristic treatment of passion. Although the

Roman tragedian was never much concerned with dramatizing romantic love, he was interested in depicting individuals in the grip of some overwhelming emotion. As a Stoic, he distrusted anything that threatened to corrupt the rule of reason; his dramatization of reason in retreat may have been intended as cautionary. At the same time, Seneca seems not only horrified but also fascinated by the exhibition of powerful feelings; his portrayal of passion has a lurid quality, as though he were unable to avert his eyes from what intellectually repelled him. Something of the same ambivalence characterizes *Gismond of Salerne*, where the severest kind of moral condemnation is juxtaposed with the most eloquent pleas for the fulfillment of physical desire.

The English dramatists, of course, brought to the play their own attitudes, which their reading of Seneca may simply have reinforced. They were certainly no less concerned with the sovereignty of reason than was their Roman predecessor. It is interesting that despite the range of passion they depict—Gismond's grief, Guishard's love, Tancred's rage—the characters remain in other respects stubbornly rational. However torn by emotion they may be, the various characters seldom fail to exercise their mental faculties. We witness Gismond choosing her course of action, Guishard contemplating the consequences of his, and Tancred pondering his response to both. We even hear, by way of Megaera, about the deliberations of the gods. The tragedy seems, oddly since a love story, more cerebral than sensual. Law instead of nature appears to represent the greatest good. Gismond may lament the fading of her "fresh grene youth" and wonder aloud "whearto hath nature decked / me with so semely shape?" (II.i.27,28-29). However, the playwrights do not invite us to condone her surrender to desire. The actions of Gismond and Guishard, they remind us, are consciously and deliberately taken. These are no mere victims of circumstance, buffeted by the irresistible winds of passion.

This rationalistic bias is, in all likelihood, chiefly responsible for the playwrights' modification of their source, particularly for their rendering of Love as grotesque and for their suppression of Fortune. As a violation of virtue, Gismond's passion has to be made unattractive; it must offend by its excess. And in this drama devoted no less to castigating the lovers than to heralding their love, the role of Fortune must remain circumscribed. Adversity, inflicted by enigmatic Fortune in Boccaccio's novella, is no longer especially mysterious in *Gismond of Salerne*. It results from transgression against human and divine law; and it is applied with an almost mathematical precision. By neutralizing Fortune, the dramatists shift the burden to the individual, suggesting that the lovers have the capacity to resist unreason and that their failure to do so precipitates their catastrophe. Robert Wilmot's prefatory letter to his revision of the play hints at this motive. There he writes that "my purpose in this Tragedie, tendeth onely to the exaltation of vertue, & suppression of vice." Even allowing for a certain degree of exaggeration, Wilmot's declaration conveys the earnestness of his moral bent. And it suggests the nature of the sentiment which allowed Boccaccio's Love and Fortune to be purged in the interests of a grim moral didacticism.

II

The Love-Fortune topos, suppressed in *Gismond of Salerne*, may have taken on greater prominence in plays (now lost) of the 1570s and 1580s based on romance. This, at least, is one conclusion to be drawn from the survival of such a play as *Clyomon and Clamydes* (c. 1575; printed in 1599).[14] The prologue anticipates the play's treatment of Love and Fortune by telling us that "the froward chances oft, of Fortune you shall see" and that "true lovers findeth joy, with hugie heapes of care."[15] Romances, which commonly deal both with romantic love and harsh adversity, provide naturally for the expression of the Love-Fortune motif. Thus it is not surprising that Love and Fortune together should first come to the stage as characters in a play based on romance: *The Rare Triumphs of Love and Fortune*, printed in 1589. (This anonymous comedy is probably *A History of Love and Fortune*, performed for the Queen in 1582.) Although the play does not have its source in a novella, it merits brief consideration here nonetheless, since it almost certainly influenced the treatment of Love and Fortune in *Soliman and Perseda* which, in turn, helped to shape *Romeo and Juliet*.

The relationship between Love and Fortune is inherently dramatic: although sometimes allies, they are more frequently adversaries.[16] Capitalizing on this strife, the author of *The Rare Triumphs* makes it the very

basis of his plot. The drama begins with a dispute, the issue being hegemony over mankind. Before a conclave of the gods, Venus argues her
might and challenges Fortune's power: "divers thinges there be that
Fortune cannot tame, / As are the riches of the minde, or else an honest
name" (129-30).[17] In reply, Fortune asserts her own claims:

> Is not the wonder of the World a woork that soon
> > decayes?
> Therfore, ye see all earthly thinges are wearing out
> > alwaies,
> As brittle as the glasse, unconstant like the minde,
> As fickle as the whirling wheele, as wavering as the winde.
> Loe, such am I that overthrowes the hiest reared tower.
> > (165-69)

As the rival boasts grow more bitter, Jupiter commands a series of dumb
shows, illustrating the different hegemony exercised by Venus (Troilus
and Cressida; Dido) and by Fortune (Alexander; Caesar and Pompey).
But when, in the last show, Hero and Leander appear, Venus and Fortune once again begin to wrangle. And with the matter undecided, Jupiter puts their boasts to the test. He calls their attention to a young prin-
cess and her beloved "On whom I meane your soverainties to
prove":

> Venus, for that they love thy sweet delight,
> Thou shalt endevor to encrease their joy;
> And, Fortune, thou to manifest thy might,
> Their pleasures and their pastimes shalt destroye,
> Overthwarting them with newes of freshe anoye;
> And she that most can please them or dispight,
> I will confirme to be of greatest might. (260-66)

Vulcan anticipates the pleasure which this contest will afford when he
says to the audience, "And you will be quiet, sirs, they will make ye
good sport with their scolding anon" (275).

The subsequent acts, containing a plethora of romance materials, tell a
convoluted story of wandering and separation, of accidental meetings

and overheard conversations. And the audience meets a number of characters common to romance: a foundling, an exiled nobleman, a magician. All of these belong to the story of Fidelia, daughter of King Phizantius, and Hermione, the man she loves. Like Tancred in *Gismond of Salerne*, Phizantius considers his daughter's suitor unworthy of her social position. And, like Gismond, Fidelia thinks at first that Fortune may prove friendly: "Fortune, when and where it likes her majestie, / With cloudes can cover birth and highest degree" (337-38). In time, however, she and her beloved discover the depth of Fortune's enmity.

Although the focus of the drama shifts to the human characters after the first act, the playwright brings back the deities at the conclusion of subsequent acts. There they continue the conflict established earlier in the play and, of course, contribute to the spectacle. At the conclusion of Act II, for example, after Hermione has been banished, Fortune appears amid great panoply: "Strike up Fortunes triumphes with Drummes and Trumpets."[1] And she exults over her handiwork:

> Heerin consisteth Fortunes soveraintie,
> That Fortune can on earth doo what she will.
> When men have builded on the surest grounds,
> Their strong devises Fortunes power confoundes. (563-66)

Venus must look to the future for evidence of her power: "Not all in haste; you doo not so intend; / You have begun, but I must make an end" (568-69). As this prediction suggests, the pattern of victory and defeat is reversed in the next act when Hermione is reunited with his father and is assured, "all thinges shalbe well" (963). This time Venus' triumphs are celebrated (to the sound of viols), and Fortune is confined to threats: "my sport is not begun" (977).

After further adventures, the oscillation of emphasis between now Love, now Fortune, is finally brought to an end by Jupiter, who decides that henceforth Venus shall not hinder those who enjoy Fortune's favor, and Fortune shall cease to afflict those blessed by Venus: "whome soever one of you preferre, / The other shall be subject unto her" (1580-81). The deities at once accede, and in their new-found amity they actually appear to the young lovers and their families. Venus tells Phizantius, "Knowe that it is the pleasure of our will / That they together be

171

conjoyned still" (1755-56). Allaying the king's fears, Venus reveals that Hermione, whose low birth the king once contemned, is actually of noble lineage. Obstacles overcome, the lovers are at last able to marry. And with the commingling of deities and men, the play concludes in an atmosphere of harmony and joy.

III

Even such an essentially happy story as that told in *The Rare Triumphs of Love and Fortune* contains potentially tragic material. Suppose that Love and Fortune were utterly without regard for their subjects and there were no benevolent deity presiding over the conflict? The result would be calamitous rather than comic. The plaintive note heard in the speeches of the lovers would come to dominate the tone of the play. The antipathy of Love and Fortune, untrammeled by any superior power, would grow more and more intense. Such an outcome characterizes another drama of romantic love, *Soliman and Perseda, Wherein is laid open, Love's constancy, Fortune's inconstancy, and Death's triumphs* (c. 1588-92). This tragedy, ascribed to Thomas Kyd, almost certainly borrows, as its subtitle suggests, from the earlier comedy.[18] Like the author of *The Rare Triumphs*, Kyd brings Love and Fortune to the stage. And they, together with a third figure—Death—serve as chorus. The presence of Death clearly sets this play apart from its predecessor. But Death's jibe, near the end of *Soliman and Perseda*, may well be a veiled allusion to *The Rare Triumphs*: "Packe, *Love* and *Fortune*, play in Commedies; / For powerfull *Death* best fitteth Tragedies" (V.v.28-29).[19]

The chorus in *Soliman* is not necessarily dependent upon *The Rare Triumphs* alone. It may be inspired too by Kyd's chief source, a story in Jacques Yver's *Printemps d'Iver* (1572), translated into English by Henry Wotton under the title *A Courtlie controversie of Cupids Cautels* (London, 1578).[20] There, along with the tale of Erastus and Perseda and their adventures at the hands of the Emperor Soliman, are found two of the personifications who serve as Kyd's chorus: Love and Fortune. Their power over mankind and their hostility toward one another characterize the figures of both French story and English play. But since

Yver does not personify Death, it seems unlikely that his narrative alone inspired the chorus in *Soliman*. And the suggestion that the chorus owes its origin to a sentence appearing in the epitaph following Wotton's translation ("By *Fortune, Envie,* and by *Death,* / This couple caughte their bane") seems doubtful,[21] for while two of Kyd's personifications are mentioned here, the third is not.

In all likelihood the chorus, while prompted most immediately by the example of *The Rare Triumphs* and, to some extent, by Yver's narrative, has ultimately an even broader inspiration: it lies in the topos which, since the Middle Ages, linked Love, Fortune, and Death. Erwin Panofsky, noting that all three are depicted as sightless, suggests the nature of their common bond: "these three were blind both in an intransitive and in a transitive sense. They were blind, not only as personifications of an unenlightened state of mind, or of a lightless form of existence, but also as personifications of an active force behaving like an eyeless person: they would hit or miss at random, utterly regardless of age, social position and individual merit."[22] The conjunction of these three seems to occur most often in love poetry. Thus, for example, Petrarch begins one of his poems with this question:

> Datemi pace, o duri miei pensieri!
> non basta ben ch'Amor, Fortuna et Morte
> mi fanno guerra intorno e 'n su le porte,
> senza trovarmi dentro altri guerreri?
> (Give me peace, O my cruel thoughts!
> Is it not enough that Love, Fortune, and Death
> besiege me around and at the very gates,
> without having to find other enemies within?)[23]

Gilles Corrozet includes a poem entitled "D'Amour Fortune et Mort" in *Les blasons domestiques* (Paris, 1539):

> Amour assault en desirant la gloire,
> D'avoir vaincu les mortelz par ses mains:
> Fortune aussi guerroye les humains,
> Mais sur les deux Mort obtient la victoire. (fol. 43ᵛ)
> (Love assaults, desiring the glory

173

Of having vanquished mortals by his hands:
Fortune also wars against humans,
But against the two Death obtains the victory.)

And in sonnet 44 of his *Tears of Fancie or, Love Disdained* (London,
1593), Thomas Watson treats the triangular relationship of Love, Fortune, and Death:

> Long have I sued to fortune death and love,
> But fortune, love, nor death will daine to heare me:
> I fortunes frowne, deaths spight, loves horror prove,
> And must in love dispairing live I feare me.
> Love wounded me, yet nill recure my wounding,
> And yet my plaints have often him invoked:
> Fortune hath often heard my sorrowes sounding,
> Sorrowes which my poore hart have welnigh choked,
> Death well might have beene moved when I lamented,
> But cruell death was deafe when I complained:
> Death, love and fortune all might have relented,
> But fortune, love, and death, and all disdained.
> To pittie me or ease my restles minde,
> How can they choose since they are bold and blinde.
>
> (sig. D1^v)

It was Kyd's genius, guided by iconographic tradition and by
the dramatic precedent of *The Rare Triumphs*, to see the possibility of
applying this topos to the stage.

Like *The Rare Triumphs, Soliman and Perseda* begins with the
conversation of competing deities. From their earliest moments on
stage, they dispute heatedly the extent of one another's power:

> *Love.* What, *Death* and *Fortune* crosse the way of *Love?*
> *Fortune.* Why, what is *Love* but *Fortunes* tenis-ball?
> *Death.* Nay, what are you both, but subjects unto *Death?*
>
> (I.i.1-3)

At the end of each act, they return to tally their successes, grumble over their opponents' claims, and engage in contentious exchanges. As in *The Rare Triumphs*, these figures point to incidents occurring in the lives of their earthly subjects to demonstrate the scope of their hegemony. No one figure, however, seems clearly victorious, at least not until the conclusion of the last act.

The lovers, like their counterparts in *The Rare Triumphs*, are aware that their felicity depends on external forces. As though conscious of the machinations of Love, Fortune, and Death, the characters of the play proper attribute their fate to maneuvering from without. When, for instance, Erastus loses the chain that Perseda had given him as a token of her love, he asks, "Ah, treacherous *Fortune*, enemy to *Love*, / Didst thou advance me for my greater fall?" (I.iv.114-15). And fearing that, with the chain gone, his beloved is lost, he adds, "Come therefore, gentle death, and ease my griefe; / Cut short what malice *Fortune* misintends" (126-27).[24] When the chain comes into the possession of another woman, Lucina, Erastus reflects, "Fortune made the fault, not Love" (II.i.171). By gambling with Lucina, Erastus manages to recover the object, but on the way home he encounters the man who earlier had found the chain and given it to Lucina. They begin to quarrel and suddenly Erastus slays the fellow. Forced to flee Rhodes, he laments:

> Ah, if but time and place would give me leave,
> Great ease it were for me to purge my selfe,
> And to acuse fell *Fortune*, *Love*, and *Death*;
> For all these three conspire my tragedie. (II.i.258-61)

Such speeches indicate that while Love, Fortune, and Death may not actually interact with the characters of the play, as do Venus and Fortune in the last act of *The Rare Triumphs*, the lovers interpret their experience as though they were directly influenced by the three personifications.

It is this juxtaposition—if not interaction—of choral figures and other characters that contributes so largely to the tragic tone of the play. For the role of Love, Fortune, and Death in the lives of the lovers and the recognition by the latter of that involvement heighten the sense of estrangement between them. Although Kyd stresses their interconnection by the comments that each group makes about the other, he also makes clear that Love, Fortune, and Death are disinterested sovereigns. That is, they pursue their ends with no thought of the cost to their earthly victims. However preoccupied they may seem with minutiae in the lives of the lovers, the choral figures are concerned only with themselves. And there is no Jupiter to temper their strife. Knowledge of this indifference instills in Erastus, Perseda, and Soliman the feeling that they are at the mercy of events they can neither control nor comprehend.

Through the contention between Love, Fortune, and Death, the spectators in the theater are led to share the sense of consternation felt by the characters on stage. The physical presence of the chorus conveys, better than words alone, the claustrophobic nature of the world of the play. Men and women seem little more than pawns to be manipulated by Love, Fortune, and Death in a private game; the world is their chessboard, humankind the pieces. The choral figures, then, serve Kyd's dramatic purpose by demonstrating the helplessness (and thus the vulnerability) of the lovers — their inability to chart their own destiny.

IV

The tragedy of love, pioneered by Wilmot and further developed by Kyd, reached an apotheosis of sorts in *Romeo and Juliet* (c. 1595). Shakespeare conveys, as no English dramatist had before, the intensity of youthful passion. Through the language, the pace of the action, and the sheer attractiveness of the lovers, he engages the audience immediately and powerfully. At the same time, however, Shakespeare applies conventions which impose a pattern upon the violent, brawling story. As Nicholas Brooke observes, *Romeo and Juliet* "in many ways seems to be a formal exercise in romantic tragedy, given the kind of overt formality of structure and verse which rather suggests the order of a stately dance."[25] This formal quality, achieved in *Soliman and Perseda* by the chorus, is created here in part by Shakespeare's adoption of the Love-Fortune-Death topos.

Love, Fortune, and Death do not, of course, take the form of actual characters in *Romeo and Juliet*: they are refined into a sophisticated imagistic motif. Frequently on the minds and lips of the characters, the three are variously invoked, petitioned, and decried. References to each personification, however, instead of appearing consistently throughout Shakespeare's play, are clustered at those points where they are most appropriate to the mood and the dramatic action.

Cupid, or Love, figures most prominently in the first two acts, in which are dramatized Romeo's infatuation with Rosaline, his meeting with Juliet, and their falling in love. These are not merely fleeting references but detailed allusions that have an almost pictorial quality. In the first scene, for instance, Romeo envisages the weapons of Cupid when he says of Rosaline:

> she'll not be hit
> With Cupid's arrow, she hath Dian's wit;
> And in strong proof of chastity well arm'd,
> From Love's weak childish bow she lives uncharm'd.
> (I.i.208-11)

Benvolio too calls to mind the accouterments found in iconographic representations of Cupid when he remarks comically, "We'll have no Cupid hoodwink'd with a scarf, / Bearing a Tartar's painted bow of lath, / Scaring the ladies like a crow-keeper" (I.iv.4-6). Mercutio mentions still another feature of Cupid's appearance when he bids Romeo "borrow Cupid's wings, / And soar with them above a common bound" (I.iv.17-18). Similarly, in the so-called balcony scene Romeo tells his beloved: "With love's light wings did I o'erperch these walls, / For stony limits cannot hold love out, / And what love can do, that dares love attempt" (II.ii.66-68). Juliet envisions both Cupid and Venus in vivid terms when she contemplates her wedding night:

> Love's heralds should be thoughts,
> Which ten times faster glides than the sun's beams,
> Driving back shadows over low'ring hills;
> Therefore do nimble-pinion'd doves draw Love,
> And therefore hath the wind-swift Cupid wings. (II.v.4-8)

Collectively, these evocations of Cupid's (and Venus') appearance build up an elaborate mental image of the force that Kyd had personified and placed on stage in *Soliman and Perseda*.

Toward the end of the second act, Love gives way to Fortune in prominence. The references are not so elaborate or numerous as those to Cupid, but they appear at important turning points of the story.[26] For example, when Romeo kills Tybalt and thereby precipitates his banishment from Verona, he cries, "O, I am fortune's fool!" (III.i.136). And at the lovers' parting, Juliet entreats the favor of Fortune:

> O Fortune, Fortune, all men call thee fickle;
> If thou art fickle, what dost thou with him
> That is renowm'd for faith? Be fickle, Fortune:
> For then I hope thou wilt not keep him long,
> But send him back. (III.v.60-64)

Chance continues to play a major role in the remainder of the drama, as Friar John is detained by quarantine, Romeo meets Paris at the tomb, Friar Lawrence arrives late at the tomb, and Juliet fails to awaken until Romeo is already dead. References to hap, accident, adventure, and mischance abound. Explicit mention of Fortune, however, is confined chiefly to the middle act of the play where she looms largest in the minds of the lovers.

The third member of the trio, although not entirely absent earlier in the play, predominates in the latter part of *Romeo and Juliet*. There, as the lovers' happiness is thwarted, Death assumes ever more authority. Juliet anticipates Death's victories when, after Tybalt's death, she says, "Come, cords, come, nurse, I'll to my wedding-bed, / And death, not Romeo, take my maidenhead!" (III.ii.136-37). Later Romeo entreats Death too: "Come, death, and welcome! Juliet wills it so" (III.v.24). A more elaborate evocation of Death is that spoken by Capulet. Witnessing the effect of the potion upon his daughter, he says, "Death lies on her like an untimely frost / Upon the sweetest flower of all the field" (IV.v.28-29). And, turning to Paris, he adds,

> O son, the night before thy wedding-day
> Hath Death lain with thy wife. There she lies,
> Flower as she was, deflowered by him. (35-37)

The references to Death multiply as Romeo and Juliet approach their end. At the tomb Romeo conjures up the image of Death when he addresses his wife's form, "Death, that hath suck'd the honey of thy breath, / Hath had no power yet upon thy beauty" (V.iii.92-93), and when he asks,

> Shall I believe
> That unsubstantial Death is amorous,
> And that the lean abhorred monster keeps
> Thee here in dark to be his paramour? (102-5)

Such allusions, in the aggregate, paint a vivid picture of Death, the lover and destroyer.

The inspiration for Shakespeare's personification of Love, Fortune, and Death may have come from his chief source, Arthur Brooke's *Tragicall Historye of Romeus and Juliet* (1562 and 1587), itself an adaptation of Continental novelle.[27] But it seems unlikely that Brooke alone prompted the poetic rendering of Love, Fortune, and Death in the play, for although he personifies all three in the poem, one of these predominates. Brooke creates a Dame Fortune whose hegemony over human affairs is unchallenged and whose authority is recognized by all of her subjects. Shakespeare, however, does not emulate Brooke's example; some figures in *Romeo and Juliet* acknowledge Fortune's sovereignty while others do not.[28] Moreover, Shakespeare confines explicit reference to Fortune principally to the middle section of the play. He thus greatly diminishes the prominence enjoyed by Fortune in *Romeus and Juliet.* At the same time, he increases the prominence of Love and Death,[29] who in Brooke's poem receive scant attention. As a consequence of these modifications, Love, Fortune, and Death attain a roughly co-equal status.

In his diminution of Brooke's omnipresent Fortune and in his enlargement of Love and Death, Shakespeare may well have been influenced by the chorus in *Soliman and Perseda.* There is no question that he knew Kyd's play, for he borrows from it in *King John* and in *The Merchant of Venice.*[30] It is, however, also possible that, like Kyd, Shakespeare was inspired not merely by a single work but by the larger literary and iconographic tradition which had long given representation to Love, Fortune, and Death.

One of the most impressive contributions to that tradition is *La Danse aux aveugles*, a poem by Pierre Michault which recounts a man's journey through a series of gardens wherein Love, Fortune, and Death preside.[31] A fifteenth-century manuscript of Michault's work contains an illumination that bears an interesting imagistic parallel to Shakespeare's play.[32] The design presents a landscape which the viewer sees through three arches, connected one to another. In the compartment formed by the arch on the left, Cupid holds his bow and arrow; in the center, Fortune sits beside her turning wheel; and, on the right, Death rides his ox and brandishes his spear. In this portrayal the artist has sought to depict the essential narrative structure of the poem — the itinerary of the protagonist as he moves through a series of gardens. The poem and painting have, in addition, a more universal application, for they express the history of anyone who experiences love, adversity, and finally death. Indeed, the progress of Romeo and Juliet, as they move from the felicity of courtship to disastrous mischance and thence to their demise, may be said to match that of Michault's protagonist. In his tragedy Shakespeare, of course, paints no literal picture. But by clustering the references to Love, Fortune, and Death successively at the beginning, middle, and end of the play, he establishes an imagistic background against which the lovers move. In a sense, then, Shakespeare creates the dramatic counterpart of a triptych. And by so doing he subordinates the unruly phenomena of passion, accident, and sudden death to a formal pattern, familiar and explicable.

This is not to say that the triptych dominates the play in the same way as the chorus in *Soliman and Perseda*, for Shakespeare's tripartite cluster of symbols is articulated chiefly by the lovers. Other characters see other forces at work. Thus instead of perceiving the hand of Love, Fortune, or Death in what befalls the lovers, the Friar and the Prince offer a more orthodox explanation. The Friar may, like the lovers, experience accident, chance, coincidence. He may even perceive in these phenomena evidence of divine intervention; at the tomb he says, "A greater power than we can contradict / Hath thwarted our intents" (V.iii.153-54). However, the Friar — although speaking at one point of "unhappy fortune" (in the sense of "condition") — by his references to heaven attests to his faith in the Christian deity. If Romeo and Juliet believe their travail to be undeserved, Friar Lawrence regards adversity as the fate of the heedless. If they are bewildered by their experience and look outward for some explanation, he looks inward to discern the connection between human wrongdoing and divine displeasure. He perceives that "rude will" may overwhelm "grace" (II.iii.28), that the lovers may invite destruction by their own headstrong behavior. Similarly, at the conclusion of the play, the Prince gives support to the notion of providential design when he tells the feuding families: "Capulet! Montague! / See what a scourge is laid upon your hate, / That heaven finds means to kill your joys with love" (V.iii.291-93). Through the character of the Friar and, to a lesser extent, the Prince, *Romeo and Juliet* is touched, if only lightly, by the moralism that dominates *Gismond of Saleme*. Interestingly, it is Shakespeare who emphasizes the retributive element of the story; Brooke, despite the harsh tone of his Preface, portrays the lovers in a very sympathetic manner.

How are we to reconcile the viewpoint of the lovers with that of the authority figures? H. B. Charlton suggests, in effect, that we discount the latter: "the whole universe of God's justice, vengeance and providence is discarded and rejected from the directing forces of the play's dramatic movement. In its place, there is a theatrical resuscitation of the half-barbarian, half-Roman deities of Fate and Fortune."[33] Franklin M. Dickey, by contrast, would subordinate the vision of the lovers to that of the Friar and the Prince: "In *Romeo and Juliet* . . . fortune may be considered not the prime mover but the agent of a higher power [i.e., providence]."[34] Neither of these interpretations, on reflection, seems very satisfactory. Romeo and Juliet go to their deaths convinced that they are the victims of a cruel world. Their suicides scarcely betoken faith in divine plan. Nor do the authority figures, for their part, claim that Fortune serves providence; they are in fact silent about Dame Fortune. What Shakespeare does is neither to assign Fortune the role of executrix (as Dickey suggests) nor to banish providence from the play (Charlton). The playwright chooses a less rigid course. He allows the lovers to express an outlook appropriate to their youth, inexperience, and passion; in their world, as they see it, Dame Fortune wields great power. At the same time, the Friar and the Prince express a view consistent with their age, wisdom, and social station. Their assertion of providential design does not obliterate the lovers' view; nor does the lovers' obliterate theirs. The two are juxtaposed.

By allowing the characters to conceive of their milieu in sharply individualized fashion, Shakespeare creates a dramatic world of much greater complexity than that envisioned by his predecessors. Such complexity would probably have been impossible had Shakespeare emulated Kyd and imposed upon the play a chorus consisting of machinators. The author of *Soliman and Perseda*, as we have seen, seeks to create a world in which the lovers are doomed to stumble from crisis to crisis. By contrast, Shakespeare fashions characters who possess a far larger measure of autonomy. He affirms their power of choice and their accountability for their actions. Such a dramatist would naturally find the personified characters less useful than Kyd, for the direct, explicit authority exercised by Love, Fortune, and Death would necessarily undercut the independence of the human characters. And Shakespeare does not envision Romeo and Juliet merely as helpless victims of a cosmic game. At the same time, he recognizes the awesome power of hostile circumstance, for he portrays with sensitivity the lovers who believe themselves to be the victims of Love, Fortune, and Death. By combining at once the lovers' lamentations and the Friar's admonitions, Shakespeare strikes a balance between individual responsibility and external compulsion.

Shakespeare's Love, Fortune, and Death may lack the intrinsic interest of Kyd's choral figures, who exert an immediate appeal by virtue of their physical presence and contentiousness. But the personifications of *Romeo and Juliet* ably serve the artistic purposes of the dramatist. After all, for Shakespeare the topos is less a means of achieving striking theatrical effect than of creating a richly varied dramatic texture. And as expressions of the characters' attitudes and personalities, Love, Fortune, and Death effectively suggest the diversity of human experience; by making implicit what Kyd renders explicitly, Shakespeare conveys the lovers' sense of doom without requiring the audience to accept Love, Fortune, and Death as the sole arbiters of human destiny. Shakespeare's treatment of the topos also permits a more subtle delineation of Love, Fortune, and Death themselves. For if he gives them a less concrete form than does his predecessor, Shakespeare nevertheless preserves something that Kyd, by his very theatricality, sacrifices: the essential mystery of the forces personified.

V

The juxtaposition of cosmic forces in *Romeo and Juliet* has puzzled many readers, who detect an apparent inconsistency between Fortune and fate, the contingent and the determined. A. C. Hamilton calls attention to this problem when he writes, "the succession of tragic events that proceeds inexorably in *Titus Andronicus* combines in *Romeo and Juliet* with fortuitous circumstance, which suggests that events need not happen as they do."[35] G. I. Duthie would account for the difficulty by arguing that the seemingly fortuitous events are actually determined: "Shakespeare does not want us to think of these 'accidents' as merely fortuitous. We cannot avoid the impression that he asks us to think of them as intentionally arranged by Fate."[36] Shakespeare, to be sure, does create an atmosphere of fatality, beginning with the choral reference to "star-cross'd lovers" in the Prologue. And this mood is strengthened by the premonitions of the lovers. Thus Romeo, before Capulet's party, says, "my mind misgives / Some consequence yet hanging in the stars" (I.iv.106-7). Similarly, Juliet, after her wedding night, says: "Methinks I see thee now, thou art so low, / As one dead in the bottom of a tomb" (III.v.55-56). And the sense of astral determinism is underscored when Romeo hears the news (false, as it turns out) that his wife is dead: "Then I defy you, stars!" (V.i.24). Despite these remarks, however, there seems little doubt that chance operates within the world of the play, from Romeo's fortuitous encounter with Capulet's servant to the detainment of Friar John. Indeed, Friar Lawrence himself points to the contingency when he exclaims, "Ah, what an unkind hour / Is guilty of this lamentable chance!" (V.iii.145-46).

The inconsistency posed by the operation of both Fortune and fate appears particularly acute in the death of Mercutio, an incident that abruptly alters the tone and direction of the play. The victim seems to blame his mortal wound on the feud: "A plague a' both houses! I am sped" (III.i.91). And the feud, as H. B. Charlton remarks, is "the means by which Fate acts."[37] The Prologue, of course, had earlier linked the feud with fate by the reference to "the fatal loins of these two foes." At the same time, there is undeniably an element of chance in Mercutio's death, for had Romeo not stepped between Mercutio and Tybalt, and had Tybalt not happened at that particular moment to stab his foe, Mercutio might never have been slain. Romeo's cry, after the killing of Tybalt, attributes his death to the mistress of chance: "O, I am fortune's fool!" (III.i.136).

It may be argued that in mingling Fortune and fate Shakespeare merely perpetuates the dualism of his source, Brooke's *Romeus and Juliet*. And Shakespeare's practice is hardly unique in Elizabethan literature: other poets and dramatists occasionally link Fortune and fate.[38] Moreover, Fortune had long been associated with the stars, themselves identified with fate. Willard Farnham explains how this came about: "the ancient world had made a natural association between the power of Fortune and the power of the stars. Fortune began to take prominent place as a deity at the same time that acceptance of Chaldean astrology spread through all ranks of men under Greco-Roman culture."[39] There were, then, precedents for the mixture of Fortune and fate. This does not, however, make the play any more satisfying aesthetically. The confusion felt by readers and spectators of *Romeo and Juliet* is genuine: characters speak repeatedly of determinism, yet incidents point to a world of contingency. As T. J. B. Spencer observes, "The verbal emphasis is frequently on fate; but the logic of the play seems to be, rather more than we should like, on chance."[40] How may this dissonance be explained?

Perhaps an explanation is to be found in Shakespeare's comparative youth when he wrote *Romeo and Juliet*. At that point, about 1595, he had little experience in writing tragedy. In adapting Brooke's poem to the stage, he sought to create an atmosphere that his audience would deem appropriate to tragedy. And so, in addition to suggesting the responsibility of the lovers for their plight, he included in his play the paraphernalia customarily associated with tragedy: premonitions, astral influence, invocations of fate and Fortune and the heavens—the kind of thing he parodies in the Pyramus and Thisbe episode of *A Midsummer Night's Dream* (also written about 1595). However, lacking the skill smoothly to combine such disparate materials, Shakespeare failed to subordinate them to a consistent vision. The result was what Clifford Leech calls "the casualness of the play's cosmology."[41]

The depiction of Fortune in the three love tragedies suggests that playwrights were familiar with pictorial representations of Fortune. And because those representations help us to understand Fortune's meaning in the drama, the next chapter treats Fortune's appearance in the visual arts.

NOTES TO CHAPTER 6

1. See T. J. B. Spencer, Introduction to *Elizabethan Love Stories* (Baltimore, Md.: Penguin Books, 1968), pp. 7-37; Max Bluestone, *From Story to Stage: The Dramatic Adaptation of Prose Fiction in the Period of Shakespeare and His Contemporaries* (The Hague and Paris: Mouton, 1974); Robert J. Clements and Joseph Gibaldi, "The Novella and the Elizabethan Drama," Appendix B of *Anatomy of the Novella: The European Tale Collection from Boccaccio and Chaucer to Cervantes* (New York: New York Univ. Press, 1977), pp. 232-41.

2. The names of the authors, indicated by initials appended to each of the five acts, are generally assumed to be: Roderick Stafford (I), Henry Noel (II), G. Al. (III), Christopher Hatton (IV), and Robert Wilmot (V).

3. See Irving Ribner, "Then I Denie You Starres: A Reading of *Romeo and Juliet*," in *Studies in the English Renaissance Drama in Memory of Karl Julius Holzknecht*, ed. Josephine W. Bennett et al. (New York: New York Univ. Press, 1959), pp. 269-86; Annette T. Rottenberg, "The Early Love Drama," *CE*, 23 (1962): 579-83. Leonora Leet Brodwin's treatment of *Gismond of Salerne*, in *Elizabethan Love Tragedy, 1587-1625* (New York and London: New York Univ. Press, 1971), does not deal with the relationship between the novella and the play.

4. William Painter, *The Palace of Pleasure* (London, 1566). Painter's translation of the story was probably available to the playwrights. John W. Cunliffe, however, in "Gismond of Salerne," *PMLA*, 21 (1906): 435-61, argues that they worked directly from the original Italian. In any case, Painter's translation adheres closely to the original; all of the quotations cited here have been checked against the Italian in Vittore Branca's edition of the *Decameron* (1960; reprint ed., Florence: Le Monnier, 1965).

5. Howard R. Patch discusses the medieval background of the topos in *The Goddess Fortuna in Mediaeval Literature* (1927; reprint ed., New York:

Octagon Books, 1974), "The Fortune of Love," pp. 90-98. Samuel C. Chew treats the iconographic expression of the topos in *The Pilgrimage of Life* (1962; reprint ed., Port Washington, N.Y. and London: Kennikat Press, 1973), pp. 44, 67-68.

6. See *Seneca: The Tragedies*, ed. and trans. Frank Justus Miller, LCL (1917; reprint ed., Cambridge, Mass.: Harvard Univ. Press, 1968), 2: 454, ll. 561-65.

7. *The Roman de la Rose: A Study in Allegory and Iconography* (Princeton: Princeton Univ. Press, 1969), p. 112.

8. Virtually all commentators on the play believe that the figure of Cupid was borrowed from Lodovico Dolce's *Didone* (Vinegia, 1547).

9. I have used the text edited by John W. Cunliffe, in *Early English Classical Tragedies* (Oxford: Clarendon Press, 1912).

10. In *The Tudor Play of Mind: Rhetorical Inquiry and the Development of Elizabethan Drama* (Berkeley and Los Angeles: Univ. of California Press, 1978), Joel B. Altman writes that the lovers "are presented between choruses as noble and innocent" (p. 259). This judgment seems too sweeping, for while Gismond and Guishard are poignant figures, the comments of both Lucrece and Tancred in the play proper qualify the lovers' innocence.

11. Aldo D. Scaglione, *Nature and Love in the Late Middle Ages* (Berkeley and Los Angeles: Univ. of California Press, 1963), pp. 81-82.

12 The general significance of Continental Senecan tragedy for the English stage is discussed by Cunliffe in his Introduction to *Early English Classical Tragedies*. The most comprehensive treatment of Senecan influence is that by H. B. Charlton, *The Senecan Tradition in Renaissance Tragedy* (Manchester: Manchester Univ. Press, 1946). (This study originally appeared as the Introduction to *The Poetical Works of William Alexander, Earl of Stirling*, ed. L. E. Kastner and H. B. Charlton, 2 vols. [Manchester: Manchester Univ. Press, 1921, 1929].) See also Frederick Kiefer, "Seneca's Influence on Elizabethan Tragedy: An Annotated Bibliography," *RORD*, 21 (1978): 17-34. It is possible that the Senecan quality of *Gismond of Salerne* may, in part, derive from an earlier Italian dramatization of the story, Antonio da Pistoia's *Filostrato e Panfila* (performed in 1499). In this earliest of Italian tragedies of romantic love, the ghost of Seneca speaks the prologue. Whether the English dramatists were familiar with *Filostrato e Panfila* is, however, uncertain. Marvin T. Herrick, *Italian Tragedy in the Renaissance* (Urbana: Univ. of Illinois Press, 1965), writes, "There is no evidence that the English authors knew Pistoia's play, but one wonders if they might have heard of it" (p. 32). Herbert G. Wright, less tenta-

tive than Herrick, suggests a number of resemblances between Pistoia's work and the English play, in *Ghismonda, A Seventeenth-Century Tragedy* (Manchester: Manchester Univ. Press, 1944), pp. 63-65.

13. *The Tragedy of Tancred and Gismund, 1591-92,* ed. W. W. Greg, MSR (Oxford: Oxford Univ. Press, 1914), sig. [*3]. This later version of the play differs in several respects from the original. When Wilmot rewrote *Gismond,* he substituted blank verse for rhyme, added more extensive stage directions and four dumb shows, gave the chorus a greater role, made more use of dialogue in place of set speeches, substituted Christian allusions for pagan, made Tancred a more sympathetic figure, and accentuated the moralizing of the earlier version. For comparisons between *Gismond of Salerne* and the revision, *Tancred and Gismund,* see David Klein, "'According to the Decorum of These Daies,'" *PMLA,* 33 (1918): 244-68; John Murray, "*Tancred and Gismund,*" *RES,* 14 (1938): 385-95; Herbert G. Wright, *Boccaccio in England from Chaucer to Tennyson* (London: Athlone Press, 1957), pp. 178-84; and Wright, *Ghismonda, A Seventeenth-Century Tragedy,* pp. 66-80.

14. Betty J. Littleton, in *Clyomon and Clamydes: A Critical Edition* (The Hague and Paris: Mouton, 1968), observes, "*Clyomon and Clamydes, Common Conditions,* and *The Rare Triumphs of Love and Fortune* are the only surviving representatives of a large group of romantic plays which were produced during the period from about 1570 to about 1585" (p. 53).

15. *Clyomon and Clamydes,* ed. W. W. Greg, MSR (Oxford: Oxford Univ. Press, 1913).

16. The treatment of Love and Fortune in the visual arts may have influenced the composition of *The Rare Triumphs.* Albrecht Dürer exemplifies accord between Love and Fortune in his composition known as "Das kleine Glück." The design, reproduced in Edgar Wind, *Giorgione's Tempesta, with Comments on Giorgione's Poetic Allegories* (Oxford: Clarendon Press, 1969), fig. 23, shows Fortune standing upon the globe symbolic of her inconstancy. But she steadies herself with a staff; and at the top of the staff appears an eryngium, a flower signifying love. Otho Vaenius (Octavio van Veen) chronicles an alliance between Love and Fortune in his *Amorum Emblemata* (Antwerp, 1608). Reprint ed. Stephen Orgel, New York and London: Garland, 1979. There Cupid and Fortune work together to drive away Envy (p. 107). Another of the emblems, however, portrays Fortune with one foot on her globe while she ties a scarf around Cupid's head; the looming figure of Fortune dominates the diminutive Cupid whose feet rest upon the globe (p. 157). Jean Cousin, in his *Liber Fortunae,* depicts Fortune sitting on her globe and holding

in her outstretched hand a clock. A reclining Cupid grasps his quiver and bow in one hand while he touches the clock with his other hand. A sense of quietude characterizes the emblem, even if the precarious balance of the clock suggests that the purposes of Love and Fortune may not always be congruent. See *The Book of Fortune, Two Hundred Unpublished Drawings [Liber Fortunae]*, ed. Ludovic Lalanne, trans. H. Mainwaring Dunstan (London and Paris: Librairie de l'art, 1883), pl. LXIX.

17. *An Edition of The Rare Triumphs of Love and Fortune*, ed. John Isaac Owen, Renaissance Drama: A Collection of Critical Editions (New York and London: Garland, 1979).

18. In "The Debate Element in the Elizabethan Drama," in *Anniversary Papers by Colleagues and Pupils of George Lyman Kittredge* (Boston and London: Ginn, 1913), James Holly Hanford writes that the "mythological contention" in Kyd's drama "must certainly have been suggested by that in *The Rare Triumphs*" (p. 450). Thelma N. Greenfield, in *The Induction in Elizabethan Drama* (Eugene: Univ. of Oregon Books, 1969), writes that the personifications and debate of *Soliman and Perseda* are "similar enough" to those of *The Rare Triumphs* "to suggest direct borrowing" (p. 48).

19. *Soliman and Perseda*, in *The Works of Thomas Kyd*, ed. Frederick S. Boas (Oxford: Clarendon Press, 1901).

20. For a discussion of Yver's work, see Henri Clouzot, "Le 'Printemps' d'Yver (1572)," *Revue du seizième siècle*, 18 (1931): 104-29.

21. The suggestion is made by Arthur Freeman, in *Thomas Kyd: Facts and Problems* (Oxford: Clarendon Press, 1967), p. 148.

22. *Studies in Iconology: Humanistic Themes in the Art of the Renaissance* (1939; reprint ed., New York: Harper and Row, 1972), p. 112.

23. *Petrarch's Lyric Poems: The Rime sparse and Other Lyrics*, ed. and trans. Robert M. Durling (London and Cambridge, Mass.: Harvard Univ. Press, 1976), poem 274, pp. 452-53.

24. The Fortune-Death topos, long expressed in the visual arts, perhaps influenced Kyd's play. A fifteenth-century German woodcut shows Death turning the wheel of Fortune (reproduced in Chew, fig. 145). Another German woodcut of about the same date depicts Fortune, on the left, turning a wheel on which are four figures in various stages of ascent and descent. As the wheel turns, the victims of Fortune fall into the grave that spans the center of the picture. Meanwhile, on the right, Death points his bow and arrow at the Tree of Life. For this representation, see Alfred Doren, "Fortuna im Mittelalter

und in der Renaissance," *Vorträge der Bibliothek Warburg*, ed. Fritz Saxl, 2 (1922-23), part 1, pl. V, fig. 13. Jean Cousin, in his *Liber Fortunae*, portrays Fortune and skeletal Death side by side (pl. CXCIX): Fortune stands with one foot on her globe and a hand on Death's arm. Death, in turn, grasps Fortune's wheel with one of his hands. The topos also appears in Elizabethan drama. For instance, a character in Samuel Daniel's *Cleopatra* (1594) speaks of "that inexorable Monster Death / That followes Fortune" (*The Complete Works in Prose and Verse of Samuel Daniel*, ed. Rev. Alexander B. Grosart [London: Hazell, Watson, and Viney (for the Spenser Society), 1885], 3: 86, ll. 1525-26). And in *The Weakest Goeth to the Wall* [c. 1599-1600], ed. W. W. Greg, MSR (Oxford: Oxford Univ. Press, 1912), a character, addressing Fortune, says: "thou would'st send / Death, to fill up the measure of thy spight" (ll. 971-72). See also Patch, "The Fortune of Death," in *The Goddess Fortuna in Mediaeval Literature*, pp. 117-20; and Chew, pp. 247-48.

25. *Shakespeare's Early Tragedies* (London: Methuen, 1968), p. 81.

26. In addition to the invocations of Dame Fortune, there are references to "fortune" in the middle of the play. Thus when the Nurse brings news of the marriage plan to her mistress, Juliet exclaims, "Hie to high fortune!" (II.v.78). And Friar Lawrence upbraids Romeo, saying, "like a mishaved and sullen wench, / Thou pouts upon thy fortune and thy love" (III.iii.143-44).

27. For a discussion of Shakespeare's sources, see Brian Gibbons, ed. New Arden *Romeo and Juliet* (London and New York: Methuen, 1980), pp. 32-42.

28. Cf. discussions of Fortune in the play by G. I. Duthie, ed., [with J. Dover Wilson] New Cambridge *Romeo and Juliet* (Cambridge: Cambridge Univ. Press, 1955), pp. xxii-xxiv; and John Lawlor, "*Romeo and Juliet*," in *Early Shakespeare*, Stratford-upon-Avon Studies 3 (London: Edward Arnold, 1961), 123-43.

29. Perhaps the best general discussion of Love and Death remains that by Edgar Wind, "Amor as a God of Death," in *Pagan Mysteries of the Renaissance*, rev. and enlarged ed. (London: Faber and Faber, 1958), pp. 129-41. See also Denis de Rougemont, "The Love of Death," in *Love in the Western World*, trans. Montgomery Belgion, rev. and augmented ed. (New York: Pantheon, 1956), pp. 42-46. Pictorial representations of Love and Death are treated by Horst W. Janson, "A 'Memento Mori' among Early Italian Prints," *JWCI*, 3 (1939-40): 243-48; and Chew, *Pilgrimage of Life*, pp. 190-92. For Shakespeare's treatment of Love and Death, see Norman Rabkin, "Eros and Death," in

Shakespeare and the Common Understanding (New York: Free Press, 1967), pp. 150-91; H. A. Mason, *Shakespeare's Tragedies of Love* (New York: Barnes and Noble, 1970), pp. 42-45; and Roger Stilling, *Love and Death in Renaissance Tragedy* (Baton Rouge: Louisiana State Univ. Press, 1976), pp. 67-81. See also Charles R. Forker, "The Love-Death Nexus in English Renaissance Tragedy," *ShakS*, 8 (1975): 211-30; and Theodore Spencer, *Death in Elizabethan Tragedy: A Study of Convention and Opinion in the Elizabethan Drama* (1936; reprint ed., New York: Pageant Books, 1960).

30. In "Shakespeare and 'Solyman and Perseda,'" *MLR*, 58 (1963): 481-87, an article that explores the dating of *Soliman and Perseda, Romeo and Juliet*, and *King John*, Arthur Freeman points out a number of structural parallels between Shakespeare's love tragedy and Kyd's. For Shakespeare's specific borrowings, see E. A. J. Honigmann, ed., New Arden *King John*, 4th ed. rev. (London: Methuen, 1954), p. xliv and notes to I.i.244 and II.i.75; and John Russell Brown, ed., New Arden *Merchant of Venice*, 7th ed. rev. (London: Methuen, 1955), note to II.i.25-26.

31. For a discussion of Michault's work, see M. l'Abbé Goujet, *Bibliothèque françoise, ou histoire de la littérature françoise* (Paris: Pierre-Jean Mariette and Hippolyte-Louis Guerin, 1745), 9: 345 ff.; and Howard R. Patch, "Fortuna in Old French Literature," *Smith College Studies in Modern Languages*, 4 (1923): 29-30. For the text of the poem, see Pierre Michault, *La Dance aux Aveugles, et autres poësies du XV siècle extraites de la bibliothèque des ducs de Bourgogne* (Lille: A. J. Panckoucke, 1748), pp. 1-118.

32. The illumination is reproduced by Panofsky, pl. XLVI, fig. 82. See also A. de Laborde, *La mort chevauchant un boeuf: origine de cette illustration de l'office des morts dans certains livres d'heures de la fin du XVe siècle* (Paris: Francisque Lefrançois [for the Librairie de la Société des Bibliophiles François], 1923), pls. VIII, IX, X, XI. The conjunction of Love, Fortune, and Death also sometimes appears in pictorial representations of Petrarch's *Triumphs*, a work that records this sequence of victories: Love, Chastity, Death, Fame, Time, and Eternity. Engravings of Chastity's triumph sometimes include Fortune as part of the design. Thus the viewer, looking at the first three in the series of engravings celebrating the triumphs, finds that his eye moves from Cupid to Fortune to Death. See Arthur M. Hind, *Early Italian Engraving: A Critical Catalogue with Complete Reproduction of All the Prints Described* (London: Bernard Quaritch [for M. Knoedler, N. Y.], 1938-48), 2: pl. 24. See also D. D. Carnicelli, ed., *Lord Morley's Tryumphes of Fraunces Petrarcke: The First English Translation of the Trionfi* (Cambridge, Mass.: Harvard Univ. Press, 1971), pp. 38-46.

33. *Shakespearian Tragedy* (London and New York: Cambridge Univ. Press, 1948), p. 51.

34. *Not Wisely but Too Well: Shakespeare's Love Tragedies* (San Marino, Calif.: Huntington Library, 1957), p. 95. Similarly, J. M. R. Margeson, in *The Origins of English Tragedy* (Oxford: Clarendon Press, 1967), writes: "The seeming opposition between fortune and providence in the play disappears in this final view of a world ruled by fortune and the evil passions of men, but subject in the long run to the laws established by providence" (p. 100).

35. *The Early Shakespeare* (San Marino, Calif.: Huntington Library, 1967), p. 206.

36. Introduction to the New Cambridge *Romeo and Juliet*, p. xviii.

37. *Shakespearian Tragedy*, p. 52.

38. For instance, in *The Mirror for Magistrates*, ed. Lily B. Campbell (1938; reprint ed., New York: Barnes and Noble, 1960), one speaker says: "Among the ryders of the rollyng wheele, / That lost theyr holdes, Baldwin forget not me, / whose fatall threede false Fortune nedes would reele, / Ere it were twysted by the systers three" (p. 82). Also, Fortune is linked with the Fates in *Old Fortunatus* (*The Dramatic Works of Thomas Dekker*, ed. Fredson Bowers, 1 [Cambridge: Cambridge Univ. Press, 1953]), where this stage direction appears: "*Enter* Fortune: *after her three* Destinies *working*" (II.ii.213).

39. *The Medieval Heritage of Elizabethan Tragedy* (1936; reprint ed., with corrections, Oxford: Basil Blackwell, 1970), p. 105.

40. Introduction to the New Penguin *Romeo and Juliet* (Baltimore, Md.: Penguin Books, 1967), p. 21. Not everyone, of course, is equally troubled by the inconsistency that Spencer notices. James H. Seward, in *Tragic Vision in Romeo and Juliet* (Washington, D. C.: Consortium Press, 1973), argues that both contingency and determinism in the play are really nothing more than the outcome of character. He writes that "chance which seems such an important element in the play, . . . is in one sense nothing more than an extension of character" (pp. 221-22). Similarly, "it would have been clear to an Elizabethan audience that the net which tightens around the lovers is one which they have woven for themselves and from which, should they choose, escape was always possible" (p. 223). H. A. Mason, in "Fate or Fortune?", the first chapter of his *Shakespeare's Tragedies of Love*, notes that Fortune is much less prominent in the play than in Brooke's poem, and he dismisses all talk of fatality by the characters: "all these scattered references to fate do not amount to very much . . ." (pp. 22-23).

41. "The Moral Tragedy of *Romeo and Juliet,*" in *English Renaissance Drama: Essays in Honor of Madeleine Doran and Mark Eccles,* ed. Standish Henning et al. (Carbondale and Edwardsville: Southern Illinois Univ. Press, 1976), p. 73.

Chapter 7

FORTUNE AND OCCASION

*A*RTISTS AND ARTISANS have, since antiquity, altered the portrayal of Fortune, but perhaps never more sharply than in the late fifteenth and early sixteenth centuries. During that period Fortune came to be represented with a sail and dolphin; she acquired accouterments that in antiquity had belonged to Occasion—forelock, razor, and wings; and she acquired a clock or hourglass as well. Concomitantly, people began to conceive of Fortune's nature in a strikingly new way; they came to regard her as a less menacing and more tractable figure than she seemed in the Middle Ages.[1] Since playwrights—as well as artists, philosophers, and poets—reflected in their work this new Fortune, we need to look closely at the iconographic changes that Fortune underwent in the Renaissance and the conceptual transformation that shaped them.

I

Medieval Fortune was, of course, depicted in a variety of ways, as Howard R. Patch and others have demonstrated.[2] But typically she was a regal figure, fully clothed, wearing a crown or hat, and turning a wheel on which men were arrayed in various stages of ascent and descent. In his major work on Fortune, Patch reproduces an illumination from the twelfth-century *Imago Mundi* which may be considered representative of Fortune's appearance in the Middle Ages (Patch, pl. 5). It shows a standing Fortune, who turns a wheel nearly as large as herself.

Fig. 4. The coat of arms of Giovanni Rucellai in the Palazzo Rucellai, Florence.

Four figures ride the wheel in the manner of the medieval formula: *regnabo, regno, regnavi, sum sine regno* (I shall reign, I reign, I have reigned, I am without reign). It is appropriate that the wheel should be so prominent in this and other depictions, since it was by far the most important accouterment belonging to Fortune in the Middle Ages. The wheel helped to dramatize man's vulnerability to sharp and devastating change, the lot of all who refused to abjure worldly possessions and

worldly aspirations. To underscore the need for man to embrace trans-
cendent values, medieval thinkers and artists often opposed Fortune to
some form of virtue.³ Thus in the manuscript illumination from the *Imago Mundi*, Fortune stands opposite a figure named Sapience.

From such representations, with their cautionary import, portrayals
of Fortune changed drastically during the latter part of the fifteenth century. These changed depictions are typified—and in some instances
probably inspired—by the impresa or coat of arms of the Florentine
merchant Giovanni Rucellai (fig. 4). The impresa is located in the court-
yard of the Palazzo Rucellai, designed by Leon Battista Alberti and
constructed in the late 1440s and early 1450s.⁴ Cut by Bernardo
Rosellino, the impresa depicts, above a shield and helmet, a nude
woman standing in a boat. As though she were the mast of the
vessel, she holds in her left hand the mainyard and in her right
the lower section of a sail inflated by the wind. And she wears a
forelock. This depiction would probably be recognizable to the
fifteenth-century viewer as Fortune, who was customarily associated
with the sea in antiquity (she usually held a rudder or prow, symbolic of
her capacity to direct the course of man's life)⁵ and in the Middle Ages,
which continued to find in the sea an apt symbol of Fortune's mercurial
nature. Nevertheless, Rucellai's impresa would almost certainly have
struck the contemporary observer as unusual both in design and
meaning.⁶

First, the nearly ubiquitous accouterment of Fortune in the Middle
Ages—the wheel—has been discarded. Its absence suggests that there is
nothing mechanical about the course of man's life, that he is not
necessarily bound to trace an arc from prosperity to adversity or
vice versa. The absence of the wheel, moreover, may signify that
Fortune's hegemony is not so absolute as had once been feared;
there is no figure in the impresa compelled to suffer or joy at the whim of
Fortune. Also, Fortune wears no crown and carries no orb of her
dominion. She is no forbidding matron but a youthful woman. Her attractiveness suggests that she is to be sought after rather than shunned,
although her swift movement renders her elusive.

The sail held by Rucellai's Fortune would also probably have struck
the observer as unusual, although it has its inspiration, ultimately, in antiquity. Cicero said of Fortune, "When we enjoy her favouring breeze,

we are wafted over to the wished for haven; when she blows against us, we are dashed to destruction."[7] And both Ovid (*Ex Ponto*, II.iii.21 ff.) and Seneca (*Hercules Oetaeus*, lines 692 ff.) liken Fortune to a breeze filling the sails of a ship. This association of Fortune with the wind made it natural that the sail should appear in her representations, although it is not certain that the sail of Rucellai's Fortune was directly inspired by classical precedent.[8] In Renaissance imprese a sail sometimes appears, independent of Fortune. In fact, Giovanni Rucellai employs an inflated sail alone on the facade of Santa Maria Novella and on other buildings.[9] Whatever its immediate inspiration, the sail, rare in ancient depictions of the goddess but commonplace by the sixteenth century, implies something important about man's relationship to Fortune. For if the wind represents Fortune, then the sail signifies man's capacity to adjust himself to her force.[10] Rucellai's impresa, then, suggests that man, like the mariner who speeds his voyage by hoisting or trimming his sail, can successfully tailor his conduct to circumstance.

This notion is underscored by the presence in the impresa of the forelock. This feature, so far as I can determine, was never part of Fortune's depiction in antiquity.[11] The forelock is unquestionably derived from the ancient embodiment of opportunity—Kairos in Greek, Occasio in Latin—who wore a forelock to symbolize the auspicious moment that the aspirant must grasp.[12] The forelock in Rucellai's impresa suggests that man can attune himself to the forces that Fortune represents and thereby prosper.

Collectively, the elements of the impresa suggest a Fortune very different in nature from that envisioned in the Middle Ages. In the impresa Fortune may be formidable, but not all-powerful; she is attractive but elusive, swift-moving but also potentially approachable; she may bring adversity but also pose challenges. Clearly, the "medieval" relationship to Fortune has been modified. The coat of arms is not meant to inculcate a fear of Fortune's might; nor is it intended to inspire a spiritual defiance of her power. Instead, it is meant to suggest that a kind of collaboration between man and Fortune is possible and desirable.

The inspiration for Rucellai's impresa may well have come from the traditional association of Fortune with sea and storm. In Italian the very word *fortuna* can signify a tempest. Thus Leonardo da Vinci, providing instructions for representing a storm, calls it *una fortuna*.[13] Of course, the designer of Rucellai's impresa may have been prompted by classical writers who speak of Fortune's resemblance to the wind. Or he may, as Aby Warburg has suggested, have found inspiration in a contemporary, such as the Florentine philosopher Marsilio Ficino. It is known that Rucellai corresponded with the eminent Neoplatonist, asking his opinion of man's relationship to Fortune. To what extent, Rucellai wondered, was it within man's power to counteract Fortune's caprice?

Ficino replied in a letter characterized chiefly by a spirit of resignation.[14] Although initially he acknowledges Rucellai's accomplishments and although he claims to be of two minds, Ficino finally argues that it is better to flee the struggle with Fortune altogether than to be overwhelmed in a contest in which few can prevail. And he offers the standard remedies for adversity: namely, the exercise of prudence and patience. However, Ficino also makes a significant allusion to Plato's *Laws*, in which the Greek philosopher ponders much the same question that vexed Rucellai: What forces govern man's life? Plato suggests three possible answers: (i) pure chance; (ii) chance and occasion co-operating with God in the control of human affairs; and (iii) man's skill in conjunction with these other forces. In this third suggestion, Plato introduces the image of a pilot directing the course of a vessel during a storm.[15] And Ficino, in his commentary on Plato's *Laws*, writes this of the third proposition:

> [When God] moves the sea by a storm and the storm rocks the ship, God also moves the ship through the mind of the pilot, that is, by the exercise of his skill which is continuously dependent on God. When the ship is therefore directed by skill to a certain harbor, and is also carried there by the storm, then skill is in perfect agreement with chance (*tunc ars simul cum fortuna consentit*).[16]

Edgar Wind, convinced of a connection between this passage and Ficino's allusion to Plato in the letter to Rucellai, comments: "It was surely with this argument in mind that Rucellai chose the nautical Fortuna as his emblem."[17]

Despite the significance of Ficino's allusion to Plato, Rucellai's impresa probably owes less to the Florentine philosopher and more to

Rucellai's own character than is generally supposed. For if that letter represents Ficino's most deeply held views on Fortune, then the coat of arms can scarcely be interpreted as a simple embodiment of his advice.[18] After all, Ficino concludes the epistle by recommending a life of contemplation and wisdom, a retreat into the inner self where Fortune cannot reach. In contrast, the coat of arms, especially by its sail and forelock, implies the pursuit of a vigorously active and even adventuresome life. And this, of course, is entirely in keeping with what we know of Giovanni Rucellai's career.[19] He made his way in a secular world and, as a successful merchant, took risks every day that exposed him to the adversity of Fortune. For such a man, Ficino's advocacy of caution cannot have been the ruling impulse—either in life or in the commissioning of a coat of arms. Rucellai's impresa, whatever it may owe to Ficino, is the creation of a self-reliant pragmatist. His Fortune may draw inspiration from traditional iconography and philosophy, but it is undeniably innovative in its implications for man and his place in the world.

II

The confidence in man's powers implicit in Rucellai's coat of arms had found even stronger expression in the work of Leon Battista Alberti, who believed that man should aggressively pursue worldly goals and could actually prevail over Fortune. In the Preface to his *Della famiglia* (1432-34), Alberti writes: "I see that many who have come to grief through their own stupidity blame Fortune and complain of being tossed about by her stormy waves, when the fools have actually cast themselves into them."[20] In Alberti's eyes, Fortune need not be feared: "So long as we assert our dominion and power over everything we do not choose to abandon to the whims of external forces, no one can say that uncertain and fickle Fortune has the power to consume and destroy."[21]

It may seem that Alberti's attitude toward Fortune would lead to a conflation with Occasion, for the concept of Occasion presumes that man possesses power to achieve success by choosing wisely and acting skillfully.[22] In my view, however, Alberti's sentiments, logically extended, would lead not so much to the transformation as to the obliteration of Fortune. For Alberti, at least in his Preface to *Della famiglia*, seems skeptical whether Fortune poses any real problem to the determined individual. What underlies the conflation with Occasion, however, is not the idea that Fortune is powerless, but rather that Fortune is potentially tractable, that man can, at least sometimes, wrest advantage from her mutability. In short, the conflation with Occasion rests upon the assumption that, while Fortune impinges upon him in powerful and perhaps dangerous fashion, man still has the capacity to decide how he will respond to change; and that his response may lead to self-aggrandizement. Such a world view assumes a Fortune more formidable than Alberti's, but less so than Ficino's. And such a view, which strikes a balance between self-determination and fatalism, finds its most cogent expression in the work of another Florentine thinker, Niccolò Machiavelli, who more than any other individual articulated a concept of Fortune that facilitated the conflation with Occasion.

Machiavelli's best-known pronouncements about Fortune appear in the twenty-fifth chapter of *The Prince* (c. 1513). There he displays, not unlike Ficino, a healthy respect for Fortune's capacity to inflict adversity. However, while at times nearly resigned to Fortune's caprice, he draws back from any thoroughgoing fatalism, sharply demarcating the scope of Fortune's power: "in order not to annul our free will, I judge it true that Fortune may be mistress of one half our actions but that even she leaves the other half, or almost, under our control."[23] By way of explanation, Machiavelli enlists this metaphor:

> I compare Fortune with one of our destructive rivers which, when it is angry, turns the plains into lakes, throws down the trees and the buildings, takes earth from one spot, puts it in another; everyone flees before the flood; everyone yields to its fury and nowhere can repel it. (p. 90)

Man's freedom of will, however, allows him to adopt countermeasures:

> Yet though such it is, we need not therefore conclude that when the weather is quiet, men cannot take precautions with both embankments and dykes, so that when the waters rise, either they go

off by a canal or their fury is neither so wild nor so damaging. The same things happen about Fortune. She shows her power where strength and wisdom do not prepare to resist her, and directs her fury where she knows that no dykes or embankments are ready to hold her. (p. 90)

That Machiavelli should liken Fortune to a river, rather than the sea, is most unusual. It seems reasonable to suppose that he chose this comparison because a river conveys, better than the sea, a sense of Fortune's limitations and thus man's capacity to avert the ravages of Fortune.[24]

It is, of course, not merely avoidance of Fortune's adversity (so far as possible) that Machiavelli counsels, for he also believes that men can actually prevail over circumstance. This assumption is apparent in the second comparison he draws — of Fortune to a woman with whom man struggles:

it is better to be impetuous than cautious, because Fortune is a woman and it is necessary, in order to keep her under, to cuff and maul her. She more often lets herself be overcome by men using such methods than by those who proceed coldly; therefore always, like a woman, she is the friend of young men, because they are less cautious, more spirited, and with more boldness master her. (p. 92)

The qualities which allow man to succeed, Machiavelli subsumes in the term *virtù*, a word he neglects to delimit with precision. *Virtù* has been interpreted as meaning, singly or in combination, ability, power, forcefulness, industry, valor, strength, energy, foresight, self-discipline, fortitude, determination, and decisiveness.[25] The term is elusive because Machiavelli uses it in widely differing contexts. Moreover, he often counterposes it to the word Fortune, which may also convey different meanings. Depending on the context, Fortune may signify not merely contingency and the incalculable element in life, but also the whole world of circumstance within which man moves.

Machiavelli's concept of man's relationship to Fortune, Allan H. Gilbert has suggested, may be understood by considering an iconographic counterpart: an early sixteenth-century woodcut. The design portrays Fortune seated on a sphere and holding in her hand a wheel to which four figures cling. Opposite her sits Sapientia, in her hand a mirror, symbolizing self-knowledge, and beneath her a square block to indicate her constancy. According to Gilbert, the woodcut "illustrates Machiavelli's conception of Fortune and Wisdom or Virtue as it appears throughout *The Prince*, especially in chapter 25."[26] Undoubtedly, Gilbert is correct in suggesting that the ancient antinomy between Fortuna and Virtus helped to shape Machiavelli's formulation.[27] But I do not think that the pictorial design corresponds very closely to the ideas set forth in *The Prince,* for the static rendering of the woodcut fails to express the dynamic relationship that, in Machiavelli's view, exists between man and Fortune. The woodcut does not convey either Fortune's susceptibility to human endeavor or the nature of the qualities that render her pliant.

A certain pageant, performed in Rome in January 1501, seems to Sydney Anglo a more apt iconographic counterpart to Machiavelli's thought. The pageant presents a conflict between Fortuna and Virtus, but in very different terms from the woodcut just described. According to a letter recounting the entertainment, Fame awards *virtù* the prize over Fortune, "saying that Cesare and Ercole (Caesar and Hercules) by *virtù* had overcome Fortune; thereupon he described a number of the heroic deeds performed by the illustrious Duke of Romagna."[28] Subsequently, Fortune is sent by Juno to attack Hercules, is overcome, and is released only when she promises never to "do anything which might injure the house of Ercole or that of Cesare Borgia." What is striking about this pageant is not the assumption that Fortune can be vanquished, but rather the conception of the attributes responsible for victory. In Anglo's words, "*Virtù* has shed all its contemplative connotations and its association with moral virtues"; here, *virtù* signifies "simply military prowess and strength of arms."[29] Similarly, Machiavelli in *The Prince* uses the term *virtù* not usually in a moral sense, but in the ancient Roman sense of manliness. For him, *virtù* signifies secular qualities primarily. Thus he conceives of the struggle with Fortune not as a spiritual contest, requiring the practice of self-denial, detachment, and restraint, as did Seneca or, for that matter, Ficino, but rather as a worldly conflict requiring entirely different qualities.

Joseph Anthony Mazzeo suggests some of these when he writes that *virtù* denotes "the power of constant adaptability to circumstances, the power to operate in conditions which men are not responsible for and on realities which they did not bring into being."[30] *Virtù*, then, presupposes flexibility together with boldness. What is needed to prevail against Fortune is not a retreat into the fortress of the mind, but rather a readiness to respond quickly and decisively to circumstance, a willingness to pursue aggressively any opening. Essentially, what Machiavelli advocates is a presence of mind, force of will, and adroitness of action sufficient to recognize and exploit the vagaries of Fortune.

Machiavelli's delineation of the relationship between *virtù* and Fortune may call to mind the ancient Roman adage, "Fortuna audentes juvat" ("Fortune favors the bold"), revived with some frequency during the late fifteenth and the sixteenth centuries. Indeed, a contemporary of Machiavelli's, Giovanni Pontano, in his *De Fortuna* bases his concept of the *fortunati* upon it.[31] For Pontano, the *fortunati* are men who let impulse be their guide and who are invariably favored by Fortune. Despite some similarity between their philosophies, however, it would be inaccurate to claim that Pontano's view coincides with Machiavelli's. In Machiavelli's view, success is not usually dependent simply on being naturally lucky. To a much greater extent than Pontano, Machiavelli stresses the active exercise of *virtù* in securing a goal; he insists that man must react to changing circumstance with all the ingenuity and energy he commands. Felix Gilbert observes: "In contrast to the static quality inherent in the belief in the existence of *Fortuna*'s elect, Machiavelli's formulation presumed the dynamism of a constantly changing scene in which sudden action can bring about the assistance of *Fortuna*."[32]

Machiavelli, then, believes that Fortune provides man not with an irreversible situation, but rather with possibilities that he must exploit. As he writes in chapter six of *The Prince*, in a discussion of Cyrus and other princes who gained power through their own ability, "on inspecting their actions and their lives, we see that they had from Fortune nothing more than opportunity [*l'occasione*], which gave them matter into which they could introduce whatever form they chose" (p. 25). Admittedly, without at least potentially favorable circumstance, a man cannot prevail. But unless he energetically utilizes his capabilities, he will not succeed: "without opportunity, their strength of will [*virtù*] would have been wasted, and without such strength the opportunity would have been useless."[33]

Machiavelli does not actually conflate Fortune and Occasion in *The Prince*, but in his undated poem, the "Capitolo di Fortuna," he closely links the two.[34] The poem, which sums up much of his thinking about Fortune, describes Fortune's palace. There one finds, not a single wheel of Fortune, but an extraordinary series of wheels: "Within her palace, as many wheels are turning as there are varied ways of climbing to those things which every living man strives to attain" (61-63). Each individual may choose the wheel he would mount, but having committed himself, he may easily fall prey to Fortune's caprice, for she may reverse the wheel in midcircle. The sheer number of wheels, however, offers at least the prospect of escaping sudden reversal; if one could only study Fortune's behavior and never lose sight of her wiliness, he "could leap from wheel to wheel" and "always be happy and fortunate" (116-17).

The tension between the desire to diminish one's vulnerability to circumstance and the knowledge that one can never fully achieve such a goal characterizes the allegorical tableau which unfolds as Machiavelli describes the inhabitants of Fortune's palace. The identities and activities of these figures recall attributes and values formulated elsewhere in Machiavelli's works. His discussion of *virtù* in *The Prince*, for example, is recalled by these lines: "Among the strange and varied crowd of fellow servants whom that building holds, Audacity and Youth make the highest showing" (73-75). If success favors the bold, disaster waits upon the hesitant and timorous: "We see Anxiety prostrate on the floor, so full of fears that he does nothing; then Penitence and Envy make war on him" (76-78). Among those who inhabit Fortune's palace only one figure thrives. And she not only prospers but even revels in the challenge posed by Fortune's wheels: "Here Opportunity [l'Occasione] alone finds sport, and always frisking about among the wheels is that tousel-haired and simple maiden" (79-81). In these lines Machiavelli expresses a doctrine implicit in *The Prince* and in his histories: namely, that only one who nimbly and vigorously seizes the propitious moment whenever it presents itself will prosper in an uncertain and dangerous world. Clearly, Machiavelli suggests that Fortune represents not a source of ready-made blessings or ineluctable afflictions, but rather a profusion of challenges. As such, Fortune resembles Occasion herself.

III

Despite the celebrity of his works, even Machiavelli's qualified optimism must have seemed too bold to some contemporaries. Indeed, two of his friends, Francesco Vettori and Francesco Guicciardini (especially in his later years) both came to doubt man's capacity to prevail over circumstance.[35] Neither, therefore, was as inclined as Machiavelli to align Fortune with Occasion. Nevertheless, confidence in man's *virtù* appears to have gained in the later fifteenth and early sixteenth centuries in Italy. The near conflation of Fortune and Occasion, implicit in Machiavelli's writings, has its counterpart in the myriad engravings, medals, and other artistic representations of the time. Many of these seem related in design to Rucellai's coat of arms. And, like it, they evoke a Fortune very different from that envisioned in the Middle Ages.

Two Florentine engravings by an unknown hand and dating from 1465-80 typify the break with medieval representations of Fortune.[36] Both depict Fortune without clothing, without crown, and without a wheel. As in Rucellai's coat of arms, Fortune floats above the waves of the sea. Here, however, she does not appear in a vessel. Instead, in one of the engravings, Fortune stands upon a dolphin. And in both, Fortune holds a sail inflated by the breeze, blown by a wind-cherub.

To account for the presence of the sail and dolphin in such engravings, scholars postulate a conflation with the Venus Marina, who was also depicted nude, standing upon a dolphin, and holding a sail. According to John Doebler, for instance, Fortune owes her sail to sea-born Venus: "The sail is a curious development of the draperies associated with the birth of Venus in the sea. Fortune is an alluring woman and thus conflated with Venus as an ideal of feminine beauty."[37] And Guy de Tervarent attributes the dolphin in representations of Fortune to confusion with the Venus Marina.[38] Unquestionably, Doebler, Tervarent, and others are correct in detecting confusion between Fortune and the sea-born Venus.[39] However, Fortune's acquisition of the sail and dolphin would never have become so popular were it not for the conflation with Occasion.

In antiquity, as we have seen, Fortune's association with the sea and with ships was commonplace. Horace in his *Odes* (I.35.6) calls Fortune "empress of the ocean," and other classical authors compare Fortune with the breezes that fill the sails of a vessel. Nevertheless, the sail itself was evidently not a customary part of Fortune's iconography until the Renaissance. Vincenzo Cartari, in *Le imagini con la spositione de i dei de gli antichi* (Venice, 1556), writes of Fortune: "Adunque oltre alli disegni fatti della Fortuna trovo che alcuni l'hanno dipinta in mare far vela tra le turbate onde. . . . E credo che queste siano state dipinture moderne, perche non ne trovo fatta mentione da gli antichi . . ." (sigs. AA4^{r-v}). It is no accident that the sail should have become associated with Fortune in the same period when Fortune's conflation with Occasion occurred. For, as we have seen, the sail suggests that man has the capacity to take advantage of forces in his environment. The connection between the sail and the idea of opportunity is evident in Giulio Cesare Capaccio's *Delle imprese* (Naples, 1592). One of his designs juxtaposes two Fortunes: on the left, Fortune is characterized by a waving forelock and a billowing sail; on the right, Fortune has a drooping forelock and a rent sail (Book III, fol. 19). Plainly, Capaccio means to identify the sail with opportunity won and lost.

Although the dolphin is less obviously linked with Occasion, there are several points of correspondence between the two. First, since antiquity the dolphin had been recognized as an extraordinarily swift creature. Thus in the famous device of the Aldine press, the dolphin is counterposed to the anchor.[40] Second, the dolphin may represent a phenomenon which makes its appearance to man only under certain conditions. According to tradition, the dolphin appeared on the surface of the sea as tempests began. Giovanni Pierio Valeriano Bolzani writes in *Les Hieroglyphiques* (Lyons, 1615), a work originally published in Latin in 1556: "le Dauphin est un infallible prejugé de la tempeste à-venir," for as warm water rises from the bottom of a turbulent sea, the dolphin rises in a search for cooler water (p. 341). Finally, although the dolphin may be associated with the adversity of a tempest, the dolphin also represents, potentially, a friend of man. From ancient times, stories circulated about the dolphin's penchant for rescuing mariners in distress. To quote Valeriano again, "cest animal s'est maintes fois offert de son plein gré pour rendre service à des personnes qui se trouvoyent en extreme peril de leur vie" (p. 340). Given, then, the dolphin's swiftness, variability, and friendliness, it is not surprising that the sea creature should become a common feature of Fortune's iconography as Fortune came increasingly to represent opportunity.

There is something else as well about many representations of Fortune with sail and dolphin that suggests a link with Occasion: namely, the artistic treatment of Fortune's hair. Several Italian medals, dating from around 1500 and attributed to Niccolò Fiorentino, portray Fortune with dolphin and sail — and with her hair disheveled in a most peculiar fashion by the wind.[41] The hair, which seems to fly outward from her head, probably represents an intermediary stage between the traditional hairstyle worn by Fortune (hair combed and sometimes braided: fig. 6) and the depiction of Fortune with a forelock. Other medals of the early sixteenth century depict Fortune with an unmistakable forelock (Hill, nos. 532, 599).

As the representations cited above suggest, the late fifteenth and early sixteenth centuries were a period of considerable experimentation in the portrayal of Fortune. And at times a single engraver might depict Fortune in strikingly different ways. A case in point is the Florentine artisan Nicoletto da Modena (active 1500-12). One of his engravings, similar to those discussed above, presents a nude Fortune amid the waves, riding a dolphin, and holding a sail (Hind, 6: pl. 683, fig. 84). Another engraving also shows Fortune floating on the waves, but instead of riding a dolphin Fortune rests upon her ancient accouterments, one foot on a sphere (symbolic of her mutability and dominion), the other on a rudder (pl. 651, fig. 24). Around her body billows not a sail, but a sail-like veil or cloak. And cradled against her right arm is a staff at the top of which appears a head sporting a prominent forelock. Clearly, Modena has equipped Fortune with her classical appurtenances. Equally clearly, he is working toward a new way of representing Fortune, for the forelock is unmistakably allied with Occasion. The conflation of Fortune and Occasion may not be fully accomplished here, but the viewer senses that such a conflation is imminent.

What lies behind engravings like Modena's is, of course, a conceptual development: the growing conviction that what happens to a man in this world depends to a considerable extent on his own decisions and deeds rather than on some purely external force acting upon him. Significantly, when Vincenzo Cartari introduces a discussion of Occasion in his chapter on Fortune, he does so by speaking of man's responsibility for his fate: "Percioche quando al male ci appigliamo di tutte le disaventure, che ci intravengono poi habbiamo da dolerci della dapochezza nostra, e del nostro poco vedere, non della Fortuna, come mostrarono pur'anche gli antichi nella imagine della Occasione, laquale fanno alcuni essere una medesima con la Fortuna . . ." (sigs. AA2^{r-v}). That some writers should in the mid 1550s think Fortune the same as Occasion testifies to how profoundly attitudes had changed since the middle of the preceding century.

It was not, however, books of mythography like Cartari's which were responsible for the conflation of Fortune and Occasion. Those works, after all, were printed when the conflation was already well advanced; Lilius Gregorio Gyraldus' *De Deis Gentium* appeared in 1548, Natale Conti's *Mythologiae* in 1551. Nor do these compilations contain evidence of a significant contribution on the part of the authors to the evolution of a new Fortune. Instead, such creativity is evident in the Renaissance emblem book, the development of which in the 1530s helped to accelerate the conflation with Occasion. Emblem books, which combined pictures, mottoes, and poems, enjoyed enormous popularity and were widely disseminated in Europe. Designers of emblems freely borrowed from one another, thus making available to their readers new artistic treatments of old subjects. And one of the favorite topoi was Fortune, who in the emblem books gradually took on virtually all the features of the classical Occasion.

The first emblem book, Andrea Alciati's *Viri Clarissimi . . . Emblematum Liber* (published in Augsburg in 1531, but apparently ready for the press a decade earlier) does not include a depiction of Fortune but does portray Occasion (fig. 5), who wears a forelock and carries a razor, which in antiquity evidently symbolized the "narrowness" of the

Fig. 5. Andrea Alciati,
Viri Clarissimi . . .
Emblematum Liber

auspicious instant, the edge of the moment between opportunity approaching and opportunity past (sig. A8). In other emblem books Fortune frequently acquires both forelock and razor. Sometimes, however, the acquisition of one of these symbols occurs between successive editions of a single work. For instance, the 1539 Paris edition of Guillaume de la Perrière's *Le Théâtre des bons engins* includes two representations of Fortune, one of which is meant to exemplify the folly of allowing oneself to be guided by Fortune, the other her indifference to merit (emblems XX and XXIX). In neither emblem does Fortune wear a forelock, but in the 1549 Lyons edition, Fortune has a forelock in both. (Usually in the emblem books Fortune—like the classical Occasion—

Fig. 6. Achille Bocchi, Symbolicarum Quaestionum (p. cxxx)

has, behind the forelock, a bald head to symbolize the aspirant's inability to recover an auspicious moment once past.)

A single edition of an emblem book may include several representations of Fortune, some traditional, others innovative. For instance, one of the engravings by Giulio Bonasone in Achille Bocchi's *Symbolicarum Quaestionum . . . Libri Quinque* (Bologna, 1555) depicts Fortune as a fully clothed matron (fig. 6), holding a rudder in one hand and a cornucopia in the other (p. cxxx); the design is obviously inspired by Roman statues of the goddess. But another engraving shows a nude Fortune (fig. 7) whom Industry lifts from the waves (p. ciiii). This Fortune, with her forelock, her veil, and dolphin in the sea behind her, unmistakably belongs to the Renaissance.

Fig. 7. Achille Bocchi, Symbolicarum Quaestionum (p. ciiii)

In Principio Fabricii's *Delle allusione, imprese, et emblemi* (Rome, 1588), Fortune not only wears a forelock but also carries a razor (Book III, p. 179). Similarly, a design in Giulio Cesare Capaccio's *Delle imprese* (Naples, 1592) portrays Fortune standing on her sphere, wearing a forelock, and carrying the razor in her outstretched hand (Book III, fol. 58ᵛ). Renaissance emblematists and mythographers interpret the razor of Occasion in a bewildering variety of ways. Alciati, in his *Emblematum Liber*, cites the classical epigram of Posidippus: "In dextra est tenuis dic unde novacula? acutum / Omni acie hoc signum me magis esse docet" (sig. A8ᵛ). Geoffrey Whitney in *A Choice of Emblemes* (Leyden, 1586) accounts for the implement of Occasion (fig. 8) this way: "Why doest thou houlde a rasor in thy hande? / *That men maie knowe I cut on*

Fig. 8. Geoffrey Whitney, A Choice of Emblemes

everie side, / And when I come, I armies can devide" (p. 181). La Perrière in
Le Théâtre des bons engins (Paris, 1539) writes: "Et que tient elle? ung
rasoir en sa main. / Pourquoy? pourtant que tout tranche soubdain"
(sig. I5). And Cesare Ripa in his *Iconologia* (Siena, 1613) explains: "Tiene
il rasoio in mano, perche deve essere subito a troncare ogni sorte
d'impedimento" (Part 2, p. 105). In these explanations the Renaissance
iconographers demonstrate their powers rather of ingenuity than
of understanding.

In the emblem books, Fortune also increasingly acquires a feature
which she possessed infrequently in antiquity and in the Middle Ages —
wings. To be sure, the wings are not exclusively due to the conflation
with Occasion, for both the classical Victory and Nemesis, with whom
Fortune was sometimes confused, also wore wings.[42] Among classical
authors, moreover, both Horace (*Odes*, I.34.15) and Plutarch ("On the
Fortune of the Romans," 318) speak of Fortune herself as having wings;
the wings suggest Fortune's swiftness, her fleeting quality. Nevertheless,
relatively few representations of winged Fortune are extant before the
Renaissance. And it is probably no coincidence that, as the conflation
with Occasion advanced, the depiction of Fortune with wings became
more common. An engraving by the "Master of 1515" (probably Agos-
tino Busti, called il Bambaia) portrays Fortune standing upon a winged
sphere.[43] And an emblem that appears in Hadrianus Junius' *Emblemata*
(Antwerp, 1565) depicts Fortune herself as winged and standing on a
sphere (emblem XXVI). A winged Fortune, who holds in her hands a
sail, also appears in Achille Bocchi's *Symbolicarum Quaestionum* (p.
cxxxvi). And in both of La Perrière's emblems, discussed above,
Fortune has wings.

Even this brief survey of the emblem literature reveals that the distinction between Fortune and Occasion was blurred if not obliterated altogether by the middle of the sixteenth century. And to the materials already assembled the following evidence may be added. The motto above
La Perrière's representation of Occasion (fig. 9) in his 1549 *Le Théâtre des
bons engins* reads: "Ne refusons Fortune, quand à nous se presente"
(emblem LXIII). One of the emblems in Bocchi's *Symbolicarum Quaestionum* depicts Occasion clinging to the wheel of Fortune (p. cxlvi). The
mythographer Valeriano in *Les Hieroglyphiques*, discussing the sphere
and wheel which appear in so many representations of Fortune, writes:

*Ne refuſons Fortune, quand à
nous ſe preſente.*

Fig. 9. Guillaume de la Perrière, Le Théâtre des bons engins

"Il est donc certain que la boule & la rouë sont l'hieroglyphique de la volubilité, ce que l'on cognoit par un gentil epigramme Grec de Posidippe touchant l'Occasion, laquelle exerce quasi une mesme function que la Fortune" (p. 515). And the emblematist Jacobus Typotius, who in one design of his *Symbola Divina et Humana* (Prague, 1642) depicts a nude woman standing on a sphere, holding a sail, and wearing a forelock, speaks of "fortunam vel occasionem in pila volubili" (I, 129) — "Fortune or Occasion on a spinning ball."

Such identifications of one personification with another may well lead the modern reader to wonder whether the emblematists truly distinguished any longer between Fortune and Occasion. Since most emblem books do not present separate representations of the two, it is difficult to arrive at a firm conclusion. However, Gilles Corrozet's *Hecatomgraphie* (Paris, 1543), an early emblem book that contains emblems both of Fortune and of Occasion, does provide an answer of sorts. Corrozet differentiates the two, but he does so in such a way that a fundamental similarity between Fortune and Occasion is (perhaps unconsciously) affirmed.

Corrozet's Fortune (fig. 10) lacks the most distinctive accouterments of Occasion: the forelock, razor, and wings. Nevertheless, his Fortune is clearly a creation of the Renaissance: the nude figure floats above the waves, one foot on a dolphin, the other on a sphere. Around her billows a veil, while wind-cherubs appear at the upper corners of the design (sig. F7ᵛ). Corrozet evidently conceives of Occasion (fig. 11) as a different personification, for she has a forelock, winged feet, and, beneath her, a wheel that lies flat (sig. M2ᵛ). (The wheel derives from the famous poem by Ausonius, who describes Occasion as standing upon a wheel to indicate her instability.) However, although Corrozet means to distinguish the two symbols, there remains an essential similarity, for Occasion too floats above the waves — though in a boat — and holds in her hands a sail. Since mythographers prior to the sixteenth century had not given Occasion a boat and sail, it would appear that these features are derived from Fortune, who had been and continued to be associated with ships at sea.[44]

There is something else too, admittedly more tenuous, that links Corrozet's Occasion with Fortune, and that is the resemblance of his emblem to a much earlier engraving of Fortune (c. 1460-70), sometimes

Lymage de Fortune.

Fortune eſt vn euenement
Inopiné & treſſoubdain,
Ne luy donne doncques (mondain)
Effect deſſus toy nullement.

Fig 10. Fortune in Gilles Corrozet, Hecatomgraphie

L'ymage d'occaſion.

Haſte toy bien toſt d'attrapper
L'occaſion quand el' f'auance,
Sy tu la laiſſes eſchapper
Tu en feras la pœnitence.

Fig. 11. Occasion in Gilles Corrozet, Hecatomgraphie

attributed to Baccio Baldini. The Florentine engraving shows Fortune standing in the middle of a vessel and holding a sail into which wind gods are blowing (Hind, 2: pl. 6). This Fortune, who seems rather masculine in appearance, was probably meant to represent Bernardo Rucellai (son of Giovanni), who in 1466 married Nannina de' Medici (granddaughter of Cosimo); Nannina is represented by the woman who sits in the stern of the vessel.[45] Corrozet, for his part, also portrays a woman in his emblem of Occasion; she sits in the stern and represents Penitence, who in Ausonius' epigram is said to accompany Occasion. And as in the "impresa amorosa," the woman in the emblem sits to the (viewer's) left of the figure holding the sail. Since there was, so far as I can discover, no depiction of Occasion and Penitence in a boat prior to Corrozet's, one wonders if the unusual Florentine rendering of Fortune inspired his depiction. Whether or not the French emblematist was indebted to the Italian engraving, it would appear that while Corrozet intended to distinguish between Fortune and Occasion, he demonstrated an essential similarity by placing both upon the sea.

A consideration of Corrozet's emblems indicates that while Fortune underwent a transformation in the Renaissance, so too did Occasion. The latter's identification with the sea, so much a part of Corrozet's conception, was a creation of the Renaissance. Interestingly, the very first emblem book, Alciati's *Emblematum Liber*, portrays Occasion against the background of the sea, and this association remained common throughout the history of the emblem book; often a ship or ships appear behind Occasion herself. This method of representation probably came about because the tide was recognized as an apt expression of Occasion. That is, seizing the tide was regarded as parallel to the idea of seizing the forelock. Like the forelock, the tide represents the swiftly moving forces in man's environment which offer possibilities for gain. And, like the forelock, the tide cannot be easily recovered once it is past.

This association of Occasion with the sea is an important development because it suggests that the significance of the sea in representations of Fortune may be broader than initially appears. That is, the sea of Fortune signifies not only Fortune's variability and her power, but also her cyclicity, her penchant for providing man with periodically favorable conditions. The notion that Fortune's tide can and should be seized by the capable to win prosperity is implicit in Gabriel Rollenhagen's *Selectorum Emblematum, Centuria Secunda* (Utrecht, 1613); engravings by Crispijn van de Passe. Here Fortune (fig. 12) holds in her hand a crescent moon, which suggests control over the tides (emblem 40); the motto is "Fortuna ut Luna" ("Fortune is like the Moon"). Fortune's other accouterments are nearly all related to the idea of seizing opportunity: she floats upon the sea, stands on a winged sphere, holds a veil or cloak that billows in the wind, and wears a forelock. Moreover, in the background appear ships under sail. Such representations suggest that the sea symbolizes not merely Fortune's mutability but also her accessibility and her potentially favorable attitude toward human endeavor.

Fig. 12.
Gabriel Rollenhagen,
Selectorum
Emblematum,
Centuria Secunda

IV

Those Renaissance thinkers who were convinced of man's capacity for wresting advantage from Fortune not surprisingly responded enthusiastically to the ancient Roman adage that each man is the maker of his own fortune. Francis Bacon, for example, begins his essay "Of Fortune" by saying, "It cannot be denied, but outward accidents conduce much to fortune; favour, opportunity, death of others, occasion fitting virtue. But chiefly, the mould of a man's fortune is in his own hands. *Faber quisque fortunae suae*, saith the poet [Plautus]."[46] This notion also found expression in Renaissance emblem books. Thus Guillaume de la Perrière interprets the topos in *La Morosophie* (Lyons, 1553) by depicting a man carving with mallet and chisel the figure of Fortune (fig. 13) on a tablet (emblem 78). Interestingly, this cannot be mistaken for a medieval Fortune. Like so many of the figures allied with Occasion and discussed above, this Fortune is nude and carries a sail.

If man is the maker of his fortune, then it follows logically that he cannot presume upon Fortune: in adversity he cannot hope to ride Fortune's wheel passively to prosperity; and in prosperity he certainly cannot assume Fortune's continued favor. In a world where man bears considerable responsibility for his fate, any absolute dependence upon Fortune is useless. As Machiavelli writes in *The Prince*, "any prince who relies exclusively on Fortune falls when she varies" (p. 90). Furthermore, "a prince succeeds who adapts his way of proceeding to the nature of the times, and conversely one does not succeed whose procedure is out of harmony with the times."

Machiavelli's words underscore the importance of timing for one who would prevail in a relentlessly challenging world. It is self-evident, Machiavelli would say, that not all times are equally propitious. And since it is man's endeavor that may chiefly determine his success, it is crucial that he choose the proper moment for action. For Machiavelli and for others who came to share his views, *when* man acts is scarcely less urgent than *that* he acts.

This recognition of the essential role of timing helps to explain why the Renaissance added a new meaning to the classical adage, "Fortune favors the bold." Nearly all Renaissance pictorial representations of the

Fig. 13. Guillaume de la Perrière, La Morosophie

topos portray Fortune with a forelock and sail. For instance, in Girolamo Ruscelli's *Le imprese illustri* (Venice, 1566), Fortune stands upon a
sphere, holds a sail, and wears a forelock (Book II, p. 92). Beneath her
feet are the words "Audaces juvo." An emblem in Florentius Schoonho-
vius' *Emblemata* (Gouda, 1618) shows Fortune with one foot on a
sphere, the other on a wheel; she wears a forelock and holds a veil or
cloak which billows out toward two suppliants (emblem V). In the accompanying poem appear the words, "Audentes Fortuna juvo." And
Jacobus Typotius in *Symbola Divina et Humana* (Prague, 1642) portrays
Fortune with a sail, while each of her feet rests upon a dolphin; once
again she wears a forelock (II, 98). The motto reads, "Audaces Fortuna
Juvat." Such emblems suggest that while Fortune may favor the bold,
nevertheless the aspirant must manifest his boldness by aggressively
seizing the propitious moment.

In view of the importance of timing for those who hope to profit from
Fortune, it is readily understandable that symbols relating to time
should appear in Renaissance representations of Fortune.[47] Thus, for instance, a sixteenth-century Italian woodcut of Fortune's castle depicts,
at the summit, a nude Fortune carrying her sail.[48] To her immediate left
flies a winged Father Time, holding an hourglass. An emblem in Jean
Cousin's *Liber Fortunae* illustrates Fortune's connection with time by
means of the Love-Fortune topos. Here, sitting opposite Cupid, Fortune holds in her hand a clock; the motto reads, "Fortuna et Amor.
Tempus et Locus" ("Fortune and Love. The time and the place").[49] A
painting by Hans Schäufelin, a student of Dürer, represents a very different illustration of Fortune's association with time.[50] The painting,
which depicts a wheel to which four men cling, seems at first
glance an entirely conventional representation of Fortune's most
famous accouterment. Near the base of Fortune's wheel, however,
stands an hourglass. A sixteenth-century French printer's device contains a still more unusual embodiment of the topos, for, according to
Samuel C. Chew, "Fortune has Time's escapement on her head."[51]
Finally, a German broadsheet (c. 1642), entitled "The Great World
Clock of the Roman Empire," presents yet another demonstration of
Fortune's relationship to time.[52] In the center of the design appears a
tower representing the Empire. Around it is a wheel, and inscribed on
each semicircle are the numerals from one to twelve. Four men cling to

the wheel and along the rim are the words applied by medieval thinkers and artisans to the four positions on Fortune's wheel: *regnabo, regno, regnavi, sum sine regno*. Next to one of these figures stands an hourglass.

Fortune's representation in the literature of the Renaissance also suggests how closely she became associated with time. Shakespeare, for example, in *The Rape of Lucrece* writes that one of Time's appointed tasks is to "turn the giddy round of Fortune's wheel" (line 952). And a contemporary of Shakespeare's, George Chapman, seems to conflate the wheel of Fortune with the wheel of life, traditionally turned by Father Time.[53] In his play *Bussy D'Ambois* (c. 1604), Chapman writes: "There is a deep nick in Time's restless wheel / For each man's good, when which nick comes it strikes."[54]

It seems clear that this association of Fortune with time followed logically the conflation of Fortune with Occasion. Occasion herself, of course, had been linked with time since antiquity. "Occasio est pars temporis" ("Occasion is a part of time"), writes Cicero in *De Inventione*.[55] During the Renaissance it was not uncommon for writers to confuse the two. Thus Erasmus, for example, translates the Greek word *kairos* by the Latin *tempus* in his *Adagia*. Hence his verbal portrait of Occasion appears under the heading, "Nosce tempus" ("Know the time").[56]

This coalescence is easily understood, for the very essence of Occasion is auspicious timing, as a printer's device of the Elizabethan era illustrates. The device portrays Occasion holding a razor and standing above the waves of the sea. Surrounding her is this motto: "Aut nunc aut nunquam" ("Either now or never").[57] The coalescence is demonstrated at much greater length in Jan David's *Occasio Arrepta, Neglecta* (Antwerp, 1605), a work containing a series of plates by Theodore Galle. In one of them a group of men successfully grasp the forelock of Occasion while Father Time hovers close by (p. 116). Another plate shows a less enterprising group of figures who fail to seize the forelock; Occasion has turned her back and Time has flown off (p. 172).[58]

The significance of this Occasion-Time nexus for Fortune is perhaps best revealed in the emblem literature. An emblem in Jean Cousin's *Liber Fortunae* depicts a winged Father Time who holds an hourglass, wears a forelock (which undoubtedly derives from Occasion), and clings to a revolving wheel of Fortune (pl. XVII). Cousin's English commentary makes explicit the connection between Time and Occasion: "Time is as it were the husbande of occasion."[59] However, despite the prominence of Time in both the picture and the commentary, the motto, interestingly, fails to mention Time at all. Instead, it announces, "Fortuna sive occasionis deus" ("Fortune or the god of opportunity"). What is significant here is not only the identification of Fortune as the god of opportunity, but also Fortune's relationship to time. Evidently, Fortune has become so closely linked with time that, at least in her role as dispenser of opportunity, she can be virtually represented by Father Time himself.

A measure of how deeply the concept of Fortune was modified by the association with time — as early as the late fifteenth or the early sixteenth century — is provided by an interesting visual treatment of the Fortuna-Virtus topos, located in the city of Mantua. Traditionally, Fortune was, of course, depicted sitting or standing upon a sphere, symbolic of her inconstancy, while opposite her sat or stood a figure on a square block, symbolic of stability. A fresco of the school of Mantegna (sometime after 1490) represents a profound change in the topos. It shows, on the left, a Renaissance Fortune, who wears a forelock; one of her winged feet touches a sphere as she moves rapidly forward. Opposite her on a square pedestal stands an elderly matron representing Virtue.[60] Most unusual is the addition of a third figure to the traditional topos: a boy whose hands are outstretched toward Fortune, but who is impeded by the matron. The boy and the forelock toward which he reaches suggest the dynamism that informs this innovative work. And central to the dynamism is the passage of time. Indeed, Edgar Wind theorizes that the boy's action constitutes "a perfect embodiment of *festina lente*" ("make haste slowly").[61]

Much of the evidence assembled thus far has been pictorial in nature, but perhaps the best way of concluding this study of Fortune's transformation is to consider a literary representation by Shakespeare. At the opening of *The Tempest* (c. 1611), the playwright creates a vivid storm scene. The audience envisions a ship tossed by wind and waves, its sails rent. It may be too facile to suggest that the vessel recalls the vessels which appear in so many pictorial representations of Fortune and Occasion. But there can be no mistaking the nature of the Fortune whom Prospero invokes as he witnesses the storm:

By accident most strange, bountiful Fortune
(Now my dear lady) hath mine enemies
Brought to this shore; and by my prescience
I find my zenith doth depend upon
A most auspicious star, whose influence
If now I court not, but omit, my fortunes
Will ever after droop. (I.ii.178-84)

The reference to the star may remind us of Machiavelli's advice in his "Capitolo di Fortuna" that man take Fortune "for his star" (line 124). And, like Machiavelli, Prospero has a keen sense of opportunity. The magician knows that he must act (and quickly) to secure his goals. His success or failure depends upon his own decisions and conduct. Fortune provides only the opportunity. The rest is up to him.

Shakespeare's treatment of Fortune in *The Tempest*, it should be noted, is by no means typical of Fortune's representation in his other plays. In fact, Shakespeare sometimes evokes a distinctively medieval Fortune as, for example, when the Poet in *Timon of Athens* speaks of Fortune enthroned on a hill (I.i.63-72). Such passages remind us that Fortune's representation remained varied, that older ways of thinking about Fortune persisted alongside the new, that a century and a half after the creation of Giovanni Rucellai's coat of arms, medieval Fortune had not perished. Generalizations about an emerging new Fortune need, therefore, to be tempered by a realization that it never entirely supplanted the Fortune of old.

Nevertheless, it is also true that the Fortune of Prospero and Rollenhagen and Corrozet and Modena and Machiavelli and Rucellai constitutes an important departure from earlier ways of representing Fortune. And their Fortune had enormous vitality. Merchants, artisans, historians, emblematists, poets, and playwrights alike responded enthusiastically to a concept of Fortune based not only upon a recognition of the awesome power of changing circumstance, but also upon confidence in man's powers. The intensity of interest in this symbol is demonstrated both by the number of appearances made by Fortune in words and pictures and by the multiplicity of forms that Fortune took. Not content merely to perpetuate inherited concepts and images, Renaissance thinkers sought to adapt Fortune to a changing world view. Admittedly, they fashioned their Fortune out of traditional materials, but they assembled those materials in a distinctively new manner. The Fortune they created differs profoundly from both medieval and classical antecedents.

NOTES TO CHAPTER 7

1. For the connection between Fortune's changing iconography and underlying cultural attitudes, see Aby Warburg, "Francesco Sassettis letzwillige Verfügung," in *Kunstwissenschaftliche Beiträge August Schmarsow gewidmet* (Leipzig, 1907); reprinted in Warburg, *Gesammelte Schriften: Die Erneuerung der heidnischen Antike* (Leipzig and Berlin: B. G. Teubner, 1932), 1: 127-58. All references in my text are to this reprint. See also Alfred Doren, "Fortuna im Mittelalter und in der Renaissance," *Vorträge der Bibliothek Warburg*, ed. Fritz Saxl, 2 (1922-23), part 1, 71-151; Ernst Cassirer, *Individuum und Kosmos in der Philosophie der Renaissance* (Leipzig and Berlin: B. G. Teubner, 1927). Translated into English by Mario Domandi under the title, *The Individual and the Cosmos in Renaissance Philosophy* (New York: Harper and Row, 1964); see esp. pp. 73 ff. More recently, Maurizio Bonicatti has dealt with the subject, although tangentially, in "Dürer nella storia delle idee umanistiche fra Quattrocento e Cinquecento," *JMRS*, 1 (1971): 131-250. Also useful is the study by Mario Santoro, *Fortuna, ragione e prudenza nella civiltà letteraria del Cinquecento* (Naples: Liguori, 1967).

2. *The Goddess Fortuna in Mediaeval Literature* (1927; reprint ed., New York: Octagon Books, 1967). See also Patch, "The Tradition of the Goddess Fortuna in Medieval Philosophy and Literature," *Smith College Studies in Modern Languages*, 3 (1922): 179-235; Raimond van Marle, *Iconographie de l'art profane au Moyen-Age et à la Renaissance* (The Hague: Martinus Nijhoff, 1932), 2: 189-202; F. P. Pickering, *Literature and Art in the Middle Ages* (London: Macmillan, 1970), pp. 168-222 (originally published as *Literatur und darstellende Kunst im Mittelalter* [Berlin: E. Schmidt, 1966]).

3. For the history of the Fortuna-Virtus topos, see Ida Wyss, *Virtù und Fortuna bei Boiardo und Ariost* (Leipzig and Berlin: B. G. Teubner, 1931); Klaus

Heitmann, *Fortuna und Virtus: Eine Studie zu Petrarcas Lebensweisheit* (Cologne: Böhlau, 1958); Oskar Roth, *Studien zum "Estrif de Fortune et Vertu" des Martin Le Franc* (Bern: Herbert Lang, 1970).

4. The date of the Palazzo Rucellai is usually put c. 1446-51. However, Charles Randall Mack, in "The Rucellai Palace: Some New Proposals," *Art Bulletin*, 56 (1974): 517-29, argues that the facade of the building was not completed until after 1461. (Mack also attributes the design of the palazzo to Bernardo Rossellino rather than to Alberti.) Mack's arguments for a later date of completion have been sharply challenged by Kurt W. Forster, in "The Palazzo Rucellai and Questions of Typology in the Development of Renaissance Buildings," *Art Bulletin*, 58 (1976): 109-13.

5. For representations of Fortune in antiquity, see Patch, "The Tradition of the Goddess Fortuna in Roman Literature and in the Transitional Period," *Smith College Studies in Modern Languages*, 3 (1922): 131-77; Roger Hinks, *Myth and Allegory in Ancient Art* (London: Warburg Institute, 1939), pp. 76-83; John Ferguson, *The Religions of the Roman Empire* (London: Thames and Hudson, 1970), pp. 77-87.

6. In addition to the discussions of the coat of arms by Warburg and Doren, see Felix Gilbert, "Bernardo Rucellai and the Orti Oricellari: A Study on the Origin of Modern Political Thought," *JWCI*, 12 (1949): 103-4.

7. *De Officiis*, ed. and trans. Walter Miller, LCL (New York and London: Macmillan, 1913), p. 187.

8. Warburg (p. 149, *n*2) cites the representation of Fortune with sail on a Roman medal, reproduced by Wilhelm Froehner, *Les Médaillons de l'empire romain* (Paris: J. Rothschild, 1878), p. xiii. See also other reproductions in Froehner, pp. 124-25. Doren believes that the sail is due, at least in part, to Fortune's ancient conflation with Isis (p. 135, *n*130).

9. Rucellai's use of the sail in various imprese is discussed by Volker Herzner, in "Die Segel-Imprese der Familie Pazzi," *Mitteilungen des kunsthistorischen Institutes in Florenz*, 20 (1976): 13-32.

10. Gilbert theorizes: "The Fortuna, to which the Rucellai are willing to adapt themselves, may represent the Medici" (p. 104).

11. However, Fortune sometimes, though rarely, was said to have a forelock in the Middle Ages. See George Lyman Kittredge, "To Take Time by the Forelock," *MLN*, 8 (1893): 230-35; Karl Pietsch, "On the Source of the Italian and English Idioms meaning 'to take time by the forelock,' . . . by J. E. Matzke," *MLN*, 8 (1893): 235-38. Jacob Burckhardt also notes the

appearance of Fortune with forelock in a pageant performed in 1443 to celebrate the entry of Alfonso the Great into Naples: *The Civilization of the Renaissance in Italy*, trans. S. G. C. Middlemore (1929; reprint ed., New York: Harper and Row, 1958), 2: 417.

12. In addition to the forelock, the famous statue of Kairos by the Greek sculptor Lysippus, according to Callistratus, represented the figure as a young nude male possessing these features: a sphere upon which he stood, winged feet, and (behind the forelock) a bald head. According to Posidippus, Kairos also held in his right hand a razor. And, according to Himerius, Kairos held in his left hand a scale, winged and balanced on a sphere. When the Greek personification of opportunity was adapted by the Romans, it became known as Occasio (a feminine noun) and portrayed as a woman. A poem by Ausonius describes a personification much like that created by Lysippus, but Occasio stands upon a wheel instead of a sphere. The texts of the relevant poems by these classical authors are included in John E. Matzke, "On the Source of the Italian and English Idioms meaning 'To Take Time by the Forelock,'" *PMLA*, 8 (1893): 303-34. Studies of Kairos-Occasio include: Daremberg-Saglio, *Dictionnaire des antiquités grecques et romaines* (Paris: Hachette, 1877-1919), 3: part 1, 787-88; Pauly-Wissowa-Kroll, *Real-Encyclopädie der classischen Altertumswissenschaft* (Stuttgart: J. B. Metzler, 1893-1919) 20: cols. 1508-21; W. H. Roscher, *Ausführliches Lexikon der griechischen und römischen Mythologie* (Leipzig: B. G. Teubner, 1884-1937), 2: part 1, cols. 897-901.

13. *The Literary Works of Leonardo da Vinci*, ed. Jean Paul and Irma A. Richter, 3rd ed. (New York: Phaidon, 1970), 1: 351 (1st ed. 1883). Also, in *Giorgione's Tempesta, with Comments on Giorgione's Poetic Allegories* (Oxford: Clarendon Press, 1969), Edgar Wind writes: "In Sigismondo Fanti's *Triompho di Fortuna* (Venice, 1526), Fortuna is pictured in twelve types that are named after twelve winds" (pp. 20-21, *n*9). Wind reproduces two of these depictions (figs. 21-22 of his book).

14. The text of the letter appears in *Supplementum Ficinianum*, ed. Paul Oskar Kristeller (1937; reprint ed., Florence: L. S. Olschki, 1973), 2: 169-73. Warburg also reproduces the letter, pp. 147-48, *n*2. Doren discusses it, p. 121.

15. *Plato: Laws*, ed. and trans. R. G. Bury, LCL (London and New York: G. P. Putnam's Sons, 1926), 1: 269-71.

16. Quoted by Edgar Wind, "Platonic Tyranny and the Renaissance Fortuna: On Ficino's Reading of Laws IV, 709A-712A," in *De Artibus Opuscula*,

XL: Essays in Honor of Erwin Panofsky, ed. Millard Meiss (New York: New York Univ. Press, 1961), 1: 492.

17. Ibid.

18. Ficino has confidence in man's capacity to contend with Fortune only to the extent that the individual proceeds in accord with Christian precepts. Ficino makes the assumption, common in the Middle Ages, that Fortune exists only as an extension of divine providence. As Paul Oskar Kristeller observes in *The Philosophy of Marsilio Ficino,* trans. Virginia Conant (New York: Columbia Univ. Press, 1943), "Ficino does not attribute an unlimited power to fortune, but from the outset subordinates it to nature and God" (p. 298).

19. For an account of Giovanni Rucellai's life, see Luigi Passerini, *Genealogia e storia della famiglia Rucellai* (Florence: M. Cellini, 1861), pp. 117-21.

20. *The Albertis of Florence: Leon Battista Alberti's Della Famiglia,* trans. Guido A. Guarino (Lewisburg, Pa.: Bucknell Univ. Press, 1971), p. 28. Cassirer, in *The Individual and the Cosmos,* notes that for Alberti, "the current of Fortune will not drag away a man who, trusting his own strength, makes his way in the current as an able swimmer" (p. 77).

21. Ibid., p. 30.

22. The conflation of Fortune and Occasion in the Renaissance has been noted by Erwin Panofsky, *Studies in Iconology* (1939; reprint ed., New York: Harper and Row, 1962), p. 72, *n*5; Edgar Wind, *Pagan Mysteries in the Renaissance,* rev. ed. (New York: W. W. Norton, 1968), p. 101, *n*15; Samuel C. Chew, *The Pilgrimage of Life* (1962; reprint ed., Port Washington, N.Y.: Kennikat Press, 1973), pp. 26-27 and 59-60. For more extensive treatments of the conflation, see Rudolf Wittkower, "Chance, Time and Virtue," *JWI,* 1 (1937-38): 313-21; "Patience and Chance: The Story of a Political Emblem," ibid., pp. 171-77; Erwin Panofsky, "'Good Government' or Fortune?: The Iconography of a Newly-Discovered Composition by Rubens," *Gazette des Beaux-Arts,* 68 (1966): 305-26.

23. In *Machiavelli: The Chief Works and Others,* trans. Allan Gilbert (Durham, N.C.: Duke Univ. Press, 1965), 1: 90.

24. Machiavelli's concept of man's relationship to Fortune is illuminated by comparison with Seneca's. See Joseph S. M. J. Chang, "'Of Mighty Opposites': Stoicism and Machiavellianism," *RenD,* 9 (1966): 37-57.

25. Discussions of *virtù* include: Leonardo Olschki, *Machiavelli the Scientist*

(Berkeley, Calif.: The Gillick Press, 1945), pp. 35-41; Ernst Cassirer, *The Myth of the State* (New Haven: Yale Univ. Press, 1946), pp. 156-62; J. H. Whitfield, *Machiavelli* (Oxford: Blackwell, 1947), pp. 92-105; Felix Gilbert, "On Machiavelli's Idea of *Virtù*," *Renaissance News*, 4 (1951): 53-55; Federico Chabod, *Machiavelli and the Renaissance*, trans. David Moore (Cambridge, Mass.: Harvard Univ. Press, 1958), pp. 21-23, 69-70, 145-47; Burleigh Taylor Wilkins, "Machiavelli on History and Fortune," *BuR*, 8 (1959): 225-45; Giuseppe Prezzolini, *Machiavelli*, trans. Gioconda Savini (New York: Farrar, Straus and Giroux, 1967), pp. 21-25 and 61-66; Neal Wood, "Machiavelli's Concept of *Virtù* Reconsidered," *Political Studies*, 15 (1967): 159-72; Charles D. Tarlton, "The Symbolism of Redemption and the Exorcism of Fortune in Machiavelli's *Prince*," *Review of Politics*, 30 (1968): 332-48; Thomas Flanagan, "The Concept of *Fortuna* in Machiavelli," in *The Political Calculus: Essays on Machiavelli's Philosophy*, ed. Anthony Parel (Toronto: Univ. of Toronto Press, 1972), pp. 127-56; John Plamenatz, "In Search of Machiavellian *Virtù*," in *The Political Calculus*, pp. 157-78; I. Hannaford, "Machiavelli's Concept of Virtù in *The Prince* and *The Discourses* Reconsidered," *Political Studies*, 20 (1972): 185-89; Russell Price, "The Senses of *Virtù* in Machiavelli," *European Studies Review*, 3 (1973): 315-45.

26. *Machiavelli's Prince and Its Forerunners: The Prince as a Typical Book de Regimine Principum* (1938; reprint ed., New York: Barnes and Noble, 1968), description of frontispiece.

27. In antiquity the competing claims of Fortuna and Virtus had been explored by Livy, Polybius, Plutarch, Seneca, and others. In addition, a number of medieval and early Renaissance works chronicled the familiar dualism. These include the *De Remediis Fortuitorum* (once ascribed to Seneca), Guillaume de Machaut's *Le Remède de Fortune*, Martin Le Franc's *L'Estrif de Fortune et de Vertu*, Petrarch's *De Remediis Utruisque Fortunai*, and Poggio Bracciolini's *De Varietate Fortunae*. For discussions of the works by Petrarch, Bracciolini, and others, see Clarence William Kerr, "The Idea of Fortune in Italian Humanism from Petrarch to Machiavelli," Diss. Harvard Univ. 1957.

28. Quoted by Sydney Anglo, *Machiavelli: A Dissection* (London: Gollancz, 1969), pp. 228-29.

29. Ibid.

30. *Renaissance and Revolution: The Remaking of European Thought* (1965; reprint ed., London: Secker and Warburg, 1967), p. 93.

31. Pontano's philosophy is discussed by Doren, pp. 121-28; Don Cameron

Allen, "Renaissance Remedies for Fortune: Marlowe and the *Fortunati*," *SP*, 38 (1941): 188-97; and Gilbert, *Machiavelli's Prince and Its Forerunners*, esp. pp. 216-19.

32. *Machiavelli and Guicciardini: Politics and History in Sixteenth-Century Florence* (Princeton: Princeton Univ. Press, 1965), p. 194.

33. Machiavelli's concern with the idea of opportunity also issued in his poem, "Dell' Occasione," actually a rendering of Ausonius' poem on Occasion. See *Ausonius*, ed. and trans. Hugh G. Evelyn White, LCL, 2 (London and Cambridge, Mass.: Harvard Univ. Press, 1949), 174-77.

34. The poem appears under the title "Tercets on Fortune," in *Machiavelli: The Chief Works and Others*, ed. Gilbert, 2: 745-49.

35. See Peter E. Bondanella, *Francesco Guicciardini* (Boston: Twayne, 1976), pp. 115-22.

36. Reproduced by Arthur M. Hind, *Early Italian Engraving: A Critical Catalogue with Complete Reproduction of All the Prints Described* (London: B. Quaritch [for M. Knoedler, N.Y.], 1938-48), 2: pl. 157.

37. *Shakespeare's Speaking Pictures: Studies in Iconic Imagery* (Albuquerque, N.M.: Univ. of New Mexico Press, 1974), p. 209, *n*10.

38. *Attributs et symboles dans l'art profane, 1450-1600* (Geneva: E. Droz, 1958), cols. 143-45.

39. See, for example, Campbell Dodgson, "Rare Woodcuts in the Ashmolean Museum—I," *Burlington Magazine*, 63 (1933): 21-24 and 288-89.

40. Reproduced by Wind, *Pagan Mysteries*, fig. 52.

41. See George Francis Hill, *A Corpus of Italian Medals of the Renaissance before Cellini* (London: British Museum, 1930), nos. 958, 968, and 981.

42. See Tervarent, cols. 9-14.

43. Reproduced by Van Marle, 2: fig. 216.

44. See, for example, a design by Bernard Van Orley (d. 1542), which depicts Fortune holding a boat in her hand (reproduced by Van Marle, 2: fig. 210); Girolamo Ruscelli, *Le imprese illustri* (Venice, 1566), where Fortune appears in a boat and holds a sail (Book III, p. 517); and Jean Jacques Boissard, *Emblematum Liber* (Frankfurt, 1593), where Fortune also appears in a boat and holds a sail (emblem LI).

45. The "impresa amorosa" is discussed briefly by Warburg, pp. 149-51, and reproduced (fig. 36). The usual identification of the couple in the boat has been

challenged by Edgar Wind, who in "Platonic Tyranny and the Renaissance Fortuna" writes: "Whether it is right to identify the happy pair with the young Bernardo . . . is doubtful" (p. 492, *n7*).

46. In *The Works of Francis Bacon*, ed. James Spedding et al. (London: Longman, 1858), 6: 472. And see Rexmond C. Cochrane, "Francis Bacon and the Architect of Fortune," *Studies in the Renaissance*, 5 (1958): 176-95.

47. See Chew, "Time and Fortune," *ELH*, 6 (1939): 83-113. Chew's article concerns the Time-Fortune nexus chiefly as it appears in Elizabethan and Jacobean literature.

48. Reproduced by Doebler, pl. 14.

49. *The Book of Fortune, Two Hundred Unpublished Drawings [Liber Fortunae]*, ed. Ludovic Lalanne, trans. H. Mainwaring Dunstan (London and Paris: Librairie de l'art, 1883), pl. LXIX.

50. Reproduced by S. Arthur Strong, *Critical Studies and Fragments* (London: Duckworth, 1905), pl. VIII, fig. 1.

51. *The Pilgrimage of Life*, p. 27. The device is reproduced by G. Van Havre, *Marques typographiques des imprimeurs et libraires Anversois*, 2 (Antwerp: J. E. Buschmann, 1884), 201, fig. 1.

52. Reproduced by Pickering, pl. 6b.

53. Chew discusses briefly the two wheels, in "'This Strange Eventful History,'" in *Joseph Quincy Adams Memorial Studies*, ed. James G. McManaway et al. (Washington, D. C.: The Folger Shakespeare Library, 1948), pp. 157-82.

54. *Bussy D'Ambois*, ed. Nicholas Brooke, The Revels Plays (London and Cambridge, Mass.: Harvard Univ. Press, 1964), I.i.130-31.

55. *De Inventione, De Optimo Genere Oratorum, Topica*, ed. and trans. H. M. Hubbell, LCL (Cambridge, Mass.: Harvard Univ. Press, 1949), p. 78.

56. *Adagia* (Basel, 1540), 2: 252-53.

57. Reproduced by Ronald B. McKerrow, *Printers' and Publishers' Devices in England and Scotland, 1485-1640* (London: Chiswick Press for the Bibliographical Society, 1913), no. 281.

58. These two plates by Galle, along with others from David's work, are reproduced by Chew, *The Pilgrimage of Life*, figs. 44 and 46.

59. MS. 1910, catalogued under the title *Le Livre de Fortune*, in the Bibliothèque de l'Institut de France.

60. Reproduced by Wittkower, "Chance, Time and Virtue," pl. 51c. Witt-

kower identifies the figure as "Virtus-Constantia" (p. 318); Wind, *Pagan Mysteries*, identifies her as "Wisdom" (p. 101). Another innovative treatment of the topos appears in the pavement of Siena Cathedral. The design was conceived by Pinturicchio and executed probably in 1505-06. It portrays a seated Wisdom on a hill, situated on an island. Beneath, at the shore, stands Fortune, who has apparently just discharged a group of passengers. Fortune is nude, carries a sail and cornucopia, and stands with one foot on a sphere, the other on the prow of a boat. Reproduced by Van Marle, 2: fig. 213.

61. *Pagan Mysteries*, p. 103.

Chapter 8

FORTUNE AND OCCASION IN SHAKESPEARE: *RICHARD II, JULIUS CAESAR,* AND *HAMLET*

PLAYWRIGHTS SELDOM PROVIDE an elaborate description of Dame Fortune—certainly no counterpart in words to the vivid depictions of Continental emblematists. Nevertheless, their plays reflect the changing concept of Fortune in the Renaissance. And in the work of one playwright in particular, Shakespeare, we can actually observe the transition away from the traditional view of Fortune.[1] In three tragedies written during the closing years of the sixteenth century, Shakespeare manifests a growing interest in Occasion.

The plays are *Richard II* (c. 1595), *Julius Caesar* (c. 1599), and *Hamlet* (c. 1600). In the earliest of these the protagonist expresses an attitude toward Fortune that seems characteristically medieval. King Richard sees himself as Fortune's victim, inescapably vulnerable to her whim. By contrast, his antagonist represents an emerging new order. As confident as he is skilled, Henry Bolingbroke determines to shape his own future. Moving with events rather than against them, he cooperates with the time to advance his purposes and to vanquish Richard. The psychology of a man who would pursue Occasion is explored yet more deeply in *Julius Caesar*. Brutus, like Bolingbroke, has a highly developed sense of opportunity, which he expresses in his speech on the tide in the affairs of men. Unlike Bolingbroke, however, Brutus lacks the skill to realize his aspirations: instead of capitalizing upon the world's mutability, he destroys himself. More adept is Hamlet, perhaps because he possesses a greater capacity for adaptability than Brutus. Initially, Hamlet's view of Fortune is conventional, hardly distinct from Richard's; and he blunders in his efforts to fulfill the Ghost's command. After a series of remarkable personal experiences, however, Hamlet adopts a new outlook. He begins to attune himself to the time and, locating opportunity under the aegis of providence, at last pursues his goal successfully.

I

Shakespeare's treatment of Fortune in *Richard II*, it is generally agreed, both draws inspiration from and transcends *de casibus* tragedy. The play has been called "an almost perfect example of *de casibus* tragedy in its formal structure and in its technical mastery."[2] The pattern of rise and fall evokes the traditional progression dictated by Fortune in the *de casibus* stories of Boccaccio, Chaucer, and Lydgate. Richard, of course, undergoes a spectacular transition from prosperity to adversity, ascribing it, at least in part, to a perverse Fortune. For his part, Bolingbroke, according to Irving Ribner, is "made to appear as a minion of fortune who rises to fill a position which Richard vacates."[3] At the same time, readers of *Richard II* see evidence of a turning away from convention on Shakespeare's part. Arguing that the king attains considerable insight into his own culpability, they claim that Richard's characterization transcends that typical of *de casibus* tragedy. Peter G. Phialas, for example, suggests that "from a *de casibus* concept of his fall Richard advances to full awareness and acceptance of his own moral involvement."[4] And, according to S. C. Sen Gupta, "by making Richard personally responsible for his disasters, Shakespeare seems to stress his independence of the medieval idea of tragedy and show in the true Renaissance spirit that man is the architect of his fate and not a victim of the blind goddess Fortune."[5]

Richard II undoubtedly represents a step toward what today is called tragedy of character. Nevertheless, Richard's characterization remains profoundly shaped by *de casibus* tradition, for throughout the play Richard harbors the conviction that he has been victimized by circumstance, undone by Fortune. Characterization in *Richard II* may transcend the pattern common to metrical tragedy, but it is Bolingbroke, not Richard, who diverges sharply from that precedent. Indeed, much of what readers say about Richard's perception of the connection between one's deeds and one's fate applies more properly to Boling-broke, who sees himself as master, not servant, of circumstance. Confident of what he can achieve through his own efforts, Bolingbroke never directly acknowledges Dame Fortune. Shakespeare's characterization of these two antagonists, then, represents the juxtaposition of the traditional and the innovative: he preserves *de casibus* convention in the portrayal of Richard while rejecting it for something newer in the depiction of Bolingbroke.[6]

The attainment of self-knowledge is, in the view of most readers, the most profound change that Richard undergoes. Richard's request for a mirror in IV.i is seen as "a move towards self-knowledge, and even repentance."[7] One critic speaks of Richard's "increasingly bitter self-awareness,"[8] while another finds a gradual but clear development in Richard's understanding of himself: "At first Richard sees himself exclusively in the light of a victim of fortune's wheel; only very slowly does he accept the moral of the *specula principis* that kings must be virtuous or they may be punished, even deposed, by the vengeance of God."[9]

Actually, it is Richard's histrionic flair that creates the impression of a deeper self-knowledge than he really attains. Upon close reading his speeches reveal, at most, a seriously deficient understanding and an unwillingness to assume responsibility for his plight. The king may occasionally express regret over his words or deeds. Upon his return from Ireland, for instance, he laments that "this tongue of mine" ever banished Bolingbroke (III.iii.133). This remark represents, however, concern over a tactical error rather than a profound acknowledgment of wrongdoing. And even on those occasions when Richard castigates himself more vigorously, he seems unable to do so without sharing the blame liberally with his enemies. Thus while he concedes that he is a traitor to himself, he also in the same breath complains bitterly of the traitors who surround him (IV.i.244-48). And he cannot speak of his "weav'd-up follies" (IV.i.229) without in the same speech comparing himself to Christ and his enemies to Pilate. Here, as elsewhere, Richard displays an indulgent self-pity scarcely synonymous with true self-knowledge, much less contrition.

If Richard's attitude toward personal responsibility is ambivalent, so too is his attitude toward the divine power that exacts retribution for wrongdoing. The king may express confidence in providential justice when he tells Aumerle that "The breath of worldly men cannot depose / The deputy elected by the Lord" and that "heaven still guards the right" (III.ii.56-57, 62), but he seems not to recognize that the divine dispensation subjects him also to its strictures. Carlisle tells him that "The means that heavens yield must be embrac'd, / And not neglected" (29-30). Yet this reproof works little change in Richard, who, oblivious to the responsibilities he should fulfill, succumbs to torpor and despair. Despite his penchant for likening himself to Christ, Richard offers little evidence that the providence with which he threatens others has personal meaning for himself.

Significantly, when Richard is overtaken by adversity, he looks for explanation not to providence but to a capricious power that seems to frustrate his own purposes and to favor those of his opponents. In these words, for example, Richard in the deposition scene invites Bolingbroke to grasp the crown:

> Here, cousin, seize the crown;
> Here, cousin,
> On this side my hand, and on that side thine.
> Now is this golden crown like a deep well
> That owes two buckets, filling one another,
> The emptier ever dancing in the air,
> The other down, unseen, and full of water:
> That bucket down and full of tears am I,
> Drinking my griefs, whilst you mount up on high.
>
> (IV.i.181-89)

There is little here to suggest that Richard's understanding of either himself or his world is very profound. The lines evince no sense of accountability. Based on the medieval figure of Fortune's buckets,[10] they in effect transfer responsibility for what is happening away from Richard and to an external force.

In this case, then, far from abandoning the *de casibus* mode, Shakespeare draws his inspiration from it. For Richard's speech almost certainly is in the tradition of metrical tragedy, where the notion that one man's rising dictates another's fall is ascribed to Fortune. The idea survives in the foremost *de casibus* work of Shakespeare's era, the *Mirror for Magistrates*, where a complainant observes, "Fortune can not raise, / Any one aloft without sum others wracke."[11]

Richard's references to Fortune may be appropriate in the sense that chance seems to work against him; his return from Ireland, for instance, is delayed by adverse weather, and his discouraged army disperses prematurely. Moreover, the caprice of the London crowds may, as J. M. R. Margeson suggests, be interpreted as signifying the fickleness of Fortune.[12] Nevertheless, when Margeson writes that "the law of change in earthly kingdoms governed by indifferent fortune seems almost as probable an interpretation of these events as any providential order,"[13] he fails to note Richard's inconsistency: the king threatens his enemies with the justice of God, yet blames capricious Fortune for his own reverses.

In so doing Richard is not necessarily being insincere. He may honestly believe himself to be a victim of circumstance. Despite the admonitions of royal counselors and despite even his own self-recrimination, Richard seems to remain baffled by the relationship between cause and effect. Certainly his language reveals no particular comprehension of the underlying principles at work in his deposition. The image of the buckets, for example, tends to blur, if it does not altogether obscure, the reason for the political upheaval. Fortune may be the only notion that allows a bewildered Richard to explain to himself how he could fall so far so fast.

Most readers contend that Richard moves beyond bewilderment, that eventually he sees beyond the caprice of Fortune and comes to accept responsibility for his plight. Irving Ribner, for example, finds evidence of maturation when Richard tells his wife, "I am sworn brother, sweet, / To grim Necessity, and he and I / Will keep a league till death" (V.i.20-22). Ribner comments: "Richard's awareness of his brotherhood to 'grim necessity' may be regarded as the culminating evidence of a growth in self-knowledge which had begun with his first awareness of Bolingbroke's inevitable triumph."[14] Yet Richard himself does not specify the source of that necessity as being within; in fact, he repeatedly locates causality outside of the individual.[15] The fact that Richard has come to think of the world as governed by inflexible laws does not necessarily mean that he perceives his own role in creating his destiny. His remark about necessity suggests, rather, an abject surrender to circumstance.

Nor does Richard discard the image of himself as victim. Indeed, only moments before his death he continues to speak of Fortune, and he intimates that his relationship remains one of thralldom: "Thoughts tending to content flatter themselves / That they are not the first of fortune's slaves, / Nor shall not be the last—" (V.v.23-25). Here, virtually at the end of his life, he still employs the terminology of the *de casibus* narrative. And even Richard's eloquent admission in this last speech, "I wasted time, and now doth time waste me," recalls the tragedies of Boccaccio, Chaucer, and Lydgate, for implicit in the lines that follow the admission is the image of the wheel of Fortune:

> For now hath time made me his numb'ring clock:
> My thoughts are minutes, and with sighs they jar
> Their watches on unto mine eyes, the outward watch,
> Whereto my finger, like a dial's point,
> Is pointing still, in cleansing them from tears.
> Now, sir, the sound that tells what hour it is
> Are clamorous groans, which strike upon my heart,
> Which is the bell. So sighs, and tears, and groans
> Show minutes, times, and hours; but my time
> Runs posting on in Bullingbrook's proud joy,
> While I stand fooling here, his Jack of the clock.
>
> (V.v.50-60)

The shape of the clock's face corresponds to that of Fortune's wheel. The steady progress of "minutes, times, and hours" suggests the ceaseless revolution of the wheel. And the motion of Richard, or rather his finger, around the circumference as a "dial point" evokes the conventional representation of a man bound to Fortune's wheel. The image, then, undercuts Richard's acknowledgment of his prodigality. To the very end he portrays himself as acted upon by hostile forces. Thus, to the extent that the tragedy is seen through Richard's eyes, it is a "Boccacesque tragedy of Fortune."[16]

Richard, of course, bears responsibility for his demise: the speeches of Gaunt (II.i.31-68, 93-115), Carlisle (III.ii.27-32, 178-85), and York

(II.i.186-208, II.ii.77-85) demonstrate the connection between his deeds and his downfall. Collectively, they suggest that Richard is insensitive to both people and custom, that he is ineffectual in dealing with political crises, that his thralldom to circumstance stems largely from his own deficiencies.[17] Richard, however, does not share the view of Gaunt or Carlisle or York—or of the reader or audience.

And it remains unclear whether Richard even seeks to look within himself very deeply. Although his request for a mirror in the deposition scene may constitute an outward sign of such a desire, the smashing of that mirror, as Wilbur Sanders observes, signifies a "renunciation of self-knowledge."[18] Perhaps self-recognition is too difficult for one who has customarily looked outward to discover the source of his predicaments. Perhaps his histrionics, his violent moods, prevent him from ever gaining the quiet stability and perspective from which he might sensibly assess his plight. Or perhaps his rigidity of character simply will not allow Richard to look forthrightly at himself. Whatever the nature of the impediment, Richard fails to achieve any greater understanding of himself or of causality than the ghostly figures of the *Mirror for Magistrates* had in life.

Although critical opinion has tended to minimize Richard's link with metrical tragedy, a long critical tradition has identified Richard's antagonist with Fortune. J. Dover Wilson, who argues that the wheel of Fortune "determines the play's shape and structure," describes Bolingbroke as "borne upward by a power [Fortune] beyond his volition."[19] E. M. W. Tillyard writes that the usurper "having once set events in motion is the servant of fortune."[20] And Raymond Chapman claims that at the beginning of the play Bolingbroke is so situated that "The next turn of the Wheel must draw him up and cast Richard down."[21] Source material is sometimes cited to buttress this argument. Dover Wilson, for instance, quotes one of Shakespeare's sources, Daniel's *Civil Wars*, which links Bolingbroke's return from exile and subsequent activity with Fortune:

> Then fortune thou art guilty of his deed
> That didst his state above his hopes erect,
> And thou must beare some blame of his great sin
> That left'st him worse then when he did begin.[22]

M. M. Reese believes that Shakespeare "allows" Daniel's view to be a possible interpretation of the play, and perhaps the dramatist does.[23] This interpretation, however, does not sufficiently take into account Bolingbroke's dynamism and his conception of himself as one who largely determines his own destiny.

Never in the play does Bolingbroke see himself as a passive agent of Fortune. Nor does he directly acknowledge the existence of the Fortune whom Richard and his queen contemplate.[24] When Bolingbroke uses the term, it is "fortune," his personal lot, to which he refers, not the goddess Fortune.[25] Consider, for example, his conversation with his followers upon his return from exile. When Henry Percy meets Bolingbroke, he pledges his "service . . . Which elder days shall ripen and confirm / To more approved service and desert" (II.iii.41-44). To this Bolingbroke replies in kind:

> I thank thee, gentle Percy, and be sure
> I count myself in nothing else so happy
> As in a soul rememb'ring my good friends,
> And as my fortune ripens with thy love,
> It shall be still thy true love's recompense. (45-49)

And in conversation with Ross and Willoughby, Bolingbroke again employs the image. Responding to Ross' comment, "Your presence makes us rich," Bolingbroke says:

> Evermore thank's the exchequer of the poor,
> Which, till my infant fortune comes to years,
> Stands for my bounty. (65-67)

The expressions, "fortune ripens" and "infant fortune," are no less revelatory of Bolingbroke's self-image than Richard's references to the buckets and clock. Bolingbroke's words indicate that he sees his situation, at any moment, not as unalterably fixed, but rather as temporary and capable of amelioration. The epithets "infant" and "ripening" also suggest growth from within rather than constraint from without. Indeed, a "ripening" fortune is one that holds within itself the promise of improvement and fulfillment. This language, then, reflects Bolingbroke's sense of his own capacity for change and development, his sense of responsibility for the shape that his career takes.

Bolingbroke, of course, has to contend with external forces, just as Richard must. Unlike Richard, however, he perceives those forces as natural rather than mechanical, and this attitude allows for a more amicable and productive relationship with them. They are to be accommodated, not merely endured. Cooperation is Bolingbroke's watchword, for he perceives that he can capitalize on those forces and employ them to advance his own purposes.

Nowhere is this sense of cooperation more apparent than in his relationship to time. The Gardener comments upon this collaboration when he compares his own tending of the plants according to the "time of year" (III.iv.57) with Bolingbroke's tending of the kingdom. In his actions, of course, Bolingbroke demonstrates himself to be a master of timing. For example, he delays his return from exile until Richard has left for Ireland. And, later, having managed to secure York's promise of neutrality, Bolingbroke immediately persuades the duke to accompany him to Bristow Castle where he will seek to dislodge Bushy, Bagot, and Green (II.iii.162-67). Even Bolingbroke's opponents acknowledge his sensitivity to the exigencies of the moment. Berkeley, sent to learn of his intentions upon his return, declares that he has come "to know what pricks you on / To take advantage of the absent time, / And fright our native peace with self-borne arms" (II.iii.78-80). The query suggests Bolingbroke's aggressive seizing of opportunity, his confidence that dependence upon circumstance need not mean passivity.[26]

Admittedly, Bolingbroke sometimes appears resigned to events. When York tells him that "the heavens are over our heads," Bolingbroke replies, "I know it, uncle, and oppose not myself / Against their will" (III.iii.18-19). But this seems merely a pose, calculated to assuage the qualms of those uneasy about the prospect of usurpation. There is no evidence that the heavens are any more real to Bolingbroke than they are to Richard.[27] And Bolingbroke, for all his outward obeisance, is certainly not slow to capitalize on his opponent's errors.

In view of Bolingbroke's aggressiveness and resolute spirit, it seems inappropriate to regard him as a passive figure, "whom the Wheel of Fortune . . . carries aloft as it carries Richard down."[28] In fact, the image of Fortune's wheel, which never explicitly appears in the play, should, it seems to me, be discarded in describing Bolingbroke and his relationship to Richard.[29] What is required is a different formulation, one that indicates Shakespeare's indebtedness to *de casibus* tradition in the characterization of Richard (and Richard's Fortune) and, at the same time, his departure from that tradition in the characterization of Bolingbroke. The Fortuna-Virtus topos provides the basis for just such a formulation. Imagine the rivals in *Richard II* as each identified with one side of the antinomy. Together, they form a composite of the old and the new: Fortuna as conceived in such a "medieval" work as the *Mirror for Magistrates*, Virtus as conceived in such a distinctively Renaissance work as *The Prince*.

Throughout the play Richard is, by his own words, associated with Fortune. And his remarks seem not an expression of conventional sentiment for the sake of convention; rather, they seem to grow naturally out of his character. Richard's is, in fact, the sort of personality that by its very nature gives life to Fortune. His obtuseness leads him to ascribe events to Fortune that a more discerning and conscientious individual might himself claim responsibility for. Moreover, Richard's association with Fortune is subtly underscored in another way as well: his mercurial temperament resembles that of the moody goddess he describes. His rapid oscillation between confidence and despair in III.iii rivals any caprice of Dame Fortune; his behavior upon his return from Ireland may, like Fortune's, best be described in terms of antitheses.

Shakespeare makes the relationship between character and Fortune even more explicit when in the deposition scene Richard calls for the mirror. The use of this hand prop evokes the very image of Fortune, for as Samuel C. Chew explains, "when the King dashes the mirror to the ground and comments upon the brittleness of glory, we remember the figures of *Fortuna Vitrea* and those representations of the goddess where . . . she holds in her hand a brittle globe of glass."[30] The very physical presentation of Richard on stage no less than his temperament recalls the image of Fortune, who wields such awesome power in the realm of *de casibus* tragedy.

On the other hand, Bolingbroke's association with Fortune is minimal. He is so determined and energetic that, one imagines, Fortune (at least of the traditional kind) can scarcely exist for him. And while Richard seems to have stepped from the pages of *de casibus* tragedy,

Bolingbroke draws his values and outlook from another source altogether. Irving Ribner suggests the likely inspiration when he writes, "The political activity of Bolingbroke in Shakespeare's *Richard II* closely adheres to Machiavelli's political philosophy as contained in *The Prince*."[31] In the twenty-fifth chapter of that work, Machiavelli argues that man need not remain at the mercy of Fortune, that he can by his skill and daring prevail, at least at times, over circumstance. What Machiavelli urges is the practice of those traits that make for success. And these he sums up in the word *virtù*. As we have seen in Chapter 7, this is not virtue in any moral sense, for Machiavelli, guided by his reading of Roman authors and by his own experience, recasts the medieval Fortuna-Virtus antinomy by defining Virtus in a thoroughly secular light.

Like the model of success for Machiavelli, Shakespeare's Bolingbroke never surrenders to circumstance; he finds in adversity not catastrophe but challenge. In contrast to Richard's penchant for contemning the world when adversity strikes, Bolingbroke retains a stubborn determination to persevere. Clever and resilient, he is an embodiment of energy and purpose. His is a spirit of indomitable strength and resolution; he incarnates Machiavelli's *virtù*.

The application of the Fortuna-Virtus topos to *Richard II* is suggested through the stage imagery. For when the king and the usurper jointly hold the crown at IV.i.181-83, they evoke the figures of Fortuna and Virtus (fig. 14), who jointly hold a crown above a monarch's head in Guillaume de la Perrière's *La Morosophie* (Paris, 1553). Shakespeare may not seek to make the emblematist's point—that a king, ideally, needs to combine happy circumstance with his own integrity; Shakespeare, like Machiavelli, interprets Virtus in a secular sense. But Richard's identification with Fortune and Bolingbroke's with *virtù* suggest that Shakespeare may well have intended to realize the topos in emblematic terms.

The composite formulation suggested above (old-fashioned Fortune and new-fangled *virtù*) provides a more useful means of characterizing the profound shift in power that takes place during *Richard II* than does the wheel of Fortune. For when the crown passes from Richard to Bolingbroke, it passes from a man intimidated by Fortune and doubtful of his capacity to prevail over hostile circumstance, to a man confident of

Fig. 14. Guillaume de la Perriere, La Morosophie

his *virtù*, secure in his belief that he can achieve whatever he sets his will to. The crown, then, passes not merely from one individual to another but also from a figure who embodies one set of assumptions and attitudes to a figure who embodies quite different values; Richard and Bolingbroke are each representative of a distinctive world view. Richard's is a world that views ambition with horror, that prizes acquiescence over aggressiveness, that takes pride and comfort in the observance of ritual. His fall marks the demise of a habit of mind and a political climate as well as that of a man. As Robert Ornstein observes of Richard, "When he falls, a way of life and a world seem to fall with him."[32] The world coming into being is one that prizes adroitness, audacity, and pragmatism, above all. The triumph of Bolingbroke, champion of these attributes, signals the sharp displacement of traditional values.

In triumphing, Bolingbroke remains enigmatic, never overtly alluding to the skill with which he seizes the right opportunity at the right time. Not until *1 Henry IV* is there any explicit evocation of Occasion in connection with Bolingbroke. And there it is not Henry but a disgruntled former confederate who makes the point. Recalling events in the latter part of Richard's reign, Worcester reminds Henry, "from this swarm of fair advantages / You took Occasion to be quickly wooed / To gripe the general sway into your hand" (V.i.55-57).

II

Were Bolingbroke a more voluble character, we might know more about his concept of opportunity. But he is as taciturn as the king is loquacious. And we learn almost nothing of his private thoughts. Not until Shakespeare's next tragedy do we meet a figure whose speeches and soliloquies permit a fuller consideration of Occasion. The character is Marcus Brutus, who while very different from Bolingbroke in temperament, faces a similar task — the removal of a head of state and the substitution of a new regime. Though Brutus is only partially successful, his character permits an especially detailed treatment of the quest for opportunity.

In one of the earliest studies seeking to relate Renaissance literature to iconography, Henry Green suggested that Brutus' image of "a tide in the affairs of men" resembles the emblem of Occasion,[33] and in this century the correspondence has been widely noticed. Occasion, however, has significance not only for the imagery of Brutus' speech but also, more generally, for his character. That is, the concept of Occasion underlies a cluster of Brutus' traits, including his penchant for predicting the future, timing his actions with precision, and staking chances of success upon a single daring move. All of these stem from Brutus' profound sense of opportunity, which informs his psyche throughout the play, from his early meditation on Caesar's "tyranny" to his last orders on the plains of Philippi.

Brutus' "tide" speech is essentially a plea for action, designed to convince a dubious Cassius that the struggle with the enemy has reached a critical point, that the time for battle is now:

> Our legions are brimful, our cause is ripe:
> The enemy increaseth every day;
> We, at the height, are ready to decline.
> There is a tide in the affairs of men,
> Which taken at the flood, leads on to fortune;
> Omitted, all the voyage of their life
> Is bound in shallows and in miseries.
> On such a full sea are we now afloat,
> And we must take the current when it serves,
> Or lose our ventures. (IV.iii.215-24)

The speaker's sense of urgency is expressed in part through the language of height and declination. And for some readers this imagery, together with the reference to "fortune" (meaning simply "success"), suggests Fortune and her wheel. But the playwright eschews the image of a mechanical wheel which raises a man to the top only to begin a steady and inexorable downfall. Instead, he constructs the passage upon the nautical image of a ship riding the waves and seizing the tide. And this belongs, more properly, to Occasion.[34]

There is much in Brutus' speech that recalls pictorial representations of Occasion—more even than Henry Green recognized. As we have already seen, the "sea" almost always appears in emblems of Occasion, and sometimes Occasion actually stands above the waves. In addition, Brutus' assertion that they are "afloat" recalls the vessels that sail on the sea of Occasion, driven by the force of wind and tide. Brutus' references to "fortune" and "ventures," moreover, express the element of contingency associated with Occasion and made manifest by one of her accouterments, the wheel lying flat beneath her feet. Brutus' speech, then, incorporates several features associated with Occasion.[35]

The assumptions on which Occasion is predicated (that powerful forces are at work in the world but that man may, if skillful, harness them) inform Brutus' very character. His experience of prophecies, portents, and visions undoubtedly contributes to his belief that man's powers are circumscribed, and he expresses this notion after the assassination when he says, "Fates, we will know your pleasures. / That we shall die, we know, 'tis but the time, / And drawing days out, that men stand upon" (III.i.98-100). Later, after his vision of the Ghost, he speaks of "the providence of some high powers / That govern us below" (V.i.106-7). This conviction does not, however, deter Brutus from acting decisively. A resolute figure, he displays a fixedness of purpose befitting one who believes he is the master of events, not their servant. His confidence is nourished by his association with Cassius, a forceful embodiment of man's autonomy. For his part, Cassius is an Epicurean, who believes that even if the gods exist, they take no interest in humankind. Thus man is, or should be, free to assert himself as he wishes. Brutus may not display the pugnacious arrogance before men and gods that characterizes his friend. But by his tacit acceptance of Cassius' arguments, his participation in the conspiracy, and his active role in the assassination itself, Brutus affirms his capacity to shape his own future and thus history as well.

The balance between fatalism and self-determination that characterizes Brutus is perhaps most apparent in his attitude toward time, which he sees as both imposing constraints and offering opportunities. Typically, time (of the month and the day) is much on his mind the night before Caesar's death. Reflecting on the warning that he had heard along with others that day ("Beware the ides of March"), Brutus asks his servant, "Is not to-morrow, boy, the ides of March?" (II.i.40), and he directs Lucius, "Look in the calendar, and bring me word" (42). Later, as the details of Caesar's murder are plotted with the other conspirators,

Brutus remains mindful of the hour. When he hears a clock strike, he interjects, "Peace, count the clock" (192). This anxiety is prompted in part by his fear that Caesar may not leave home the next day. And although Decius assures them, "I will bring him to the Capitol" (211), the nervous Brutus seeks to fix the exact hour. When Cassius says, "We will all of us be there to fetch him," Brutus responds, "By the eight hour; is that the uttermost?" (213). In the morning Brutus is obviously mindful of the hour, for when Caesar at his home inquires the time, Brutus quickly replies, "Caesar, 'tis strucken eight" (II.ii.114).

Collectively, these references to time betray Brutus' reservations about man's ability to control his own destiny. For him, successful endeavor is not guaranteed by immediate, straightforward action. Man's capacity is limited by circumstance; some times are more propitious than others. In the words of Cassius, "Men *at some time* are masters of their fates" (I.ii.139). By embracing this view, Brutus manifests his sense of opportunity, the very essence of which is astute timing.[36]

For all his sensitivity to the exigencies of circumstance, however, Brutus has great difficulty capitalizing on his opportunities. In fact, whenever he faces a decision that requires a deft handling of the time, he makes a calamitous error. For example, the decision to allow Antony to deliver an oration—and over Caesar's body—proves to be lamentably inopportune. At this point the fortunes of the assassins are at a crucial stage, for they need to appease the multitude and thus to consolidate their political gains. To permit Antony, a well-known friend of Caesar's, to address the populace at such a volatile moment is to court disaster. Similarly, the decision made near Sardis to commit the troops proves to be a fateful error. It plays into the hands of an enemy awaiting an opening to strike; Octavius greets the sight of the conspirators' forces with the words, "Now, Antony, our hopes are answered" (V.i.1). And Brutus' actions at Philippi are singularly ill-timed. Taking advantage of initial success, Brutus, heedless of the disaster overtaking Cassius' forces, precipitously charges the enemy. As Titinius explains to Cassius after the battle:

> O Cassius, Brutus gave the word too early,
> Who, having some advantage on Octavius,
> Took it too eagerly. His soldiers fell to spoil,
> Whilst we by Antony are all enclos'd. (V.iii.5-8)

Since Plutarch attributes the error chiefly to the impatience of the soldiers,[37] it is clear that Shakespeare has accentuated Brutus' failure in timing. This departure from the source is, however, entirely consistent with the playwright's conception of the character. In *Julius Caesar* Brutus' habits of thinking and acting are such that they dictate errors in timing.

The way in which Brutus arrives at his resolution for action reveals why he so often errs. Consider the first critical decision that Brutus makes in the play:

> 'tis a common proof
> That lowliness is young ambition's ladder,
> Whereto the climber-upward turns his face;
> But when he once attains the upmost round,
> He then unto the ladder turns his back,
> Looks in the clouds, scorning the base degrees
> By which he did ascend. So Caesar may;
> Then lest he may, prevent. And since the quarrel
> Will bear no color for the thing he is,
> Fashion it thus: that what he is, augmented,
> Would run to these and these extremities;
> And therefore think him as a serpent's egg,
> Which, hatch'd, would as his kind grow mischievous,
> And kill him in the shell. (II.i.21-34)

Here Brutus indulges his predilection for anticipating the behavior of others and tailoring his own deeds to that expectation. In this instance he decides that Caesar is a tyrant in embryo whose maturation must be thwarted. It is his confidence that he knows what the future holds for Caesar and for Rome that leads him to attach such importance to the present and to believe that, if the Republic is to be preserved, his decisive action now is necessary.

The soundness of Brutus' proposed action, however, depends upon the accuracy of his prediction. And that is highly questionable, for Brutus' premise seems dubious. Indeed, he himself admits that "the quarrel / Will bear no color for the thing he is." But Brutus somehow manages to evade the implications of this admission. Suppressing his personal feeling for Caesar, Brutus resorts to an austere cerebration that takes on a life of its own.[38] His rationalism is apparent in the progression of his thought from general truth to specific instance to deduction; in the use of such words as "since" and "therefore," indicating logical relationships; and in his framing of the simile, a consciously thought-out correlation, likening Caesar to a serpent. By relying so confidently on rational processes and by denying the promptings of his own instincts, Brutus dooms himself to misconstrue the futures of others and to construct a seriously flawed design for his own future conduct.[39]

Reason, as exercised by Brutus, is an imperfect guide to prediction and to the formulation of action in a capricious, tumultuous, even mysterious world. And its inadequacy is underscored by the other decisions that punctuate his career, none of which is more important than that to commit the troops at Philippi. The decision has its origins in Brutus' anxiety over the allegiance of the populace. Only grudgingly have they aided the forces of Brutus and Cassius. And this reluctance signifies to Brutus a sympathy with the enemy. In the future, Brutus tells his comrade, this will render their military position precarious:

> The enemy, marching along by them,
> By them shall make a fuller number up,
> Come on refresh'd, new-added, and encourag'd;
> From which advantage shall we cut him off
> If at Philippi we do face him there,
> These people at our back. (IV.iii.207-12)

When Cassius interrupts to voice his own opinion, Brutus silences him with the speech on "a tide in the affairs of men."

Here, as in the earlier meditation on Caesar, Brutus bases a momentous course of action on a personal prediction; in this instance he gauges the likely behavior of the populace. And here, too, he fails to question closely the premise that underlies that prediction. The people near Sardis may or may not favor the forces of Antony. What Brutus interprets as their hostility may simply be their resentment against the intrusion of any military forces in their land. It is not clear that Brutus and Cassius need do anything at present to secure their safety; Cassius seeks not a battle, but a campaign of attrition. By forcing the issue and seeking a confrontation, Brutus may be attempting to seize an opportunity that does not truly exist.

If that opportunity is genuine, it is certainly mishandled. In the field Brutus proves an erratic general. His orders are given, as we have seen, "too early." Indefatigable, he decides on a second contest with the enemy. He tells his men: "'Tis three a' clock, and, Romans, yet ere night / We shall try fortune in a second fight" (V.iii.109-10). Like the first encounter, this one also ends short of success, and no less inevitably. When Brutus should respond to the rhythm inherent in events, his rationality leads him to look to the regular, precise measurements of clock time. Norman Rabkin, commenting on Brutus' speech on "a tide in the affairs of men," succinctly points to the nature of his problem: "His wisdom here is undercut only by his failure to realize that the flood cannot be gauged by the reasoning mind."[40]

Brutus' plight demonstrates that the individual who conceives of time as containing specially propitious moments for action faces a burdensome difficulty, for his world view requires him to select a certain moment for action and to concentrate all his energies then. But which moment? How is it to be recognized? And, once recognized, how precisely should it be handled? It was just such questions—and the possibility of failure—that led thinkers traditionally to link Occasion with another personification, Regret or Penitence. In antiquity Ausonius linked the two in his poem, "In Simulacrum Occasionis et Paenitentiae."[41] (In the Renaissance Machiavelli translated the poem into Italian; his version is entitled "Dell' Occasione.") Renaissance emblematists vividly expressed the same idea. For example, in Gilles Corrozet's *Hecatomgraphie* (Paris, 1543), Penitence sits in the stern of Occasion's vessel (fig. 11). And in Jean Jacques Boissard's *Emblemes latins* (Metz, 1588), Penitence, holding a whip in her hands, walks immediately behind Occasion (fig. 15). These representations are meant to suggest that for some aspirants the self-reproach and the public opprobrium of missed or bungled opportunities could be severe indeed. And such is the case of Marcus Brutus who, unwilling to face the disgrace of capture, follows Cassius' example and takes his own life.[42]

Brutus' death constitutes, in effect, an eloquent commentary on his quest for opportunity and, in particular, on his speech on "a tide in the affairs of men." That speech aptly expresses the possibilities open to the individual who moves swiftly and decisively, the fleeting quality of the opportune moment, and the inevitable disaster that awaits

Fig. 15. Jean Jacques Boissard, Emblemes latins

the action taken at an inauspicious time. Perhaps no passage in Elizabethan drama captures so well the meaning of Occasion. Yet those lines, in their context, must surely be ironic, for Brutus is precisely that figure in *Julius Caesar* who consistently misjudges the "right" moment. His tragedy is that of a man convinced of the existence of opportune moments, yet lacking the qualities of personality and mind needed to assess and exploit them effectively.

To deepen the irony, Shakespeare surrounds Brutus with friends and enemies who possess a far surer sense of opportunity than he. Thus the pragmatic Cassius realizes his compatriot's error in allowing Antony to survive the assassination and to deliver the funeral oration. And it is Cassius who would dissuade Brutus from waging war at Philippi. Appropriately, Cassius expresses his anxiety before battle in a nautical metaphor that seems to evoke Occasion: "Why now blow wind, swell billow, and swim bark! / The storm is up, and all is on the hazard" (V.i.67-68). Similarly, Mark Antony has a keener sense of opportunity than Brutus, which allows him to capitalize on circumstance following

Caesar's murder and turn the people against the assassins. Over Caesar's body he speaks of "the tide of times" (III.i.257), and after the oration he calls to mind a distinctively Renaissance Fortune when, flushed with success, he tells a servant, "Fortune is merry, / And in this mood will give us any thing" (III.ii.266-67).

III

Calling him "the sensitive philosopher misgivingly impelled to action," Harley Granville-Barker remarks on Brutus' similarity to Hamlet: "The likeness is distinct."[43] Like Brutus, Hamlet is an intellectual, a man whose cerebration is perhaps the most salient feature of his character. Like Brutus, moreover, Hamlet is called to action of a particularly violent kind, the killing of a head of state; and such a deed runs counter to his cautious nature. To be sure, Hamlet can be impulsive. But his celebrated delay in exacting revenge is the product of a mind that weighs things with great care and of a temperament that tends naturally toward meditation. When, for example, Hamlet finds Claudius at prayer, he ponders the situation, considers the possible consequences of killing the king at this moment, and finally deems the circumstances unsuitable to the deed. Hamlet's soliloquy at III.iii.73-96 is as revealing of his character as is Brutus' reflection on Caesar-as-serpent the night before the assassination.

For Hamlet, as for Brutus, some times are more propitious than others. These moments of opportunity are, however, difficult to locate. And in his pursuit of them Hamlet, like Brutus, lurches and stumbles. Hostile Fortune, rather than responsive Occasion, dominates Hamlet's mental world. During the play, however, Hamlet profoundly alters his world view, replacing Fortune with something more benign. With his acceptance of divine providence, he perceives opportunity where formerly he saw only opposition.

The transition is thrown into bold relief by the specifically visual way in which Hamlet conceives of his world.[44] This trait manifests itself in a variety of ways: in his reference to miniature painting; his use of actual portraits in the bedroom scene ("Look here upon this picture, and on this"); and his habit of speech ("By the image of my cause, I see / The portraiture of his"). Even more important, this trait expresses itself in Hamlet's vivid description of those forces which he perceives as dominating his world, forces which he personifies and describes in an almost painterly fashion.[45] Among these none is more important than Fortune.

The first important description of Fortune occurs in the context of the players' visit to Elsinore. A playgoer himself, Hamlet welcomes them warmly and asks a player to recite a speech about the killing of Priam, a speech which the prince had heard on some earlier occasion. After Hamlet declaims the lines that he remembers, the player obligingly continues.[46] From its beginning the narrative is richly descriptive—and gruesome. The Greek warrior is a ghastly figure: his arms are "Black as his purpose" (II.ii.453); he is "total gules, horridly trick'd / With blood of fathers, mothers, daughters, sons" (457-58). This appearance mirrors the horror of the deed he is about to commit: the slaying of an aged king, a figure presented sympathetically. As the Player speaks, Hamlet's purpose in requesting the recital becomes clear: he seems to feel a kinship with the bloody warrior. Life parallels art, for just as Pyrrhus is engaged in avenging his father, Achilles, so too Hamlet is embarked on avenging *his* father. The correspondence between Pyrrhus and Hamlet is hardly exact; we witness no soul-searching on the part of the Greek. But there is this similarity: both revengers pause before claiming their victims. Although the hesitation of Pyrrhus may have nothing of Hamlet's complexity, it is nonetheless pronounced:

> lo his sword,
> Which was declining on the milky head
> Of reverent Priam, seem'd i' th' air to stick.
> So as a painted tyrant Pyrrhus stood
> And, like a neutral to his will and matter,
> Did nothing. (477-82)

Only after this does "A roused vengeance" set Pyrrhus in motion; finally, the sword falls.

The parallel between Pyrrhus and Hamlet goes even further, for the deeds of both revengers are identified with the will of Fortune. Notice that the Player's speech proceeds to castigate not Pyrrhus but the power ultimately responsible for the killing of Priam:

> Out, out, thou strumpet Fortune! All you gods,
> In general synod take away her power!
> Break all the spokes and fellies from her wheel,
> And bowl the round nave down the hill of heaven
> As low as to the fiends! (493-97)

Pyrrhus, the speech suggests, is Fortune's agent, executing her decrees. Like him, Hamlet too feels impelled by Fortune, and so he shares vicariously in the vitriolic denunciation directed at Fortune by the Player: "Who this had seen, with tongue in venom steep'd, / 'Gainst Fortune's state would treason have pronounc'd" (510-11). In Hamlet's mind, as in the Player's speech, revenge is associated with a malign Fortune.

In the next scene Hamlet's tone is subdued. His passion has spent itself, but he is still thinking about his response to Fortune:

> To be, or not to be, that is the question:
> Whether 'tis nobler in the mind to suffer
> The slings and arrows of outrageous fortune,
> Or to take arms against a sea of troubles,
> And by opposing, end them. (III.i.55-59)

Although these most famous of Shakespearean lines concern Dame Fortune, few listeners or readers are truly conscious of the personification; editors seldom capitalize Fortune's name here. Yet the attributes that Hamlet assigns to Fortune are traditional parts of her iconography. From at least the time of Dante, Fortune was associated with arrows, and sixteenth-century emblem books depict Fortune brandishing those arrows.[47] Moreover, the "sea of troubles" also belongs to depictions of Fortune. As we have seen, Fortune in the Renaissance is often pictured standing just above the waves or riding in a vessel.

Unless we recognize Hamlet's personification of Fortune, we are likely to construe his thinking as more abstract than it actually is. Critics commonly cite the "To be, or not to be" soliloquy as evidence of Hamlet's philosophic bent. One even concludes that "Hamlet is a metaphysician."[48] Admittedly, Hamlet is given to cerebration; he accuses himself

254

of thinking too precisely on the event. Yet when he speaks of Fortune here, he is not speaking vaguely of some generalized condition; rather, he has in mind a specific antagonist, one armed with slings and arrows. So direct and intense is his response to his situation that it issues in this particular image of Fortune. Despite his intellectuality, then, there is an immediacy and vividness about the way Hamlet conceives his world. One can almost imagine him as Seneca and Machiavelli envision man: in hand-to-hand combat with Fortune.

What Wolfgang Clemen has said of Hamlet's image-making applies as well to his thinking about Fortune: "When he begins to speak, the images fairly stream to him without the slightest effort—not as similes or conscious paraphrases, but as immediate and spontaneous visions."[49] Hamlet's way of envisioning Fortune, then, differs from, say, Fluellen's. In *Henry V* Fluellen ticks off Fortune's features as though he were taking an iconographic inventory (III.vi.30-38). He tells us that Fortune "is painted blind," that she is "painted also with a wheel," that her foot "is fixed upon a spherical stone which rolls, and rolls, and rolls." By contrast, there is nothing laborious about Hamlet's description of Fortune. She springs quickly to his mind's eye. She is a familiar part of the cosmic furniture, as much a part of his world as the sun and moon.

Hamlet's way of envisioning Fortune is distinctive in another way as well: rather than enumerating several of her accouterments in the manner of Fluellen, he suggests her power by naming only one. Marvin Spevack's observation about Hamlet's method of constructing images is apposite: "Hamlet is like a caricaturist who dwells on some ruling trait or feature . . . and makes the part stand for the whole."[50] It is this characteristic which manifests itself in his speech to Horatio:

> thou hast been
> As one in suff'ring all that suffers nothing,
> A man that Fortune's buffets and rewards
> Hast ta'en with equal thanks; and blest are those
> Whose blood and judgment are so well co-meddled,
> That they are not a pipe for Fortune's finger
> To sound what stop she please. (III.ii.65-71)

The only visual counterpart to this passage that I have discovered shows Fortune not only with a pipe, which she plays while a man dances to the tune, but also with other familiar accouterments—blindfold, globe, and sail. The representation appears as an emblem in Guillaume de la Perrière's *La Morosophie* (fig. 16). If Shakespeare knew this emblem or some other like it, he has chosen to simplify it drastically so as to focus on only one of Fortune's features.

Artistic constructions of one kind or another—portraits, theatrical speeches, even an entire play—form an integral part of Hamlet's expression. They function as a screen onto which he projects his emotions of anger or depression or admiration. Maurice Charney remarks that Hamlet "thinks of experience as a work of art that can only be mastered by aesthetic means."[51] Hamlet habitually locates himself within the confines of an already created artistic world. Art enables him to recapture his past, define his situation, and express his most intense feelings.

Such an application of art is apparent in the play-within-the-play, where Hamlet's personal feelings find a parallel. When the Player King declares, "What to ourselves in passion we propose, / The passion ending, doth the purpose lose" (III.ii.194-95), Hamlet must be reminded of the difficulty he has in marshalling and sustaining emotional resolution. He keenly appreciates the problem of directing one's action in a perilously uncertain world; he knows how riddled with contingency is the human condition. The Player King's line, "Grief joys, joy grieves, on slender accident" (199), must strike a responsive chord in Hamlet whose entire life has been irrevocably changed by the discovery of his father's murder. So too this recognition of man's bondage to circumstance must strike Hamlet as particularly apt to his own situation:

> Our wills and fates do so contrary run
> That our devices still are overthrown,
> Our thoughts are ours, their ends none of our own. (211-13)

In so many of these lines we seem to hear Hamlet's own sentiments. Indeed, it is entirely possible that these are meant to be Hamlet's own words, the "speech of some dozen lines, or sixteen lines" (II.ii.541-42) which he asked the Player to insert in *The Murder of Gonzago*.

If Hamlet detects accident in his own life, he sees it also in the

Fig. 16. Guillaume de la Perrière, La Morosophie

lives of others, especially those of his parents, whose relationship is reflected in that of the Player King and Queen. Contemplating the gulf between present resolve and future action, the Player King says:

> This world is not for aye, nor 'tis not strange
> That even our loves should with our fortunes change:
> For 'tis a question left us yet to prove,
> Whether love lead fortune, or else fortune love. (200-3)

The speaker knows that although the queen may vow eternal fidelity, human behavior is unpredictable. And he expresses his sense of contingency by personifying Fortune.[52] Like the references to Fortune by Hamlet, this one has a pictorial counterpart, for in Jean Cousin's *Liber Fortunae* Dame Fortune quite literally leads Cupid (or Love) by the hand.[53]

The series of references to Fortune in the play convey, collectively, Hamlet's sense of victimization. To him circumstance seems always to favor predatory figures. It is the innocent—Hamlet's father, Priam, the Player King—who fall prey to their adversaries.[54] It is inevitable, then, that Hamlet should feel demoralized and that, consequently, he should find it difficult to act decisively. With the success of the play-within-the-play, however, Hamlet gains a new sense of belligerency, one that leads him to rebuff Rosencrantz and Guildenstern: "'Sblood, do you think I am easier to be play'd on than a pipe?" (III.ii.370-71). Compared with his comments on Fortune's pipe earlier in the scene, this remark bespeaks new resolve to resist intimidation from without. And Hamlet's killing of Polonius manifests, in an even more vivid way, his determination to act. When he sees the body, Hamlet says, "I took thee for thy better. Take thy fortune" (III.iv.32). These words underscore his changed disposition. For the first time, he speaks of "fortune" rather than Fortune. That is, he speaks of a person's individual lot rather than the goddess.

Nevertheless, this new aggressiveness does not immediately issue in the fulfillment of the Ghost's command, for Hamlet proves singularly inept. The killing of Polonius fails to advance his purpose; it only jeopardizes Hamlet's already precarious position at Claudius' court. He seems dimly to recognize his inability to find or to seize opportunity when, just before leaving Denmark, he sees the doughty Fortinbras and says:

> How all occasions do inform against me,
> And spur my dull revenge! (IV.iv.32-33)

That Hamlet should admire a soldier who has been termed an "opportunist" is not surprising, for despite his preoccupation with the time, Hamlet lacks any sense of timeliness. He resorts to quick, jerky, ineffectual action. He has no sense of the rhythm of events, no sense of what is opportune. Instead of cooperating with the time, he thinks of himself as correcting the time: "The time is out of joint—O cursed spite, / That ever I was born to set it right!" (I.v.188-89).

Hamlet's antagonism toward and fear of time parallels and perhaps derives from his attitude toward Fortune. These two are closely allied in the Renaissance and, as we have seen, are sometimes conflated iconographically. To Hamlet both are implacable foes. In the same speech in which he talks of the slings and arrows of Fortune, he also complains of "the whips and scorns of time" (III.i.69). And a whip, Samuel C. Chew has shown, was actually carried by Father Time in the Renaissance.[55] When, later on, Hamlet's attitude toward Fortune alters, he also modifies his attitude toward time.

The change takes place on Hamlet's voyage to England, one of the most mysterious journeys in Shakespeare. Since it occurs offstage, we are denied first-hand knowledge. We perceive its effects as soon as we see the returned Hamlet, but the nature of the change we learn only gradually through Hamlet's words to Horatio.

Hamlet recounts to his friend his experience of several events involving chance: the discovery of the royal commission intended to work his death; the substitution of one letter for another; and the capture by pirates. The series of coincidences is striking: that he should have chanced to discover the contents of Claudius' letter; that he should have had his father's signet with him; that he alone should have been captured at sea. We might expect Hamlet to perceive the hand of Fortune in all of this. After all, as recently as his last speech before leaving Denmark, he was still talking about Fortune, expressing his admiration of Fortinbras for "Exposing what is mortal and unsure / To all that fortune, death, and danger dare" (IV.iv.51-52). Moreover, Hamlet's journey takes place upon the sea, associated with the operation of chance. Indeed, Hamlet has himself invoked the symbolism when he spoke of the "sea of troubles." But Hamlet defies our expectation. Instead of ascribing events to Fortune, he says to Horatio:

> Rashly—
> And prais'd be rashness for it—let us know
> Our indiscretion sometime serves us well
> When our deep plots do pall, and that should learn us
> There's a divinity that shapes our ends,
> Rough-hew them how we will— (V.ii.6-11)

And in answering Horatio's inquiry about the signet, Hamlet again cites divine agency: "Why, even in that was heaven ordinant" (48). Clearly, Hamlet places an entirely different interpretation on contingency than he did previously. Why?

Hitherto Hamlet has considered himself the victim of "slender accident." He has been tormented by Fortune—her slings and arrows, her pipe, her wheel. From his earliest reference (to Fortune's star), every mention of Fortune has been negative, and understandably so. But now, on the voyage, chance begins to work in his favor. He finds himself guided rather than manipulated; the power responsible he deems benign. Contingency emerges as part of an overarching pattern. John Holloway writes, "Over and over in *Hamlet,* chance turns into a larger design, randomness becomes retribution."[56] Believing God to be the author of that design, Hamlet supplants Fortune with providence in his cosmology. Never again will he mention Fortune.

Concomitantly, Hamlet gains a wholly new attitude toward time. No longer does he complain of Time's whips and scorns. Nor does he shrink from action. There is now no flailing about in search of the right moment. He has a sense of opportunity which he had not previously possessed. It is appropriate that this should be owing to his experience on the voyage, for in the Renaissance Occasion was usually depicted on the sea, sometimes riding in a vessel. Earlier in the play Laertes implicitly links Occasion with the sea when, about to embark, he says to Ophelia, "A double blessing is a double grace, / Occasion smiles upon a second leave" (I.iii.53-54).[57] And Hamlet, on his voyage, seizes an opportunity that presents itself quite literally on the sea. It is perhaps not too much of an exaggeration to say that Hamlet re-enacts the shift from Fortune to Occasion that was taking place in so much Renaissance thought and iconography. That is, he moves from a world dominated by an antagonistic Fortune, to one inhabited by a more responsive Occasion.

When Hamlet returns to Denmark, his demeanor has utterly changed. Despite the brief altercation with Laertes at Ophelia's funeral, Hamlet seems invested with quiet confidence, even in the face of peril. When the duel with Laertes is proposed, Horatio urges caution. But Hamlet refuses to delay:

> Not a whit, we defy augury. There is special providence in the fall of a sparrow. If it be now, 'tis not to come; if it be not to come, it will be now; if it be not now, yet it will come — the readiness is all.
> (V.ii.219-22)

To some, this marks the nadir of Hamlet's life. H. B. Charlton, for instance, interprets Hamlet's utterance as "merely the courage of despair."[58] In my judgment, however, Hamlet expresses neither despair nor indifference. His attitude, after all, is based upon faith in providence, a benevolent force which invites man's cooperation. Providence allows him to fulfill his potential by aligning himself with a larger design. Acknowledgment of providence thus inspires a mood of calm, rather than despondency. Hamlet no longer needs or wants to play the malcontent. His demeanor takes on the subdued aspect of one who believes himself acting in accord with some greater power.

Hamlet's readiness should not be confused with passivity.[59] Readiness involves an alertness to the rhythm of events. It implies a willingness to respond actively to circumstance. It presupposes an ability and a disposition to cooperate with the time, for readiness signifies "both prompt compliance and a state of preparation."[60] Believing himself an instrument of God's will, Hamlet can act with equanimity and at the right moment. He will not now plot revenge as he had earlier done. Yet "it will come" — as the unpremeditated response to Claudius' device of the poisoned sword.

By the end of the play, when Hamlet has come to accept the role of providence in his life, not only has Fortune been expunged from Hamlet's world view but also from the play itself. This is owing to the fact that, earlier, the representation of Fortune was so completely an expression of Hamlet's personal vision. Apart from the Player and the Player King, who describe Fortune "in character" so to speak and implicitly at Hamlet's direction, only the prince speaks of Fortune repeatedly. Since Hamlet is the chief source of Fortune's representation and since it is through him that we so largely perceive the world of the play, it is natural that she should disappear when Hamlet revises his picture of the world. Fortune, whose image has loomed so prominently for so long, must vanish as suddenly as she first appeared.

NOTES TO CHAPTER 8

1. General studies of Fortune in Shakespearean tragedy include: Paul Reyher, *Essai sur les idées dans l'oeuvre de Shakespeare*, Bibliothèque des langues modernes (Paris: Marcel Didier, 1947); Soji Iwasaki, *The Sword and the Word: Shakespeare's Tragic Sense of Time* (Tokyo: Shinozaki Shorin, 1973), esp. pp. 13-49; J. Leeds Barroll, "Structure in Shakespearean Tragedy," *ShakS*, 7 (1974): 345-78. See also Robert Kilburn Root, *Classical Mythology in Shakespeare*, Yale Studies in English, 19 (New York: Henry Holt, 1903), pp. 61-64. For Shakespeare's treatment of time, see Frederick Turner, *Shakespeare and the Nature of Time: Moral and Philosophical Themes in Some Plays and Poems of William Shakespeare* (Oxford: Clarendon Press, 1971). A wide-ranging study of time in the Renaissance has been made by Ricardo Quinones, *The Renaissance Discovery of Time*, Harvard Studies in Comparative Literature, no. 31 (Cambridge, Mass.: Harvard Univ. Press, 1972).

2. Virgil K. Whitaker, *The Mirror up to Nature: The Technique of Shakespeare's Tragedies* (San Marino, Calif.: Huntington Library, 1965), p. 119.

3. *Patterns in Shakespearian Tragedy* (London: Methuen, 1960), p. 51. Ribner makes much the same point in *The English History Play in the Age of Shakespeare*, rev. ed. (London: Methuen, 1965), p. 162.

4. "*Richard II* and Shakespeare's Tragic Mode," *TSLL*, 5 (1963): 350.

5. *Shakespeare's Historical Plays* (London: Oxford Univ. Press, 1964), p. 119.

6. Studies of Fortune in *Richard II* and in the other histories include: Reyher, *Essai sur les idées dans l'oeuvre de Shakespeare*, esp. pp. 245-52; and Walter F. Schirmer, "Glück und Ende der Könige in Shakespeares Historien," *Arbeitsgemeinschaft für Forschung des Landes Nordrhein-Westfalen*, 22 (1954): 5-18.

7. Peter Ure, ed., New Arden *King Richard II*, 5th ed. (London: Methuen, 1961), p. lxxxii.

8. H. M. Richmond, *Shakespeare's Political Plays* (New York: Random House, 1967), p. 134.

9. Rolf Soellner, *Shakespeare's Patterns of Self-Knowledge* (Columbus: Ohio State Univ. Press, 1972), p. 99.

10. According to Peter Ure, ed., *King Richard II*, "The figure of buckets and well is adapted from the medieval and Elizabethan figure of Fortune's buckets..." (p. 136). Howard R. Patch discusses the figure, in *The Goddess Fortuna in Mediaeval Literature* (1927; reprint ed., New York: Octagon Books, 1967), pp. 53-54. Guillaume de Machaut uses the image of Fortune's buckets in *Remède de Fortune* (c. 1342), printed in *Oeuvres*, ed. Ernest Hoepffner, 2 vols. (Paris: Firmin Didot, 1911), 2: 35-36.

11. *The Mirror for Magistrates*, ed. Lily B. Campbell (1938; reprint ed., New York: Barnes and Noble, 1960), p. 163.

12. *The Origins of English Tragedy* (Oxford: Clarendon Press, 1967), p. 109.

13. Ibid., p. 124.

14. *Patterns in Shakespearian Tragedy*, pp. 49-50.

15. Richard's most memorable images—the buckets and, later, the clock—while implying some sort of cause and effect, locate the cause without rather than within.

16. Willard Farnham, *The Medieval Heritage of Elizabethan Tragedy* (1936; reprint ed. with corrections, Oxford: Basil Blackwell, 1970), p. 415.

17. Samuel Schoenbaum, in "'Richard II' and the Realities of Power," *ShS*, 28 (1975): 1-13, has argued that the king is actually more astute, at least in the trial-by-combat scene, than readers of the play recognize. Diane Bornstein, however, in "Trial by Combat and Official Irresponsibility in *Richard II*," *ShakS*, 8 (1975): 131-41, argues that the scene demonstrates serious error on Richard's part.

18. *The Dramatist and the Received Idea: Studies in the Plays of Marlowe and Shakespeare* (Cambridge: Cambridge Univ. Press, 1968), p. 178.

19. Ed., New Cambridge *King Richard II* (Cambridge: Cambridge Univ. Press, 1939), p. xx.

20. *Shakespeare's History Plays* (1944; reprint ed., New York: Barnes and Noble, 1969), p. 260.

21. "The Wheel of Fortune in Shakespeare's Historical Plays," *RES*, NS 1 (1950): 3.

22. Quoted in the New Cambridge *King Richard II*, ed. Wilson, p. lxii.

23. *The Cease of Majesty: A Study of Shakespeare's History Plays* (London: Edward Arnold, 1961), p. 251.

24. Like her husband, the queen speaks of Fortune, using imagery in keeping with her sex: "methinks / Some unborn sorrow, ripe in fortune's womb, / Is coming towards me" (II.ii.9-11). There is an interesting parallel in Fulke Greville's *Life of Sir Philip Sidney*, Intro. Nowell Smith (London: Clarendon Press, 1907): "these Tyrannicall encrochments doe carry the images of Hell, and her thunder-workers, in their own breasts, as fortune doth misfortunes in that wind-blown, vast, and various womb of hers" (p. 109).

25. The distinction is expressed in this line of Sidney's: "Nor Fortune of thy fortune author is" (*The Poems of Sir Philip Sidney*, ed. William A. Ringler, Jr. [Oxford: Clarendon Press, 1962], sonnet 33, p. 181). Editors of Shakespeare and many commentators as well frequently fail to observe this distinction in their handling of capitalization.

26. Shakespeare's treatment of Bolingbroke probably was inspired, in part, by this passage in Holinshed regarding the departure of the Welsh troops: ". . . wheras if the king had come before their breaking up, no doubt, but they would have put the duke of Hereford in adventure of a field: so that the kings lingering of time before his comming over, gave opportunitie to the duke to bring things to passe as he could have wished, and tooke from the king all occasion to recover afterwards anie forces sufficient to resist him." Quoted in *Narrative and Dramatic Sources of Shakespeare*, ed. Geoffrey Bullough, 3 (New York and London: Columbia Univ. Press, 1960), 400.

27. Holinshed's *Third Volume of Chronicles* (1587) interprets the rise and fall in providential fashion: "in this dejecting of the one, & advancing of the other, the providence of God is to be respected, & his secret will to be woondered at." Quoted in *Narrative and Dramatic Sources of Shakespeare*, 3: 402. R. Mark Benbow, in "The Providential Theory of Historical Causation in *Holinshed's Chronicles*: 1577 and 1587," *TSLL*, 1 (1959): 264-76, argues that the 1587 edition

is more insistently providential in emphasis than the earlier edition and that this shift is largely due to the additions of Abraham Fleming (additions which include, according to Benbow, the sentence quoted above in this note). Benbow also makes the point that "Fleming attempts to subordinate the concept of Fortune to that of Providence" (p. 267). Evidently, the providential interpretation found in the *Chronicles* was not shared by Shakespeare. As Henry Ansgar Kelly writes, in *Divine Providence in the England of Shakespeare's Histories* (Cambridge, Mass.: Harvard Univ. Press, 1970), "After viewing the providential themes in *Richard II*, we may ask if there is any indication that Shakespeare intended us to feel that God was active in bringing about any of the actions of the play, or in aiding any of the characters. It would seem that we must answer in the negative, for not even the characters themselves are dramatized as considering any of the play's vicissitudes to have been brought about by God" (p. 214).

28. A. R. Humphreys, *Shakespeare: Richard II* (London: Edward Arnold, 1967), pp. 43-44.

29. Moody E. Prior, in *The Drama of Power: Studies in Shakespeare's History Plays* (Evanston: Northwestern Univ. Press, 1973), writes that the "evidently calculated absence" of the wheel of Fortune suggests that Shakespeare "was trying to avoid a reductive cliché" (p. 165).

30. *The Virtues Reconciled: An Iconographic Study* (Toronto: Univ. of Toronto Press, 1947), p. 15. See also Heinrich Schwarz, "The Mirror in Art," *Art Quarterly*, 15 (1952): 105-06.

31. "Bolingbroke, A True Machiavellian," *MLQ*, 9 (1948): 183.

32. *A Kingdom for a Stage: The Achievement of Shakespeare's History Plays* (Cambridge, Mass.: Harvard Univ. Press, 1972), p. 102.

33. *Shakespeare and the Emblem Writers: An Exposition of Their Similarities of Thought and Expression* (London: Trübner, 1870), pp. 260 ff.

34. John W. Velz, in "Undular Structure in 'Julius Caesar,'" *MLR*, 66 (1971): 21-30, has suggested that the imagery of Brutus' speech may have been inspired by a passage in Plutarch dealing with "the small boat which carried 'Caesar and his fortune' to safety through an adverse surf and a dangerous storm when he made his secret journey to Brundisium" (24). This seems to me unlikely.

35. Brutus does not, of course, actually describe the figure of Occasion. George Lyman Kittredge, however, writes in his edition of *Julius Caesar*

(New York: Ginn, 1939) that Brutus' speech "gives superb expression to a philosophical commonplace that Shakespeare had read in one of his earliest schoolbooks — *Cato's Distichs*, ii, 26:

> Rem tibi quam noris aptam dimittere noli:
> Fronte capillata, post est Occasio calva" (p. 176).

A translation, in *Preceptes of Cato with annotacions of D. Erasmus of Roterodame* (London, [1553]), Book II, sigs. G_5^V-G6, reads:

> A thing that thou knowest mete for thy purpose.
> See in no case, thou dooest it lose.
> Occasion in the forehead hath heare
> And the polle, balde and bare.

36. The connection between Time and Occasion is suggested in *The Bloody Brother, or Rollo, Duke of Normandy*, in which a character says: "Blest Occasion / Offers herself in thousand safeties to you; / Time standing still to point you out your purpose. . . ." See *The Works of Beaumont and Fletcher*, ed. Rev. Alexander Dyce, 10 (London: Edward Moxon, 1846), 391. So closely related are Occasion and Time that Shakespeare sometimes conflates the two. In *Much Ado About Nothing*, for instance, a character speaks of Time when the metaphor, referring to a topknot or forelock, properly demands Occasion: "if he found her accordant, he meant to take the present time by the top. . ." (I.ii.14-15). Similarly, in *All's Well That Ends Well* a character says, "Not one word more of the consumed time. / Let's take the instant by the forward top" (V.iii.38-39).

37. See *Plutarch's Lives of the Noble Grecians and Romanes*, in *Narrative and Dramatic Sources of Shakespeare*, ed. Geoffrey Bullough, 5 (New York and London: Columbia Univ. Press, 1964), 122.

38. Among those who find Brutus' reasoning seriously flawed are Virgil K. Whitaker, who writes of Brutus' soliloquy, in *Shakespeare's Use of Learning: An Inquiry into the Growth of his Mind and Art* (San Marino, Calif.: Huntington Library, 1953), "Shakespeare has done his best to make the fallacies in the reasoning obvious" (p. 245) and Kenneth Muir, who writes, in *Shakespeare's Tragic Sequence* (London: Hutchinson Univ. Library, 1972), that "in this crucial soliloquy Brutus is not given a single valid argument" (p. 48).

39. This soliloquy is not so explicitly informed by the concept of Occasion as is the speech on "a tide in the affairs of men." However, Douglas L. Peterson, in *Time, Tide, and Tempest: A Study of Shakespeare's Romances* (San Marino, Calif.: Huntington Library, 1973), observes that Brutus' images of the serpent

and of seizing the tide resemble those in a poem by Robert Southwell "on the importance of seizing occasion when it presents itself" (p. 67, *n*31).

40. *Shakespeare and the Common Understanding* (New York: Free Press, 1967), p. 117.

41. See *Ausonius*, ed. and trans. Hugh G. Evelyn White, LCL, 2 (Cambridge, Mass. and London: Harvard Univ. Press, 1949), 174-77.

42. Brutus' suicide was a popular subject among emblematists. Andrea Alciati, for example, in *Viri Clarissimi . . . Emblematum Liber* (Augsburg, 1531), depicts Brutus plunging a sword into his chest (sig. C1). And Geoffrey Whitney, in *A Choice of Emblemes* (Leyden, 1586), portrays Brutus falling on his sword (p. 70). Both interpret the action in similar fashion; their common motto reads, "Fortuna virtutem superans" ("Fortune conquering virtue"). In Shakespeare's treatment, however, it would be more accurate to say that Brutus falls victim to Occasio rather than Fortuna.

43. *Prefaces to Shakespeare*, 1 (Princeton: Princeton Univ. Press, 1946), 30. Granville-Barker had made essentially the same point earlier, in "From Henry V to Hamlet," in *Proceedings of the British Academy*, 11 (1924-25), 283-309.

44. For Shakespeare's interest in the visual arts, see Margaret Farrand Thorp, "Shakespeare and the Fine Arts," *PMLA*, 46 (1931): 672-93; and Arthur H. R. Fairchild, *Shakespeare and the Arts of Design*, Univ. of Missouri Studies, 12 (Columbia: Univ. of Missouri Press, 1937).

45. For discussions of the world of the play, see Maynard Mack, "The World of *Hamlet*," *YR*, 41 (1952): 502-23; and Bernard McElroy, *Shakespeare's Mature Tragedies* (Princeton: Princeton Univ. Press, 1973), pp. 29-88.

46. For analyses of the Player's speech, see Harry Levin, "An Explication of the Player's Speech," in *The Question of Hamlet* (New York: Oxford Univ. Press, 1959), pp. 138-64; Arthur Johnston, "The Player's Speech in *Hamlet*," *SQ*, 13 (1962): 21-30; Harold Skulsky, "Revenge, Honor, and Conscience in *Hamlet*," *PMLA*, 85 (1970): 78-87.

47. For Dante's suggestion that arrows belong to Fortune, see the *Paradiso*, Canto XVII, 23-26. For the pictorial rendering of Fortune with arrows, see Jean Cousin, *The Book of Fortune, Two Hundred Unpublished Drawings*, ed. Ludovic Lalanne, trans. H. Mainwaring Dunstan (London and Paris: Librairie de l'art, 1883), pls. VII and XIII. Alfred Woltmann, in *Holbein and His Time*, trans. F. E. Bunnètt (London: Richard Bentley, 1872), notes that a design by Ambrosius Holbein, brother of the painter, associates Fortune with the arrow of Death (p. 257). And the title page of a German work, published in 1564, depicts

the figure of Fortuna-Occasio-Tempus holding in her hand an arrow. In this design by Heinrich Lautensack, the figure is identified as "Die Zeit," but may more accurately be called Occasion: she is winged, carries a razor, wears a forelock, and stands on a winged hourglass. Reproduced in *Hollstein's German Engravings, Etchings and Woodcuts*, ed. Fedja Anzelewsky, 21 (Amsterdam: Van Gendt, 1978), 128. As for the slings of Fortune, I think it likely that the bridle held by Fortuna-Nemesis in many Renaissance representations was mistakenly interpreted as a sling. Erwin Panofsky, in "'Virgo et Victrix': A Note on Dürer's *Nemesis*," in *Prints*, ed. Carl Zigrosser (New York: Holt, Rinehart and Winston, 1962), pp. 13-38, notes that "the excellent Joseph Hilarius Eckhel (1737-1798) found it necessary to devote a whole page to proving that her [Nemesis] most frequent and distinctive attribute, the bridle ('frenum'), is indeed a bridle and not a sling ('funda') . . ." (p. 17).

48. H. B. Charlton, *Shakespearian Tragedy* (Cambridge: Cambridge Univ. Press, 1948), p. 97.

49. *The Development of Shakespeare's Imagery* (London: Methuen, 1951), p. 106.

50. "Hamlet and Imagery: The Mind's Eye," *NS*, 15 (1966): 208.

51. *Style in Hamlet* (Princeton: Princeton Univ. Press, 1969), p. 318.

52. Fortune in the Player King's speech is discussed by James I. Wimsatt, in "The Player King on Friendship," *MLR*, 65 (1970): 1-6.

53. See *The Book of Fortune [Liber Fortunae]*, pl. LXVII. There is an interesting parallel in Webster's *Duchess of Malfi*, ed. John Russell Brown, The Revels Plays (London: Methuen, 1964). In the "marriage" scene the Duchess says to Antonio, "I would have you lead your fortune by the hand, / Unto your marriage bed" (I.i.495-96). Webster may be indebted to the lines in *Hamlet* or perhaps to some pictorial representation like that of Jean Cousin.

54. One of these adversaries, Claudius, has been linked to Fortune by his own self-description. Beatrice White, in "Claudius and Fortune," *Anglia*, 77 (1959): 204-07, writes: "the reference of Claudius to his 'one auspicious and one dropping eye,' in an ancient antithesis supported by paradoxes reminiscent of those used by writers on Fortune to stress her fickleness, stamps him from the first as a hypocrite, underlines the dubious nature of his real intentions, and marks him out at once as a potentially 'treacherous villain'" (206).

55. *The Pilgrimage of Life* (1962; reprint ed., Port Washington, N.Y. and London: Kennikat Press, 1973), p. 18.

56. *The Story of the Night: Studies in Shakespeare's Major Tragedies* (London: Routledge and Kegan Paul, 1961), p. 35.

57. Nigel Alexander, in *Poison, Play, and Duel: A Study in Hamlet* (Lincoln: Univ. of Nebraska Press, 1971), finds a correspondence between Hamlet's lines at III.i.85-87 and Brutus' speech in *Julius Caesar* about "a tide in the affairs of men" (pp. 74-75). Doris V. Falk, in "Proverbs and the Polonius Destiny," *SQ*, 18 (1967), sees a reference to the wheel of Occasion in Ophelia's mention of a wheel at IV.v.172 (35).

58. *Shakespearian Tragedy*, p. 103.

59. J. V. Cunningham usefully assesses the meaning of "readiness," in *Woe or Wonder: The Emotional Effect of Shakespearean Tragedy* (Denver: Univ. of Denver Press, 1951), pp. 9-13.

60. S. F. Johnson, "The Regeneration of Hamlet," *SQ*, 3 (1952): 205.

Chapter 9

FORTUNE AND NATURE
IN *SEJANUS* AND *KING LEAR*

T HE MOST CONFIDENT—and brazen—of Renaissance men believed themselves capable of turning change and chance to their advantage. In its most intense form this preoccupation with self-aggrandizement, with achievement in this world, fostered an indifference not only to man's fate in the next but also to the whole notion of divine purpose. Thus Machiavelli's pragmatic philosophy, as it directed man's efforts to his immediate surroundings, ignored providential design and implicitly denied it. So long as the aspirant remained successful in attuning himself to the fluctuations of time and circumstance, he could retain a large measure of optimism. But what if the forces that shift and re-shift the world's affairs proved intractable, even hostile? Suppose those forces had a life and direction of their own, which man could control only intermittently, if at all? What once looked like opportunity would come to appear less promising. And the world, lacking the stamp of God's design, and resistant to man's, would seem to the bewildered observer increasingly anarchic.

At the end of the Elizabethan era and the beginning of the Jacobean, the specter of just such a world came to haunt poets and playwrights. In the drama two works in particular—Ben Jonson's *Sejanus His Fall* and Shakespeare's *King Lear*—reflect the pessimism that characterizes so much of the era. Although they differ widely in setting, structure, and style, the plays have a similar theme and tone. In both, frustration is everywhere: the virtuous swiftly fall prey to the machinations of others; the villainous find their successes difficult to sustain. Men seem unable to impose their will upon the world for long. Confidence gives way to dismay, and dismay to despair. The characters speak of a falling off: the sureties and principles that once guided conduct no longer hold. Corruption envelops society. Human nature seems increasingly mean. Nature herself appears disordered. And implicated in this disorder is Fortune. Not Occasion, but the Fortune of old, intractable, capricious, malign.

I

As depicted in *Sejanus* (c. 1603), the Rome of Tiberius has little in common with the Rome of the Republic; the imperial epoch would be unrecognizable to Cato, Brutus, or Cassius—all named in Jonson's play as exemplars of Roman virtue. The extent of the change that has occurred is apparent in the trial of Cremutius Cordus, the annalist whose compilation of historical records is deemed to reflect adversely on Tiberius' reign. One of the censors seeks to justify the indictment by arguing, "It fits not such licentious things should live / T'upbraid the age" (III.467-68).[1] Arruntius, a kind of choral figure, growls in an aside, "If th' age were good, they might" (468). But as Arruntius' colleague, Marcus Lepidus, notes sadly, the age is not: "It is an argument the times are sore, / When virtue cannot safely be advanced, / Nor vice reproved" (481-83). The decision to burn the writings of Cordus underscores the self-consciousness of this peculiar era, which sees itself—accurately—as fundamentally unlike its predecessors.

The despair of Arruntius, Lepidus, and others over the present inspires a wistful remembrance of the past. The mere mention of the name Germanicus, in life a paragon of honor, is sufficient to induce in Caius Silius a melancholy reverie over lost virtue: "He was a man most like to virtue, 'in all / And every action, nearer to the gods / Than men in nature" (I.124-26). His loss would be less dispiriting were it not for the dim prospect of any amelioration in the state of things; Arruntius notes, "If there were seeds of the old virtue left, / They lived in him" (I.119-20). Little hope, therefore, remains of the present redeeming itself. A blight has settled upon the human condition and no one has entirely escaped. So calamitous is the degeneration that it elicits this hyperbolic comment: "There's nothing Roman in us, nothing good, / Gallant, or great" (102-3).

Rome is not, to be sure, completely devoid of virtuous men. The values of the noble Arruntius provide a counterpoint to the values of Tiberius, Sejanus, and their army of sycophants. Sabinus and Silius also deplore eloquently the conditions that prevail in Rome. Yet much as we may applaud their imprecations, we must concede that Arruntius and his colleagues are not those who decisively shape the world of the play. They are almost entirely located on the fringes of the action. And on those occasions when they come stage center—as Cordus and Silius do at their trials—it is invariably in the role of victim. For the most part, they are onlookers. They deplore injustice, rail at vice, condemn corruption—almost always, however, in quiet asides to the audience; they seem unable to combine moral outrage with bravery.

The ineffectuality of Arruntius, Lepidus, and others of their party prevents the play from becoming chiefly a struggle of good and evil. More intense and dramatically interesting is the conflict between unremitting villains, especially between Tiberius and Sejanus. Its essence is captured by the emperor as he reflects on his plan to counter Sejanus' ambition by enhancing the stature of Sertorius Macro:

> I have heard that aconite,
> Being timely taken, hath a healing might
> Against the scorpion's stroke. The proof we'll give,
> That, while two poisons wrestle, we may live. (III.651-54)

Tiberius does not intend to purge the body politic of its bane: one evil will simply be substituted for another.

Tiberius bases his strategy upon a shrewd insight into the laws that govern the interaction of people in the state. He accurately gauges the interconnectedness of human beings, the intricate pattern of relationships that constitute a society. In particular, he understands that augmentation of power in one sector must be accompanied by diminution in another, that the rise of one man must be linked with the fall of another, and vice versa. In this perception Tiberius is not alone, for a variety of other figures also recognize the principle. In the opening scene, for example, Sabinus refuses "to raise / Ourselves a fortune by subverting theirs" (I.17-18). In his more ambitious moments Sejanus envisions the emperor's fall as a necessary corollary of his own elevation: "I will rise, / By making him the public sacrifice" (II.403-4). And Macro too sees this governing principle at work when he ruminates over his newly attained stature:

> If then it be the lust of Caesar's power
> T'have raised Sejanus up, and in an hour
> O'erturn him, tumbling down from height of all,
> We are his ready engine, and his fall
> May be our rise. (III.744-48)

The phenomenon described by Sabinus, Sejanus, and Macro is clearly an integral part of the state of things. If it has the force of a "natural law," however, it is one that involves—and perhaps derives its impetus from—Fortune. For the pattern of ascent and descent coincides precisely with that traditionally ascribed to Dame Fortune in the literature of the Middle Ages and Renaissance.

As Sejanus falls and Macro rises, Fortune assumes extraordinary prominence. And Jonson ransacks the work of Tacitus, Dio Cassius, Juvenal, Suetonius, and Seneca for *sententiae* expressive of Fortune's role in raising up and hurling down her victims. In addition, Jonson draws upon the medieval and Renaissance tradition which represented Nature and Fortune as rivals.[2] In imaginative literature they are typically conceived as antithetical, Fortune encroaching upon Nature's domain, gradually beginning to dominate, bringing turmoil and decay where order formerly prevailed. In *Sejanus* this topos is expressed chiefly through the activities of Tiberius and Sejanus, who are identified with Fortune and who plot to transgress what, in the words of Tiberius, "nature, blood, and laws of kind forbid" (II.170).

Robert Ornstein has called Tiberius "the secular god in the empire of Rome who rigs Fortune's wheel and punishes overreaching ambition when it threatens his own security."[3] His resemblance to Fortune is suggested, for example, by his letter (read to the senate in the last act) which toys with Sejanus in the way that Fortune vexes her victims, alternately raising and dashing their hopes. Sejanus himself also may be termed a "secular Fortune," for clients are said to mimic his moods in the way that suppliants tailor their actions to the humor of Fortune. And Sejanus, no less than Tiberius, knows well how to perplex those who occupy lower rungs on the social ladder. Moreover, when he plans strategy against his enemies, he seems almost to control Fortune: "The course must be to let 'em still swell up, / Riot and surfeit on blind Fortune's cup" (II.260-61). Sejanus even acquires the very features of Fortune when Silius says of him:

> We talk of Rhadamanth,
> Furies, and firebrands, but 'tis his frown
> That is all these, where, on the adverse part,
> His smile is more than e'er yet poets feigned
> Of bliss, and shades, nectar—. (I.208-12)

The frowns and smiles of Sejanus evoke those that characterize Fortune's countenance in scores of literary and pictorial works. Only at the end of the play is Sejanus' identification with Fortune nullified. There he orders a sacrifice to Fortune, whose statue he has placed in his home. But Fortune literally turns her face from the man whose rise to power she once favored:

> *Terentius.* See, see the image stirs!
> *Satrius.* And turns away!
> *Natta.* Fortune averts her face! (V. 185-86)

Enraged by the rejection, Sejanus overturns the icon, signalling his estrangement from the goddess whose might he once seemed to command.[4]

It is, of course, not merely Sejanus and Tiberius who contribute to the transgressions of Nature. Other elements of society are involved, and they too are identified with Fortune. The senate, for example, called the "hands of Fortune" by Silius (III.324), ratifies the decisions of Sejanus and Tiberius. And the general populace is implicated as well when, at the conclusion of the drama, the multitudes of Rome run amok. The mob dismembers Sejanus' body, destroys his statues, and even breaks the wheels of his chariot. When Lepidus hears of the depredations, he exclaims, "Oh, violent change / And whirl of men's affections!" (V.701-2). Arruntius adds, "Like as both / Their bulks and souls were bound on Fortune's wheel, / And must act only with her motion" (702-4). The anger of the rabble reaches past its chief target and engulfs his children too. Sejanus' daughter is raped and strangled; his son also is murdered. Lepidus is forced to confess in wonderment:

> How Fortune plies her sports, when she begins
> To practice 'em! Pursues, continues, adds!
> Confounds, with varying her impassioned moods! (888-90)

This exclamation and the communal nature of the events that elicit it suggest that if Fortune has a human dimension, it is to be found not in Tiberius or Sejanus alone, but in the collective acts of the society—from the emperor, to his agents, to the court sycophants, to the senators, to the ordinary citizens who constitute the mob. In Jonson's tragedy, then, Fortune serves not merely as an explanation for the adversity or prosperity experienced by any one figure. Fortune symbolizes the larger currents that swirl through the Rome of Tiberius, affecting every element of society.

Despite the actual presence of Fortune's statue on stage in Act V, the numerous speeches on Fortune by Sejanus himself, and the exclamations over Fortune uttered by Sejanus' antagonists, modern readers of Jonson's tragedy commonly minimize the significance of Fortune.[5] They point to Lepidus' dismissal of the goddess: "Fortune, thou hadst no deity if men / Had wisdom. We have placèd thee so high / By fond belief in thy felicity" (V.733-35). This sentiment, however, scarcely negates the power of Fortune, for if the play demonstrates anything it is that men lack the wisdom and courage to deprive Fortune of her "deity." The mere intellectual rejection of the goddess is insufficient to banish her from the world of the play. Her victims are many. If Silius triumphs over her ("She herself, / When virtue doth oppose, must lose her threats" [III.324-25]), it is only at the cost of his life. Arruntius and Lepidus manage to escape the worst of her scourge only by retreating within themselves. Collectively, these characters serve to remind us that to contemn something is not necessarily to deprive it of its power to inflict adversity.

Those critics who slight Fortune's importance also overlook Jonson's departure from those writers—ancient, medieval, and Renaissance—who are acknowledged as having been especially influential on his tragic art. His treatment of Fortune, for instance, differs from Seneca's, whom scholars have long perceived as an important inspiration for Jonsonian tragedy.[6] For Seneca, Fortune constitutes one part of a large and varied cosmos; and Fortune is counterbalanced by other forces. If Fortune represents a principle of irrationality, fate, though sometimes enigmatic and harsh, guarantees a measure of design. In *Sejanus*, by contrast, Fortune shares her authority with no other power. Alone, she affects the course of every life. Thus although Jonson may draw inspiration from Seneca, he refrains from depicting Fortune within the full context of the Senecan cosmology. By default, then, Fortune assumes a hegemony which even Seneca probably never envisioned.

If Jonson's treatment of Fortune is not precisely Senecan, neither may it be termed, without qualification, medieval. Admittedly, the play by its subject and title evokes the world of *de casibus* tragedy. Herford and Simpson write of Jonson: "What he felt to be tragic in the story of Sejanus was in part that which the whole medieval world understood by tragedy, and the authors of the *Mirror for Magistrates* still exemplified in their tragic tales,—the sudden passage from prosperity to adversity."[7] Jonson, however, does not allow us (as, say, Lydgate sometimes does) the comforting assumption that Fortune is an expression of providential design. Nor does he suggest that Fortune uses her power to requite evil. In the last act of *Sejanus*, Arruntius asks: "Dost thou hope, Fortune, to redeem thy crimes? / To make amends for thy ill-placèd favors, / With these strange punishments?" (891-93). Were Fortune granted a voice, she would certainly respond in the negative. For there is never any suggestion that her activity in casting down one man and elevating another is meant to reward virtue or punish vice. Those who rise do so not on account of their probity. And the wicked fall not on account of their crimes, but because they cannot escape the vicissitude that plagues all of life.[8] When Sejanus dies, evil is not banished from Rome; Macro is no less villainous than the man he replaces. And as a keen student of history, Jonson knew that the emperors who succeeded Tiberius—Caligula and Nero—were no less depraved than he.

Nor does Jonson's treatment of Fortune correspond to Machiavelli's, though the Italian theorist undeniably influenced Jonson's tragedy, particularly the portrayals of Sejanus and Tiberius.[9] In *Sejanus* men may skilfully exploit, for their personal aggrandizement, the situation in which they find themselves. Sejanus and Macro on one level, Afer, Satrius, and Natta on another, display a capacity for enhancing their worldly position. But the illusion that they are in control of events is just that. Their dominion over Fortune is precarious, their triumph short-lived. The behavior of her statue suggests that Fortune cannot be conciliated or won over for long, no matter how wily or adventuresome the aspirant. We do not find here the confidence of a Machiavelli, for the shape of vicissitude does not permit people to capitalize for long on the vagaries of time and circumstance. Neither the men of virtue, who retreat from the struggle, nor the men of *virtù*, who engage in it, prove adequate to the goddess' challenge. In Jonson's tragic world, Fortune assumes unprecedented power.

II

That Fortune's mutability could be cruelly destructive was hardly a new discovery of Jonson's; men in every age have known this. And they have expressed it in their literature, especially in tragedy. In one sense, however, dramatists of the early seventeenth century depart from precedent, for with unusual force they give dramatic form to the idea that mutability, in society and perhaps in Nature herself, is inseparable from decay.[10]

Mutability and decay are in theory disparate processes. Renaissance thinkers could contemplate mutability without subscribing to the notion that Nature was decaying. Jean Bodin's *Methodus ad Facilem Historiarum Cognitionem* (1566) declines to associate change with decay. And the same may be said of Louis Le Roy's exploration of cyclical recurrence, *De la Vicissitude, ou varieté des choses en l'univers* (1575), translated by Robert Ashley as *Of the Interchangeable Course, or Variety of Things in the Whole World* (1594). Nevertheless, in the early seventeenth century, the assumption of general decay began to gain greater currency, inspired by renewed interest in a literary tradition that stretched back to antiquity; by a religious preoccupation with man's sinfulness; and by scientific observation (in 1572 a new star had been discovered in the heavens, formerly thought immutable).[11] This belief received its best known expression in Godfrey Goodman's brooding work, *The Fall of Man, or the Corruption of Nature* (1616; other edd. 1618, 1629). George Hakewill vigorously rejected Goodman's opinions in *An Apologie of the Power and Providence of God in the Government of the Whole World. Or an Examination and Censure of the Common Error touching Nature's perpetual and universal Decay* (1627; enlarged edd. 1630, 1635). But the very fact that Hakewill found it necessary to write such a lengthy rejoinder suggests the appeal that Goodman's arguments must have had.

Ben Jonson's position in this controversy is not entirely clear. In *Timber: Or, Discoveries* he expresses a view akin to Hakewill's: "I cannot thinke Nature is so spent, and decay'd, that she can bring forth nothing worth her former yeares. She is always the same, like her selfe: And when she collects her strength, is abler still."[12] In the very next sentence, however, Jonson, while maintaining Nature's stability, makes a concession regarding mankind: "Men are decay'd, and *studies*: Shee is not." The words recall Arruntius' in *Sejanus*: "The men, / The men are not the same! 'Tis we are base, / Poor, and degenerate from th'exalted strain / Of our great fathers" (I.86-89). It may be that Arruntius (and Jonson) do not intend this indictment of men to include all of Nature as well. But so thoroughgoing is the power of destructive change in the play, so widespread the evidence of debasement, so remote the prospect of regeneration, that it is difficult to imagine Nature standing apart from man and retaining her orderliness undiminished.

Unquestionably, Jonson portrays men's actions in *Sejanus* as a deliberate assault upon Nature's canon. Thus during a discussion of policy to be followed against their enemies (policy that includes the murder of Germanicus' children), Tiberius raises an objection, saying, "That nature, blood, and laws of kind forbid" (II.170). Sejanus replies, "Do policy and state forbid it?" And when the emperor answers in the negative, Sejanus declares, "The rest of poor respects, then, let go by. / State is enough to make th'act just, them guilty" (172-73). Tiberius asks, "Are rites / Of faith, love, piety, to be trod down? / Forgotten? And made vain?" (175-77). Sejanus responds, "All for a crown."

In such a world natural bonds, filial, parental, and marital, collapse with alarming swiftness. Livia, for instance, intrigues with Sejanus to murder her husband Drusus. To the extent that he is disgusted with the favored position of Sejanus, Drusus, we assume, is alienated from his father. The emperor, in turn, shows little concern over the death of his son, murdered by Sejanus. Sexual relationships, meanwhile, are singularly tawdry. Livia commits adultery with Sejanus, in his youth "the noted pathic of the time" (I.216). Tiberius is as depraved as his power allows. Arruntius calls him "An emp'ror only in his lusts" (IV.376) and catalogues the deeds committed on the imperial island. There, at Tiberius' direction, families are torn apart: youths

> by their friends detained,
> Are ravished hence like captives, and in sight
> Of their most grievèd parents, dealt away
> Unto his spintries, sellaries, and slaves,
> Masters of strange and new commented lusts,
> For which wise nature hath not left a name. (IV.396-401)

By their depredations, men have perverted the patterns established by "wise nature," creating mutations which Nature cannot recognize.

That Shakespeare, like Jonson, should have been drawn to the controversy over mutability and decay seems almost inevitable, given the climate of ideas in the early seventeenth century. His interest in the subject may even have been stimulated, in part, by Jonson: we know that Shakespeare acted in *Sejanus* in 1603.[13] The playwright has left no record of his personal views of the sort preserved in Jonson's *Timber: Or, Discoveries*. But we can look briefly at the more influential works that treated Nature and Fortune in the sixteenth century and that may well have helped to shape *King Lear*, a tragedy in which convulsive change affects all things: human life, the physical world, and the heavens.

Sixteenth-century writers could have looked back to John Lydgate, who in *The Fall of Princes* observed that strife between Nature and Fortune began with the primal sin of man in the Garden of Eden. It was this sin that resulted in Fortune's gaining a hitherto unknown power over mankind:

> We hadde nevir stondyn in dau*n*geer
> Off worldly stryff nor p*er*ellys ful mortal,
> Nor dreed of deth, nat in a thousand yeer,
> Nor of Fortune that tournyth as a bal,
> Yiff Adam hadde in Paradys had no fal;
> Touch of an appyl and inobedyence,—
> Cause that Fortune is had in suych rev*er*ence.[14]

Fortune thus represents an intrusion, one that would afflict Nature as well as man himself. Once having entered the world, Fortune aggressively seeks to extend her influence.

Stephen Hawes treats this subject in *The Example of Virtue* (1510). The conflict pits Nature against Fortune, the issue being sovereignty over man. With her customary bravado, Fortune makes this claim:

> I Fortune am the rule and steere
> Of every persone lyke to my wyll
> That in this worlde now lyveth here
> Whan that I lyst for to fulfyll
> My mynde ryght sone I can dystyll
> The dewe of comfort welth and rychesse
> To man exaltynge hym to noblenesse. (sig. dd2ᵛ)[15]

In addition, Fortune boasts that neither Dame Hardiness nor Dame Sapience can avail anything without her. But Nature counters:

> That nature gyveth by her power
> Wysedome nor hardynes may not defete
> For I to man am the chefe doer
> Durynge his lyfe without retrete
> Also dame fortune may not well lete
> Me of my course though she it thought. . . . (sig. dd3ᵛ)

The conflict of claims is not really resolved in Hawes's work. Justice settles the quarrel by having Nature and Fortune, together with Hardiness and Sapience, agree to cooperate. Henceforth, they will join forces in aiding mankind.

The happy view of *The Example of Virtue* did not entirely disappear later in the sixteenth century. Thus in a London pageant of 1547, the figures of Nature and Fortune, along with Grace and Charity, saluted Edward VI on the way to his coronation.[16] And in a royal progress of 1591, Queen Elizabeth was called "Nature's glory, Fortune's empress."[17] An amicable relationship between Nature and Fortune also prevails in George Peele's *Descensus Astraeae* (1591), a pageant intended to honor the Lord Mayor of London, William Web. According to the allegory, "In the hinder part of the Pageant did sit a Child, representing Nature, holding in her hand a distaffe, and spinning a Web, which passed through the hand of Fortune and was wheeled up by Time. . . ."[18] Time explicates the meaning of the action: "Fortune doth enrich what Nature spinnes." Similar cooperation is envisaged in Shakespeare's *King John*, when Constance tells her son Arthur, "at thy birth, dear boy, / Nature and Fortune join'd to make thee great" (III.i.51-52). If Nature and Fortune are less amicable in Marlowe's *Tamburlaine*, it is only because each seeks to exalt the protagonist: "Nature doth strive with Fortune and his stars / To make him famous in accomplish'd worth" (II.i.33-34).[19] Sometimes the more serious implications of the strife are concealed by a jocular tone, as for example when Rosalind and Celia playfully debate the proper realms of Nature and Fortune in *As You Like It* (I.ii.31-55).

Giordano Bruno's *Expulsion of the Triumphant Beast* (1584) manages to preserve a light tone while conceding to Fortune extraordinary power. Bruno's work recounts the appearance of Fortune before an assembly of the Olympian gods. At issue is not so much Fortune's sovereignty over man as Fortune's place in the universe at large. It seems that the deities have decided to remove from the heavens the old constellations (with their history of Jove's transgressions); and Fortune announces her desire to take the place of Hercules (the Great Bear). Objections are raised, but Fortune argues forcefully. Eventually, Jove is forced to concede that fortune has presented her case well and seems deserving of a place in the heavens. He points out, however, that because of Fortune's nature, it would be improper to restrict her to a single place. She may not gain exactly what she covets, but Jove's rebuff is very gentle: "I leave you with that power that you seem to have throughout heaven, since you, in your own right, have so much authority that you open for yourself those places that are closed to Jove himself as well as to all the other gods."[20]

Bruno's work was known in England; the author himself travelled there and met notable men of letters, including Sir Philip Sidney and Fulke Greville. *The Expulsion of the Triumphant Beast* may even have influenced Spenser's *Mutabilitie Cantos* (c. 1598-99; printed 1609).[21] Both describe a conclave of deities over which Jove presides. Both concern the effort by a figure identified with change to seek a new recognition of her power. (Spenser calls this figure Mutabilitie, a trait that Fortune embodies; and the "ever-whirling wheele / Of Change" which Spenser mentions in his opening stanza recalls the wheel of Fortune.) Bruno's Fortune and Spenser's Mutabilitie also display a similar personality; each is ambitious, argumentative, confident.

Spenser's pugnacious Mutabilitie is described as breaking the laws of Nature on earth:

> For she the face of earthly things so changed
> That all which Nature had establisht first
> In good estate, and in meet order ranged,
> She did pervert, and all their statutes burst.
>
> (VI.5)[22]

Having demonstrated her power over things sublunary, she climbs to the circle of the moon where she bids Cynthia surrender her throne. Jove, troubled by the commotion in the heavens, summons her to his palace. There Mutabilitie claims, "I greater am in bloud (whereon I build) / Then all the Gods, though wrongfully from heaven exil'd" (VI.26). Rebuffing the challenge, Jove declares, in effect, that the gods are not about to surrender their power to a usurper: "we by conquest of our soveraine might, / And by eternall doome of Fates' decree, / Have wonne the empire of the heavens bright; / Which to our selves we hold" (VI.33). Mutabilitie shrewdly observes that as a usurper who is himself threatened, Jove can scarcely render an impartial decision, and so she appeals to "the god of nature."

At an assembly of the gods, Mutabilitie argues that everything on earth (including mankind) is subject to change. To prove her point, Mutabilitie calls for an appearance by the Seasons of the Year, the

Months, Day and Night, the Hours, Life and Death. Finally, Mutabilitie addresses Nature:

> "Lo, mighty mother, now be judge and say
> Whether in all thy creatures more or lesse
> Change doth not raign and beare the greatest sway.
> For who sees not that time on all doth pray?
> But times do change and move continually,
> So nothing here long standeth in one stay.
> Wherefore this lower world who can deny
> But to be subject still to Mutabilitie?" (VII.47)

Jove interjects that "these / And all things else that under heaven dwell / Are chaung'd of time," but he adds that the gods, since they "doth move and still compell" Time, are superior to Mutabilitie (VII.48). She claims, in reply, that the gods are themselves changeable: "Then are ye mortall borne, and thrall to me, / Unlesse the kingdome of the sky yee make / Immortall, and unchangeable to be" (VII.54). Still unresolved, the dispute goes to Nature for adjudication. After a pause Nature renders her verdict:

> "I well consider all that ye have sayd,
> And find that all things stedfastnes doe hate,
> And changed be. Yet, being rightly wayd,
> They are not changed from their first estate,
> But by their change their being doe dilate,
> And turning to themselves at length againe,
> Doe worke their owne perfection so by fate.
> Then over them Change doth not rule and raigne;
> But they raigne over Change, and doe their states
> maintaine."
>
> (VII.58)

S. P. Zitner comments, "At last Nature declares that all things are indeed subject to alteration, but that alteration involves no change of their essence, only an unfolding of their potentialities."[23] But is Mutabilitie entirely vanquished by Nature's decree? More specifically, is Mutabili-

tie's claim that she exerts her power in the heavens as well as on earth refuted? Lewis J. Owen argues persuasively that it has not been: ". . .
whatever her role was called — ruler or agent — nothing Nature had said
refuted her claim to operate in the heavens as well as on earth — and this,
in one sense, is to rule."[24] According to Owen, Spenser has here implicitly made an important concession to Mutabilitie, for the poet has failed
"to reaffirm the old and comfortable distinction between the perfect
heavens and the imperfect regions below the moon."[25]

John Norden's *Vicissitudo rerum, An Elegiacall Poeme, of the interchangeable courses and varietie of things in this world* (1600), resembles
The Mutabilitie Cantos in its concern with a stable world threatened by
disorder. Unlike Spenser, however, Norden seems to treat the result of a
conflict rather than the conflict itself. And instead of dealing with a personification called Mutabilitie or Fortune, he presents a Nature already
afflicted by "fearefull alterations" (sig. B4ᵛ). By this expression Norden
obviously means something more than mere temporary fluctuation, for
the phenomena he records are, he believes, without precedent. In words
that seem to anticipate those of Gloucester in *King Lear*, Norden
writes:

> The *Sunne* and *Moone* eclipsed ne're so much,
> *Comets* and strange *impressions* in the ayre:
> The *tydes* and swelling *flouds* were never such:
> The *earth* doth tremble, *Nature* doth impayre,
> Hid'ous *monsters* now possesse the chayre,
> Where erst dame *Natures* true begotten seede
> Sate truely graced in her proper weede. (sig. B4ᵛ)

This dislocation characterizes not only the physical universe, but also
humankind. Of society Norden writes apprehensively:

> Such changes never have beene seene of yore,
> In *Countries* and in *Kingdomes*, as of late,
> *Manners*, and *Lawes*, and *Religions* lore,
> Never were prized at so meane a rate. (sig. B4ᵛ)

In the poet's view, natural relationships are disordered by a "contrariness" which disturbs what should be close ties:

> What passionate *inconstancie* have *men*,
> Which shew *affections* so contrarie?
> No *creature* to a *creature* worse hath ben,
> Then man to man, who in hot enmitie,
>   Hath wrought each other deadly destinie.
>   Yea, some that deerely lov'd before, comes foes,
>   And foes come friends: some work themselves their
>   woes. (sig. D4ᵛ)

For Norden the culprit is time. Instead of providing reassurance, as time
seems to do in *The Mutabilitie Cantos*, time takes a heavy toll, denying
man happiness:

> Who doth not see the state of fickle *man*,
> His changing courses and his divers turnes,
> Tweene aged yeeres, and time he first began,
> How *time* his termes from time to time adjurnes?
>   *Time* tries him still, to triumph him he wurnes,
>   And will not let him glorie long in blisse,
>   In this short *progresse* where no *glorie* is. (sig. F2ᵛ)

A variation on the "Tempus edax rerum" motif ("Time the devourer of
things"), this is the melancholy assessment of a poet preoccupied with
transience.

   Norden would like to locate all such change under the aegis of providence. In one stanza he declares in the most fervent terms his faith in
God and concludes that the turbulence of the world constitutes an
expression of divine design: "Yet are the *Heavens* and the *Earth* maintain'd / By *discord* excellent, that hee ordain'd" (sig. D2). Despite this
profession of confidence, however, in the essential orderliness of "*discord* excellent," the reader senses that Norden's faith is precarious, increasingly difficult to sustain in a world that seems quite literally in danger of dissolution. There is an unmistakably plaintive note, particularly
in Norden's contemplation of man's subjection to mutability:

Man never standeth, but like a waving *tyde*,
That comes and goes, now calme, then full of ire:
Now sings he sweete, all sorrowes layd aside,
Then groweth *griefe*, welcome to no desire,
 Heav'd up, hurl'd downe, dismay'd, or in aspire:
 Grac'd now, then in disdaine, now in the sunne
 Of sweetest *savour:* then eclips'd, undonne. (sig. F3)

Norden's modern editor writes that the poet "tries desperately to hold on to his belief in the divine reason of Providence among the evident marks of decay and disintegration which races, nations, and kingdoms bear."[26] Norden's tone, however, betrays the tenuousness of that belief; his work is marked by deep pessimism.

It is Norden's bleak outlook rather than Spenser's declared confidence that characterizes the treatment of Nature on the early seventeenth-century stage. In the drama Nature often seems to be reeling, Fortune ascendant. Thus in *Bussy D'Ambois* by George Chapman, who may have collaborated with Jonson on the stage version of *Sejanus*,[27] Nature is apparently dominated by Fortune. In fact, Nature has actually taken on characteristics of the capricious deity:

Now shall we see, that Nature hath no end
In her great works, responsive to their worths,
That she who makes so many eyes and souls,
To see and foresee, is stark blind herself. (V.iii.1-4)[28]

This "blind" Nature creates, "Not knowing what she does" (17). And even when Nature manages to fashion an individual with "all the wondrous fabric man should have" (32) — in this instance, the protagonist — her work is completely undone. Thus the Monsieur can tell the Guise: "this full creature now shall reel and fall, / Before the frantic puffs of purblind chance / That pipes through empty men, and makes them dance" (46-48). Faster than the sea churns the ocean bottom, he continues, "Fortune swings about the restless state / Of Virtue" (55-56). These words are prophetic, for the man who opened the play, saying, "Fortune, not Reason, rules the state of things," falls victim to purblind Fortune. Even the grandest of Nature's works succumbs to a Fortune whose influence has become pervasive.

A still more powerful depiction of Nature in turmoil occurs in *King Lear*, probably written soon after *Bussy D'Ambois*.[29] (Chapman's tragedy is thought to have been written about 1604; *King Lear* about 1605.) In Shakespeare's play the storm on the heath, commonly interpreted as an outward symbol of Lear's inner distress, epitomizes the tumult felt throughout the natural world and society as well. When the aged Lear, rejected by his daughters, wanders onto a bleak landscape, he experiences at first hand the fury of a Nature gone berserk. He is stricken by wind and rain. The wild power "tears his white hair, / Which the impetuous blasts with eyeless rage / Catch in their fury, and make nothing of" (III.i.7-9). Neither orderly nor benign, these forces belong to a chaotic Nature: the blasts are "eyeless," that is, without direction. And they are "impetuous" — sudden and mercurial. The word "rage," moreover, suggests an impulse utterly without restraint. This Nature, at best indifferent to man, seems driven by uncontrolled and uncontrollable forces. It is the Nature envisaged with foreboding by Spenser, the Nature that Norden, perhaps subconsciously, feared had become a *fait accompli*, the Nature that Chapman knew as a reality.

The descriptions of turmoil by both Chapman ("frantic puffs of purblind chance") and by Shakespeare ("impetuous blasts with eyeless rage") evoke Fortune not only because Fortune is herself blind, but also because "puffs" and "blasts" are symbols of her power. In the visual arts, wind and rain sometimes accompany or even stand for Fortune. In Giorgione's *La Tempesta*, for instance, the storm in the background has been interpreted as a symbolic representation of Fortune.[30] (In Italian the very word *fortuna* may signify a storm.) Another picture, an engraving by Wenceslaus Hollar in the early seventeenth century, also makes the identification of Fortune with Nature in turmoil (fig. 17). The engraving depicts Dame Fortune at the center of a stormy nautical scene. Fierce gales sweep the waters while lightning streaks across the sky; rain falls in torrents. And on either side of Fortune, ships are buffeted. In this picture, Edgar Wind observes, "Fortuna appears literally as Storm personified, mistress of a violent tempest."[31] With its portrayal of man at the mercy of unrestrained natural forces, Hollar's engraving seems a pictorial counterpart of the Nature that Lear experiences on the heath, a Nature in disarray, a Nature inseparable from Fortune's fury.

Fig. 17. Wenceslaus Hollar, engraving of Fortune.

III

Instead of Nature disordered, many commentators find in *King Lear* "two contradictory views of Nature": Nature as a "divinely ordained cosmic scheme"; and Nature as "vital force, the physical drive and the impulses of the individual, the totality of unfettered and uncriticized urgencies."[32] This interpretation may seem to suit the play since most of the characters divide into two groups, each of which has been identified with one of these attitudes. Thus critics speak of "the Nature of Edmund and the Nature of Cordelia"[33] as though one or another view of Nature could be matched with each figure in the *dramatis personae.* The trouble with this scheme is that it fails to apply equally well to all of the characters. Where, for example, are we to locate Gloucester in this antinomy? On the one hand, he belongs, like Cordelia and Kent, with the more benevolent figures of the play. On the other hand, the Nature he perceives can scarcely be described as part of some orderly cosmic design. There is, as well, another and more important difficulty: the notion of "contradictory views of Nature" fails to tally with the evidence suggesting not so much two clashing theories (Nature as cosmic scheme vs. Nature as vital force) as a once stable Nature in collapse.

From the opening scene, the audience beholds Nature—as it operates in mankind—faltering. Normally harmonious relationships—between father and daughter, father and son, sister and sister, brother and brother—are sundered by antagonism and hatred. Characters display a willful quality which frustrates common understanding and, in the case of Lear and Cordelia, masks underlying affection. Moreover, the antipathy develops so suddenly as to defy comprehension and to preclude resolution. In wonderment Gloucester asks,

> Kent banish'd thus? and France in choler parted?
> And the King gone to-night? Prescrib'd his pow'r,
> Confin'd to exhibition? All this done
> Upon the gad? (I.ii.23-26)

Events take on a rapidly developing momentum which even the wisdom of counselors and the ties of family are powerless to slow.

After the so-called love-test, Gloucester reflects upon the rending of social ties. Looking to the heavens as well as to society, he says:

These late eclipses in the sun and moon portend no good to us. Though the wisdom of nature can reason it thus and thus, yet nature finds itself scourg'd by the sequent effects. Love cools, friendship falls off, brothers divide: in cities, mutinies; in countries, discord; in palaces, treason; and the bond crack'd 'twixt son and father. This villain of mine comes under the prediction; there's son against father: the King falls from bias of nature; there's father against child.

We have seen the best of our time. Machinations, hollowness, treachery, and all ruinous disorders follow us disquietly to our graves. (I.ii.103-14)

Because he is, to many, an unattractive figure, insensitive to a son's bastardy, excessively credulous, and given to formulating opinions according to his most recent experience or conversation, Gloucester is usually dismissed as an unreliable observer; his sins are deemed to invalidate the accuracy of his perceptions.[34] What is more, his discourse on Nature is immediately challenged by the Machiavellian Edmund, whose rational bias, as it happens, accords with that of a modern audience.[35] Nevertheless, Gloucester's words remain telling. Although we may object, with Edmund, to Gloucester's linking of cause and effect, we cannot question the phenomena that he catalogues. There *is* antagonism between father and child: between Lear and Cordelia, later between Lear and Goneril, then between Lear and Regan; also, between Gloucester himself and Edgar, later between Gloucester and Edmund. Moreover, "brothers divide" — and so do sisters. "Discord" there is aplenty. A social order which formerly prevailed is now jeopardized as families split apart. Nor is the end in sight. The process observed by Gloucester continues, and it is one that, ironically, the contemptuous Edmund will himself foster. The remainder of the drama offers copious evidence of "Machinations, hollowness, treachery, and all ruinous disorders."

An image used by the Fool captures the precarious state of human relationships. Warning Kent, he says:

Let go thy hold when a great wheel runs down a hill, lest it break thy neck with following; but the great one that goes upward, let him draw thee after. (II.iv.71-74)[36]

The words recall those of Rosencrantz to Claudius in *Hamlet*. There too the image of the wheel conveys societal mutability:

The cess of majesty
Dies not alone, but like a gulf doth draw
What's near it with it. Or it is a massy wheel

Fix'd on the summit of the highest mount,
To whose huge spokes ten thousand lesser things
Are mortis'd and adjoin'd, which when it falls,
Each small annexment, petty consequence,
Attends the boist'rous ruin. (III.iii.15-22)

Implicit in both speeches is man's vulnerability to other people, the awful momentum of flux, and the inevitable destruction of anyone who fails to distance himself from the vortex of change. The Fool's advice to Kent contains, additionally, this irony: although the Fool is solicitous, the action he counsels would fracture society still further, for to seek safety in isolation is to contribute to the general fragmentation. It is to adopt the lonely stance of Arruntius and Lepidus in *Sejanus*.

To be sure, complete disintegration never occurs in *King Lear*. Indeed, Arthur Sewell writes, "None other of Shakespeare's plays contains such moving and dramatic references to personal loyalty and love."[37] Kent disregards the Fool's advice and stays with the ruined king; so too does the Fool himself. Similarly, Edgar remains with his father after the blinding; Gloucester defies Goneril and Regan in order to help the king. The Gentleman agrees to help Kent; Cornwall's servant rebels against his master on Gloucester's behalf; an Old Man ministers to the victim of blinding. And yet, despite the example of those who at personal risk aid others, the social order remains constantly under attack. The king, symbol of that order, is treated with contempt. So too are those in his service. And what should be the closest of natural bonds break down. The individual instances of affection and human decency are not to be denied. But they loom large precisely because they contrast so vividly with the enveloping savagery, madness, and warfare.

Even the closest of human ties seems doomed. Thus the reconciliation of Lear and Cordelia is shadowed by the fear that such communion must perish. Indeed, it is Lear's perception of the flux that besets all human relationships that causes him actually to look forward to prison (V.iii.8-19). Only there, he mistakenly believes, will he find protection against the virulent mutability of the world. Lear's endeavor to find surcease from the "ebb and flow" is frustrated because walls cannot exclude the turbulence. Disorder proceeds only partially from external forces; it also comes from within. And, ironically, the very people who seek to cherish familial bonds may themselves be responsible for the upheaval, as Lear discovers. His madness arises at least partly from the recognition that he has somehow contributed to his daughters' transgressions. D. G. James notes that "at the centre of Shakespeare's intention in this play" is "the sense, which Lear frequently conveys, that the source of his children's evil is in himself."[38] Consider his words to Goneril:

> I will not trouble thee, my child; farewell:
> We'll no more meet, no more see one another.
> But yet thou art my flesh, my blood, my daughter—
> Or rather a disease that's in my flesh,
> Which I must needs call mine. Thou art a bile,
> A plague-sore, or embossed carbuncle,
> In my corrupted blood. (II.iv.219-25)

At the height of the storm this perception leads the king to reflect, "'twas this flesh begot / Those pelican daughters" (III.iv.74-75). Perhaps it is this painful recognition that causes Lear to wish to annihilate part of Nature:

> And thou, all-shaking thunder,
> Strike flat the thick rotundity o' th' world!
> Crack nature's moulds, all germains spill at once
> That makes ingrateful man! (III.ii.6-9)

No longer may disorder be considered merely temporary. So totally has human nature been infiltrated by a malignant force that it cannot be extirpated without the destruction of "nature's moulds."

Lear, of course, is as much a victim of Nature as are his daughters. Gloucester, when he encounters the mad Lear, exclaims, "O ruin'd piece of nature!" (IV.vi.134). And Gloucester goes on to predict that the decay already manifest in Lear is but the prelude to a wider decay involving the entire world: "This great world / Shall so wear out to nought" (134-35). Gloucester does not speculate on the source of Lear's plight, but Lear points to Fortune's role: "I am even / The natural fool of fortune" (190-91). This self-description and Gloucester's remark on Lear's "ruin'd" nature, closely juxtaposed in the same scene, are not irreconcilable; they overlap. As Northrop Frye observes, Nature and Fortune "interpenetrate in a very complex way."[39] One's fortune, Lear discovers, may be shaped not only by Fortune directly, but also by one's own nature, itself the product of aberrant Nature.[40]

IV

Despite evidence of ever-widening chaos, there are characters in the play who remain convinced that, beneath the veil of disorder, lies an order instilled by divinity. Only with the greatest reluctance do they acknowledge the darker implications of their experience. The deities that others believe hostile or indifferent they consider benevolent. And it is these optimistic voices which, for many modern critics, most fully embody the overall vision of the tragedy. Because an understanding of Nature in *King Lear* is so closely related to an interpretation of the deities who preside, we need to consider briefly the cosmic setting of the play, especially the treatment of the gods and Fortune.[41]

The most forceful exponent of an orderly and benevolent Nature, one consonant with divine design, is Albany. But even he is forced momentarily to entertain the vision of Nature and society in total disarray. When he learns of Goneril's vicious treatment of her father, his first impulse is to invoke divine intercession:

> If that the heavens do not their visible spirits
> Send quickly down to tame these vild offenses,
> It will come,
> Humanity must perforce prey on itself,
> Like monsters of the deep. (IV.ii.46-50)

In his attitude Albany approaches that of John Norden at his most pessimistic, envisaging "monsters" in possession of Nature's throne. (The persistent animal imagery of *King Lear* suggests that human nature may already have become monstrous.) Albany, however, almost immediately dismisses this bleak prospect. Hearing that a servant sought to prevent the blinding of Gloucester and that Cornwall subsequently died of wounds sustained in the struggle, Albany concludes that the heavens not only watch over but also actually take a part in human affairs:

> This shows you are above,
> You justicers, that these our nether crimes
> So speedily can venge! (78-80)

Albany may be satisfied that the essential orderliness of the heavens has been demonstrated; the audience, however, is permitted no such certitude. For the sequence of events undercuts any affirmation of retributive justice ordained by the gods.

More than any other scene, the last in the play exposes the fatuity of Albany's confidence. There he, with Edgar, speaks of divine design. For his part, Edgar has no difficulty finding evidence of justice in the world, even in his father's blinding:

> The gods are just, and of our pleasant vices
> Make instruments to plague us:
> The dark and vicious place where thee he got
> Cost him his eyes. (V.iii.171-74)

The smugness of this simplistic analysis is appalling. Edgar's faith in the gods, moreover, is soon shown to be misplaced. Moments later, when Edgar and the others hear that Cordelia's life is in jeopardy, Albany (as he had earlier) invokes divine solicitude: "The gods defend her!" (257). Scarcely have the words left his mouth, however, when Lear enters with the dead Cordelia in his arms. By any rational standard of cause and effect, Cordelia has done nothing to merit her death. Samuel Johnson's pained reaction to the murder points to its flagrant injustice: "Shakespeare has suffered the virtue of Cordelia to perish in a just cause, contrary to the natural ideas of justice, to the hope of the reader, and, what is yet more strange, to the faith of chronicles."[42] Dr. Johnson thus underscores the thematic import and dramatic impact of the single most disturbing incident in the play, one that assumes all the more significance when we consider how sharp a departure it represents from Shakespeare's chief source, *The True Chronicle History of King Leir*.[43] By rejecting the happy conclusion of the earlier play, Shakespeare undercuts the confident assertions of divine design made by Albany and Edgar.

This is not to say that Gloucester's opinion ("As flies to wanton boys are we to th' gods, / They kill us for their sport" [IV.i.36-37]) or Kent's ("It is the stars, / The stars above us, govern our conditions" [IV.iii.32-33]) is supported by events more convincingly than Edgar's. For surely what the play calls into question is whether any design—ordained by God, the gods, or the stars—may truly be said to govern the world or to take any interest in its inhabitants. Admittedly, references to various gods of Olympus appear from time to time. In fact, in no other play of Shakespeare's are "the gods" invoked more often. In no other play, however, are they more remote. And, interestingly for a drama concerned with the activities and very existence of the gods, the play lacks any sort of supernatural manifestation. There is no evidence of magic, no witchcraft, no portents (unless we include the disturbances cited by Gloucester), no ghosts or other spirits, and no miracles.

Who or what, then presides over the events of the play? Nature, apostrophized as goddess by characters as diverse as Lear (I.iv.275) and Edmund (I.ii.1), undoubtedly has the best claim. The words "nature" and "natural" appear more often in *King Lear* than in any other play of Shakespeare's; the synonymous "kind" and "kindness" also appear frequently. Such references suggest that Nature is felt as a presence. But how are we to describe this Nature? After all, some readers would argue, not all the characters envision Nature in precisely the same way.

The characters, diverse though they may be, are actually more alike in their vision of Nature than is usually acknowledged by those critics who insist on seeing "rival theories of Nature" in *King Lear*. Consider, for instance, the Nature addressed as goddess by Lear and Edmund. These two characters are certainly very different from one another. Yet when they invoke Nature, they envision a curiously similar force. Reuben A. Brower notes that when Lear calls upon Nature as goddess, "he cries on Order to produce the kind of disorder he deplores." Brower makes a similar point about Edmund: "Although the Nature Edmund hails . . . seems so different from the purposeful and fruitful power to which Lear prays, its workings are not very different from the corruption of order that Lear unconsciously wills."[44] Likewise, this disorderly Nature is not so very different from that which Gloucester contemplates when he speaks of the "ruinous disorders" all around him (I.ii.113). Nor is this very different from the Nature Edgar sees when, stunned by the sight of his blind father, he speaks of the world's "strange mutations" (IV.i.11). And this, in turn, seems not unlike the Nature that Albany envisages when he momentarily surrenders his confidence in an orderly world and imagines men preying on one another "Like monsters of the deep" (IV.ii.50). All of these characters, at one time or another, come to see Nature as tumultuous, unstable, disordered.

That all of these characters should also at some point call upon Fortune is no coincidence, for Nature in *King Lear* cannot be described without acknowledging the extraordinary role played by Fortune. In no other of Shakespeare's plays do characters invoke Fortune so insistently; from first scene to last they speak of her power. And in no other play of Shakespeare's do characters cite Fortune so frequently at pivotal points of the action. Not only is Fortune mentioned more often than any other deity, but she accounts more readily for the events witnessed by the audience. Unlike other explanations proffered for adversity, Fortune is supported by the pattern of upheaval that characterizes the play; no other force is so compatible with the sharp and sudden reversals that affect the virtuous and villainous alike. Scarcely a character in the play fails to experience some unlooked-for setback. And the most brutal reversal of all, Cordelia's murder, is entirely consistent with the operation of Fortune. A. C. Bradley has written of that climactic incident: "this catastrophe, unlike those of all the other mature tragedies, does not seem at all inevitable. It is not even satisfactorily motived. In fact it seems expressly designed to fall suddenly like a bolt from a sky cleared by the vanished storm."[45] Such unpredictability is, of course, the characteristic mode of Fortune's behavior. And, appropriately, Cordelia herself speaks of Fortune shortly before her death. She tells her father:

> We are not the first
> Who with best meaning have incurr'd the worst.
> For thee, oppressed king, I am cast down,
> Myself could else out-frown false Fortune's frown.
>
> (V.iii.3-6)

And when Lear enters with the body of his daughter, Kent says, "If Fortune brag of two she lov'd and hated, / One of them we behold" (281-82).[46]

The play does not, of course, require us to see the hand of a deity named Fortune behind every action we witness. Events, after all, can be explained in human terms. Each evil, vicious act in *King Lear*, as in *Sejanus*, may be attributed to the quirk or malice of some person. But the characters of Shakespeare's play, like those of Jonson's, find a naturalistic interpretation inadequate, at least at those points when they can no longer comprehend what they experience, when they are stunned by the sequence of events. The usually confident Edgar, for instance, speaks of Fortune after he has been betrayed by his brother and become estranged from his father:

> To be worst,
> The lowest and most dejected thing of fortune,
> Stands still in esperance, lives not in fear.
> The lamentable change is from the best,
> The worst returns to laughter. (IV.i.2-6)

In a development characteristic of this play, the blind Gloucester enters while Edgar speaks. And what the son beholds makes even his speech on Fortune seem complacent:

> My father, parti-ey'd? World, world, O world!
> But that thy strange mutations make us hate thee,
> Life would not yield to age. (10-12)

This horror fails to crush Edgar's spirit; he can still encourage his father to replace despair with patience. Yet a residue of the jarring experience remains, as we learn when Gloucester asks, "Now, good sir, what are you?" and Edgar replies, "A most poor man, made tame to fortune's blows" (IV.vi.220-21). For Edgar, as for Lepidus in *Sejanus*, the concession of Fortune's power is the grudging response of the bewildered and buffeted.[47]

Like Edgar, Kent in adversity also invokes the name of Fortune. Placed in the stocks by Regan and Cornwall, he says, "Fortune, good night; smile once more, turn thy wheel" (II.ii.173). To a modern audience, Kent's remark may mean simply that change is inevitable and, given his present dire state, things will probably change for the better; Fortune may be interpreted as shorthand for those forces in the world that cause ceaseless flux. The Jacobean audience, however, while perhaps understanding Kent's words in much the same way, could not fail to envision Dame Fortune herself, whose smiles and frowns were the most conspicuous parts of her physiognomy and whose wheel was her most famous accouterment. Seeing in the mind's eye that figure embodying caprice, the audience might well suspect that the forces at work in Kent's world are more unpredictable and destructive than even the speaker recognizes. And indeed they are. Kent in the stocks does not guess the horrors to come: the madness of Lear, the blinding of Gloucester, the murder of Cordelia. For Kent, as for Edgar, change will take the form of "strange mutations."

Audiences are doubtless pleased by one sort of change: Cornwall and Oswald, Goneril and Regan, Edmund and the Captain responsible for Cordelia's death — all die. Spectators may feel that Fortune cannot be so terrible if she contributes to the destruction of the wicked. Recall that Edmund, apparently acquiescent in his brother's assertion of retributive justice, says, "The wheel is come full circle, I am here" (V.iii.175). But even if Edmund (who earlier apostrophized Fortune: "Briefness and fortune, work!" [II.i.18]) is brought low by Fortune's wheel, the audience can take little comfort in this since Fortune destroys the good and the evil alike. The overthrow of a villain by Fortune is no guarantee that the world is ultimately rational, a divinely ordered place.

The wheel mentioned by Edmund is, of course, not explicitly identified as Fortune's.[48] And for the Jacobean audience it might well evoke the wheel of Time, sometimes conflated with Fortune's wheel. We may compare Edmund's remark with that of Cassius in *Julius Caesar:* "This day I breathed first: time is come round, / And where I did begin, there shall I end; / My life is run his compass" (V.iii.23-25). Perhaps too the audience would envision what Spenser in the opening lines of *The Mutabilitie Cantos* calls "the ever-whirling wheele / Of change." Whether the wheel mentioned by Edmund is that of Fortune or Time or Mutabilitie or of some other force, seems to have been left purposely vague. And this very imprecision makes it difficult to know whether the wheel has any retributive significance at all.

The wheel may signify merely the operation of natural forces, unconnected with any divine impetus. Indeed, Edmund had earlier spoken of rising and falling in a way entirely in keeping with his pragmatic and godless philosophy: "The younger rises when the old doth fall" (III.iii.25). If Edmund falls victim to a morally neutral wheel of vicissitude, then we are allowed little satisfaction in his defeat. For he is undone not so much by the might of virtue as he is by the permutations of time and circumstance which he sought to capitalize on and which indifferently strike down the good and the evil. G. Wilson Knight has written: "It is Edgar's trumpet, symbol of natural judgement, that summons Edmund to account at the end, sounding through the Lear-mist from which right and wrong at this moment emerge distinct. Right wins, surely as the sun rises: but it is a natural, a human process."[49]

In this connection it is interesting to note that in the Renaissance the wheel is sometimes explicitly identified with the processes of Nature. One of the emblems in Jean Jacques Boissard's *Emblemes latins* (Metz, 1588) depicts a wheel virtually identical in design to those found in representations of Fortune (fig. 18). Along the outer rim, however, the emblem portrays the history of a flower from bud to full bloom to decay. The revolution of the wheel thus coincides with the process of maturation and dissolution. The emblem, whose motto reads, "Omnium rerum vicissitudo" ("The vicissitude of all things"), inextricably links mutability with decay and death.

Shakespeare's tendency to align the activity of Fortune with the process of decay in *King Lear* is not without precedent in his earlier drama. He anticipates this conjunction in *Richard II*, where Bolingbroke speaks of his "ripening fortune." Edgar's words to his father about ripeness are thus, in a sense, a culmination of the vision expressed in the dramatist's work a decade earlier. Edgar says:

> Men must endure
> Their going hence even as their coming hither,
> Ripeness is all. (V.ii.9-11)

An air of assurance characterizes this declaration.[50] Edgar's words even contain a hint of the optimism that one associates with Occasion. But

Fig. *18. Jean Jacques Boissard,* Emblemes latins

Edgar does not exude the vitality of a Bolingbroke. Nor does "ripeness" evince the air of charged energy that animates Hamlet's "readiness"; "ripeness" connotes greater passivity.[51] And coming on the heels of Gloucester's remark, "No further, sir, a man may rot even here," Edgar's has a more melancholy resonance. For, as Jacques in *As You Like It* reminds us, ripeness presages decay and death (II.vii.26-27). Edgar's gnomic utterance, moreover, is much less definitive than it sounds.[52] Indeed, considered within the dramatic context of the last act, it is inaccurate. William R. Elton observes: "Edgar appears shortly to undercut the crucial expression when, in an aside [V.iii.185-87], he admits that endurance and ripeness are *not* all and that, indeed, suicide or death might be preferable to the drawn-out calamity of so long life."[53] Ripeness, then, and the natural processes it implies are not in themselves reassuring in the world of this play. If Shakespeare treats the forces of time and circumstance as phenomena promising growth and progress in an earlier drama like *Richard II*, he reveals these same forces as instruments of destruction in *King Lear*.

V

Destruction in *King Lear*, it may be argued, is balanced by regeneration: in society, love may atone for hatred, loyalty for treachery. In the person of Cordelia we meet a character whose benevolence may be termed restorative. As a Gentleman tells Lear, "Thou hast one daughter / Who redeems nature from the general curse / Which twain have brought her to" (IV.vi.205-7). Whether this is more than a transitory redemption is, however, unclear. Certainly Cordelia, through her filial devotion, compensates to some extent for the horrors perpetrated by her sisters. But does that compensation survive her death? Kent is so moved by the sight of the dead Cordelia in Lear's arms that he asks, "Is this the promis'd end?" and Edgar adds, "Or image of that horror?" (V.iii.264-65). These questioners envisage nothing less than the end of the world. And although Doomsday could be regarded as a necessary part of providential history,[54] the descent into chaos in *King Lear* is unrelated to any divine scheme. Cordelia's death signals no impending divine judgment; nor does it seem to herald a rebirth of goodness. We leave the theater with Lear's cries in our ears and with the sight of the dead Cordelia in our mind's eye.

The dramatic action of *Sejanus*, like that of *King Lear*, concludes with a harrowing portrayal of the parent-child relationship. At the end of his play, Jonson depicts a grieving mother, rather than father, but the emotion experienced is surely the same. In Jonson's tragedy it is Sejanus' wife who must endure the murder of her children, described as being of "unripe years" (V.843). And just as the death of Cordelia leads others to envision general conflagration, so too the death of son and daughter leads Sejanus' wife to utter such cries

> As might affright the gods, and force the sun
> Run backward to the east—nay, make the old
> Deformèd Chaos rise again, t'o'erwhelm
> Them, us, and all the world—. (V.867-70)

In what was once the citadel of the civilized world, this mother in her agony evokes in her listeners the prospect of a return to primal chaos.

Her desolation is complete. She cannot look to the heavens for solace. Although one of Sejanus' agents earlier claimed that "The gods are wise and just (IV.481), the only deity (Fortune) whose presence is felt at the end of the play, as earlier, is willful, capricious, unjust.

There are, to be sure, differences between the dramatic impact of *Sejanus* and that of *King Lear*. We are likely to feel that goodness is a more potent force in Shakespeare's play: we witness genuine sacrifice in *Lear* and we feel that it is meaningful even if it fails to rescue others from misery and death. Affection and indignation result in positive action in *Lear*, while in *Sejanus* those impulses are often smothered by fear and helplessness. Virtue in *King Lear* may not readily achieve the destruction of evil, but there can be no doubt that the courage of Cornwall's servant and the dignity of Cordelia, the devotion of Kent and of Edgar, are preferable to the cringing of Arruntius and Lepidus in *Sejanus*. Many spectators, as a result, experience a kind of exaltation in a performance of *King Lear* that seems largely missing from *Sejanus*. Nevertheless, the two tragedies have in common this essential similarity: at the end of each play, there seems no turning back from the point that has been reached, no way of recovering what has been lost. Jonson and Shakespeare both create a dramatic world where Fortune's power can no longer be checked. They depict a world where justice remains the ideal of the few, where caprice riddles the body politic, where man discerns an even deeper vicissitude behind the mutability immediately apparent in Nature, a world, in short, where irrational forces frustrate man's most determined efforts to prevail.

NOTES TO CHAPTER 9

1. *Sejanus*, ed. Jonas A. Barish, The Yale Ben Jonson (New Haven and London: Yale Univ. Press, 1965).

2. For a survey of the medieval background of the topos, see Barbara Bartholomew, *Fortuna and Natura: A Reading of Three Chaucer Narratives* (London and the Hague: Mouton, 1966), Introduction, pp. 9-45. See also R. M.

Lumiansky, "The Bereaved Narrator in Chaucer's *The Book of the Duchess*," *TSE*, 9 (1959): 5-17; James I. Wimsatt, "Chaucer, Fortune, and Machaut's 'Il m'est avis,'" in *Chaucerian Problems and Perspectives*, ed. Edward Vasta and Zacharias P. Thundy (Notre Dame and London: Univ. of Notre Dame Press, 1979), pp. 119-31. Several studies of Shakespeare's *As You Like It* also deal with the topos: John Shaw, "Fortune and Nature in *As You Like It*," *SQ*, 6 (1955): 45-50; Geoffrey Bullough, ed., *Narrative and Dramatic Sources of Shakespeare*, 2 (New York and London: Columbia Univ. Press, 1958), 150 ff; John Mac-Queen, "*As You Like It* and Mediaeval Literary Tradition," *FMLS*, 1 (1965): 216-29. See also Samuel C. Chew, *The Pilgrimage of Life* (1962; reprint ed., Port Washington, N.Y. and London: Kennikat Press, 1973), pp. 33 and 57; S. C. Sen Gupta, "Nature and Fortune," in *Shakespeare's Historical Plays* (London: Oxford Univ. Press, 1964), pp. 30-54; John Wilders, "Fortune and Nature," in *The Lost Garden: A View of Shakespeare's English and Roman History Plays* (London: Macmillan, 1978), pp. 29-52.

3. *The Moral Vision of Jacobean Tragedy* (Madison: Univ. of Wisconsin Press, 1960), p. 96.

4. The behavior of Fortune's statue has a parallel in the phenomena reported about the statue of Sejanus in Pompey's theater. First, smoke pours out, and, when the head is removed so that the source of the fire can be located, "A great and monstrous serpent" leaps out. When a new head is set upon the statue, "a fiery meteor" appears (V.218-21). These prodigies epitomize the turmoil that afflicts Nature. Coinciding with the strange demeanor of Fortune's statue, they may be meant to suggest a similarity between Nature and Fortune.

5. Gary D. Hamilton, in "Irony and Fortune in *Sejanus*," *SEL*, 11 (1971): 265-81, claims: "The idea that it is man who makes Fortune a deity informs the moral outlook of *Sejanus*" (267). Similarly, J. W. Lever, in *The Tragedy of State* (London: Methuen, 1971), writes: "that equivocal deity Fortune, both invoked and defied by Sejanus in Act V, exercises no influence and may be dismissed as a mental construct" (p. 68).

6. Una Ellis-Fermor, in *The Jacobean Drama: An Interpretation*, 4th ed. (1957; reprint ed., New York: Vintage Books, 1964), writes, "it is evident that the poetry of Seneca was in his mind throughout, at least, the early parts of the play" (pp. 111-12, *n3*). Similarly, Moody E. Prior, in *The Language of Tragedy* (1947; reprint ed., Bloomington and London: Indiana Univ. Press, 1966), argues that "the play itself is in some ways a throwback to those early days of adaptations of Seneca . . ." (p. 114). For Robert E. Knoll, in *Ben Jonson's Plays: An Introduction* (Lincoln: Univ. of Nebraska Press, 1964), *Sejanus* is "festooned with Senecan drapery" (p. 68).

7. C. H. Herford and Percy and Evelyn Simpson, eds., *Ben Jonson*, 2 (Oxford: Clarendon Press, 1925), 24.

8. Some readers, interpreting the play in a more retributive light, may cite a sentence that appears in the Argument of the 1605 Quarto: "This do we advance as a mark of terror to all traitors and treasons, to show how just the heavens are in pouring and thundering down a weighty vengeance on their unnatural intents, even to the worst princes, much more to those for guard of whose piety and virtue the angels are in continual watch, and God himself miraculously working" (Barish, p. 183). Explicit as this may be, there is good reason to believe that the sentence does not represent Jonson's thinking. We may note that the sentence is the last in the Argument and that it appears in a different kind of type from that used on the rest of the page. It is possible that the sentence was added as an afterthought. As Barish observes, "*Sejanus* had evidently been thought subversive, to judge from the fact that it apparently caused Jonson to be summoned before the Privy Council on charges of treason" (p. 183). That final sentence, then, may have been intended to placate the authorities. Significantly, Jonson omitted the sentence from the Folio edition.

9. See Daniel C. Boughner, "*Sejanus* and Machiavelli," *SEL*, 1 (1961): 81-100; reprinted in *The Devil's Disciple: Ben Jonson's Debt to Machiavelli* (New York: Philosophical Library, 1968), chapter 5.

10. Even so seemingly orthodox a play as *The Atheist's Tragedy* (published in 1611) by Cyril Tourneur evinces uncertainty about Nature. In "*The Atheist's Tragedy* and Renaissance Naturalism," *SP*, 51 (1954): 194-207, Robert Ornstein argues that the play fails to refute fully the challenges to a traditional concept of Nature: "the obvious fallacies of Levidulcia's 'naturalism' are never anatomized. Similarly D'Amville's view of nature as consisting of the physical forces of the universe is never seriously challenged. Only once is it suggested that D'Amville degrades nature by his arguments, and even then Castabella's main point is that he argues 'meerely out / Of Nature'" (204).

11. The debate and its background have been treated by Victor Harris, *All Coherence Gone* (Chicago: Univ. of Chicago Press, 1949). See also George Williamson, "Mutability, Decay, and Seventeenth-Century Melancholy," *ELH*, 2 (1935): 121-50; Don Cameron Allen, "The Degeneration of Man and Renaissance Pessimism," *SP*, 35 (1938): 202-27; Arnold Williams, "A Note on Pessimism in the Renaissance," *SP*, 36 (1939): 243-46; Ernest Lee Tuveson, *Millennium and Utopia: A Study in the Background of the Idea of Progress* (Berkeley and Los Angeles: Univ. of California Press, 1949); Hiram Haydn, *The Counter-Renaissance* (New York: Scribner's, 1950); Raymond Chapman, "Fortune

and Mutability in Elizabethan Literature," *Cambridge Journal*, 5 (1952): 374-82; Herschel Baker, *The Wars of Truth: Studies in the Decay of Christian Humanism in the Earlier Seventeenth Century* (Cambridge, Mass.: Harvard Univ. Press, 1952), pp. 43-78.

12. *Ben Jonson*, ed. Herford and Simpson, 8: 567.

13. See S. Schoenbaum, *William Shakespeare: A Compact Documentary Life* (London and New York: Oxford Univ. Press, 1977), p. 203. *Sejanus*, acted in 1603, was published in Quarto in 1605. *King Lear*, probably written in 1604-05, was published in Quarto in 1608. Geoffrey Ashe, in "William Strachey," *N&Q*, 195 (25 November 1950): 508-11, argues that in writing *King Lear* Shakespeare was influenced by a dedicatory sonnet included in the published version of *Sejanus*; that poem speaks of "Fortune's ruinous blasts."

14. *Lydgate's Fall of Princes*, ed. Henry Bergen (Washington, D.C.: The Carnegie Institution of Washington, 1923), part 3, Book IX, ll. 3520-26.

15. *The Example of Virtue*, in *The Works of Stephen Hawes*, Facsimile Reproductions with an Introduction by Frank J. Spang (Delmar, N.Y.: Scholars' Facsimiles and Reprints, 1975).

16. See *Joannis Lelandi Antiquarii de Rebus Britannicis Collectanea*, Editio Altera, 4 (London: Benj. White, 1774), 315.

17. See David M. Bergeron, *English Civic Pageantry, 1558-1642* (Columbia: Univ. of South Carolina Press, 1971), p. 56.

18. *The Life and Minor Works of George Peele*, ed. David H. Horne (New Haven: Yale Univ. Press, 1952), p. 218.

19. *Tamburlaine the Great, Parts I and II*, ed. John D. Jump, RRDS (Lincoln: Univ. of Nebraska Press, 1967).

20. *The Expulsion of the Triumphant Beast*, trans. and ed. Arthur D. Imerti (New Brunswick, N.J.: Rutgers Univ. Press, 1964), p. 176.

21. Oliver Elton, in "Giordano Bruno in England," *Modern Studies* (London: Edward Arnold, 1907), pp. 1-36, first suggested Bruno's influence on *The Mutabilitie Cantos*: "The fragment certainly recalls part of the *Spaccio* in its machinery, and some other works of Bruno in its ruling idea" (p. 33). Ronald B. Levinson, in "Spenser and Bruno," *PMLA*, 43 (1928): 675-81, also argues for Bruno's influence. By contrast, Angelo M. Pellegrini, in "Bruno, Sidney, and Spenser," *SP*, 40 (1943): 128-44, argues against it. Of course, it is possible that both Bruno and Spenser are indebted to the same work, perhaps that of the mythographer Natale Conti (or Natalis Comes). In *Classical Mythology in the*

Poetry of Edmund Spenser (Princeton: Princeton Univ. Press, 1932), Henry G. Lotspeich writes: "N.C. offers the information, from what source does not appear, that at one time Fortuna, like Mutability, almost succeeded in ousting Jove from his throne . . ." (p. 86).

22. *The Mutabilitie Cantos*, ed. S. P. Zitner, Nelson's Medieval and Renaissance Library (London: Thomas Nelson, 1968).

23. Ibid., p. 15.

24. "Mutable in Eternity: Spenser's Despair and the Multiple Forms of Mutabilitie," *JMRS*, 2 (1972): 59.

25. Ibid., p. 67.

26. D. C. Collins, ed., *Vicissitudo Rerum*, Shakespeare Association Facsimiles, no. 4 (London: Oxford Univ. Press, 1931), p. viii. Kathrine Koller, in "Two Expressions of the Idea of Mutability," *SP*, 35 (1938): 228-37, shows that while Norden versifies entire sections of Louis LeRoy's work (in translation), he ignores LeRoy's confidence in progress. For a discussion of LeRoy, see Werner L. Gundersheimer, "Louis LeRoy's Humanistic Optimism," *JHI*, 23 (1962): 324-39.

27. In his address to his readers, Jonson writes that "this book, in all numbers, is not the same with that which was acted on the public stage, wherein a second pen had good share . . ." (p. 28). Jonas A. Barish comments: "Sometimes thought to have been that of George Chapman, for whom Jonson had considerable respect, and whose own historical tragedies resemble Jonson's more closely than any others of the period. But no real clue exists as to the identity of the collaborator, or as to which portions of the original play were his work" (p. 183).

28. *Bussy D'Ambois*, ed. Nicholas Brooke, The Revels Plays (Cambridge, Mass.: Harvard Univ. Press, 1964).

29. Useful discussions of Nature in Shakespeare's time generally or in *King Lear* specifically include the following: Theodore Spencer, *Shakespeare and the Nature of Man* (New York: Macmillan, 1942), pp. 1-50 and 135-52; E. M. W. Tillyard, *The Elizabethan World Picture* (London: Chatto and Windus, 1943); John F. Danby, *Shakespeare's Doctrine of Nature: A Study of King Lear* (London: Faber and Faber, 1949); H. B. Parkes, "Nature's Diverse Laws: The Double Vision of the Elizabethans," *SR*, 58 (1950): 402-18; Robert Speaight, *Nature in Shakespearian Tragedy* (London: Hollis and Carter, 1955), pp. 89-121; Russell A. Fraser, *Shakespeare's Poetics in Relation to King Lear* (1962; reprint ed., Nashville, Tennessee: Vanderbilt Univ. Press, 1966),

pp. 30-45 and 85-102; George C. Herndl, *The High Design: English Renaissance Tragedy and the Natural Law* (Lexington: Univ. Press of Kentucky, 1970), pp. 44-48; James Daly, "Cosmic Harmony and Political Thinking in Early Stuart England," *Transactions of the American Philosophical Society*, 69, part 7 (October, 1979), 1-41.

30. See Edgar Wind, *Giorgione's Tempesta, with Comments on Giorgione's Poetic Allegories* (Oxford: Clarendon Press, 1969), p. 3.

31. Ibid.

32. Robert Bechtold Heilman, *This Great Stage: Image and Structure in King Lear* (Baton Rouge: Louisiana State Univ. Press, 1948), p. 115.

33. Danby, *Shakespeare's Doctrine of Nature*, p. 198.

34. Virgil K. Whitaker, in *Shakespeare's Use of Learning: An Inquiry into the Growth of his Mind and Art* (San Marino, Calif.: Huntington Library, 1953), finds Gloucester "detestable beyond any villain in Shakespeare" (p. 307). Michael Long, in *The Unnatural Scene: A Study in Shakespearean Tragedy* (London: Methuen, 1976), echoes the judgment of Edmund and calls Gloucester "foppish" (p. 177).

35. Of Edmund's speech, R. C. Bald writes, in "'Thou, Nature, art my goddess': Edmund and Renaissance Free-Thought," in *Joseph Quincy Adams Memorial Studies*, ed. James G. McManaway et al. (Washington, D. C.: Folger Shakespeare Library, 1948), pp. 337-49, "Such sentiments find so ready an endorsement in the modern mind that one scarcely stops to examine them or consider them in relation to the speaker and the situation. Yet it is far from certain that these lines represent Shakespeare's own attitude" (p. 347).

36. Is the Fool referring to the wheel of Fortune in this passage? Possibly. Elsewhere he speaks of Fortune: "Fortune, that arrant whore, / Ne'er turns the key to th' poor" (II.iv.52-53). For a discussion of Fortune and the Fool, see William Willeford, *The Fool and His Scepter: A Study in Clowns and Jesters and Their Audience* (Evanston: Northwestern Univ. Press, 1969), chapter 13.

37. *Character and Society in Shakespeare* (Oxford: Clarendon Press, 1951), p. 112.

38. *The Dream of Learning* (Oxford: Clarendon Press, 1951), p. 93.

39. *Fools of Time: Studies in Shakespearean Tragedy* (Toronto: Univ. of Toronto Press, 1967), p. 13.

40. The connection between one's nature and one's fortune is suggested in another of Shakespeare's tragedies, *Coriolanus*, when a Patrician says, "This

man has marr'd his fortune," and Menenius replies, "His nature is too noble for the world" (III.i.253-54). In *King Lear* that connection is suggested by the characters' speaking of a person's fortune as something organic and diseased. Edmund, for instance, dismisses Gloucester's concern over the disturbances in Nature, saying, "This is the excellent foppery of the world, that when we are *sick in fortune* . . . we make guilty of our disasters the sun, the moon, and stars" (I.ii.118-21). Later, Oswald rebukes Edgar with this warning: "Wherefore, bold peasant, / Durst thou support a publish'd traitor? Hence, / Lest that th' *infection of his fortune* take / Like hold on thee" (IV.vi.231-34).

41. J. C. Maxwell, in "The Technique of Invocation in 'King Lear,'" *MLR*, 45 (1950): 142-47, wrote that "*King Lear* is a Christian play about a pagan world" (142). Whether the play is more pagan than Christian is still perhaps the most controversial question that surrounds Shakespeare's tragedy. Those who tend toward a Christian interpretation (with an emphasis on man's regeneration and on divine justice) or who explicitly endorse it include the following: Hardin Craig, "The Ethics of King Lear," *PQ*, 4 (1925): 97-109; Geoffrey L. Bickersteth, "The Golden World of *King Lear*," Annual Shakespeare Lecture of the British Academy for 1946 (printed 1947); Robert B. Heilman, *This Great Stage* (1948); Oscar James Campbell, "The Salvation of Lear," *ELH*, 15 (1948): 93-109; John F. Danby, *Shakespeare's Doctrine of Nature* (1949); Danby, *Poets on Fortune's Hill* (London: Faber and Faber, 1952), pp. 108-27; Alwin Thaler, "The Gods and God in *King Lear*," *RenP* (1955): 32-39; Irving Ribner, "The Gods are Just: A Reading of King Lear," *TDR*, 2 (1958): 34-54; Paul N. Siegel, *Shakespearean Tragedy and the Elizabethan Compromise* (New York: New York Univ. Press, 1957), pp. 161-88; Kenneth Myrick, "Christian Pessimism in *King Lear*," in *Shakespeare, 1564-1964: A Collection of Modern Essays by Various Hands*, ed. Edward A. Bloom (Providence, R.I.: Brown Univ. Press, 1964), pp. 56-70; Roy W. Battenhouse, *Shakespearean Tragedy: Its Art and Its Christian Premises* (Bloomington and London: Indiana Univ. Press, 1969); James P. Driscoll, "The Vision of *King Lear*," *ShakS*, 10 (1977): 159-89. Among those who see *King Lear* as essentially a non-Christian play are the following: H. B. Charlton, *Shakespearian Tragedy* (Cambridge: Cambridge Univ. Press, 1948); W. R. Keast, "Imagery and Meaning in the Interpretation of *King Lear*" [a review article of Heilman's *This Great Stage*], *MP*, 47 (1949): 45-64; D. G. James, *The Dream of Learning* (1951); Sylvan Barnet, "Some Limitations of a Christian Approach to Shakespeare," *ELH*, 22 (1955): 81-92; Barbara Everett, "The New King Lear," *CritQ*, 2 (1960): 325-39; Nicholas Brooke, "The Ending of *King Lear*," in *Shakespeare, 1564-1964*, ed. Bloom, pp. 71-87; William R. Elton, *King Lear and the Gods* (San Marino, Calif.: Huntington Library, 1966).

42. *Johnson on Shakespeare*, ed. Arthur Sherbo, The Yale Edition of the Works of Samuel Johnson (New Haven: Yale Univ. Press, 1968), 8: 704.

43. *The True Chronicle History of King Leir* was registered and published in 1605, but evidently written much earlier.

44. *Hero and Saint: Shakespeare and the Graeco-Roman Heroic Tradition* (New York and Oxford: Oxford Univ. Press, 1971), p. 391. Similarly, Maurice Charney, in "'We Put Fresh Garments on Him': Nakedness and Clothes in *King Lear*," in *Some Facets of King Lear*, ed. Rosalie L. Colie and F. T. Flahiff (Toronto and Buffalo: Univ. of Toronto Press, 1974), observes: "There are striking similarities between Edmund's 'Nature' and that of Lear . . ." (p. 85).

45. *Shakespearean Tragedy*, 2nd ed. (London: Macmillan, 1905), pp. 252-53.

46. In the first scene of the play, numerous comments associate Cordelia with Fortune or fortune. For instance, Lear tells his daughter, "Mend your speech a little, / Lest you may mar your fortunes" (I.i.94- 95). Cordelia says, "Peace be with Burgundy! / Since that respects of fortune are his love, / I shall not be his wife" (247-249). And Goneril says to her sister, "Let your study / Be to content your lord, who hath receiv'd you / At fortune's alms" (276-78). It is interesting that this same character in Shakespeare's source, *The True Chronicle History of King Leir* (in *Narrative and Dramatic Sources of Shakespeare*, ed. Geoffrey Bullough, 7 [London and New York: Columbia Univ. Press, 1973]), also is linked with Fortune. Among Cordella's remarks are these: "How may I blame the fickle Queene of Chaunce, / That maketh me a patterne of her power?" (603-04); "And in this day of tryumph to my sisters, / Doth Fortune tryumph in my over throw" (656-57); "Thus ile mock fortune, as she mocketh me" (704). In keeping with the Christian world of *Leir*, the believer must repudiate Fortune as an explanation of adversity. Thus Cordella rebukes herself: "But why accuse I fortune and my father? / No, no, it is the pleasure of my God: / And I do willingly imbrace the rod" (609-11).

47. Toward the end of the play, references to Fortune or fortune become more numerous, even in the speeches of characters who have previously affirmed divine design. Edgar tells Albany, "Fortune love you!" (V.i.46). Albany says to Edmund, "Sir, you have show'd to-day your valiant strain, / And fortune led you well" (V.iii.40-41). Edgar speaks of Edmund's "fire-new fortune" (V.iii.133).

48. The wheel has been variously interpreted. Geoffrey L. Bickersteth, in "The Golden World of *King Lear*," identifies it as Fortune's (p. 9). But Virgil K. Whitaker, in *Shakespeare's Use of Learning*, writes: "The wheel is no longer

Fortune's. It almost belongs to the world machine of a coming age" (p. 313). Ruth Nevo, in *Tragic Form in Shakespeare* (Princeton: Princeton Univ. Press, 1972), identifies it as "the wheel of nemesis" (p. 302). Alan Hobson, in *Full Circle: Shakespeare and Moral Development* (London: Chatto and Windus, 1972), writes: "That the wheel referred to is not Fortune's wheel is made evident by Edgar's insistence upon the justice of this causal relation between deed and consequence established by 'The Gods,' and by the fact that Edmund agrees with him. Fortune's wheel symbolises the mere alternation of prosperity and adversity, not causal necessity" (p. 222, *n1*). John Doebler, in *Shakespeare's Speaking Pictures: Studies in Iconic Imagery* (Albuquerque: Univ. of New Mexico Press, 1974), sees in the posture of the fallen Edmund a victim of Fortune's wheel (p. xii).

49. "The *Lear* Universe," in *The Wheel of Fire: Essays in Interpretation of Shakespeare's Sombre Tragedies* (London: Humphrey Milford, 1930), p. 213.

50. Among the most useful discussions of Edgar's words are these: J. V. Cunningham, *Woe or Wonder: The Emotional Effect of Shakespearean Tragedy* (Denver: Univ. of Denver Press, 1951), Introduction; Edgar Wind, *Pagan Mysteries of the Renaissance*, rev. and enlarged ed. (New York: Norton, 1968), chapter 6; William R. Elton, *King Lear and the Gods*, pp. 99-107; Martha Andresen, "'Ripeness is All': Sententiae and Commonplaces in *King Lear*," in *Some Facets of King Lear*, ed. Colie and Flahiff, pp. 145-68.

51. William R. Elton, in *King Lear and the Gods*, relates the passivity implicit in Edgar's remark to Stoic attitudes: "The acceptance of passive resignation and endurance in a universe of suffering is both characteristically Stoic and an element of the Christian outlook, in both early times of Roman admixture and neo-Stoic Renaissance times of disintegration and crises" (p. 103).

52. Maynard Mack has noted that the predominant mood of the play is imperative; speakers voice with conviction views that contrast totally with those of others around them. See *King Lear in Our Time* (Berkeley and Los Angeles: Univ. of California Press, 1965), p. 89.

53. *King Lear and the Gods*, p. 107.

54. John Holloway, in *The Story of the Night: Studies in Shakespeare's Major Tragedies* (London: Routledge and Kegan Paul, 1961), has written: "Disruption in the kingdom, disruption in the family, linked by tradition, were facets of that universal disruption of Nature, that Descent into Chaos, which for millennia had been a standing dread of mankind and at the same time one of mankind's convictions about providential history in the future" (p. 79).

Chapter 10

FORTUNE IN *TIMON OF ATHENS* AND *ANTONY AND CLEOPATRA*

HAKESPEARE'S LATE TRAGEDIES display his undiminished capacity for experimentation. *Timon of Athens* (c. 1607-1608) and *Antony and Cleopatra* (c. 1606-1607) are as different from one another as they are from his earlier plays. In *Timon* the action seems schematized, the characters limited mostly to types, the setting (Athens and environs) claustrophobic. Even the language is constrained: "We miss the ardour, the poetic wealth and complexity characteristic of the imagery in *Antony and Cleopatra*."[1] As the language indicates, the world of *Antony* is expansive: the action—political, military, and personal—is diverse; the characters of the large cast not only represent well-defined individuals but also rival cultures; and the setting embraces much of the Mediterranean. "Shakespeare's eyes," writes Granville-Barker, "swept no wider horizon."[2] There is also a cosmic dimension in *Antony and Cleopatra*; we hear of soothsayers and diviners, daemons and the old gods of Egypt.

Disparate as they are, *Timon of Athens* and *Antony and Cleopatra* both reflect the continuing appeal of tragedy as it had been understood for centuries. The action of *Timon* reminds Rolf Soellner of "the old wheel Boccaccio imprinted on medieval and Renaissance conceptions of tragedy."[3] And Maynard Mack has noted that *Antony and Cleopatra* "would have delighted Chaucer's Monk. For it obviously owes much, at least in its general outline, to the medieval tragic formula of the fall-of-princes and mirror-for-magistrates tradition, which the Monk enunciates to the Canterbury pilgrims, and which was still, in 1607, . . . far better known than Plutarch to playhouse audiences."[4] The two plays, then, outwardly so different, draw inspiration from a traditional concept of tragedy, one that had not lost its power to move contemporary audiences.

This is not to say that the plays perpetuate unchanged a formula Shakespeare found in Lydgate, Baldwin, and others. The playwright's imagination remakes what it finds, shaping new emphases while preserving the basic pattern. A key to Shakespeare's concern in both these plays is provided by the Poet's allegory of Fortune in *Timon*. Although he evokes medieval iconography when he speaks of Fortune's hill, the Poet names a Jacobean concern when he describes the multitudes that throng that hill. As the allegory suggests, *Timon*—and, as we shall see, *Antony* too—is not so much about an individual's relationship to Fortune as it is about man's relationship to other men in consequence of Fortune's activity. The two plays deal with the societal implications of Fortune and, despite their crowd scenes, especially with the isolation engendered by adversity.

This thematic concern is reflected in the frequent reference by characters to their own or others' "fortunes." The term has a special implication in these plays since, whether it signifies the material (e.g. wealth) or the intangible (reputation, the prospects for success), it represents something that others may exploit for their own ends or something that may present a danger to them. This application of the term "fortunes" also points to the important, if indirect, role that Fortune plays in *Timon* and *Antony*. For what the characters recognize is that Fortune acts through other people. Friends and associates are quick to spot the signs of Fortune's favor or hostility in Timon and Antony, and they tailor their actions accordingly. Literally and figuratively they reach out to others or draw back, convinced that by forging friendships they may obtain Fortune's bounty or by abjuring them avert Fortune's hostility.

I

Timon of Athens is, to many readers, a Renaissance Everyman who makes serious mistakes in handling money and people and, consequently, loses his wealth and gains the contempt of his friends. One reader, who finds "thematic and structural similarities" between *Timon* and *Everyman*, writes that Timon's generosity "finally becomes prodigality."[5] Another critic, who sees *Timon* as "the medieval morality play, only so much altered as to bring it very near to perfection," calls the protagonist "Ideal Bounty and Friendship."[6] To be sure, the play has about it a highly abstract quality,[7] but Timon himself is less a misguided idealist and more a pragmatist than is usually acknowledged. Even though he may spend money lavishly, Timon is not so naive as to think himself immune to adversity. In fact, his generosity springs, in large measure, from this very realization. That is, he showers gifts upon others because in time of adversity he means to be protected by their fellowship.

Timon's relationship to Ventidius demonstrates this intent. By pledging a sum needed to satisfy the man's debt, Timon secures his release from prison. Ventidius, however, has not been completely freed, since he substitutes one obligation for another. Thus when Timon announces, "I'll pay the debt and free him" (I.i.103), the Messenger shrewdly observes, "Your lordship ever binds him." Similarly, Timon binds Lucilius by providing the money that allows him to marry. The happy recipient expresses his gratitude in terms that reveal his awareness of the debt:

> Humbly I thank your lordship. Never may
> That state or fortune fall into my keeping,
> Which is not owed to you! (I.i.149-51)

By these actions Timon establishes a network of social ties defined by financial indebtedness. Such is his method for coping with the prospect of change. What to others may seem generosity amounting to profligacy is to him a form of prudence.

The blend of altruism and calculation that characterizes Timon is evident at his banquet. There Ventidius, having come into an inheritance, offers to repay his debt. Timon, however, generously assures him that the money was given without strings: "I gave it freely ever, and there's none / Can truly say he gives if he receives" (I.ii.10-11). Nevertheless, in this same scene Timon tells his guests, "O, no doubt, my good friends, but the gods themselves have provided that I shall have much help from you: how had you been my friends else?" (88-90). Timon's notion of friendship, then, entails reciprocal obligation: "We are born to do benefits; and what better or properer can we call our own than the riches of our friends?" (101-103). From this idea Timon derives a sense of security: "O, what a precious comfort 'tis to have so many like brothers commanding one another's fortunes!" (103-105).

That Timon envisages himself as "commanding" the resources of others becomes clear when his creditors demand payment. His first impulse is to seek aid from those whom he has helped in the past. Believing that he need only ask to receive, he assures Flavius:

> If I would broach the vessels of my love,
> And try the argument of hearts, by borrowing,
> Men and men's fortunes could I frankly use
> As I can bid thee speak. (II.ii.177-80)

A few moments later he tells this servant, who has criticized his largesse, "You shall perceive how you / Mistake my fortunes; I am wealthy in my friends" (183-84). This is more than a figure of speech, for Timon sincerely believes not only that he has many friends, but also that they will, on request, deliver the cash he seeks.

So confident is Timon of their help that he cannot comprehend his friends' refusal. When Flavius returns with news of the first rejection, Timon's response is to send him out again, this time to Ventidius: "Nev'r speak or think / That Timon's fortunes 'mong his friends can sink" (II.ii.230-31). But the new entreaties fail too. And with that failure Timon is forced to confront the perfidy of his supposed friends and the error of his own assumptions.

All along Timon has valued friendship because it seemed to offer a bulwark against the world's mutability: if a man were needy, he could reach out to others for help. Now Timon discovers that men are no more constant than Dame Fortune. They are themselves merely "fools of fortune" (III.vi.96). And with this realization Timon turns his hostility against those who emulate Fortune's inconstancy.

Timon's anger is directed not only against the individuals who have spurned him but also against society at large. In his rage he invites the destruction of those institutions designed to preserve social order:

> Piety, and fear,
> Religion to the gods, peace, justice, truth,
> Domestic awe, night-rest, and neighborhood,
> Instruction, manners, mysteries, and trades,
> Degrees, observances, customs, and laws,
> Decline to your confounding contraries;
> And yet confusion live! (IV.i.15-21)

If this reminds us of King Lear on the heath, it is because Timon has made essentially the same discovery as Lear: that man's nature is weak, that Nature itself has been corrupted by Fortune:

> Not nature
> (To whom all sores lay siege) can bear great fortune
> But by contempt of nature. (IV.iii.6-8)

Like Lear before him, Timon comes to see that Fortune's hostility dissolves even the closest of human ties, while Fortune's favor fosters relationships based tenuously upon greed:

> every grize of fortune
> Is smooth'd by that below. The learned pate
> Ducks to the golden fool. All's obliquy;
> There's nothing level in our cursed natures
> But direct villainy. (IV.iii.16-20)

By his experience Timon confirms the vision of the Poet who, near the beginning of the play, sees all mankind clustered round Fortune's hill.[8]

> Sir, I have upon a high and pleasant hill
> Feign'd Fortune to be thron'd. The base o' th' mount
> Is rank'd with all deserts, all kind of natures,
> That labor on the bosom of this sphere
> To propagate their states. Amongst them all,
> Whose eyes are on this sovereign lady fix'd,

One do I personate of Lord Timon's frame,
Whom Fortune with her ivory hand wafts to her,
Whose present grace to present slaves and servants
Translates his rivals. (I.i.63-72)

And in a foreshadowing of Timon's anguish, the Poet sees Fortune's influence as invariably baleful:

When Fortune in her shift and change of mood
Spurns down her late beloved, all his dependants
Which labor'd after him to the mountain's top
Even on their knees and hands, let him slip down,
Not one accompanying his declining foot. (84-88)

After Timon "slips down," the First Servant seems to recall these words
of the Poet when he remarks in wonderment on the desertion of Timon:
"So noble a master fall'n, all gone, and not / One friend to take his fortune by the arm, / And go along with him" (IV.ii.6-8). In his anguish
Timon comes to envy Apemantus precisely because Fortune never
reached out to help him: "Thou art a slave, whom Fortune's tender arm
/ With favor never clasp'd, but bred a dog" (IV.iii.250-51). Not to enjoy
Fortune's favor (and thus the adulation of the crowd) is never to suffer
the sharp transition from happiness to misery and, concomitantly, from
celebrity to isolation.

Of course, the Poet's (and Timon's) vision scarcely represents a com-
plete description of the world of the play. After all, some human ties re-
sist destruction in *Timon of Athens* just as they do in *King Lear*. The First
Stranger, for example, says, "Had his necessity made use of me, /
I would have put my wealth into donation, / And the best half
should have return'd to him, / So much I love his heart" (III.ii.82-85).
Moreover, Flavius serves his master no less faithfully than Kent serves
Lear. And he is willing to bestow on his friends what little he possesses:

Good fellows all,
The latest of my wealth I'll share amongst you.
Where ever we shall meet, for Timon's sake
Let's yet be fellows. Let's shake our heads, and say,

As 'twere a knell unto our master's fortunes,
"We have seen better days." Let each take some;
                              [*Giving them money.*]
Nay, put out all your hand. (IV.ii.22-28)

Perhaps most impressively of all, Alcibiades, in the subplot, intercedes for a friend in distress. And he does so without thought of reward. He tells the Senators of Athens:

> It pleases time and fortune to lie heavy
> Upon a friend of mine, who in hot blood
> Hath stepp'd into the law, which is past depth
> To those that (without heed) do plunge into't.
>
> (III.v.10-13)

The Second Senator, continuing the water imagery suggestive of dangerous flux, replies later in the conversation: "he has a sin that often / Drowns him and takes his valor prisoner" (67-68). In seeking to compensate for that flux, Alcibiades does not bestow money in the manner of Timon, but he employs imagery of finance to suggest that the accused man's deeds have redeemed him. Thus his honor "buys out his fault" (17); and "His service done / At Lacedaemon and Byzantium / Were a sufficient briber for his life" (59-61). Alcibiades, moreover, uses similar imagery when he offers himself as partial recompense for his friend:

> — yet more to move you,
> Take my deserts to his, and join 'em both;
> And for I know your reverend ages love
> Security, I'll pawn my victories, all
> My honor to you, upon his good returns. (77-81)

The language conveys Alcibiades' commitment to his friend, the strength of the bond linking them. The Athenian general will not succumb to the pattern of desertion so often manifest in the main plot, where adversity has the effect of dividing one man from another.

Alcibiades, however, meets much the same fate as Timon. By persisting in his advocacy, Alcibiades prompts his own banishment and so reenacts the experience of Timon, moving from community to separation. Even though Alcibiades' long record of service to Athens would seem to offer some protection from the caprice of other people, he is enveloped by change no less than the improvident Timon. And he is left to ponder the irony of his situation: "I have kept back their foes, / While they have told their money, and let out / Their coin upon large interest—I myself / Rich only in large hurts" (III.v.105-108).

If the loyalty of Flavius and Alcibiades does not outweigh the anguish of Timon, it is because Timon dominates the play, and we recognize how incontrovertible is his pain. When an angry Alcibiades threatens to destroy Athens, Timon is offered an opportunity to rejoin his society. Two senators ask him to return and help defend their city from attack. They reason that although Timon has rejected the company of men, nevertheless one who has changed from bon vivant to misanthrope can also change back:

> At all times alike
> Men are not still the same; 'twas time and griefs
> That fram'd him thus. Time with his fairer hand,
> Offering the fortunes of his former days,
> The former man may make him. (V.i.121-25)

But Timon's bitterness cannot be exchanged for amity so easily. He remains a misanthrope, perhaps because he cannot stand the prospect of being disappointed by his fellow man yet again. At the end he is determined to live and die alone. Insofar as it betokens a self-sufficiency he once lacked, Timon's resolution may reflect a dogged strength. But his choice of a grave-site reveals his surrender to the flux that has taken such a heavy toll: he makes his "everlasting mansion / Upon the beached verge of the salt flood," which daily will cover his tomb with the "turbulent surge" (V.i.215-18).

318

II

When we first see them, Antony and Cleopatra are already overtaken by change. In the opening scene of the play, Philo describes Antony as "transform'd" (I.i.12); once a formidable soldier, he is now, Octavius tells us later, "not more manlike / Than Cleopatra" (I.iv.5-6). In frustration Antony complains to a messenger from Octavius: "he seems / Proud and disdainful, harping on what I am / Not what he knew I was" (III.xiii.141-43). Nor has Antony even now achieved stability. His present changeability reveals itself in constant irresolution: he leaves Cleopatra for Octavia, and Octavia for Cleopatra again; he pledges solidarity with Octavius, then alienates him by deserting Octavia; he commits himself to battle at Actium, then abruptly abandons the scene of conflict. In Antony Roman thoughts seem always to war with Egyptian pleasures, ensuring an oscillation between what his conscience and his impulses dictate. Cleopatra too is volatile, her nature chameleon. Antony speaks of her as one whom "every thing becomes—to chide, to laugh, / To weep" (I.i.49-50). Her capacity for contrariness and unpredictability is apparent when she tells Charmian to defy Antony's expectations: "If you find him sad, / Say I am dancing; if in mirth, report / That I am sudden sick" (I.iii.3-5). Typically, when she interrogates a messenger, in II.v, she quivers on the edge of joy and despair. "It is the unexpectedness of her transitions," writes M. W. MacCallum, "the impossibility of foreseeing what she will say or do, the certainty that whatever she says or does will be a surprise, that keeps Antony and everyone else in perpetual agitation."[9] Little wonder that Enobarbus can speak of her "infinite variety" (II.ii.235). Individually so changeable, Antony and Cleopatra find their relationship ceaselessly in flux. Sometimes intense, sometimes indifferent, their passion creates a cycle of parting and reconciliation.

"In no other play by Shakespeare," writes Ernest Schanzer, "do we meet characters given to such persistent oscillation of feelings, such violent veering between emotional extremes."[10] In this constant change, the characters seem to evince Fortune's influence. During most of the play, however, they seldom speak of Dame Fortune herself; there is nothing in *Antony and Cleopatra* to match the Poet's elaborate allego-

ry of Fortune in *Timon of Athens*.[11] Instead, they speak often of their
"fortunes," which may suggest that Fortune is immanent in their characters, a force within as much as a force without.[12] G. Wilson Knight
remarks, "In *Antony and Cleopatra* . . . any powerful divine suggestion is
blended with things natural and human. The 'gods' and 'fortune' are
vaguer than in *Lear*."[13] And, he adds, "The divine blends with the
human, the human becomes divine." Significantly, Cleopatra dresses
"In th' abiliments of the goddess Isis" (III.vi.17), who was conflated with
Fortune in antiquity and in the Renaissance.[14]

Given their volatile temperaments, it is natural that Antony and Cleopatra should spend so much of their time quite literally on or near the
water, itself a symbol of change and one identified with both Fortune
and Isis. Antony, likened to a "grand sea" (III.xii.10), undertakes a journey to Rome and back; he celebrates peace with the other triumvirs and
Pompey aboard ship; and he wages his most important battle on the
Mediterranean. Cleopatra too, called "serpent of old Nile" (I.v.25), is
linked with both river and sea. The most famous description of the
Egyptian Queen, by Enobarbus, captures her splendor on the river
Cydnus: "The barge she sat in, like a burnish'd throne, / Burnt on the
water . . ." (II.ii.191-92). Her most inglorious moment also occurs on the
water: at Actium she "Hoists sail and flies" (III.x.15), prompting Antony
to follow her and thus to lose the battle.

Water functions not only as a setting in *Antony and Cleopatra*, but also
as a recurrent image. As in *Timon of Athens*, things melt and pour, sink
and rise, dissolve and o'erflow, swell and ebb. This imagery applies both
to the protagonists and to other characters as well. Thus, for example,
when Pompey expresses confidence in his future, he does so in terms
that evoke the sea, the tide, and the moon: "The people love me, and the
sea is mine; / My powers are crescent, and my auguring hope / Says it
will come to th' full" (II.i.9-11). Octavius, reflecting on Pompey's prospects, generalizes about human destiny in language of the tide: "he
which is was wish'd, until he were; / And the ebb'd man, ne'er lov'd till
ne'er worth love, / Comes dear'd by being lack'd" (I.iv.42-44). This
insistent imagery points to a hallmark of the characters in this
play: their fickleness. Not only are the protagonists forever changing,
but so too is everyone else. Antony, for example, speaks of "Our slip-
pery people" (I.ii.185), and Octavius comments on the advantage which
the people's caprice lends Pompey:

This common body,
Like to a vagabond flag upon the stream,
Goes to and back, lackeying the varying tide,
To rot itself with motion.   (I.iv.44-47)

Something innate, it seems, drives them to incessant fluctuation. Having been quiescent for a time, they are destined, Antony remarks, to alter their allegiance: "quietness, grown sick of rest, would purge / By any desperate change" (I.iii.53-54).[15]

If everyone, from triumvir to common citizen, is subject to change, then it follows that relationships between individuals are necessarily precarious.[16] Antony and Octavius, partners and rivals, epitomize the uneasy, shifting friendships that characterize the play. Preoccupied with his memory of Antony in times past, Octavius can neither understand nor sympathize with the Antony of the present. Out of a mixture of loyalty and ambition, Octavius would preserve for a time their friendship. But Antony, so different now, is unable to sustain it. As Octavius observes, "'t cannot be / We shall remain in friendship, our conditions / So diff'ring in their acts" (II.ii.112-14). In a move to patch together their alliance — "to knit your hearts / With an unslipping knot" (125-26) — Agrippa proposes that Antony marry Octavia, the sister of Octavius. Even as the marriage is arranged, however, we sense that it will prove no more lasting than other relationships. And with its failure the alliance between Antony and Octavius gives way to hostility.

Even characters who share essentially the same interests and goals find themselves drawing apart, especially in times of adversity, as they perceive their friends changing. Consider, for instance, Pompey and Menas. The latter follows Pompey as long as he demonstrates the qualities that made his father great. But Menas comes to doubt the wisdom of Pompey's bargain with the triumvirs: "Pompey doth this day laugh away his fortune" (II.vi.104-105). On board Pompey's galley, he proposes a remedy: that the cable holding fast the ship be cut — along with the throats of Pompey's rivals. The idea appeals to Pompey, but his sense of honor inhibits him: "In me 'tis villainy, / In thee't had been good service" (II.vii.74-75). Stung by the rebuff and foreseeing the adversity that will overtake Pompey, Menas determines to sever his ties:

For this,
I'll never follow thy pall'd fortunes more.
Who seeks, and will not take when once 'tis offer'd,
Shall never find it more. (81-84)

And so this figure who only shortly before told Pompey, "I have ever held my cap off to thy fortunes" (57), now, sensing Pompey's forfeiture of opportunity, abruptly reverses himself. What is a minor incident in Plutarch has become an object lesson in loyalty and desertion, a paradigm for other relationships in the play.

What Menas is to Pompey, Enobarbus is to Antony. The Roman soldier has long served the general whose wisdom (especially military judgment) he comes to doubt. When the antipathy between Antony and Octavius leads to war, Enobarbus seeks to dissuade his superior from waging a naval battle:

> Most worthy sir, you therein throw away
> The absolute soldiership you have by land,
> Distract your army, which doth most consist
> Of war-mark'd footmen, leave unexecuted
> Your own renowned knowledge, quite forgo
> The way which promises assurance, and
> Give up yourself merely to chance and hazard,
> From firm security. (III.vii.41-48)

Although Enobarbus argues forcefully, Antony is drawn to the sea almost as though by compulsion; obstinately, he replies, "I'll fight at sea." To the dispirited Enobarbus the decision is utterly misguided, and it sets the stage for his desertion.

Initially, following the debacle at Actium, Enobarbus remains loyal. When Canidius decides to leave Antony for Octavius, Enobarbus declares, "I'll yet follow / The wounded chance of Antony, though my reason / Sits in the wind against me" (III.x.34-36). However, when he hears the defeated Antony propose hand-to-hand combat with the enemy—"sword against sword, / Ourselves alone" (III.xiii.27-28)— Enobarbus realizes that his general's judgment has become irreparably impaired:

> I see men's judgments are
> A parcel of their fortunes, and things outward
> Do draw the inward quality after them,
> To suffer all alike. (III.xiii.31-34)

And in Cleopatra's apparently favorable response to Octavius' entreaty, Enobarbus imagines her imminent capitulation: "Sir, sir, thou art so leaky / That we must leave thee to thy sinking, for / Thy dearest quit thee" (III.xiii.63-65). To remain with Antony any longer has come to seem an act of folly.

Enobarbus' change of heart is affecting not only because he is a sensitive soul but also because that change occurs against the background of Antony's need for companionship. In adversity the Roman general draws strength from the presence of friends. Thus after Actium and while contemplating another battle with Octavius, Antony makes this request: "Call to me / All my sad captains, fill our bowls once more; / Let's mock the midnight bell" (III.xiii.182-84). Only moments later, Enobarbus resolves to desert Antony: "I will seek / Some way to leave him" (199-200). Antony, meanwhile, literally reaches out to his household servants: "Give me thy hand, / Thou hast been rightly honest—so hast thou— / Thou—and thou—and thou" (IV.ii.10-12). And ever more plaintively he appeals to his followers:

> Mine honest friends,
> I turn you not away, but like a master
> Married to your good service, stay till death.
> Tend me to-night two hours, I ask no more,
> And the gods yield you for't! (29-33)

But such pleas cannot prevent the defection of his men, who see in Antony's defeat the harbinger of their own destruction. When Enobarbus finally goes over to Octavius, Antony recognizes how profoundly his adversity has affected his erstwhile friend: "O, my fortunes have / Corrupted honest men!" (IV.v.16-17).[17]

By responding to the news with forbearance, and generously sending Enobarbus' treasure after him, Antony seems the antithesis of Timon, who reacts to his friends' desertion with bitterness and thoughts of revenge. Antony's action, however, may signal an underlying kinship with Timon, for the Roman general would, perhaps unconsciously, put Enobarbus in his debt. Moreover, Antony's gesture is ultimately self-defeating, for, whatever its motive, it must appear to his followers (like the extravagance of Timon) the act of a profligate. Eugene M. Waith, discussing the offer of treasure to Antony's men after Actium and the incident with Enobarbus, writes: "from the Roman point of view these examples of Antony's bounty are as patently unreasonable as his debauches. In both cases Antony is spending his substance prodigally—in effect, giving himself away. Looked at in this way, Antony's generosity is closely allied to the self-destructiveness which leads up to Actium. . . ."[18]

The most glaring instance of self-destructiveness, of course, is Antony's behavior at Actium. There, having decided on a sea battle against the advice of Enobarbus, Antony abandons his men when he sees Cleopatra's vessel fleeing. Plutarch bluntly characterizes the action as betrayal: "when he saw Cleopatraes shippe under saile, he forgot, forsooke, and betrayed them that fought for him, and imbarked upon a galley with five bankes of owers, to follow her that had already begon to overthrow him, and would in the end be his utter destruction."[19] Shakespeare echoes this view in the judgment of Scarus: "I never saw an action of such shame" (III.x.21). But the playwright also tempers the indictment by allowing Antony to blame his beloved:

> Egypt, thou knew'st too well
> My heart was to thy rudder tied by th' strings,
> And thou shouldst tow me after. (III.xi.56-58)

Ironically, by sustaining their love relationship, Antony severs the multitude of relationships that bind him to his troops. And by sacrificing these, he condemns himself to a lonely future. As his men desert him one by one, we may recall that on the day he first met Cleopatra, she had the effect of isolating him. At Cydnus, according to Enobarbus, as Cleopatra's barge approached, "The city cast / Her people out upon her; and Antony / Enthron'd i' th' marketplace, did sit alone" (II.ii.213-15).

Plutarch sees in the defeated Antony a parallel with Timon of Athens: "Antonius, he forsooke the citie and companie of his frendes, and built him a house in the sea, by the Ile of Pharos, . . . and dwelt there, as a man that banished him selfe from all mens companie: saying that he would lead Timons life, bicause he had the like wrong offered him, that was affore offered unto Timon: and that for the unthankefulnes of those he had done good unto, and whom he tooke to be his frendes, he was angry with all men, and would trust no man."[20] In Shakespeare's treatment we find no explicit reference to Timon. But the playwright does present Antony as an ever more isolated figure, deserted even by his divine protector: "'Tis the god Hercules, whom Antony lov'd, / Now leaves him" (IV.iii.16-17). As he dies, Antony may draw comfort from Mardian's assurance, "My mistress lov'd thee, and her fortunes mingled / With thine entirely" (IV.xiv.24-25). But Decretas epitomizes the feelings of Antony's soldiers when, as the pace of desertion accelerates, he tells the dying general: "Thy death and fortunes bid thy followers fly" (IV.xiv.111).

III

At certain points in *Antony and Cleopatra*—when Menas suggests that Pompey cut the throats of the triumvirs or when Enobarbus suggests that Antony fight by land—Shakespeare evokes the idea of Occasion: with the right decision and prompt action, we feel, Pompey or Antony could exploit a temporary strength and ensure future success. The insistent imagery of moon and tide, moreover, strengthens the suggestion that the characters are subject not to mere flux but to change conforming to some pattern, one that provides them with opportunity. Commentators have even proposed a parallel between the Fortune of *Antony and Cleopatra* and that implicit in *Julius Caesar* when Brutus speaks of "a tide in the affairs of men."[21] In my view, however, the concept of Fortune seldom appears synonymous with Occasion in *Antony and Cleopatra*. For while tantalizing opportunities seem available, most of the characters are unable to seize them. In an important sense, then, the tide in the affairs of men proves oddly elusive. Perhaps the defeated are conquered and the victorious triumphant from the very beginning.

Lepidus perceives that Antony's deficiencies are too deeply rooted to change:

I must not think there are
Evils enow to darken all his goodness:
His faults, in him, seem as the spots of heaven,
More fiery by night's blackness; hereditary,
Rather than purchas'd; what he cannot change,
Than what he chooses. (I.iv.10-15)

Admittedly, not everyone agrees with this assessment. Octavius replies, "You are too indulgent," and his opinion finds support among Antony's own men. After Actium, for example, Canidius says, "Had our general / Been what he knew himself, it had gone well" (III.x.25-26). And Enobarbus answers Cleopatra's query about who was at fault with a similar indictment: "Antony only, that would make his will / Lord of his reason" (III.xiii.3-4). Nevertheless, these judgments are made by Romans preoccupied with reason and responsibility, with duty and sacrifice. They fail to acknowledge the extent to which Antony and his adversary are beneficiaries or victims of forces beyond their control.

When Antony asks the Soothsayer, "whose fortunes shall rise higher, / Caesar's or mine?" (II.iii.16-17), the reply is "Caesar's." And the Soothsayer goes on to associate Octavius with the contingency that seems always to favor him: "of [i.e., by] that natural luck, / He beats thee 'gainst the odds" (27-28). Though irritated, Antony is forced to concede the truth of what he hears:

The very dice obey him,
And in our sports my better cunning faints
Under his chance. If we draw lots, he speeds. (II.iii.34-36)

It is ironic that Octavius, who benefits most from the external forces that shape his "chance," should be so unyielding in his judgment of Antony. Octavius is described as "fortunate Caesar" (IV.xiv.76) and as "full-fortun'd Caesar" (IV.xv.24). And Antony's ambassador addresses the victorious Octavius as "Lord of his fortunes" (III.xii.11). To be sure, Octavius supposes himself subject to risk. Before Actium he tells a lieutenant, "Our fortune lies / Upon this jump" (III.viii.5- 6). But his success seems as inevitable as Antony's failure. Octavius is truly one of the *fortunati*, always favored by Fortune.

As Antony finds himself overcome by forces he cannot master, he tends increasingly to personify Fortune and to conceive of his situation as a personal struggle with the goddess. After the loss at Actium, for example, he says, "Fortune knows / We scorn her most when most she offers blows" (III.xi.73-74). And when he puts on his armor at Alexandria before yet another battle, he tells Eros, "if Fortune be not ours today, it is / Because we brave her" (IV.iv.4-5). There is no suggestion here that Antony sees Fortune as providing opportunities to be seized. Instead, his concept of Fortune depends upon a much older vision. If Shakespeare departs from tradition in portraying Antony's relationship to Fortune, it is in the notion that Fortune is a formidable but honorable opponent whose hand Antony can shake when they come to a parting of the ways: "Fortune and Antony part here, even here / Do we shake hands" (IV.xii.19-20). This remark is, of course, in keeping with that larger pattern in the play of Antony's progressive isolation.

Ironically, while Antony has no difficulty envisioning Fortune's nature, his own identity seems unstable, even in danger of perishing. At the end he must still struggle to suppress the irresolution and vacillation that all along have marked his behavior. At moments he actually seems close to faltering, as when, in a conversation with Eros, he speaks of rapidly changing cloud formations:

Antony. That which is now a horse, even with a thought
      The rack dislimns, and makes it indistinct
      As water is in water.
Eros.   It does, my lord.
Antony. My good knave Eros, now thy captain is
      Even such a body. Here I am Antony,
      Yet cannot hold this visible shape, my knave.(IV.xiv.9-14)

The imagery evokes the predicament of Timon, but there is this important difference: Timon abjectly surrenders to the flux; he places his grave at the edge of the sea where all traces of it will be obliterated by the changing tide. By contrast, Antony would steady himself by the sheer force of his will and resist mutability.

In the last two acts Cleopatra too seems to take on a new steadiness, embodying the earlier advice of Thidias:

Wisdom and fortune combating together,
If that the former dare but what it can,
No chance may shake it. (III.xiii.79-81)

The fickle Egyptian, who has behaved as capriciously as Fortune in her daily life, repudiates the changeability that has characterized her all along, and she now condemns the goddess:

> let me rail so high,
> That the false huswife Fortune break her wheel,
> Provok'd by my offense. (IV.xv.43-45)

Like Antony, Cleopatra imagines Fortune not as a bringer of opportunity, but as an opponent. As she steels herself for death, she envisions Fortune as a challenge to her strength of character:

> 'Tis paltry to be Caesar;
> Not being Fortune, he's but Fortune's knave,
> A minister of her will: and it is great
> To do that thing that ends all other deeds,
> Which shackles accidents and bolts up change,
> Which sleeps, and never palates more the dung,
> The beggar's nurse and Caesar's. (V.ii.2-8)[22]

By standing firm, she would shackle accident and bolt up change; and by so doing she would in effect not only deprive Fortune but also Octavius (who is Fortune's favorite) of power over her. To accomplish this end, she must renounce her former nature. She must sever her connection with Isis (the moon goddess), whose costume she once wore:

> My resolution's plac'd, and I have nothing
> Of woman in me; now from head to foot
> I am marble-constant; now the fleeting moon
> No planet is of mine. (V.ii.238-41)

With this resolve the ancient Fortuna-Virtus antinomy asserts itself,

328

each of these mighty opposites affirming its strength. By imposing her will on circumstance and confronting her end with dignity, Cleopatra wins a victory of sorts, one that Baldwin and Neville and Wager and Lodge and Marlowe and Kyd and Dekker would appreciate. At the same time, however, we are made to acknowledge the cost of this victory. For Cleopatra must suppress the qualities that have made her personality so distinctive and appealing; she must adopt a Stoic rigidity; and she must forfeit her very life.

NOTES TO CHAPTER 10

1. Wolfgang H. Clemen, *The Development of Shakespeare's Imagery* (Cambridge, Mass.: Harvard Univ. Press, 1951), p. 168.

2. *Prefaces to Shakespeare*, 1 (Princeton: Princeton Univ. Press, 1946), 367.

3. *Timon of Athens: Shakespeare's Pessimistic Tragedy* (Columbus: Ohio State Univ. Press, 1979), p. 30. Soellner's book contains an extensive discussion of Fortune in the play.

4. "*Antony and Cleopatra*: The Stillness and the Dance," in *Shakespeare's Art: Seven Essays*, ed. Milton Crane (Chicago and London: Univ. of Chicago Press [for George Washington Univ.], 1973), p. 85. This essay contains an especially fine analysis of the theme of change in the play.

5. David M. Bergeron, "'Timon of Athens' and Morality Drama," *CLAJ*, 10 (1967): 182, 185.

6. A. S. Collins, "*Timon of Athens*: A Reconsideration," *RES*, 22 (1946): 98, 99.

7. Other readers who see *Timon* as resembling the morality drama include: Anne Lancashire, "Timon of Athens: Shakespeare's *Doctor Faustus*," *SQ*, 21 (1970): 35-44; Ruth Levitsky, "*Timon*: Shakespeare's *Magnyfycence* and an Embryonic *Lear*," *ShakS*, 11 (1978): 107-21; Lewis Walker, "*Timon of Athens* and the Morality Tradition," *ShakS*, 12 (1979): 159-77.

8. M. M. Mahood, in *Shakespeare's Wordplay* (London: Methuen, 1957), explores the significance of the Poet's speech: "the Poet's allegory of Fortune is a kind of dumbshow to the whole drama, and fixes *fortune* in our mind as the

key word. Three meanings of *fortune*: wealth, ill or good hap, and the fickle goddess whose caprices cause the reversal of man's lot, are used interchangeably to hold up the simple and strong theme that those who have large fortunes are seldom fortunate" (p. 49). Lewis Walker, in "Fortune and Friendship in *Timon of Athens*," *TSLL*, 18 (1977): 577- 600, uses the Poet's speech as the starting point of his analysis. Walker writes: "many of the play's peculiarities result from Shakespeare's attempt to demonstrate the operations of the goddess through dramatic action, a procedure necessitating a mingling of allegorical and naturalistic elements" (p. 577).

9. *Shakespeare's Roman Plays and Their Background* (1910; reprint ed., London: Methuen, 1967), pp. 419-20.

10. *The Problem Plays of Shakespeare* (New York: Schocken Books, 1963), p. 143.

11. Shakespeare's treatment of Fortune in *Antony and Cleopatra* is discussed by Michael Lloyd, in "Antony and the Game of Chance," *JEGP*, 61 (1962): 548-54. Lloyd contends that "Plutarch's Roman Fortune is a planning goddess beneficent to Rome," whereas Shakespeare's Fortune "is not the planning goddess who brings stability to an unstable world, but the very 'chance' that 'shakes' it" (pp. 548, 549). Marilyn L. Williamson, in "Fortune in *Antony and Cleopatra*," *JEGP*, 67 (1968): 423-29, accepts Lloyd's arguments: "though Fortune appears in Plutarch's narrative, she is not the Fortune of Shakespeare's play" (426). Charles A. Hallett, in "Change, Fortune, and Time: Aspects of the Sublunar World in *Antony and Cleopatra*," *JEGP*, 75 (1976): 75-89, also agrees with Lloyd: "As Michael Lloyd has noted, Shakespeare's concept of Fortune differs markedly from that of Plutarch" (81-82). All of these commentators, in my opinion, exaggerate the differences between Plutarch and Shakespeare. A careful reading of Plutarch yields many instances in which the historian associates Fortune with hap, chance, luck. He tells, for instance, how Antony averted disaster when his fleet was pushed away from dangerous rocks: "by good fortune, sodainely the winde turned Southwest, and blewe from the gulffe, driving the waves of the river into the mayne sea" (Plutarch's *Lives of the Noble Grecians and Romanes*, in *Narrative and Dramatic Sources of Shakespeare*, ed. Geoffrey Bullough, 5 [New York and London: Columbia Univ. Press, 1964], 259.) Similarly, Plutarch relates the surprise of Antony's men at Actium when they see him fleeing, "as if he had not oftentimes proved both the one and the other fortune, and that he had not bene throughly acquainted with the divers chaunges and fortunes of battells" (p. 302).

12. Sir William Cornwallis, writing of Fortune in *Discourses upon Seneca the*

Tragedian (London, 1601), a few years before the composition of *Antony and Cleopatra*, distinguishes between Fortune and fortunes: "though the fancy of Poets hath given a bodie to, and made her blinde, and a goddesse, yet is she neither a goddesse, nor a separated essence: for there are millions of fortunes, yea as many as there are men, every man his owne fortune . . ." (sig. E1ᵛ).

13. *The Imperial Theme* (London: Methuen, 1931), p. 338.

14. For the connection between Cleopatra and Isis, see Michael Lloyd, "Cleopatra as Isis," *ShS*, 12 (1959): 88-94; Harold Fisch, "'Antony and Cleopatra': The Limits of Mythology," *ShS*, 23 (1970): 59-67; John Adlard, "Cleopatra as Isis," *Archiv*, 212 (1975): 324-28. For the conflation of Isis and Fortune, see France Le Corsu, *Isis: mythe et mystères* (Paris: Société d'Édition, 1977), esp. pp. 180, 189, 216, 233-35. For artistic representations of Isis-Fortune, see V. Tran Tam Tinh, *Essai sur le culte d'Isis a Pompéi* (Paris: Éditions E. de Boccard, 1964), pl. VII, fig. 3; XII, 2; XIV, 2; XVIII, 1; XXII, 1; and see pp. 78-81. R. E. Witt, in *Isis in the Graeco-Roman World* (Ithaca: Cornell Univ. Press, 1971), observes that the most famous shrine of Fortune in Italy gives evidence of the conflation with Isis: "At Praeneste, the modern Palestrina, was the Temple of Fortuna Primigenia, with whom Isis in course of time must have been identified in view of the mosaic found there" (p. 34). The mosaic, which portrays all of Egypt "in a zoological map of the Nile valley at the moment of inundation," is reproduced by Witt as fig. 8. In the Renaissance the conflation of Fortune and Isis is discussed by Vincenzo Cartari, in *Les Images des dieux des anciens* (Lyons, 1581): "Apulee la [Fortune] faict une mesme chose avec Isis, quand il feinct, qu'estant d'Asne retourné homme, le prestre dit ainsi de la Deesse: Tu es maintenant sous la garde de Fortune, non de celle qui est aveugle, mais de celle qui voit, & donne lumiere aux autres Dieux, par sa splendeur. Nous pouvons dire, qu'il vouloit entendre de la bonne Fortune, souz le nom de laquelle Macrobe a entendu la Lune monstree par Isis, comme il a desia esté dict en son image: car ceste la peut beaucoup es corps d'icy bas, lesquels sont sujects à divers accidens de Fortune, & se changent continuellement" (pp. 562-63).

15. Antony's comment recalls a choral observation in Samuel Daniel's *Cleopatra*, a probable source for Shakespeare's play: "the course of things requireth / change and alteration ever: / That same continuance man desireth, / th'unconstant world yeeldeth never" (*The Tragedie of Cleopatra* [1599 edition], in *Narrative and Dramatic Sources of Shakespeare*, ed. Bullough, 5: ll. 1202-05).

16. Maynard Mack, in "*Antony and Cleopatra*: The Stillness and the Dance," notes how the staging underscores this precariousness: "*Antony and Cleopatra* in performance contains just under two hundred distinct entrances and

exits. . . . People flow to and away from each other in *Antony and Cleopatra* with relentless frequency and ease . . ." (p. 89).

17. Barbara Everett, in her edition of *Antony and Cleopatra*, Signet Classic Shakespeare (New York: New American Library, 1963), observes how Shakespeare's departure from Plutarch accentuates the emotional impact of Enobarbus' deed: "the desertion of Domitius (a minor character in Plutarch, whom Shakespeare converts into the far more important Enobarbus) is moved from before Actium to after it, accentuating Antony's isolation in defeat, and the deserter dies not of illness but of a broken heart; and the one successful sally against Caesar, Shakespeare places after, instead of before, Antony's farewell to his servants and the departure of Hercules – thus making the isolated Antony's last exhilaration of victory the more ironic and pathetic, and yet paradoxically heroic" (pp. 191-92).

18. *The Herculean Hero in Marlowe, Chapman, Shakespeare and Dryden* (New York and London: Columbia Univ. Press, 1962), p. 115.

19. *Lives of the Noble Grecians and Romanes*, in *Narrative and Dramatic Sources of Shakespeare*, ed. Bullough, 5: 301.

20. Ibid., p. 304.

21. Michael Lloyd draws the parallel in "Antony and the Game of Chance," p. 548. Similarly, Charles A. Hallett, in "Change, Fortune, and Time: Aspects of the Sublunar World in *Antony and Cleopatra*," writes: "What appeared in *Julius Caesar* merely as a wise observation, made by Brutus at a crucial moment, has become in *Antony and Cleopatra* a major strain of imagery" (p. 84). Hallett goes on to quote the beginning of Brutus' "tide in the affairs of men" speech and adds: "To a degree that would have astonished Brutus, the characters in *Antony and Cleopatra* must live by this rule."

22. Cleopatra's use of the word "knave" – with its application to playing cards – recalls an earlier speech in which Antony twice calls Eros "knave" and says of Cleopatra: "she, Eros, has / Pack'd cards with Caesar's, and false-play'd my glory / Unto an enemy's triumph" (IV.xiv.18-20). For the meaning of the words "knave," "Pack'd," and "triumph" in cards, see M. R. Ridley, ed., New Arden *Antony and Cleopatra* (London: Methuen, 1954), pp. 186-87. The association of Cleopatra with cards is perhaps meant to suggest her likeness to Fortune, who also is said to deal cards. For example, in *The Tragical Reign of Selimus, 1594*, ed. W. Bang, MSR (Oxford: Oxford Univ. Press, 1908), the protagonist says: "Will fortune favour me yet once againe? / And will she thrust the cards into my hands?" (ll. 1539-40). And in *Cupid's*

Whirligig (London, 1607) by Edward Sharpham, a character says: "Well I feare fortune hath delt mee a bad game by the shufling of hir Cardes thus, that these two Knaves should come together" (sig. H4ᵛ). Although Antony may implicitly associate Cleopatra with Fortune by his reference to card playing at IV, xiv. 18-20, Cleopatra fails to preserve that association in her speech at V.ii.2-8. In keeping with her new steadiness and with her alienation from Fortune, Cleopatra sees Caesar's card (the "knave"), evidently, as dealt by Fortune rather than by herself.

Conclusion

HAT FORTUNE PLAYS an important role in Elizabethan tragedy has been recognized from time to time. In 1922 John S. Smart declared that "Fortune . . . had become the presiding genius of Tragedy when the modern stage arose and Shakespeare began to write."[1] But assertions such as this have seldom received an enthusiastic response: Smart's contemporaries must have thought that he was taking his cue from Malvolio: "'Tis but Fortune, all is fortune." Nor have such assertions often prompted others to look closely at the Elizabethan treatment of Fortune. When scholars have studied this subject, as Campbell and Farnham did in the 1930s, they have tended to see Fortune as dwindling in significance while Elizabethan drama advanced. The prevalence of this view in the twentieth century suggests that something in our very experience and outlook predisposes us to neglect Fortune and, at the same time, to dwell on retributive justice.

The modern indifference to Fortune may be owing, in part, to something that we have lost: the experience of being surrounded by personifications, of thinking in terms of metaphors made visual. We forget that the Painter's boast in *Timon of Athens* could (if extended to include all sorts of pictorial representation) probably have been made by any knowledgeable Elizabethan: "A thousand moral paintings I can show / That shall demonstrate these quick blows of Fortune's / More pregnantly than words" (I.i.90-92). And in Shakespeare's time Fortune was to be seen not only in engravings and woodcuts and paintings, but also on public monuments and tableaux. A citizen of London could daily have encountered a statue of Fortune placed on Aldgate (the east gate of the old London wall), when it was rebuilt in 1609.[2] He could also have seen Fortune in civic pageants: for example, on an arch

334

designed to celebrate the entry of King James to London in 1604.[3] And a playgoer, entering the second Fortune theater, would pass by a representation of Dame Fortune.[4] The prevalence of this figure must have allowed Shakespeare's contemporaries to envision Fortune with an ease, immediacy, and vividness denied us today. The mention of Fortune's name on the Elizabethan stage evoked in the mind's eye of the spectator an image of Fortune; and it would thus exert a greater impact than it does today in a world of dead metaphors.

We can probably never recapture precisely the feelings of Renaissance men and women toward Fortune. We do not even know what term best describes their understanding of Fortune: is it goddess, personification, abstraction, symbol? It would be possible to say about virtually every Elizabethan author what Allan H. Gilbert says of Ben Jonson's classical deities: "A strict line can hardly be drawn between them and the personified qualities. Fortune and Fame, for example, may be considered as either allegorical or mythological."[5] Moreover, an individual might alter his view of Fortune according to his mood or circumstance. Thus E. H. Gombrich, who speaks of "a twilight zone between the gods of Olympus and the abstractions of language," notes the references to Fortune in the last will and testament of the Florentine merchant Francesco Sassetti and asks: "Did Sassetti or Giovanni Rucellai believe in the bodily existence of the goddess Fortuna? Maybe they did believe in her when they did not think about it, though surely they would have denied any such belief if asked at pistol point."[6] What Gombrich says of the two Italian merchants applies no less to the Elizabethans, for they all belonged to a culture still close enough to the Middle Ages to think spontaneously and naturally of such figures as Death, or Time, or Fortune. Living in an age of emblem books, heraldic devices, civic pageants, and masques, they would respond to symbolic figures with an enthusiasm that is difficult, if not impossible, for us to appreciate. Gilbert observes, for example, that when Machiavelli discusses Fortune in *The Prince*, "his words had as much realism as ours when we talk of Environment, and he had the advantage of bringing a well-known figure before the eyes of his readers; the concept was the more effective for being visual."[7]

A full appreciation of Fortune is impeded not only by something that we have lost but also by something that we have acquired—the notion so common today that virtually everything has an explanation. Remarkable advances in science and technology have fostered this attitude. Spacecraft send photographs and other data that permit us to analyze the makeup of distant planets and even to conjecture the origins of the universe. Studies of the world around us uncover the basis of natural phenomena — earthquakes, volcanoes, meteors — that bewildered earlier generations. Research into man's psyche reveals unconscious motivation: nothing we do, psychiatrists tell us, is arbitrary or accidental. Living in the age of psychoanalysis and the "psychological profile," we believe that a person's present may be explained by his past, that his actions, seen in the context of upbringing and experience, will appear not only explicable but virtually inevitable.

When the irrational — in the form of accident or crime — intrudes upon our lives, we are only momentarily baffled. Society's mechanisms for investigation and explanation are set in motion. Thus investigators discover the broken bolt that caused an airplane to crash; they locate the defective wiring that caused a catastrophic fire. And they analyze the criminal's past until his misdeeds come to seem a predictable response to his environment rather than a profound expression of evil.

The notion that adversity of any kind can be logically explained is so widely accepted that we seldom pause to question it. Nor do we often consider how greatly this "assumption felt as fact" (to use Basil Willey's expression) affects our expectations of and response to literature. It seems likely, for example, that the popular mystery story is the inevitable product of a culture that places its trust in reason. Ironically, the world created by the authors of these works is not very mysterious. The villain's identity is discovered through a detective's use of logic. Clues are assembled and evidence scrutinized in a laboratory. Knowledge accumulates until it points unerringly to the culprit.

Just as prevailing assumptions about the efficacy of reason shape our taste in popular literature, so too they color our reading of literature written long ago. Thus we tend to look for motives, rationales, causes. In reading tragedy we expect to find a direct connection between a person's deeds and his predicament; we look for foibles and seize upon "tragic errors"; we find most congenial the play that depicts the operation of retributive justice. Like Vindice in *The Revenger's Tragedy*, we feel that "When the bad bleeds, then is the tragedy good." We assume that a "tragedy of character" is the most profound kind of tragedy. At the same time, we look askance on tragedy precipitated by anything not readily explained, especially by anything that does not have its origin in some purposeful human action. We tend to deny, for instance, that tragedy originating in contingency is properly called tragic. Thus Robert B. Heilman writes: "a literary work that tells of destructive mischances may have its own excellence and validity, but its cosmos is a quite different one from that of tragedy."[8] Harley Granville-Barker claims: "Accidents make good incidents, but tragedy determined by them has no significance."[9] And Helen Gardner relegates the world of chance and change to comedy: "Tragic plots must have a logic which leads to an inescapable conclusion. Comic plots are made up of changes, chances and surprises."[10]

Such judgments may sound plausible until we reflect on their application to individual plays. To credit those assertions would require us to exclude from tragedy some of the greatest plays of Shakespeare and his contemporaries. Among them is *Hamlet*, which, for all its rich depiction of character, tells a story of accident as well as retribution. That, at least, is the testimony of Horatio, who sees a series

> Of carnal, bloody, and unnatural acts,
> Of accidental judgments, casual slaughters,
> Of deaths put on by cunning and forc'd cause,
> And in this upshot, purposes mistook
> Fall'n on th'inventors' heads. (V.ii.381-85)

Commenting on these lines, Clifford Leech reminds us how significant has been the role of contingency in the play: "If the players had not come to Elsinore, if the King had not been praying when Hamlet saw him, if Polonius had not been behind the arras, if Gertrude had not called for help, if Hamlet had not taken his father's seal on the voyage to England, if there had been no attack by a pirate-ship, if Gertrude had not drunk from the poisoned cup, if Hamlet and Laertes had not exchanged swords—if any one of these things had been differently disposed—the scene that greeted Fortinbras on his arrival in Elsinore might have been notably different."[11]

In *Hamlet*, as in other Elizabethan tragedies, people make errors and suffer the consequences. But the plays also depict a world of unpredictable circumstance and unmerited adversity. They dramatize the intrusion of the disorderly and anarchic into the lives of unsuspecting and often innocent people. We misrepresent and we diminish the plays when we insist that they are only about transgressions and chastisements. They are, in fact, about not only moral choice but also mere chance. They deal with both design and chaos, providence and Fortune.[12]

The tragic world created by Shakespeare and his contemporaries defies the modern impulse to construe it as eminently reasonable and retributive. As Madeleine Doran has written, "We think of Shakespearean tragedy as the tragedy of character *par excellence.* Yet Shakespeare's tragic world is not, any more than his comic world, a world of perfect logic, in which every act is motivated in character and has a strictly proportionate consequence. It is Iago's and Edmund's mistake to think it so. The world of uncontrollable circumstance always operates to heighten the mystery and deepen the irony."[13]

Such "uncontrollable circumstance" does not by itself ensure that a tragedy will prove aesthetically satisfying. An overreliance on accident, as for example in the last scenes of *Romeo and Juliet*, is likely to seem contrived. Yet a play altogether devoid of the inexplicable is just as likely to seem too pat. The plays themselves confute the notion that great tragedy proceeds exclusively from either external situation or internal resolve. Although a particular play may emphasize the one or the other, the most affecting and profound tragedies depend on both.

NOTES TO THE CONCLUSION

1. "Tragedy," *E&S*, 8 (1922): 10.

2. "On the *West* side of the *Gate*, was the Figure of Fortune curiously carved, and gilt with Gold, standing on a Mund, or Globe, with a Sail spreading over her Head, and looking towards the City" (Robert Seymour's revision of John Stow's *Survey of the Cities of London and Westminster*, 1 [London: J. Read, 1734], 16).

3. Reproduced by David M. Bergeron, in *English Civic Pageantry, 1558-1642* (London: Edward Arnold, 1971), pl. 6.

4. A character in *The English Traveller* (c. 1627) by Thomas Heywood says: "I'le rather stand heere / Like a Statue, in the Fore-front of your house / For ever; Like the picture of Dame Fortune / Before the Fortune Play-house." Quoted in Gerald Eades Bentley, *The Jacobean and Caroline Stage*, 6 (Oxford: Clarendon Press, 1968), 156. Bentley comments that the "comparison suggests that the Fortune sign was a statue of Dame Fortune rather than a picture, but either would satisfy the simile." J. A. K. Thomson, in *Shakespeare and the Classics* (London: George Allen and Unwin, 1952), speculates that the original Fortune theater was similarly decorated: "It is likely enough (though we do not know) that the Fortune theatre, built in 1600, was adorned by a figure of the goddess standing on her ball" (p. 105). And Harry Levin, in *The Overreacher: A Study of Christopher Marlowe* (Cambridge, Mass.: Harvard Univ. Press, 1952), writes: "Fortune in person, possibly symbolized by a wooden effigy, lent its name to London's largest playhouse, built by Philip Henslowe in 1600" (p. 181).

5. *The Symbolic Persons in the Masques of Ben Jonson* (Durham, N.C.: Duke Univ. Press, 1948), p. 8.

6. "Personification," in *Classical Influences on European Culture, A.D. 500-1500*, ed. R. R. Bolgar (Cambridge: Cambridge Univ. Press, 1971), p. 256.

7. *The Symbolic Persons in the Masques of Ben Jonson*, p. 15.

8. *This Great Stage: Image and Structure in King Lear* (Baton Rouge: Louisiana State Univ. Press, 1948), p. 31.

9. "Romeo and Juliet," in *Prefaces to Shakespeare*, 2 (Princeton: Princeton Univ. Press, 1947), 312.

10. "'As You Like It,'" in *More Talking of Shakespeare*, ed. John Garrett (London: Longmans, 1959), p. 21. Gardner's ideas about tragedy are expressed at greater length in *Religion and Literature* (London: Faber and Faber, 1971), pp. 13-118.

11. *The John Fletcher Plays* (London: Chatto and Windus, 1962), p. 83.

12. For a useful discussion of these mighty opposites, see John Lawlor, "Accident and Design," in *The Tragic Sense in Shakespeare* (London: Chatto and Windus, 1960), pp. 74 ff.

13. *Endeavors of Art: A Study of Form in Elizabethan Drama* (Madison and London: Univ. of Wisconsin Press, 1954), p. 333.

INDEX

341